Umkhonto we Siswe

Umkhonto we Siswe

Fighting for a divided people

Thula Bopela
Daluxolo Luthuli

GALAGO

GALAGO BOOKS

Galago Books are published by Galago Publishing (1999) (Pty) Ltd
PO Box 404, Alberton, 1450, Republic South Africa
Web address: www.galago.co.za

Galago Books are distributed by Lemur Books (Pty) Ltd
PO Box 1645, Alberton, 1450, Republic South Africa
Tel: (Int + 2711 — local 011) 907-2029. Fax 869-0890
Email: lemur@mweb.co.za

First published by Galago, November 2005 as
Umkhonto we Sizwe: Fighting for a Divided People
by Thula Bopela and Daluxolo Luthuli
© Thula Bopela and Daluxolo Luthuli
ISBN 1-919854-16-9
Maps © Madelain Davies

Thula Bopela and Daluxolo Luthuli have asserted their moral rights
to be identified as the joint authors of this work

No part of this publication may be reproduced, stored in
or introduced into any information or retrieval system, or
transmitted in any form or by any means (electronic, mechanical
photocopying, recording or otherwise) without the prior
permission in writing of the publishers. Any person who does
any unauthorised act in relation to this publication renders
themselves liable to criminal prosecution and a claim for
civil damages.

Typeset by Galago in 11 point Times New Roman
Colour and black and white photographs reproduced
by Rapid Repro Parkhurst, Johannesburg
Colour corrections by Galago
Printed and bound by CTP Book Printers, Cape

Front cover design: Madelain Davies
Photography: Justyn Davies
Model: Sandile Ngubeni, wearing Soviet Army kit
and armed with a folding butt AK

Thula dedicates this book:

To the loving memory of my late wife, Cherry Duduzile Khoza — the girl from B Section Umlazi Township. She courageously sacrificed everything and went into exile to be with me unsure if she would ever set foot in South Africa again

Daluxolo dedicates this book:

For Sibongile MaMthembu and all she has meant to me in my travails — wife, lover, comrade, friend and the mother of my children. She has no equal amongst the women of South Africa, perhaps the entire world

Guerrillas never win wars but their adversaries often lose them
        Charles W Thayer, *Guerrilla*, 1963

Changes to place names relevant to this book since Zimbabwe's independence in 1980

Old name	New name
Chipinga	Chipinge
Dett	Dete
Gatooma	Kadoma
Gwelo	Gweru
Hartley	Chegutu
Que Que	Kwekwe
Salisbury	Harare
Tjolotjo	Tsholotsho
Umtali	Mutare
Wankie	Hwange

Credits for photographs and illustrations

Thula Bopela, *Daily News*, Durban (with special thanks to Rabin Singh), Justyn Davies (front cover photograph), Madelain Davies (maps), Riaan Labuschagne, Daluxolo Luthuli, William Motau, Major-General Zolile Nqose, *Rapport*, Peter Stiff collection, Major-General Lennox Tjali and the late Henry Wolhuter. The copyright holders of a few photographs are not acknowledged, although the publishers have made every effort to establish authorship which has been lost in the mists of time or blown away by the winds of war. However, the publishers will amend or add credits in subsequent editions and make the necessary arrangements with those photographers not known at the time of going to print, or who had not been traced.

Acknowledgements

Writers of history need to be humble. They need to realise that what they record reflects a combined effort — a lot of people who didn't participate directly in the events recorded also influenced their outcomes. We are both happy to acknowledge those many unnamed people and also the many who inspired the writing of this book.

Daluxolo acknowledges his indebtedness to his father, Japhta 'Folozi' Luthuli, who recruited him into the ranks of *Umkhonto we Sizwe*. He would also like to pay tribute to his mother, Nomthandazo Majola, who had to put up with lies about his disappearance when he went for military training. He salutes his MK comrades who supported him shoulder-to-shoulder during the Wankie campaign. And never to be forgotten are the men of the IFP hit squads that he commanded in KwaZulu. They did their duty as they saw it and acted as one when the need arose to expose what had been done. It was war and many things happen in war.

Thula salutes his beloved daughters, Tshitshi, Nandi and Nombali. They were born in exile and had to cope with the life of children who found themselves in strange environments. They didn't even understand why their parents were outside South Africa, but they adjusted. They were and are great kids!

Daluxolo and Thula both recognise with gratitude the African National Congress, specifically MK, for giving them the opportunity to express their manhood. Never to be forgotten are the blacks, Indians, coloureds and the whites who stood up for the truth during the apartheid years. It cost many their lives. For some like Beyers Naude, Wilhelm Verwoerd, Madelein Malan and others of the so-called Afrikaner 'aristocracy', it meant ostracism. Thanks to them our nationhood is no longer defined in terms of tribe, race or colour, but in shared values and beliefs that South Africans will willingly die for.

The authors acknowledge their friends and drinking partners who got fed up with their 'stories from exile'. These comrades told them plainly that they wanted the full story and they wanted it in a book. The chief instigators were George 'Mjojana' Sabelo, Fo 'Vierman' Ngidi and Skhumbuzo Mthembu. The last named didn't merely say the book needed to be written, he devoted his immense computer skills to ensure that it was. Baleka Mbete is thanked because she not only insisted we put our experiences in writing, but reserved her right to differ with anything we wrote.

Finally, we acknowledge the assistance and efforts of our publisher, Peter Stiff of Galago Publishing. He went the extra mile to ensure the birth of this book and also generously allowed us to quote large sections from his own books, *Cry Zimbabwe: Independence Twenty Years On*, *The Silent War: South African Recce Operations 1969 to 1994*; *Warfare by Other Means: South Africa in the 1980s and 1990s*; and *See You in November: The story of an SAS Assassin*.

But for everyone, *Amandla Ngawethu*! (Power to the people!)

Contents

Chapter		Page
	Picture and illustration credits	6
	Acknowledgements	7
	Foreword	10
	List of illustrations	11
1	Boys to men	13
2	Weapons of today	17
3	When it's all right to lie	25
4	How a young man became a terrorist	28
5	A non-violent organisation turns to violence	35
6	Behind the Iron Curtain	38
7	Kongwa Camp	45
8	Rhodesia	52
9	When we return	59
10	Dead men don't need the time	68
11	Fighting continues	72
12	Guerrillas are to people what fish are to water	77
13	Guerrillas in school uniform	83
14	To Mozambique and back	88
15	Thula arrested	97
16	Interrogation	105

17	Death Row: The legion of the doomed	112
18	No 'thank you' for Daluxolo	121
19	'Call me *Baas*, you bastard.'	125
20	Letter from the gallows	145
21	New Lock Prison, Pretoria	151
22	Robben Island	154
23	A peep into the mind of an African leader	157
24	Khami Maximum Security Prison	164
25	Angola: betrayed and abused by one's comrades	173
26	Planting the seeds of mutual destruction	178
27	Daluxolo: double agent	186
28	Inkatha and students go to war	191
29	Daluxolo: UWUSA organiser	194
30	The Caprivi 200	199
31	Zimbabwe: bitter fruits of division	212
32	Back to basics	219
33	The Netherlands	228
34	Home in the RSA	235
35	Let's stop the killing	243
36	War clouds gather	255
37	Rocky road to peace	261
	Afterword	267
	Index	269

Foreword

This is an account of the experiences of two young men, Daluxolo Wordsworth Luthuli and Thula Osborne Bopela, who joined the South African liberation struggle in the early 1960s. Both became members of *Umkhonto we Sizwe* (MK) otherwise known as the Spear of the Nation. Both trained at the Odessa Military Academy in the Ukraine in what was then the Union of Soviet Socialist Republics (USSR). In 1967 they were soldiers in MK's Luthuli Detachment that infiltrated Rhodesia (now Zimbabwe). They operated jointly with Joshua Nkomo's guerillas of the Zimbabwe Peoples Revolutionary Army (ZIPRA).

Both were captured. Thula and six others were tried in the Salisbury High Court and given death sentences. In 1969 Thula's sentence was commuted to life imprisonment. Daluxolo was handed over to the South African Police, tried in the Pietermaritzburg Supreme Court and sentenced to ten years imprisonment which he served on Robben Island. On being released in 1979 he was instructed to join the Inkatha Freedom Party (IFP) and use it as a cover to recruit young men and women for MK.

Relations between the IFP and the ANC soured and violence erupted between the IFP and the United Democratic Front (UDF) — a pro-ANC political front — in the 1980s. Daluxolo felt that Zulus were inexplicably being targeted and murdered by the UDF. He was asked to accompany 200 men to the Caprivi for military training by the South African Defence Force (SADF) and was appointed their political commissar. On their return from the Caprivi they were deployed to various parts of Natal where they conducted hit squad activities against the UDF, financed and supported by elements of South African Military Intelligence. Daluxolo was appointed commander-in-chief of these hit squads.

It was not long before he realised that the IFP, like other political and military organisations in the Bantustan, had effectively become a surrogate army used by the National Party Government to fight the ANC. The world had come to believe that the violence in South Africa was 'black-on-black' and was not directed against the white racist regime.

Duloxolo decided to end the bloodshed in the Mpumalanga area of KwaZulu and negotiated with the UDF to do so. But the violence was countrywide and a more comprehensive strategy was necessary to bring it to a halt. By then Military Intelligence had spotted him going to the ANC offices in Durban where he tried unsuccessfully to negotiate an end to the fighting. A decision was made to assassinate him, but friends in Military Intelligence warned him.

In 1993 he sought out his old comrade Thula Bopela, who had returned from exile and was working in Durban for the electricity utility, Eskom. Thula arranged for him to meet Jacob Zuma, later deputy president, who asked him to personally explain to Nelson Mandela what was happening.

The eventual plan was for Daluxolo to defect back to the ANC and order his hit squad men to reveal all their IFP hit squad activities to the Transitional Executive Council (TEC). This was done and Daluxolo was sent overseas under the witness protection programme.

Until then the IFP had publicly refused to participate in the forthcoming democratic elections in South Africa. It had been planned that they, along with Afrikaner right wing elements including the *Afrikaanse Weerstand Beweging* (AWB), would be armed by Military Intelligence and geared to start a civil war as soon as the ANC won the elections. It would be claimed that the Zulus were diametrically opposed to ANC rule. But without an Inkatha armed hit squad, it would have become a white Afrikaner fight against the ANC. With Daluxolo's defection and his hit squad men refusing to fight, the IFP announced, virtually overnight, that it would participate in the elections.

It would be wrong to think that this book is only about those two young men. It is about those people throughout South Africa who chose to fight against apartheid. It also shows how MK found it was trying to free a divided people where chiefs and so-called traditional leaders often did everything in their power to prevent it. Instead of fighting the apartheid regime, it became a case of black fighting black to decide who would take power and capture the spoils of victory.

Photographs

Page

Black and white photographic section . . . . 129 to 144

In-text illustrations

A Russian Aeroflot boarding pass retained by a trainee as a souvenir 44

A ZIPRA leaflet calling on people to fight the white minority 56

Map: The Zambezi River and a few of its gorges downstream from Victoria Falls. Batoka Gorge was where the Luthuli Detachment crossed 62

Rewards offered for information leading to the death or capture of 'terrorists' and for the location of 'terrorist' weapons 89

Map showing Thula's and Daluxolo's movements until the former's capture 98

Letter from the Bantu Affairs Commissioner, Johannesburg, to the father of MK prisoner William Motau, advising that he had lodged an appeal against the death sentence imposed on him in Salisbury 116

Map showing Daluxolo's movements subsequent to Thula's arrest 123

1

Boys to men

This is our story, Daluxolo 'Ken Ken' Luthuli and Thula Osborne Bopela. We will tell it the way it was and not as we wish it had happened, or as somebody else might prefer us to tell it. It's not only our history, it's also a history of a people — the black people of Africa. We don't have the right to change the facts to suit us; we cannot hide the truth — if we did that we will have lied to ourselves and to our children.

Some people believe that reporting the bad things that happened within the African National Congress is tantamount to disloyalty. We disagree. To tell lies about the ANC is disloyalty. To tell the truth, however painful it might be, is an act of patriotism and loyalty because it shows the ANC is capable of self-criticism. The organisation is larger and stronger than its individual members. It cannot be judged or condemned because of the actions of individuals. It personifies the suffering and aspirations of a people, so to praise or condemn the actions of corrupt or traitorous individuals within it, leaves it untouched. It is only when it acts as an organisation, through policy, that the ANC arrives at a point where it can be condemned.

We will start at the very beginning when we were boys. We will take the reader along the road to our manhood, showing the mistakes we made and what we believed in. We will hide nothing, not even the stupid things we did, nor the senseless acts of other ANC members. The ANC survived in spite of everything and became the government in 1994 — a testimony to its resilience as an organisation. So why try to protect it? The organisation is clearly capable of looking after itself.

Let's begin with the story of Daluxolo. He was born in 1948 at Georgedale Mission in Natal. His father was Japhta Skhumbuzo Luthuli who started his adult life as a teacher, then became a minister of religion. He later became a very strong member of the ANC and MK. There was no particular reason why he trained and qualified as a minister of religion when he was already a teacher. Ministers of religion in those days ran schools and churches at the same time. The founder of the ANC, John Langalibalele Dube, was both a minister of religion and a teacher. He founded the Ohlange Institute. Japhta Luthuli followed this tradition, but problems lay ahead.

His pastoral work took him to Flagstaff in the Eastern Cape where he served both as teacher and pastor. He met and married Nomthandazo Majola, Daluxolo's mother. The family later moved to Georgedale where Daluxolo was born in 1948. Japhta worked happily there because it was not just a parish that he had been assigned to — it was also his home. His father, John Luthuli, had founded a school in Georgedale and built it with rocks collected from the fields with the willing help of his sons, Jimson, Zebulon and Japhta.

The parish priest's house had become old and dilapidated. When it rained, Nomthandazo had to put containers on the floor to catch the water that leaked into the house through the sieve of a roof. When the wind blew, its sound kept the family awake at night, but such things were accepted by those who served the Lord Jesus Christ. Sometimes the black clergy in Japhta's denomination, the Methodist Church, were invited to the houses of their white counterparts. They then saw how beautiful those houses were with their gleaming furniture, the study, the piano, and the food on the table. After lunch the leftovers were packed into parcels and handed to the wives of the black clergy who accepted this bounty with genuine gratitude. Some of the clothing no longer used by the sons or daughters of the white ministers was also given to them and it was used with care. The children of the white clergymen were educated in the best schools, often overseas, and the church paid the bills. Their stipends were generous as befitted the way of life that a white South African expected. The stipends of the black clergymen were much smaller, the argument being that in general black people needed less money to meet their daily needs. Seeing all this, Japhta reached a decision that would change his entire life.

He decided to build a better home for his family. He bought cement and sand and made bricks. He bought cheap planks and made doors and windows. Some members of the congregation saw the desperate efforts of their pastor and came to help. Slowly a structure rose from nothing. After many months the pastor and his family moved into their new house. It was a modest building made of bricks and roofed with zinc, but when the rain came it stayed dry inside. When the wind blew the family saw the trees swaying outside, but inside it was warm.

Then the church intervened. Somehow news reached the ear of the bishop (who was white of course) that Rev Japhta Luthuli had a new house. A few months passed uneventfully until one day a letter arrived from the bishopric. It notified Japhta that he was being transferred from Georgedale to another parish. It was not a suggestion but a decision. Black pastors were never consulted by their white colleagues about such matters. It was of no concern that the whole family had to move, that there were ties binding the pastor to a particular parish. There were also family, schools, friends. And the house. Japhta wrote back in protest and asked to be allowed to serve his master, Jesus Christ, in Georgedale. The church was firm and said he had to go.

Japhta was faced with another decision.

He decided to leave the church and because he had built the house himself without any assistance from the church, he could truly claim it as his own. He would no longer be a minister of the Methodist Church. But he had a family to raise, so he did what most men in his situation do — he went looking for a job. He found various jobs in and around nearby Pinetown and even went to work in factories as far from home as Durban. He soon ran into the oppression that was the lot of black people in South Africa, whether it was in the factories, the mines, the farms or the white households. He joined a trade union and became a shop steward, organising black workers.

Daluxolo began to notice that after his father stopped being a pastor, the old man frequently found himself thrown into gaol. This puzzled the son because he had learnt that people who went to gaol were criminals, bad people. But his father was not a criminal, he was good man. The family still prayed before meals and before retiring to bed at night. They went to church on Sundays and sometimes his father would preach at the request of the congregation. Why then was he being sent to prison? Unknown to Daluxolo, his father had become the kind of African that whites couldn't tolerate. He spurred workers at the factories to demand better living conditions and higher wages for their labour. He became a leader of the oppressed and people of that ilk in the South Africa of those days always finished up behind bars.

Daluxolo also noticed something else. Men who came to visit his father were different from the parish people who used to call on him when he was a pastor. Most came from outside Georgedale and Daluxolo would be sent to the railway station to meet them. They were told to look out for a boy with a dog. So he always went with his dog and brought them back to the house. The men discussed politics — a new topic in the house — and they didn't sing religious songs. Their songs were about Africa, the plight of the black man and that Africa should be returned to them. They shouted slogans like *Mayibuye I-Africa*! (Africa come back). They were passionate men who spoke in loud and angry tones. They demanded justice and freedom, not salvation.

One day Japhta went for a long walk with Daluxolo and spoke to him as he had never spoken to him before. Daluxolo was 14.

'A war will soon start between the black people of this country, our people, and the white government', Japhta said. 'We are preparing for that war and you and I will be part of it because of the way we are ruled by the government of the white people.'

He paused and they walked for a while.

'An organisation has been formed by the African National Congress, the ANC', he went on. 'It's called *Umkhonto we Sizwe* [Spear of the Nation]. It will become the fighting instrument of the ANC. I am already a member and from today you have also become one. This means you are now a soldier of the nation. Do you understand what that means, Daluxolo?'

'It means I have become a man and no longer a boy, father. I will have to fight, in the same way as my grandfathers fought against the white people. What I don't understand is how we will fight, considering we no longer have spears as our grandfathers did.'

Japhta looked at his son with a deep feeling of pride. This Daluxolo was a man. What more could someone of his culture ask of his son other than he should be man enough to rise to a challenge when the time came?

'We Zulus know no greater calling in life than to become warriors when the nation demands it', Japhta responded with pride. 'As for the weapons, you don't have to worry, my son.'

'But father, we need weapons if we are to fight the white man', Daluxolo persisted. 'White people have guns and we don't. How can we fight without guns?'

'Soon you will leave this country and join other young men who like you are soldiers of MK. In another country you will be trained in the use of the guns that the white people carry here. They might even be better guns. You will learn how to fight the way white people do and be taught how to beat them in their own arts of war. Then you will return and free the land.'

'I understand, father. I will do my duty to my clan, the Luthuli people, and to the people of South Africa. I will go and return later to free the land.'

'But, my son', Japhta said in a lowered tone, 'you cannot mention this to anybody…your mother especially. *Indaba yamadoda lena*' (This is a man thing).

Father and son retraced their steps homeward. Nomthandazo saw them coming home and was filled with happiness to see her menfolk taking an afternoon walk together. It was a rare thing. She sighed with contentment and called her daughter Nonkululeko into the house. It was time to prepare the evening meal.

2

Weapons of today

Simo Pascoe Bopela, Thula's father, was born and raised in Inanda Mission. It was a mission founded by Dr Daniel Lindley of the Congregational Church of the American Board Mission. They were American missionaries who came into the area during the reign of King Shaka and made friends with the local chief, Dube kaDabeka kaSilwane. Chief Dube allowed the Americans to start a school and he even sent his own son Langalibalele to be taught by the missionaries. Dube, however, fell from grace when Dingane murdered his half brother Shaka and became ruler of the Zulus. Chief Dube had been one of King Shaka's staunchest and earliest supporters and had despatched many regiments from his area to stiffen the fledgling army that Shaka was building. After Shaka's death Dube was attacked and defeated by Dingane. The chieftainship of the amaQadi people, as Dube's people are known to this day, passed to the Ngcobo clan. The last of that line is Chief Mzonjani of the amaQadi who rules there today.

Simo Bopela went to school at Inanda Primary and Higher Primary and then to Adams College — another American Mission. He was a brilliant student, but when he matriculated, his father Mhlathini, told him that he had no money to send him to university. Simo turned to his tutors at Adams College who obtained a bursary for him and he went to do his Bachelor of Arts at Fort Hare in the Eastern Cape. He did a university diploma in education after completing his BA and went to teach at Adams College. He married Grace Mfeka, a beautiful lady from his area who bore him four sons and a daughter. A popular movement of the time sent Simo to Ohlange Institute in his home area of Inanda.

The headmaster of Ohlange Institute was the great Dr John Langalibalele Dube, popularly known as Mafukuzela, because of his inexhaustible capacity for work, whether physical or mental. Mafukuzela had started a school, but he was short of teachers. At first he couldn't afford salaries and didn't get one himself either. The American missionaries helped him expand his school and even began paying meagre salaries. The South African government of the time was not prepared to build schools for black people, let alone pay salaries to those who taught there. Mafukuzela and other intellectuals formed the first black political organisation in Africa, the African Native Congress (later to become the African National Congress) in 1912. Mafukuzela was its first president.

Mafukuzela had a dream. He had studied for the priesthood in America and when he completed his doctorate he was offered a parish in America. He refused and insisted on returning to Africa. When the missionaries asked him why he was so keen to return he said:

> I am an educated man now, but my people are sitting in darkness. What is the use of a light if it gives light to only one man and leaves the others around him in darkness? The darkness around him will soon swallow up the light and there will be greater darkness. I will take the light you have given me back to my people and one day in Africa there will be a generation of men and women who possess the light I have to-day. That's why I must return. Africa needs education.

The Americans bought into his dream and undertook to help him advance his work in every way they could . He wrote a book, *Izikhali Zanamuhla* (Modern Weapons). The theme was interesting. Mafukuzela argued that black people had fought valiantly when resisting colonialism with the weapons they had — spears and shields. He called on them to concede that the power of naked courage and the spear had been broken. A new weapon was needed and that was education. He believed that you cannot defeat a person who knows more than you do. To mobilise people for freedom they needed to be educated first so that they could grasp, debate and understand the modern industrialised world. Even if freedom was won, it would be meaningless if people couldn't read or write.

Mafukuzela founded a weekly paper called *Ilanga Lase Natal* (The Natal Sun). It was published in Zulu, the language spoken in Natal and other parts of South Africa. He became editor and used this position to educate his people and change their thinking. He taught the Zulu people that they could never struggle successfully against colonialism while they fought against the BaSotho, the Xhosas, Shangaans and other ethnic groupings. They had to join together to provide a united front. He returned repeatedly to the theme of education — the modern weapon that would free the black peoples from oppression. Education, not violence was his dictum.

Simo volunteered to leave Adams College to teach at Ohlange, even though the salaries there were not great. Mafukuzela needed good teachers and his school couldn't be allowed to fail simply because the American missionaries paid better salaries. After all, the school was a national monument. So, Simo and other Fort Hare graduates were recruited to go and teach there. The missionaries also encouraged it because they regarded Mafukuzela as their child and they supported his dream.

Thula was born at Adams College in 1944, a year before his family left to settle at Inanda where his father took up teaching duties at Ohlange.

Simo was a top teacher. He taught mathematics, science, English, Latin, physics and chemistry. He was also a dedicated Christian. This meant at the time that he had to abandon his traditional ways — dialogue with God through ancestors, Zulu customs, beliefs and everything. The missionaries had negatively labelled the traditional ways, calling them paths of darkness, paganism and worshipping false deities like uMvelinqangi (The One who was present at the beginning) and uNkulunkulu (The Great One). Simo, as an educated Christian accepted that such systems of worship should be abandoned and he did so.

So Thula grew up in a household where Zulu religion and culture were never discussed. His father bought a piano and taught the children how to play it and how to read. They wore European clothing, prayed before meals and at night before going to bed and went to a school where the Christian faith was reinforced. They had even been given 'Christian' names. Thula was named after Sir Percy Osborne, the Mayor of Durban, and also after the American general, Dwight Eisenhower, Commander of the Allied Forces fighting against Nazi Germany in Europe. The other children had names like Newton, Conrad, Anderson and Maureen. Such names pleased the whites and made enrollment at school easier. It was part of being civilised. One man in the Bopela household, however, wielded an influence that flew in the face of all this. He was Thula's paternal grandfather, Blanjan Mhlathini Bopela.

Mhlathini was born in 1872 and was seven years old when the Zulu regiments under General Ntshingwayo kaMahole of the Khoza clan defeated the British at Isandlwana. Mhlathini was a great storyteller. The children would gather in his hut after the evening meal and listen to his stories. Some were fairy tales, where animals talked and did clever or stupid things. The children laughed and dozed around an evening fire at the feet of the old man. Frequently, though, he spoke of Zulu history. He told how his father had escaped death at the hands of Dingane's warriors. A spear flung at him pierced his side, but failed to hit vital organs. He told tales of how the impis of the amaQadi fought a retreating battle when Dube kaSilwane was attacked by Dingane because of his loyalty to the dead monarch, Shaka ka Senzangakhona. He was at his best when he recounted how King Dingane outwitted Piet Retief, lured him and his men into his great kraal and later massacred them.

Mhlathini would tower above the children as he spoke of the Zulu regiments, and how like the waves of the sea they kept rolling forward at Isandlwana, never allowing their ranks to be broken by the withering fire of Lord Chelmsford's men.

'Retreat in battle was outlawed in the Zulu army by the great Nodumehlezi himself' (one of Shaka's praise names), Mhlathini told the boys. 'When men fell, those behind rushed forward shouting: "*Uyadela wena osulapho*" (We cannot wait to join you where you are). Shaka transformed the entire fighting psychology of the Zulu army. Warriors in those days competed to reach the enemy ranks first, not by running wildly towards the enemy lines, but in straight, fast and disciplined files. Eagerness to join forces with the enemy didn't mean disorder in the ranks. The regiments on the flanks, younger men, would move at high speed to encircle the enemy, while the older and more mature regiments formed the chest in the middle. The troops in the centre marched more slowly than the horns, but once the horns had cut off the enemy from retreat, only then would the chest surge forward to complete the annihilation.

'After a battle men were singled out at a parade and their acts of valour recited before the king and the nation. The king rewarded such warriors with generous gifts of cattle.

'Cowards who had fled from battle were also singled out, paraded in front of everybody and denounced. The sentence for cowardice was death. The ones who died at the hands of the enemy were heroes. It was a stark choice...'

Mhlathini would stop for a while and find his snuff box — the part that the children liked most. He would pause, open it and pour some tobacco into his hand. It would be carefully conveyed to his mouth. After chewing it over for a while, he would spit unerringly into the fire and the children would roar with laughter. He would then order them out of his hut and settle down for the night.

It is impossible to measure how greatly this finely-honed history — a subject not discussed in the Bopela household — made an impression in the minds of the children. It is clear though that Mhlathini's stories made a great impact on my own mind. What I learnt was that my people, the Zulus, had once been a great nation. They were now a defeated people, treated with contempt by every race in South Africa. Would a chance ever come to restore their former glory? I asked my grandfather this question one day, and Mhlathini answered:

> The Zulus were great under only two of their kings, Shaka and Cetshwayo. Shaka had a clear task ... to unite the Nguni-speaking clans so that the white people would be unable to play one Nguni chief against another ... as they had done to the Xhosas. When the whites came to Zululand, there was only one king to deal with, Shaka ka Senzangakhona. The whites fought no wars against Shaka, because they would have faced a united people under a single ruler. Their divide-and-rule trick wouldn't have worked.
>
> When Dingane killed Shaka at kwaNyakamubi, he created a crack in the unity of the nation — a crack that became wider and wider as he killed more of his brothers. Mpande fled Zululand and made a pact with the English and the Boers against his brother, Dingane. Mpande's sons, Mbuyazi and Cetshwayo fought a terrible battle at Ndondakusuka where Mbuyazi was slain. After Cetshwayo's defeat at Ulundi, Zululand was placed under several chieftains, a political set-up that Shaka had tried to prevent. Since then, the Zulus haven't been anything but dogs of the white men.

The boys shivered as they imagined great groups of regiments clashing against each other and men dying.

'*Mkhulu* [Grandfather], why did Dingane kill his brother Shaka and the others? Is it right for brothers to fight and kill each other?' I asked the old man, saddened by the story.

'Among any people, there is always one person who believes that everything should belong to him. Dingane believed that amongst Senzangakhona's sons he was the one who should rule. He caused great disunity and destroyed what was once a great nation'.

I pressed on. 'Will the Zulus always be divided grandfather? Won't another Shaka appear to unite us and lead us against the government of the white people?'

'It will never happen, my boy', the old man said with finality. 'Zulus are doomed because their princes are short-sighted. Zulu princes think only of power and they fight over it. The white people support the weaker chieftain and help him to defeat the stronger one. In that way they keep the nation divided.'

Simo's eldest son Vusumuzi spoke up suddenly. 'There is an organisation called the

African National Congress. It preaches unity, not only of the Zulus, but unity between Zulus, Sothos, Xhosa and all the black people of this country. I think this organisation, because it's led by highly educated men, will one day unite us.'

'Maybe you are right, my grandson', Mhlathini responded, yawning with exhaustion. 'I'm an old man, and my knowledge is of past events. You're talking about the future. I don't know what will happen in the future, I can only tell you what happened in the past. But if what you say is true, then a new thinking must come among our people. Whoever becomes the leader will have to think of the people and what they need, rather than what he himself wants. That's where the Zulu princes failed.'

At first I didn't understand the difference in approach between my father and my grandfather. I tried to discuss things I had heard from my grandfather with my father. Mhlathini had raised my father, so what he said to me, he surely must also have told his son. But I was wrong. One day I asked my father why he went to church with us while Mhlathini always remained at home. The old man never joined in our family prayers.

'Your grandfather believes in the things of the past, my boy', he explained. 'He will tell you, for instance, that the sun rises and sets. I know that the sun does nothing of the kind. I know that it's the earth that rotates and revolves around the sun, which causes night and day and the four seasons.'

'But father, many of the things he tells us are true, like the great wars that our people fought against the white people. Those things are true, even if they happened in the past.'

'You're right, of course, my boy. It's good to understand the past, but it's even better to understand the present and the future. That's where we are and that's where we're going. Only an educated man will survive and make progress in the future, because the white man has created a new world. To survive in that world one needs education and civilisation, not Zulu history.'

'Does *Mkhulu* believe in Jesus Christ, Dad?'

'No, he doesn't.'

'Then what does he believe in?'

'He believes that his father Dambuza and his grandfather Batshazwayo and others before them are the ones he must pray to. That's his right. I believe in Jesus Christ, the Son of God, and that's my right.'

'But Dad, even the Jews pray to their ancestors, Abraham, Isaac and Jacob, and Jesus is called the son of Joseph. Why shouldn't *Mkhulu* pray to his departed fathers?'

'Because Jesus came to make peace between God and all men', my father responded. 'It's no longer necessary to pray through ancestors, whether it's Jews or Africans.'

'Will *Mkhulu* go to heaven when he dies, if he doesn't believe in Jesus?'

'Who goes to heaven and who doesn't is God's decision, my boy. There were ways that were right in the past, but we have moved beyond that. It was correct to shout messages from hilltop to hilltop before the arrival of the white people. Today we have telephones and can talk to people as far away as England. The Zulus in your grandfather's time fought with spears and assegais. The weapons of today are guns. The black people don't have guns, so the weapon they must fight with is education. That's why I send you all to school. Education is the weapon that will set you free. Even our leaders of today must be educated men.'

I went away from this discussion with a heavy heart because I liked my grandfather's stories, even if they were about the past. But I could see that my father was right. Without an education you cannot even tell the time.

The people of Inanda Mission placed a high value on education. The American missionaries built a school for girls which became known as Inanda Seminary. Many black women in leadership positions today, both in business and politics, studied at Inanda Seminary. Only a few kilometres away was the school founded by the iconic Dr John Langalibalele Dube, uMafukuzela Onjengezulu (Mafukuzela who is made in the likeness of Heaven). A person growing up at Inanda Mission had no excuses not to be educated. There was a primary school which taught kids through to standard seven. One could move on to secondary and high school education at either Inanda Seminary or Ohlange High School. Within a radius of ten kilometres a person could begin and complete a high school education.

The proud men and women of Inanda had a vision for the Mission. There was Dr Innes Gumede, a physician who studied medicine in Edinburgh, Scotland. There was Mr AWG Champion (his real surname was Mhlongo), a pioneer trade unionist and later the Natal President of the African National Congress. He was very anti-communist. A South African communist, Eric Mtshali, explained how he had met him . . .

'I had an affair with one of Champion's daughters and I visited her at home. Champion came in and found me sitting on the sofa and I stood up to greet him. He ignored me.

'Ziningi, what is this?' he asked his daughter.

'Dad, I thought that when we ask questions about people we say: "Who is this? Not what is this?"'

'Ziningi', her father continued relentlessly, 'I'm asking a very simple question. What is this?'

'I can tell you his name, father, because even though you don't think so, he has a name'.

'Don't tell me a name Ziningi. Just tell me what this thing is?'

'Father, I can't answer that question.'

'In that case I will answer the question for you. It's a communist.'

The principal of Inanda Primary School was Kenneth *Bhatata* Mnguni — nicknamed that because he had a shrill voice. As in most schools in South Africa the morning began with prayers. At those prayers Bhatata unashamedly preached politics. I was only eight when I first heard one of his political sermons and it stuck in my mind. I had never heard anybody speak like that before. He said:

> In Cape Town Dr Daniel Malan asked his parliament where he (Dr Malan) was standing. The Members of Parliament replied that Dr Malan was standing on the platform.
> *'Nee, here, ek staan nie op die platvorm nie; ek staan op die kaffer se nek!'* (No, gentlemen, I am not standing on the platform; I am standing on the kaffir's neck).

Bhatata warned us that if we didn't study hard we would never escape the harshness of life under National Party rule. Most of us were too young to properly grasp what he was saying, but his words stayed with us. Later when we were grown up we remembered and his words made sense.

Bhatata and other teachers formed a bus company called *Ukuthuthuka kwamaQadi* (The rise of the Qadi people). The buses ran for a few years before the company collapsed. Maybe it was because they didn't know how to run a transport business — or any business for that matter. Maybe they were dependant for repairs and servicing on their rivals in the transport business, the Indians. *Ukuthuthuka kwamaQadi*, for whatever reason is no longer a company and its buses have vanished. The hopes of a revival of the Qadi people vanished along with those buses.

Then there was the football club, the Natal Cannons Red and Blue. It was the aspiration of every young man in Inanda to play for the Natal Cannons. Most famous among them was the goalkeeper, Ernest Bheki
'Parachute' Majola. He was selected as goalkeeper for South Africa when the team went to play Rhodesia in 1954. They flew to Bulawayo and when Parachute returned, nobody who hadn't flown in an aeroplane could match him.

'Only Dr Innes Gumede can tell me about things I haven't seen, not you, sir', he would say.

Indeed in those days very few people had been passengers on an aeroplane.

In the 1950s there was a lot of social and sport activity in Inanda. There was a tennis team, The Lilies, made up of older and younger members of the community. There was a tennis court behind the church. There was no sponsorship but the youngsters practised regularly, especially during school vacations when they returned from their colleges. There were two choirs that provided music during church services and when there were weddings at church. One choir comprised senior members of the congregation — in my view the superior choir — and the other was made up of young school teachers.

I tell all this to preserve the memory of Inanda as it was in those years. Today it has become a slum, a dangerous place where criminals lurk and the main activities are drinking, drug-taking and crime. The vision of a better Inanda vanished when the men and women of that generation passed away. Those who remain and still strive to revive the vision are few and work against heavy odds.

My father, Simo Bopela, returned from self-imposed exile in Zimbabwe in 1993 and died three years later, the victim of a hit-and-run accident. The taxi driver who killed him dragged the injured old man for about 120 metres until he fell away from the vehicle. The taxi didn't stop. At his funeral, the master of ceremonies, Asquith Thula Goba, a former teacher, spoke about my father's death as follows:

> Mr Bopela has died of a disease that's spreading fast in our community of Inanda, and indeed the whole country: a growing insensitivity towards human suffering and little or no care for human life.

Inanda was a religious community and its story wouldn't be complete if I didn't touch on that aspect of community life. I have deliberately described it as a religious rather than a

Christian community. A religious community, in my view, is one where people believe in the existence of God, Allah or Shiva. On specific days such a community observes certain rituals, like going to a church, mosque or temple. The people of Inanda went to church every Sunday, but the true Christian teaching of loving one another, of doing unto others as you would have others do unto you, was missing. Why was that?

I think it was because they had learned their Christianity from white missionaries who put stress on formality and not deeds. They prayed and sang, but they never sought out and helped poor families, nor did they make provision for the widows and orphans in their midst. They gossiped a lot, compared their standard of living with that of the less fortunate amongst them and derived satisfaction by drawing the conclusion that they were materially better off. There were prominent families and less prominent families — the standard was material and not religious worth.

3

When it's all right to lie

People who joined MK became suddenly involved in activities they couldn't mention even to those closest to them — fathers, mothers, wives, brothers and best friends. The South African Police's Security Branch, the notorious SB, relied heavily on a widespread network of informers. The social arrangement they had created — separating races in terms of residence, schools, sports, social amenities and so on — meant that whites were isolated. When they needed to know what was happening in the black, Indian or coloured communities, they had to rely on spies. Huge sums of money were made available to the Security Police to bribe and recruit people from these communities. The informers then kept the government abreast of who was saying what or who was making plans against the apartheid state.

Japhta Luthuli reminded his son Daluxolo not to mention a word of what they had discussed about MK to anybody — even his mother. This was not because Japhta thought Nomthandazo was a government informer; it was just a standard MK precaution. During World War II, there were signs in public places that read: 'Loose lips sink ships'. This was a realisation that there were spies everywhere. People could pass on vital information and war plans without any deliberate evil intent.

MK recruits found themselves victims of unguarded chatter. For instance, a group of men from the Eastern Cape told their wives that they were going to Johannesburg to play rugby against a team there. In fact, they were leaving the country for military training. The wives became suspicious because their menfolk hadn't played rugby for years and didn't belong to any local team. It was not a well thought out lie. The women concluded that their men were running away from them, so they reported the matter to the police. The group was arrested on a train heading for Johannesburg.

The Security Branch encouraged their agents to infiltrate the ANC or the Pan Africanist Congress (PAC). Both organisations had adopted violent resistance as a policy. It's interesting to note that the PAC split from the ANC because they disagreed with the latter's political strategy of allowing whites and Indians to become members. The Security Branch recruited blacks to penetrate both the ANC and the PAC as they knew that whites or Indians would be suspect. They also didn't live in the townships where the blacks lived. It was a good example of arbitrary double-sided race classification.

Daluxolo left South Africa in 1963 with other young men from Georgedale and other townships around Durban. Japhta told his wife that their son had gone to an African traditional healer to have sores healed that chronically infected his legs. When he hadn't returned after six months, Nomthandazo expressed a wish to visit him. Japhta explained that he was making good progress, but the treatment of his sores had reached a critical stage. He told her that if she went to see him it would ruin the power of the medicine because she was a woman. 'When the boy is ready to come home, I will go with you to fetch him. Stop worrying, my wife, you will see your son soon', Japhta lied.

By then Daluxolo was in the MK's Luthuli camp in Tanzania. This was where the ANC housed cadres who were on their way to get military training. Trained cadres stayed at Mandela Camp. No one was allowed to visit either camp except members of the National Executive Committee (NEC), those delivering food supplies and drivers transporting new recruits.

Daluxolo was the youngest cadre in the camp and everybody wondered how a boy of 14 would cope with the rigours of military training, let alone fight a war. Nor did the older guerrillas want to be burdened with a young boy when the fighting started.

'*Kufuneka amadoda kulempi, hayi abantwana*' (We need men in this war, not babies), one cadre remarked.

Joe Modise — later to become Minister of Defence in Nelson Mandela's cabinet — remarked when he saw Daluxolo for the first time: 'I cannot understand why MK people would recruit an infant like you when there are so many grown men in Natal. My decision, therefore, is that you will be sent to school to study, not to a military camp. Do you understand, my boy?'

The older cadres were extremely fond of the young man and felt protective towards him. They listened to Joe Modise and wondered how the boy would respond. In some ways they agreed with Joe that Daluxolo was too young to be a soldier, although they would be sad to see him transferred to Mtoni where the ANC housed recruits who had opted for an academic education. They despised those who chose the safe and easy route of going to school while others went to fight.

'I am not an infant in the first place, and I am not your boy!' Daluxolo exploded. 'I'm a man and a soldier and it's my father who decided that. I won't go to school and you have no right to make me do something different from what my father has decided. You can take your own son to the school, but you're not taking me. I'm the son of Japhta Luthuli of the Luthuli clan and we are warriors.'

The reply was so vehement that Joe paused and looked at the young man standing before him trembling with rage. He had never met such a boy. Youngsters were usually grateful to be released from military duties and sent to an environment where there were no flying bullets. He stood there pondering for a moment.

'All right Comrade Daluxolo, I apologise for calling you an infant. Yes, you are indeed a man, but I still believe you are too young to join MK and fight. That's my position.'

'We say in my language: *Ubudoda abukhulelwa* [Manhood knows no age] and I challenge you to prove that I cannot fulfil my military tasks because of my age. Try me

Send me for training. Put a gun in my hand and Boers in front of me. See what happens.'

'Comrade Daluxolo, this is final and I won't debate the matter further. You will be moved from Luthuli Camp and placed among students. The ANC will arrange a scholarship and you'll go to school. If you still want to fight after that, I will gladly welcome you into the ranks of MK. But at the moment MK is a closed avenue for you.'

'If you exclude me from MK, I will resign from the ANC and join the PAC. They are also recruiting young men to go and fight. My father enlisted me in MK and nobody can change that.'

Daluxolo spun on his heel and walked away, leaving Joe to stare at his retreating form. Joe shook his head and after saying goodbye to the cadres standing around, he got into his Land-Rover and left.

Oliver Tambo, President of the ANC, arrived at Luthuli Camp two days later along with James Radebe, Mendi Msimang and Advocate Duma Nokwe — the Secretary-General. Tambo had come to inspire and listen to the recruits in Luthuli Camp who were leaving for the USSR within days. The cadres stood in three rows in front of him and the other leaders. Tambo addressed them.

'*Amandla*!' (Power!)

'*Ngawethu*!' (To the people!) the cadres roared back the reply.

'We are here to say farewell to you for a little while. You will be travelling to a country where you will learn the skills of war. We have faith that you will master these skills and return to Tanzania. From there we will make plans to send you home. The apartheid regime has imprisoned our leaders at home. Nelson Mandela, Walter Sisulu, Govan Mbeki, Ahmed Kathrada and others are imprisoned on Robben Island. The whole of South Africa has become one vast prison. Who will free our people? We will! Let each one of us do his or her part in the great task of national liberation. Do you have any questions, comrades?'

Daluxolo strode out of the formation and stopped in front of the President.

'My father ordered me to join *Umkhonto we Sizwe* and sent me out of the country to be trained as a soldier. A man with a big stomach has told me that he won't allow me to become a soldier because I'm too young. He says I should go to school instead. Who is this man? What makes him think that he can change my father's decision?'

'Do you want to be a soldier of *Umkhonto we Sizwe*, comrade?'

'I do, Comrade President.'

'Is it your father's decision only, or do you also want to become a freedom fighter?'

'It is my decision. I want to become a freedom fighter, Comrade President.'

'Then you shall be, comrade. All MK soldiers are volunteers. No one is forced to join or to stay out. We are a democratic organisation!'

The MK cadres roared their approval.

'*Viva* Comrade OR, *Viva*! *Viva* Chief Luthuli *Viva*! *Viva* Comrade Mandela, *Viva*!'

It was a great afternoon and the leaders mixed with the recruits, answering questions and inspiring them. That evening they ate supper at Luthuli Camp, eating the same food as the cadres, before they took their leave.

4

How a young man became a terrorist

I, Thula, left South Africa on 1 September 1963 to join my father and brother in Rhodesia. I travelled on a temporary residence permit which we hoped to renew until I could qualify for permanent residence. I left home to escape Bantu Education, an inferior system of schooling aimed specifically at black people. In Rhodesia education was never corrupted during white rule. In South Africa it was the policy of the National Party government to keep blacks at a level where they couldn't compete in the labour market with whites. This decided my father that I should leave South Africa and go to Rhodesia to learn. My father, Simo, had himself left South Africa to escape teaching under the Bantu Education system.

I stayed in Rhodesia until November of 1963 when my three month permit expired. I applied for an extension but the request was turned down. I was told to return to South Africa and re-apply to enter the country if I so wished. This was a crisis. Should I return to South Africa? If I was refused another permit, what would I do then?

From the moment I first arrived in Rhodesia, I began corresponding with a former schoolmate from Amanzimtoti Zulu Training College (formerly Adams College), Victor Mnyandu. He was then in Darmstadt, Germany, having left the country in 1962 with a group of ANC nurses. He encouraged me to consider coming to Europe to study. It was an idea that had immense appeal.

'If you can get to Dar-es-Salaam, Thula, I'll help you get a German scholarship so that you can study in Europe', Victor's letter had concluded.

I left Rhodesia in February 1964 after my final appeal for an extension of my residence permit had been turned down. I was put aboard a train for Mafikeng where the Rhodesian immigration authorities intended to hand me over to the South Africans. I was escorted by a Rhodesian immigration official. At Palapye station while travelling through Botswana, I jumped train while the official was away buying beers with money I had provided.

I stayed for a while with an uncle and his family at Serowe in Botswana, then travelled to Kazungula where I crossed into Zambia by ferry, together with some members of the South West African People's Organisation (SWAPO) I had met at Maung. I got to Lusaka by train the same day, and joined the ANC. They arranged my transit from Zambia to Tanzania. By May 1963 I was at the ANC students' residence at Mtoni, just outside Dar-es-Salaam. I resumed correspondence with Victor, telling him I had arrived in Dar. I also let my father and brother know where I was.

My travels through Botswana and Zambia into Tanzania brought me into contact with African people I had only read about before. I had grown up in Natal where everybody spoke Zulu. In Botswana I listened to the Batswana speaking their language, Setswana. It seemed like Sesotho which is spoken by the BaSotho in South Africa, so it was not utterly foreign to me. In Rhodesia I heard the Shona language for the first time — it seemed like Greek to me. In Livingstone, on the Zambian side of the Victoria Falls, I met the Barotses from Barotseland and in Lusaka I heard a language called Chibemba. When I got to Tanzania, I immediately fell in love with KiSwahili, the common language of East Africa.

'*Jambo bwana*' (Hello, sir), the Tanzanians would say in greeting.

'*Jambo*', you would reply.

'*Abari gani?* (How are you?), would come the enquiry after your health.

'*Muzuri, bwana, asante.*' (I am very well, thank you).

'*Abari yamama?*' (How is your wife doing?)

'*Mama muzuri sana.*' (My wife is fine)

'*Abari yawatoto?*' (How are the children doing?)

'*Watoto wazuri, asante*' (The children are very well, thank you).

The Tanzanian would enquire after your cattle, crops, friends and life in general. When asked why they asked one about all these things, the Tanzanians would respond in this fashion:

'Your wife, children, cattle, crops and friends are all part of your life and well-being. We cannot only hear about your personal health and stop there, because if any of the other important people and things in your life are not doing well, then your life and well-being are affected.'

South Africans, especially the urbanised ones, often lost patience when confronted with such a lengthy greeting. When they got irritated and told the Tanzanians to stop asking after all these things, the locals would apologise for having offended the guest.

'*Phole sana, ndugu, phole.*' (I'm sorry, brother, really sorry.)

Then it would be the South African's turn to be embarrassed, realising that when a person enquires after the health of your family, no offence is intended. I found the Tanzanians intelligent, humble and respectful. Most were not wealthy, but even those who were didn't openly display it. Highly educated Tanzanians speak KiSwahili like everyone else — unlike in South Africa where the educated speak English.

Parts of Tanzania are very hot for most of the year, Dar-es-Salaam in particular. The locals stayed cool by wearing a cotton garment called a *kanga* tied around their waist, a light cotton shirt and sandals. The South Africans could easily be identified by their smart western clothing, expensive shoes and caps. By midday they were sweating profusely and complaining about the heat.

I stayed at Mtoni with other ANC students waiting to go to Europe or America to study. The ANC organised bursaries and students would go to the country of their choice. The ones still waiting spent much of their time at the ANC office in town helping to compile the ANC political magazine, *The Spotlight*. This journal highlighted matters of political interest in South Africa such as the arrest, trial and conviction of top ANC leaders. It was sent to various embassies and government officials to heighten their awareness of the South African situation. The students spent the rest of their time wandering around town visiting libraries, bars and hotels.

One day I went to the ANC office to do my bit on *The Spotlight* and my life changed forever. I saw five young men sitting in the foyer. Among them was a youngish fellow of around my age and I decided to make his acquaintance.

'I'm Thula Bopela from Durban', I introduced myself.

'I'm Zoli from South Africa.'

'I can tell you're from South Africa, but where in South Africa?'

'Just South Africa will do', he told me.

I felt annoyed with him. Why was he making such a big mystery of where he came from? Before I could say anything more I was called by Tambo's secretary, Maud Manyoni (her nom de guerre). Her real name was Mate Mfusi.

'Thula, come here', she called.

I went to her desk.

'Yes?' I said.

'Stop asking silly questions'.

'What's so silly about asking where a guy comes from?'

'It's silly because you are not supposed to do it.'

'Why? I told him where I come from, so what's the big mystery?'

'Because he's an MK soldier and you're a civilian, that's why. MK soldiers don't go around telling people where they come from.'

I turned and examined the men sitting on the sofas with renewed interest. They looked very fit and most were heavily bearded. So they were MK!

'Where do they live, Sis Maud? I haven't seen them before.'

'That's another question you're are not allowed to ask.'

'I'm not a spy, so what's the big deal?'

'Because civilians aren't told where guerrillas live, whether they're spies or not. Now go find yourself something useful to do and stop asking stupid questions.'

My day felt ruined. How could I go and work on *The Spotlight* when I had discovered the most sensational news in my life? Here were young men training to fight the SADF. They were soldiers, not ninnies like me and the rest of the bunch sitting around at Mtoni. They were the guys who would free the country while the rest of us were burying our noses in books at a university somewhere. I went outside for a smoke. My mind was reeling.

I had just lit a cigarette when one of the men approached. He smiled and held out his hand in greeting.

'I'm Goodman Mhlauli and I'm from Cape Town. Where can I buy some booze?'

'Oh', I said, 'I can help you with that. Come with me.'

We walked down a few alleyways and found ourselves at a shack.

'*Hodi bwana!*' (Knock, knock, sir), I called and pushed the door open.

'*Karibuni, mabwana.*' (Welcome to you, gentlemen), someone replied as we entered.

'*Huyu bwana namimi tinataka pombe, tafadali.*' (This gentleman and I would like some beer, please) I continued showing off my KiSwahili to my new-found friend.

Bottles appeared from behind a curtain and a jug and glasses were placed in front of us. The liquor was called *pombe yamnaza*, a palm wine. It seemed very weak — milk-like — and tasted semisweet. But it was potent and had the kick of a donkey. I poured from the jug and we both drank.

'Sis Maud said that you guys are soldiers. Is it true?'

'Call me Rashidi, that's my MK name. I know you're Thula from Durban. Yes, we're soldiers, but we're not allowed to talk to anybody about it.'

'That's okay with me', I responded feeling somewhat let down because of my curiosity.

'Why don't you become a soldier yourself, Thula? There'll be no secrets then. I think that all young South Africans should become soldiers. Until now only a few of us have volunteered. The others tell you how much they hate apartheid, but they're too damned scared to go and fight for what they believe in. You don't seem that sort of chap.'

I poured myself another glass of wine, feeling I had reached a decisive stage in my life.

'No, I'm not afraid to fight, Rashidi. Some guys tried to recruit me into the ANC in 1960 at Ohlange where I went to school. I refused to join because I didn't think we could free South Africa by making fancy speeches and taking part in demonstrations. I told them I would only join when the ANC made up its mind to fight. It seems that it has now, so that puts me at my own crossroads. I will certainly become a soldier, my friend. Just give me time.'

We ordered another jug and drank quickly because Rashidi had to rejoin his comrades. A Land-Rover was coming to the office to collect and take them to their camp outside town. We paid for the wine and I thanked the old man running the place.

I didn't work at the ANC office that day but took the bus back to Mtoni. I lay on my bed sweating because of the mid-day heat. My mind was made up. I would join MK but I had no idea how to go about it. I didn't discuss it with anyone. Late in the afternoon the other students began dribbling back to Mtoni. Most were drunk and they began to sing revolutionary songs.

'*UMandela ufun amajoni, amajoni enkululeko*', (Mandela wants soldiers, soldiers of freedom), they sang.

I didn't join in but sat in the main sitting room deep in thought. One student, Mimi (Joe Nhlanhla, who after 1994 became Minister of Intelligence) asked me if I wasn't feeling well. We were friends and I had learnt a lot about the struggle from him.

'No, Mimi, I'm not sick; I'm just being quiet. Maybe I'm homesick', I lied.

'Well, if you're homesick — which we all are to a certain extent — join in the singing. It'll make you feel better.'

'Tell me something, Mimi', I heard myself saying, 'why do we sing that Mandela needs soldiers of freedom when none of us are willing to become one? What are we really singing about?'

The other students heard my question and the singing stopped. Wana Makhoba from Kimberly joined the discussion.

'Maybe that's why we're singing, Thula', Wana joked. 'It makes us feel like the soldiers that Mandela wants.'

He laughed and put his arm around me.

I shook him off and stood up.

'Mandela is on Robben Island serving a life sentence. Here we are in a free country, singing our heads off about his need for soldiers to free South Africa. Yet we all know that none of us will ever become soldiers. So who will do the fighting for us?'

'Oh, come on Thula, don't be a fool', Tebogo burst out. 'We have matric certificates and we'll be going to university to obtain degrees. Those degrees will pay off when the country is free because administrators will be needed. That will be our contribution to the struggle. What's the use of going off to fight and finding out after we remove the whites from power that we don't have anyone capable of replacing them? There are millions of people around who only got as far as standard two, three or four. They'll be available to do the fighting.'

'Look ,Thula', Wana added, 'you surely don't believe that bright boys like us should go and learn to shoot, do you? Being a soldier is about shooting and even an illiterate is capable of that. Getting a master's degree in public administration requires brains. So those with brains have a duty to go and study for their country — those with brawn will do the fighting. It's called a fair division of labour.'

'What about Fidel Castro who has just freed Cuba? Was he illiterate too, Wana? He holds an LLB but went into the Sierra Maestra mountains and fought for liberation. What about Che Guevara, the revolutionary hero? Is he also illiterate? I hear he's a medical doctor. Our own Nelson Mandela is a qualified lawyer, but he still went to Ethiopia and Algeria to train and return to free his people. Is he another illiterate? Why don't you guys just come out straight? Admit that you're cowards or just too selfish to make a sacrifice. Stop telling me about your miserable matric certificates.'

'Thula has a point, guys', Oupatjie said. 'The issue is not education — it's about whether you're afraid to fight or not. It's about whether you're too selfish to lay down your life for the freedom you claim to believe in.'

'So why don't you go and do the stupid thing, Oupatjie?' Wana shouted. 'Go and get yourself killed. Why are you sitting here with us? Thula is calling us cowards and saying we are selfish, yet he is still going to school with us. To hell with you guys.'

'I'm certainly not going to volunteer to fight as long as the leaders' sons are going to school', yelled another student. 'If it's about making sacrifices, let's all do it. Why should I go and get killed so that other people can step over my corpse into power? If Thula and Oupatjie want to become the horses on which other people will ride to power, let them do it, but I'm not.'

'I see that this subject is very painful for some of us', I remarked quietly. 'Let each man decide what he should do and then do it. If we decide that we are only willing to talk and sing about liberation, let's talk and sing. I once read a book called *Uncle Tom's Cabin*. It's about Negro slaves in South Carolina. They all hated being slaves. Some tried to escape — a perilous undertaking. Others just stayed on the plantations and continued to be abused. It seems we have a similar choice.'

I stayed awake far into the night thinking, while the other students continued the debate in the sitting room. Many had troubled consciences. Some of them went to sleep peacefully — they had already decided to take the easy road to liberation by going to school.

I got to the office early the next morning. Maud was already behind her desk and I greeted her cheerfully.

'Sis Maud, I would like to see the President, please.'

'What do you want with the President? He's a busy man and doesn't have time to talk nonsense with young boys.'

'It's not nonsense, Sis Maud, I assure you. Please ask the President to allow me ten minutes of his time. That's all I need.'

'Very well, but if he complains about me allowing a ruggamuffin like you to squander his time, I'll be very annoyed.'

Maud went into the President's office, spoke to him briefly and then returned.

'He's very busy, so keep it short and to the point.'

I entered the President's office and greeted him. He came from behind his desk and shook my hand. He held it for some time, searching my face with his piercing, kindly eyes.

'I heard what Maud said to you, Comrade Thula. But don't mind her. I like it when comrades come to see me. If they don't I feel lonely. So how can I help you?'

He waved me to a sofa where I sat down. He sat next to me.

'Thanks for seeing me, Comrade President. I have a simple request. I want to become a member of *Umkhonto we Sizwe*.'

OR (Oliver Reginald) Tambo got up, walked to the window and contemplated the view. He turned and walked back to the sofa. His eyes had hardened, but he was not angry.

'Please listen carefully to what I am about to say, Comrade Thula. Sure we want young men to join MK, but we have a problem. We haven't found a safe route to send our trained men back into South Africa. It's not difficult to train hundreds of freedom fighters. The problem is how to get them home safely. Do you understand what I'm saying, comrade?'

'Yes, Comrade President, I understand. You're saying you don't want me in your army.'

OR's eyes narrowed, then he smiled.

'You know very well that's not what I'm saying, comrade. I'm sharing a problem with you that the outside leadership is facing. Mozambique is under Portuguese control, so we cannot infiltrate South Africa through there. Rhodesia is under Ian Smith so our men cannot use that route. In places like Botswana and Swaziland security is still controlled by whites who make sure our MK men are caught once they step inside those countries.'

'So while the leadership continues to search for a safe route home, we can be training and getting ready to go there and fight.'

'It's not that simple, Comrade Thula. It may take us years to find a safe route home, so it wouldn't be wise to enlarge our army when we don't know what to do with it. My advice to you, comrade, is that you go to school and get a degree. When we're ready and able to infiltrate men safely, then by all means come and join us. Does that satisfy you, Comrade Thula?'

'The only thing that will satisfy me is your permission to join MK, so I can help to free my people. Any other answer is unacceptable, Comrade President.'

'Then I must speak like your father whom I represent. Go to school, young man, and re-apply when you have finished your degree. Then we'll send you home without danger of you being captured.'

There was no mistaking the authority in his voice. I decided to force the issue as it seemed the only hope of getting my way. I stood up, walked to the door and turned.

'If you send me to school against my wishes I will go . . . but I won't study. I will womanise, do drugs and drink myself to the devil. My blood will be on your hands, Comrade President. Your friend Nelson Mandela is in prison and relying on you to raise an army to free him. Yet when we volunteer, you send us away. Goodbye, Comrade President, I won't bother you again.'

I left without even glancing at the President and banged the door behind me. I went and got drunk. I spent a week without returning to the office, pondering on what my next move should be. That Sunday afternoon a Land-Rover arrived at Mtoni with James Radebe and Mendi Msimang aboard. They told me to pack my suitcase and get in the Land-Rover. They took me to Luthuli Camp where I joined other cadres about to undergo military training.

That's how a young man who wanted to study law became a terrorist — if that word has any meaning.

5

A non-violent organisation turns to violence

'Why did it take the ANC leaders 48 years to understand that to free our people they had to fight . . . and that it's impossible for an oppressed people to free themselves from an armed and violent oppressor merely by organising petitions and peaceful demonstrations?'

That is the question I asked in Dar-es-Salaam in 1964, just after joining MK. I was talking with one of South Africa's leading revolutionaries, ANC national executive member and senior member of the SACP, JB Marks. We were on a hill overlooking the harbour and watching ships sailing in and out. Marks was highly respected both in exile and at home, even by ordinary members of the ANC. He was immensely popular, especially among MK men who found him open and easy to approach. He often joked but there was no mistaking his seriousness, simplicity and dedication to the liberation struggle. He could answer any question on South African history or about Marxist thought. He was well read and a mine of information.

'The ANC was formed in 1912 in response to the formation of the Union of South Africa in 1910 ', JB began his response to my question. 'The African people had just emerged from a series of sometimes epic battles which they waged against colonialism. But in the end all resistance was crushed. It was the triumph of the rifle over the spear, Comrade Thula. The power of the kings was broken, their regiments smashed and disbanded. The last uprising, the Bambatha Rebellion of 1905, had been stamped out. Most people believed that armed resistance to white colonialism was useless.'

JB smiled, understanding what was going through my mind. He knew I was looking at the problem from the viewpoint of the 1960s and feeling little sympathy or understanding for the political dilemma that faced African leaders in 1912. In the 60s it was easy to understand the ANC's change of policy from non-violent to violent resistance. Now that the decision to fight the apartheid government had been made, young men like myself found it difficult to understand why non-violence hadn't been considered as a policy in the first place.

'Young people are impatient and angry', JB remarked, 'but it's the role of leaders to stop them flying off the handle. No credible African leader could have contemplated further violent resistance after the defeat of mighty kings like Cetshwayo, Dinuzulu and General Bambatha. The nation was licking its wounds. There were other reasons, Comrade Thula, that influenced the thinking of the ANC leadership at that time.

'The African people resisted colonialism as tribal entities under tribal leaders. The leaders of 1912 wanted to unite the people as a single nation, the African nation — something that couldn't be achieved under traditional tribal leadership. The ANC of the time was laying the foundation of a more effective resistance to colonialism. They wanted opposition by a united African nation rather than isolated and uncoordinated acts of defiance. Of course, time was needed to change people's thinking from tribal to national consciousness.'

'I hear what you say, Comrade JB', I answered, 'but my question still stands. Did it really have to take so long to change the policy?'

'I don't believe a change of policy from non-violence to violence would have been practicable before 1960, comrade. I'll tell you why. Let's say the ANC leadership concluded in 1930, or even in 1948 when the National Party came to power, that only violent resistance could free us. There was no Organisation of African Unity in those days. Where would the ANC have sent its cadres for military training? There were no free African states in 1930 to support the liberation of the African people in South Africa. Ghana, Nigeria, Algeria, Egypt and the rest of them were all firmly under the yoke of colonialism.

'There's another aspect that might have contributed to the choice of a non-violent strategy', continued Comrade JB. 'They were intellectuals, clergymen and pacifists. Clergymen by training and conviction are opposed to war. Intellectuals believe in solving problems by argument, debate and reason. They were the right kind of leaders at the time, but by 1960 a new kind was needed to take control.'

'Comrade JB, something puzzles me about our black clergymen and Christians in general. Black clergymen abhor violence as a principle, yet white clergymen bless their soldiers when they go into battle and even pray to God for victory. A good example of a violent clergyman is the Rev Ian Paisley in Northern Ireland, don't you agree? The SADF has salaried chaplains placed permanently with the troops. Yet nearly all black clergymen preach non-violence to our people. How so, Comrade JB?'

JB paused briefly. He was a communist and didn't want to give me the impression he was attacking Christians, but he knew he had to give the right answer otherwise I would lose faith in him.

'Take Rev Martin Luther King, Comrade Thula. Whether he supports violence as a method of freeing black Americans from racial discrimination or not, it isn't been practical for the NAACP [National Association for the Advancement of Coloured People] to adopt violence as a strategy. Black Americans are in a minority and in no position to start an insurrection. It's true, though, that our black people interpret and apply Christianity differently to their white counterparts. I really don't know why.'

'How much disagreement was there between ANC leaders who believed that violent resistance to apartheid was the right course and those who advocated a non-violent approach? I asked. 'You were involved at the time, so you must know Comrade JB.'

'Oh, yes, comrade, there was much disagreement. Arguments were advanced that if we embarked on armed resistance, the state would crush the entire liberation movement. Some ANC leaders were married to the principle of non-violence. They continually cited the example of Mahatma Gandhi who developed his creed of passive resistance while in South Africa. Others feared the reaction of the state, which could and did come down hard on our leaders. Don't imagine that the decision to form MK and to opt for violent resistance was easily reached. There are still those who oppose it, even as we speak.'

'Is this why MK tries to ensure that when it bombs a government installation nobody is killed? Is the policy of the ANC a compromise between violence and non-violence?'

'I'm afraid that's so, Comrade Thula. Some still say that when our men are armed and trained, they should be ordered to shoot to wound and not to kill. But when the day comes that we are face-to-face with the SADF, the chips will be down and those sorts of compromises will have to go.'

6

Behind the Iron Curtain

The term 'The Iron Curtain' was used by western countries to describe how difficult it was for them to know what was going on in communist countries like the USSR. In 1964 the Cold War was at its coldest and the Americans were heavily engaged in Vietnam. American foreign policy claimed to be opposed to apartheid, but gave very little support to the ANC or the PAC. It also opposed the violent overthrow of the apartheid regime and claimed that change should come through evolution and not revolution. The USSR and other socialist countries thought otherwise and supported the armed struggle in South Africa. They offered the ANC training facilities.

Daluxolo was already at the Odessa Military Academy in the Ukraine when I arrived in 1963. We had never met before, but we became friends. I was 20 years old when I began my training while Daluxolo was just 15.

Life in the USSR was an eye-opener for both of us in many ways. Black people raised in South Africa were not used to meeting white people who weren't hostile, or at least indifferent, towards them. The Soviet people were white but they were friendly. Their standard form of address was 'comrade' and not 'kaffir' as we were often referred to back in South Africa.

Whether the treatment we got indicated that Soviet society was not racist, I really don't know. What we do know is that they treated us far more decently than we were treated in our own country. The political commissars explained that the low level of racism in the USSR was because:

> This country is governed by representatives of the working class and the peasantry. Our people are taught to relate to each other and other nationals in class terms, not racial terms. This is enshrined in our slogan of 'Workers of the world Unite'. Our solidarity with the people of South Africa is that they, as workers, are exploited and oppressed by capitalists. The fact that the majority of the workers in South Africa are black and that the capitalists are white, is not the issue. We support the revolutionary workers of South Africa, not blacks against whites.

Nikolai Rokkosovsky was a major in the Red Army and he was fond of the South African cadets. He frequently held discussions with us to learn more about South Africa and to improve his English.

'It's a very rich country your South Africa, not so?' Nikolai said.

'Yes Comrade Nikolai, it's true but the wealth is only enjoyed by the whites. We blacks are the miners, the farm workers and the factory workers. We are paid peanuts compared to the whites.'

'That's a new word, comrade. You said 'wealth'. What does wealth mean? They also pay you with peanuts instead of money, huh?' Nikolai looked puzzled.

'Wealthy means riches, Comrade Nikolai. When we say peanuts we mean very little money, not that we are actually paid in real peanuts.'

The cadets laughed at Nikolai's confusion.

'I understand, I understand', Nikolai responded happily, not minding the laughter around him.

'What is the payment for white workers in South Africa? Are they also paid peanuts, comrade?'

'No, no. White workers support and vote for the government, so they always get lots of money.'

'Ah, I see it now. Only black workers get peanuts. The white workers get big money, no?'

'Yes, yes Comrade Major, that's correct.'

'What if black boy love a white *devushka*...you say girlfriend, yes?

'No, no. black boy will go to gaol if he loves a white *devushka*. It's not allowed. But if a white boy loves a black *devushka*, the black *devushka* goes to gaol.'

'Ah, ah. I see now comrade It's bad! It's racism, no?'

'We don't know, comrade. Proper racism say no love black *devushka* if you are white and no love white *devushka* if you are black. But white boys love black *devushka* very much. Where is racism now?'

'*Panyatna*! I understand! It's very confusing. Nikolai can love black *devushka*, but you no love Russian *devushka*. Nikolai get big wealth but you get peanuts, no? It's South Africa, no?'

'Yes, that's how it is Comrade Nikolai. That's South Africa.'

'Talk about football now, comrade', Nikolai would ask. He loved football.

'White boy play football with white boy, not with black boy. That's South Africa.'

'It's not good football, comrade if white boy play alone. Soviet Union plays Brazil and Brazil win 4-1, yet Soviet Union big country, no? But Pele kick football into Soviet goal past Lev Yashin our champion goalkeeper. Soviet Union learn to play better because Brazil play big football. It's good.'

'Yes, it's good, Comrade Nikolai, but it's not South Africa.'

'Ah . . . ah. I see. Thank you comrade, Nikolai now go to duty. Nikolai speak with yourself another time about South Africa, no?'

Not everything was positive during our stay in the USSR. When we arrived there was a criminal case being tried from which we were excluded. Daluxolo's group, the one before us, was involved in the case and we learned from them what it was all about.

During a visit by commander-in-chief Joe Modise, a cadet from Johannesburg, Vincent Khoza, stabbed and wounded Alfred Khombisa. When asked why he had stabbed him, Vincent explained that he had really wanted to kill Joe Modise. Khombisa just got in the way of the knife when he tried to separate Comrade Joe and Vincent.

'I wanted to kill Joe because he's a South African government spy', Vincent explained.

'Do you have proof of that?' Moses Mabhida, MK's political commissar asked.

'I have proof and if the comrades want to hear it I am ready to give evidence. Joe knows that I saw him with people who are government spies. But there is more evidence than that. If you will allow me I'll share that with you as well.'

Next to Joe, Moses was the most senior MK military officer present and he made a ruling.

'This matter must be taken before the National Executive. It cannot be discussed with the Russians, nor can it be decided by those of us here. We will report the matter to Dar-es-Salaam. Do you have anything to say, Comrade Joe?'

'I deny the charges. Vincent', he said, 'we'll meet again one dark night and I promise that only one of us will come out alive and it won't be you.'

Vincent again sprang at Joe but the other cadets grabbed him and that's how it ended. Whether Moses made a report to the National Executive Committee on reaching Dar-es-Salaam, we never heard. Whatever happened, the case just died.

Vincent and some comrades deserted from the Kongwa Camp in 1967. This was after Joe Modise sent Patrick Mosedi on a mission to the Eastern Front in Rhodesia where he was killed. Patrick was a close friend of Vincent and he believed he had been 'launched' — an MK expression for being sent on a mission of no return. Consequently, Vincent and his friends saw no future for themselves in an army commanded by Joe, so they fled to Kenya and asked for political asylum. Some time later Vincent's death was reported in Nairobi, but we never heard the cause. It was rumoured that he had been poisoned.

Daluxolo and I, like many other young MK cadres, were mystified by these events and filled with gloom. The fact that Vincent's allegations were apparently never investigated by the National Executive Committee in Tanzania, added to our despondency. The leadership never referred to the matter and rumours continued to swirl around Joe. Some believed Vincent's allegations were true, although others said that he, Patrick and their Chinese-trained clique were after Joe's position. This caused considerable confusion. We believed that the NEC should have told us their findings and not left the matter hanging. It was the beginning of a cancer of suspicion and doubts that began to cloud Joe's position as MK chief.

Daluxolo was training to be an infantryman, a detachment commander. He proved himself to be the best shot in MK. On Saturdays and Sundays when the rest of the cadets went into Odessa to look for girls and liquor, Daluxolo went to the rifle range to practise musketry. The Russians provided all the ammunition he wanted and he plugged away until he could practically shoot out the eye of a mosquito. He was not interested in Russian women, nor any women for that matter. His only love was guns and shooting. His preferred weapon was the light machine gun and the Russians nominated him to be a machine gunner when he returned to fight in South Africa. Daluxolo could also perform wonders with the SKS rifle, the AK47 and pistols. His shooting skills became legendary in MK.

In 1965 Daluxolo's group completed their training and returned to Tanzania. They bivouacked at Kongwa Camp which had been established by a Moscow-trained group of cadets. The camp commander, Ambrose Makiwane, was a Fort Hare University graduate who had trained in Cuba.

In Russia I trained as a cadet artillery officer. I learned to operate and fire mortars, anti-personnel and heavy anti-tank weapons. The mortar calibres ranged from 80mm to 120mm and the cannons from 57mm up to 101mm howitzers. The Russians worshipped the artillery arm of their service because of the role it had played in the Great Patriotic War (World War II). They referred to artillery as the God of War.

The commander of the artillery cadets was James Stuart, a coloured guy from Cape Town. He became an excellent artilleryman as did most of the group. The best artillery instructor, although a strict disciplinarian, was a Lieutenant Colonel Xobot. The map reading (topography) instructor was Lieutenant-Colonel Borisov who was fondly referred to as, *Tavarish Kursant* (Comrade Cadet). This was because Borisov always began an address with '*Tavarish Kursant…*' He was a veteran of World War II.

Artillery control is largely an exercise in geometry. It requires the calculation of angles between the guns, the commander's observation post and the target. Military maps are used extensively by artillery commanders, especially where targets are ground troops or installations like enemy camps and towns. Anti-tank guns are used to knock out tanks by direct fire — where the gun is aimed directly at the advancing target.

I used to spend much of my time with a particular friend, Templeton Mzondeni (MK name Alfred Sharp), who originated from the Eastern Cape. We liked the same things: girls, liquor and music. His friends were Goodman Mhlauli (MK name Rashidi), Gandhi Hlekani (MK name Marcus Chilemba) and Mkhaba. Mkhaba's brother Zinakile was executed by the apartheid regime in the early 1960s along with Vuyisile Mini, Khayinga and Bongco.

I liked their company and we socialised and drank together.

A small clique of Natal guys noticed this and invited me to come for a drink in Odessa one Saturday night. They asked me bluntly why I was spending so much time with Xhosas and why I had no time for my own Zulu people.

I replied that I didn't associate with them because they were Xhosas, but because we were friends. When I joined MK I didn't join as a Zulu, but as a black South African, I told them.

'You're new to MK', one commented. 'When we joined we never imagined that being Zulu was an issue but we now realise it has become one. People often say they have a problem with our history.'

'What's wrong with our history?' I demanded.

'They say they're sick and tired of reading about Zulus every time they turn the page of a history book.

'Our history was written in the blood of our ancestors at Blood River, Isandlwana and so on. Why should other tribes hold that against us?'

'They say that Zulu history gives the impression that we were the only ones who fought against colonialism. And that when the revolution comes to Natal our troops must be placed under non-Zulu commanders so it can be seen that the heroes come from other tribes.'

'You guys can't be serious. Surely there aren't people in the ANC who still think like that?'

'Some still do. They pay lip service to the ANC's doctrine of black unity, but continue to harbour ethnic aspirations and biases. Believe me, tribalism is alive and well. The leadership pretends it doesn't exist because they don't know how to deal with it.

'The tribalists want to mobilise ethnic power, an easy thing in Africa, and rise to leadership positions on the crest of an ethnic wave. That way they can gain power, influence and wealth for themselves. We are warning you Thula, that ethnic consciousness is still stronger and more powerful than national consciousness.'

'But why should being a Zulu be an issue in the ANC or MK?'

'Do you remember when the Russians lectured us about the difference between a just and an unjust war? They said a just war is when it is supported by the majority of people in a particular country. An unjust war is one conducted by a minority — like the war being fought against blacks by the Afrikaners. Imposing the will of the minority on the majority makes it unjust. That's why they support our revolution.

'Comrade George, a Masotho, asked the Russian political instructor if he regarded Shaka's wars as just or unjust. The Russian replied they were just because they were supported by the majority of the Zulu nation and because Shaka fought his wars to unite a people with a common culture, values and beliefs into one nation. I realised that George had asked the question because he hoped the Russian was going to label Shaka's wars as unjust since they had impacted on his own people. It was quite obvious that George still held a grudge against the Zulus because of what happened from 1818 to 1828.'

'But the BaSotho *were* raided and massacred by Zulu impis', I said. 'Their women *were* taken away and their cattle looted. Don't you think the BaSotho have grounds for having a grudge against us?'

'If that's the way they feel, they have no business being in the ANC. The ANC seeks to reconcile black people and unite them in the struggle against white colonial oppression. If people like George still harp back on events that occurred in the 1800s, it will be very difficult to free South Africa. That's why we say you should stick with your own people and leave the Xhosas and the rest alone.'

'I don't agree', I said. 'I no longer wish to be mobilised as a Zulu, but as a member of the black nation.'

My friend Alfred Sharp had experienced similar difficulties. We went for a long walk and I could tell that something was troubling him.

We sat under a tree and smoked but he said almost nothing. This was not the Alfred I knew, who joked, laughed easily and spontaneously broke into songs of the Eastern Cape.

'I'm afraid that after today we will no longer be able to spend much time together', he said. Some guys from my province have told me plainly that if I continue to associate with somebody from another province, I'll be excluded from their political caucuses. They reminded me that once back in South Africa, I will be operating in the Cape. If they can't trust me outside the country, they won't trust me inside.'

We were just two ordinary young men who had been caught in the grip of that spirit which has caused so much suffering in Africa — ethnic suspicion and hostility. I was filled with foreboding and could tell that Sharp felt the same way. Until then the ANC had been an almost holy institution and joining it made you feel at one with the great heroes of Africa associated with it.

You felt that you were helping to carry the burden of men like John Dube, Chief Albert Luthuli and Nelson Mandela — the burden of freeing an oppressed nation. Yet this could easily be jeopardised by people who refused to rise above ethnic loyalties and biases.

'I will continue to regard you as my comrade and friend, Thula, even though we are forced to temporarily bow to divisive forces', Sharp said. 'Although we were born and raised in different parts of the country, the ANC brought us together into a higher brotherhood that transcends culture, language and ethnicity.'

I held out my hand in a simple gesture.

'*Sala kahle*, Comrade Thula' (Farewell, Comrade Thula), Sharp said, shaking my hand.

'*Hamba kahle*, Comrade Sharp', I responded. 'We'll make a plan to meet and be friends again in a free South Africa.'

We never got the chance. Sharp died in 1967 while fighting in Rhodesia with the illustrious Luthuli Detachment. Sadly, like so many others he didn't live to see the free South Africa he had helped create.

The Russians also gave us lessons in military etiquette and we learned how soldiers should respect each other. One day the Soviet Defence Minister, Marshal Rodion Malinovsky (the defence minister was always a soldier in the USSR), was scheduled to inspect the Odessa garrison. Officers from the rank of captain upwards were ordered to parade before him. The commander of the Odessa Military Academy, General Alexei Chevchenko, paraded his officers before marching with them into town to meet the Minister.

He noticed that a lieutenant-colonel, Yuri Martinenko, was highly decorated. His medals told a story of extreme bravery and sacrifice during the Great Patriotic War. General Chevchenko immediately ordered him to take command of the parade and they marched into Odessa in that order.

'How come, comrade, that a general surrenders his command to an officer junior to him in rank?' I asked a Russian officer who was watching the parade.

'General Chevchenko is expressing his respect for the blood that Lieutenant-Colonel Martinenko must have spilt to obtain such medals. They are medals of the highest merit. The sacrifices that a soldier of the Red Army has made while defending his country are considered more important than rank.'

My artillery group went to Moldavia for a live firing exercise as part of our graduation.

They tested a cadet's abilities to direct gunfire from an observation post when the enemy is not visible from the gun position. The task had to be completed in 40 seconds from the time the enemy was identified.

I destroyed my target in 36 seconds.

'*Atlitchna, tavarish, atlitchna*' (Excellent comrade, excellent), screamed Colonel Xobot, who was there to see his former charges graduate. '*Zanyate zakonche*' (The lesson is over), he added, signifying that he had nothing left to teach us.

We flew back to Tanzania towards the end of November 1965.

We had spent a very fruitful year in the USSR.

A Russian Aeroflot boarding pass retained by a trainee as a souvenir

7

Kongwa Camp

It's possible when telling a story about a place or a person to mention only the negative side of things and ignore the positive. In that case one misses out because the image created is skewed. Kongwa was a negative experience for most of those who camped there. Ugly things happened because there were ugly people among us. But there were also positive people there and they did positive and inspiring things.

The camp was situated approximately 400 kilometres from the capital, Dar-es-Salaam. The Tanzanian government had selected it to house freedom fighters of all the political organisations in the African sub-continent. There were cadres of the Front for the Liberation of Mozambique (FRELIMO), the Popular Movement for the Liberation of Angola (MPLA), the South West African People's Organisation (SWAPO), the Zimbabwe African People's Union (ZAPU) and our own Umkhonto we Sizwe. The leaders of these organisations were a political fraternity who regarded each group as the true representatives of the people of their country.

The ANC, for instance, supported FRELIMO in Mozambique and SWAPO in South West Africa, but not SWANU. They recognised MPLA in Angola, but not Jonas Savimbi's UNITA or Holden Roberto's FNLA. In Zimbabwe it was ZAPU. In turn the favoured organisations recognised the ANC as the true representative of the people of South Africa — not the PAC. In Zimbabwe the PAC was fraternal with ZANU, not ZAPU. One accepted these unofficial alliances without the need to be told by the leadership. The Tanzanian government obviously knew this and while they didn't show open preference of one organisation over another, they made sure they placed political allies in the same camp. That's how it was in Kongwa.

The commander of the ANC camp was a chap called Archie Sibeko. He was known by his nom de guerre of Zola Zembe. In the Western Cape he had been a trade union secretary. One assumed that somebody with a trade union or communist party background would emphasise the class approach to the struggle and not a tribal one. Zola Zembe, unfortunately for everyone, was Xhosa first and ANC second. He caused division by frequently calling for meetings to be attended only by people from the Eastern Cape. What was discussed at such meetings remained a mystery to guys from the Transvaal, Natal and the Orange Free State.

Zembe was not the only one. There were individuals from all provinces whose level of consciousness remained tribal, despite claiming to be nationalists and even Marxists. This caused problems for the ANC from the outset. The fundamental ideological position of the ANC was, and still is, unity of the tribes, whether Xhosa, Sotho, Shangaan, Venda, Tsonga or Zulu.

Zembe had been swept into a nationalist working-class movement, but in his own heart of hearts he remained a Xhosa and an anomaly. The ANC called on us all to rise to the challenge of becoming nationalists, yet many people — perhaps unconsciously — brought their tribal baggage along with them.

'We are all ANC here and this is an MK camp', declared Philimon 'Pangaman' Biyela, who came from Natal. 'Why does Zembe convene meetings that only people from the Eastern Cape are allowed to attend? What if the guys from the Transvaal or the Free State did the same?'

'Maybe we should convene a meeting of Zulus from Natal and see how he takes it', responded Duncan 'Sigh No More' Khoza.

'But comrades, two wrongs don't make a right', Kenneth Malinga interjected to head off confrontation. 'What would we discuss? We're not here as Zulus. We're here as ANC and MK cadres, which goes for everybody in this camp.'

'One of these days', said Pangaman, 'I'll still announce a meeting to be attended by people from Natal. Your problem, Malinga, is that you always try to be reasonable, even when you're dealing with the unreasonable. If we announce such a meeting it will force Zembe to reconsider his divisive actions.'

Two days later Pangaman announced a meeting that would be attended only by people from Natal.

'Hey, Comrade Pangaman, what's the matter? Why are you calling a meeting of people from Natal only? What about the rest of us, *mfondini*?' Zembe asked in agitation.

'We never questioned you when you called meetings for people from the Eastern Cape only. Why are you asking me for an explanation when you do the same thing yourself?'

The meeting didn't take place because there was no agenda. Nevertheless, Zembe stopped his practice of openly calling meetings of Eastern Cape people, although he still did it clandestinely. Tribal tensions in the camp grew, fuelled by such actions. It must be mentioned that despite this, there were many men from the Eastern Cape who never attended such meetings. This included Zola Bona (later Dr Zola Skweyiya, Social Development Minister) and others. It was people like that who kept the spirit of the ANC alive.

We never understood how leaders selected and appointed people to run external camps. Certainly, there were more suitable people around than Zola Zembe and his ilk. The leadership should have ensured the appointees had the respect of the people they would be controlling. We were well aware that military leaders can't be appointed democratically, but we wondered about the criteria for their selection. People like Zembe were left in command positions even after numerous complaints had been lodged about them. There seemed to be an invisible entity who decided on these appointments and once that occurred they wouldn't be removed, even if they turned out to be abysmal failures.

During Ambrose Makiwane's tenure as camp commander at Kongwa (before Zola Zembe), a dramatic event took place. Joe Modise, the MK's commander-in-chief, came from Dar-es-Salaam to stay at the camp for a few days. Ambrose continued to run the camp as if Joe wasn't there. The soldiers saw this and asked Ambrose for an explanation. He addressed the parade the next morning with Joe standing next to him.

'Comrades, you have noticed that I have failed to hand over the direction of the camp's affairs to Joe Modise. Some of you in the spirit of this camp have raised the issue with me. Now how do we deal with camp problems, comrades? We call a general meeting and throw the problem open for everybody to discuss.'

He instructed everybody to go to The People's Hall — a zinc-covered structure where the camp's main activities like meetings and concerts were held. Once there, Ambrose plunged straight into the issue with Joe sitting next to him.

'Certain camp commanders have reported a discussion that occurred at a clandestine meeting between themselves and Joe Modise. I will not say what they told me, but will get them to do so themselves. Comrade Boysie Buciko, step forward and tell your comrades what you reported to me.'

Boysie came forward and addressed the gathering.

'Comrades, Comrade Joe invited me and other comrades here to a late night meeting in his tent. He told us we should unite as Batswana, Pedis and BaSotho because the Ngunis had plans to dominate the struggle both outside South Africa and at home after our liberation. I reported this to Comrade Ambrose. If Comrade Joe says I am lying, let him say so and I will provide more details.'

'Thank you, Comrade Boysie', Ambrose said.

He called on another commander present, Lambert Moloi (who later retired as a lieutenant-general in the SANDF) to step forward.

Lambert repeated exactly what Boysie had said. He also challenged Joe to deny it, but the latter said nothing.

Comrade Moema, real name Ramano (later South Africa's army chief), was the next to repeat the accusations.

Ambrose demanded that Joe respond to the allegations.

'I see now that my moment of death has arrived', Joe said. 'I have only one request. If you kill me, please don't harm Kapna because I took the boy from his parents.'

Joe sat down, buried his head in his hands and sobbed. The camp was stunned by his failure to deny the allegations. It seemed unbelievable that MK's commander-in-chief had been secretly engaged in dividing his own army by invoking tribal loyalties.

'What shall we do with him, comrades?' Ambrose demanded.

'We cannot pass judgement on our own C-in-C', a soldier said. 'We believe this matter should be taken to Dar-es-Salaam and placed before the NEC. They appointed Comrade Joe who is also a member of the NEC. He should be tried by his peers and not by us.'

The two commanders later left for Dar-es-Salaam. A week later JB Marks appeared at Kongwa camp. He assembled the detachment in the People's Hall and addressed us.

'The NEC has looked into the matter between Comrades Joe and Ambrose. The NEC has expressed itself in the strongest possible terms to both commanders. Comrade Ambrose, although he is the accuser, was found to be unclean himself.'

Ambrose never returned to Kongwa and Joe Modise retained his position as commander-in-chief. JB never explained what he meant by the NEC having 'expressed itself in the strongest possible terms' nor what lay behind Ambrose being 'unclean himself'. And so the matter died, but many questions remained unanswered in the minds of the detachment.

'Ambrose was not the accuser at the meeting', Sipho Mthembu remarked. 'Joe was accused by commanders he had personally invited to a meeting. Does this mean that commanders who show in an exemplary way how an MK soldier should behave are considered liars by the NEC?'

'Why was Ambrose removed from his position and Joe retained? If the NEC knew something about Comrade Ambrose that we don't know, they should both have been demoted', remarked Edgar 'Problem' Duma.

'Either they are condoning Joe's tribalism or Tambo has come up against strong opposition in the NEC that's prevented him from removing Joe. It's impossible to believe that OR failed to get to the bottom of this. Why did he send JB to give us this nonsense story?' Sipho Mthembu wanted to know.

'There's obviously a power struggle going on between people from the Cape and people from the Transvaal', Duncan Khoza said thoughtfully. 'It seems it's also a struggle between Marxists and Nationalists. This means we still have to salute a commander-in-chief who regards us as Ngunis and not MK soldiers.'

'Duncan is right', Sipho Mthembu said. 'Cough had an argument with Nhlifilili because he asked why all the external camps are controlled by Xhosa guys. Cough said he shouldn't worry as the Xhosas would continue to command outside the country and eventually they would do so at home.'

'The only thing that's going to stop this nonsense is for us to go home as soon as possible and start the fight for our liberation. When the SADF is attacking us we'll soon forget this nonsense about power struggles', Reuben 'Kulak' Nhlabathi contributed.

'We should ask for a meeting with Comrade OR and warn him about the growing hostility between tribal factions. We should insist that the solution is to send us home to fight', added Kenneth Malinga.

'The Boers don't give a damn whether you are Zulu, Xhosa, Tswana or Shangaan. To them a kaffir is a kaffir. It's us who think we are different', Reuben Nhlabathi remarked. 'We'll never defeat the Boers if we carry on like this.'

'Reuben, ask for a meeting with Comrade OR and let's place these matters before him', Edgar Duma demanded.

This resolution reflected the respect and trust that the ANC president enjoyed amongst the MK men. It was appreciated that OR often faced stiff opposition within the NEC, which sometimes probably made it difficult for him to deal effectively with problems. There was no transparency within the NEC and so rumours replaced facts and members lost trust in the leadership.

Eventually the suspicion grew that the external leaders had no intention of returning to South Africa to fight and free the people. The belief was they were living in luxury in the city while the soldiers were stuck out in bush camps with virtually no facilities. Stories filtered back about some leaders frequently wining and dining at expensive hotels. It was rumoured that some of them even had white girlfriends from Rhodesia and South Africa. The lives they were leading certainly didn't give the impression that they were laying the foundations for a hard struggle to wrench power from an immensely strong enemy.

The soldiers concluded that the leadership of both ZAPU and ANC had lost the will to fight. Joe was confronted and asked what plans he had made to attack South Africa and whether he would be coming with us when it happened.

'Comrades', he said, 'you must be unaware that when I left home I was escaping the police who were looking for me for acts of sabotage we had carried out. If I returned to South Africa and the Boers found me there, they would capture and kill me.'

'In other words, Comrade Joe, you have no intention of leading us back to South Africa', Jacques Goniwe remarked bluntly.

'Did you hear what happened to Yatuta Chisiza who commanded the liberation movement that sought to overthrow Kamuzu Banda of Malawi?' Joe asked. 'He personally led his forces back to Malawi and ran into Banda's security forces. In the ensuing battle he was killed and the entire struggle to free Malawi collapsed. It's not a wise strategy to expose the leadership to unnecessary risks, comrades.'

'But how can you conduct a revolution in South Africa from Lusaka or Dar-es-Salaam', Phooko asked.

'Technology, especially communication technology, Comrade Phooko, has made it possible for commanders to conduct wars far from the battlefield. That's why some of you were trained in advanced communication technology', was Joe's reply.

It is difficult to measure the level of demoralisation that saturated MK's ranks at Kongwa. The cadres had expected a standard of military leadership equal to that of Cuban revolutionary commanders like Fidel Castro, Che Guevara and Camillo Cienfuegos. They had been lectured on how Chairman Mao Tse-tung had inspired and led his Red Chinese revolutionaries against Chiang Kai-shek and the Kuomintang. Yet here was MK's highest ranking officer finding excuses for not venturing into the country he was supposed to liberate.

There was frequent speculation amongst cadres as to why Joe Modise wasn't removed from his position. It might have been because he was a Tswana while most of MK's leaders were Xhosas and Zulus. The only possible infiltration route the ANC had was from Zambia through Botswana. If he had been sacked he might have split from the ANC and taken the Tswana element along with him. Since Botswana was completely Tswana, he might have used his influence with the government to frustrate the MK from moving through the country.

Tambo was shocked and angry when he was confronted in the People's Hall by an old man called Gumede. Gumede was popular with the MK rank and file because he continued the ANC tradition of speaking his mind, heedless of the rank of the person he was addressing. They called him *iNtabayezulu* (smoking volcano). The underground High Command in South Africa had sent him to tell the NEC to bring the army home to fight. When Tambo said there were 'difficulties' he openly showed his disgust and spoke up in Zulu.

'*Mongameli, usasazi yini isiZulu, njengoba sewahlala kakhulu lapha ngaphandle ukhuluma isiSwahili*' (President, you have been outside South Africa for a long time speaking only KiSwahili. Do you still understand Zulu?)

'Yes, *Baba* Gumede I still understand Zulu. Feel free to speak', OR responded, not suspecting the storm that was about to break over his head.

'*Kusuke kuthiwani Mongameli uma kuthiwa umkhonto wegwala uphelela etsheni*?' (When we say a coward's spear is never sharp enough for him to attack, what do we mean?), Gumede queried.

OR got the point immediately. This old man was telling him that he had an army but he was afraid to use it to attack South Africa. OR had a reputation for keeping his temper even under serious provocation, but on that occasion he exploded.

'Listen all of you', he thundered, 'the leadership have a duty to ensure that when you are sent home the route you take will be safe. And that when you get home you will have the necessary contacts and support to keep you out of police hands. We don't want to risk your lives. We are accountable for the lives of everyone in this room. This nonsense of accusing us of having cold feet must stop.'

'Fidel Castro sailed from Mexico with his army to infiltrate Cuba', said Jimmy Mopedi. 'Their ship was spotted by the coast guard and attacked by aircraft. Many of his men died and only a few made it to the Sierra Maestra mountains to give birth to the revolution. But today Cuba is free. Yet our leadership wants to prepare every detail of the revolution in advance.'

'The Cuban example cannot always be repeated', OR responded. 'In Cuba there were thick forests, high mountains and sugarcane fields where Castro and his men could hide. Where will you hide in South Africa? There are no jungles so we will have to wage a more difficult and dangerous urban guerrilla war. Our plans are progressing and we are almost ready, but don't rush us into action just because of your impatience.'

'President, why has the leadership been given no military training whatsoever?' Victor Dlamini, an old trade unionist, asked. 'You talk about the leadership directing our operations when none of you know anything about such things. Give us the chance to plan and we'll make our own way to South Africa. Then nobody will blame you for delays, Comrade OR.'

'This amounts to an expression of no confidence in your leadership', OR said. 'But I will heed your advice and I will arrange for some of you to work at the front line to find the right routes home.'

It was an unhappy meeting, particularly because OR was loved and respected by the soldiers. When it came to the issue of going home though, nobody's feelings — not even OR's — could be spared.

The account of Kongwa Camp wouldn't be complete if the story of Samora Machel and his FRELIMO forces wasn't told. Machel commanded the FRELIMO forces at Kongwa and he lived there in a tent along with his men. The bright lights of Dar-es-Salaam were not for him. When he knew that it would not be long before fighting began in Mozambique, he set out to test the combat preparedness of his men.

He volunteered for guard duty on the midnight to morning shift. At about 02:30 he fired several long bursts with his AK47 and randomly threw grenades. He ran from place to place screaming in Portuguese to give the impression that a large force was attacking the camp. Everyone — FRELIMO, ZIPRA, MPLA, SWAPO and MK — heard the shooting and the exploding grenades. Machel's ruse worked and his men fled the camp along with some cadres from the other organisations.

Soldiers are trained to run to an assembly point where their commanders will give them orders on how to respond when a surprise attack takes place. Such an assembly point is selected on the day the soldiers first arrive at a camp. Machel's men and the rest had forgotten all about this and they ran helter skelter towards the MK camp. We asked them what was happening, but they just shouted something about grenades and kept on running.

In the morning Machel conducted a roll call. More than half couldn't be accounted for and many others had been injured while running from the imaginary Portuguese Army attack.

'What I want to know is how you are going to react to a real attack in the future', shouted Machel, livid with rage. 'If it is going to be like this I might as well disband the lot of you and send you back to your mothers. How can you be soldiers when you still fear your white masters? It's that fear that we will deal with at this camp. Next time you run away, remember that I'll be watching and I'll personally shoot you.'

Machel was later seen leaving the FRELIMO offices in Dar-es-Salaam in tears. We were aghast at the sight of such a hardened revolutionary crying.

'Why is Comrade Samora crying?' I asked a FRELIMO soldier.

'He's heard that the Portuguese General, Kaulza de Arriaga, has landed at Beira with 30 000 men and has vowed to crush FRELIMO. He's crying because the leadership is debating whether he should go to the front or not. Comrade Samora says that when the Portuguese attack he wants to be there with his troops.'

We shook our heads enviously, wishing we had a commander-in-chief like that.

As we know, Machel did get there and eventually became President of Mozambique.

8

Rhodesia

Until 1963 Rhodesia was part of a political arrangement of three states known as the Federation of Rhodesia and Nyasaland. Nyasaland was given independence and became Malawi under Dr Hastings Kamuzu Banda and Northern Rhodesia became Zambia under Dr Kenneth Kaunda. Southern Rhodesia lobbied Britain for its own independence, but there was a problem.

The independence that the whites wanted involved their tiny minority ruling millions of blacks. At the same time two nationalist organisations there were lobbying Britain for majority rule and one-man-one- vote. There was the Zimbabwe African People's Union (ZAPU) under the leadership of Joshua Nkomo and the Zimbabwe African National Union (ZANU) under Rev Ndabaningi Sithole. Sithole had caused a split in ZAPU in 1961 when he broke away to form ZANU. Later, a further split occurred and Robert Mugabe emerged as the leader of ZANU-PF. Sithole led a minority party, ZANU-Ndoga, until his death.

In 1964 the Rhodesian Front party under Ian Douglas Smith came into power. It was exclusively white and had no intention of allowing power to fall into the hands of the black majority. They began to lobby Britain to grant independence to ensure the perpetuation of white minority rule. The to and fro negotiations went on for more than a year, but the more they talked the less they saw eye to eye.

On 11 November 1965 the Rhodesian government announced a unilateral declaration of independence (UDI) to thwart Britain's moves towards granting political power to the black nationalists. Both ZAPU and ZANU decided that the only way they would win their independence would be to embark on armed struggle. Ian Smith rounded up the political leaders of both organisation and placed them in preventive detention. Not all the leaders were caught in the dragnet, however, and Advocate Herbert Chitepo took over the direction of ZANU's operations outside the country. James Chikerema, Joshua Nkomo's vice-president, began directing ZAPU's military operations from Lusaka. ZAPU's army became known as the Zimbabwe People's Revolutionary Army (ZIPRA) while ZANU's forces became the Zimbabwe National Liberation Army (ZANLA).

In 1967 the ANC formed a political/military alliance with ZAPU and it was agreed they would launch joint operations against Ian Smith's Rhodesia. The ANC would provide men on the understanding that when ZAPU grabbed power, the ANC would be given rear bases in a free Zimbabwe from which it could operate against South Africa. As a quid pro quo ZAPU agreed to field men to assist MK in its fight against apartheid South Africa.

In 1966 MK soldiers were moved from Kongwa Camp to Morogoro in Tanzania and from there to Zambia where they shared a base with ZIPRA. They jointly began a slow move southwards. The ZIPRA men puzzled the MK soldiers. They spent much of their time boasting about what they intended to do to ZANLA if they ever met up in the bush. They swore they would wipe them out. Yet they never said a word about what they intended doing when they came into contact with the Rhodesian Security Forces. It seemed they considered ZANLA the real enemy and not the Rhodesians.

This led to some MK soldiers asking for a meeting with the ZAPU leadership.

'Your men talk the whole time about attacking ZANLA if they meet them. Is that official ZAPU policy? If that is so, we in MK have a problem. We are forbidden to attack the PAC under any circumstances, but it seems that you have taught your men to regard ZANU as the enemy — not Ian Smith. Is that correct?'

'I'm glad you have asked this question, comrades', James Chikerema responded. 'We instruct our soldiers not to fight ZANU, but they continually threaten to do so. ZANLA should not be attacked if you meet them. It would be better for you to agree to launch joint operations with them. If you do that I can assure you that we politicians outside the country will accept it.'

We thanked the ZAPU leadership but we were still confused. It seemed to us that most ZAPU people were convinced that if they killed enough ZANLA soldiers they would soon free Rhodesia. Yet ZANU was not in power there — it was the Rhodesian Front. Even in 1963 when I was in the country, the newspapers were full of stories about internecine fighting between ZAPU and ZANU. The victims were invariably ZANU supporters because there were so few of them and ZAPU commanded a huge majority. The Rhodesian government played on this inter-party violence to show that Rhodesian blacks were not ready to rule themselves. Violence escalated. Gangs of ZAPU youths roamed the townships, demanding that people produce ZAPU membership cards. Those who couldn't were beaten up, sometimes killed. This ZAPU-ZANU rivalry would cause us great distress later.

Peter Stiff in his book, *See You in November*, tells how the Rhodesian Central Intelligence Organisation (CIO) cleverly exploited this ZAPU-ZANU antagonism in Zambia. They fuelled the inter-party hatred by carrying out killings and sabotage against both parties in a way that made each side believe their political rivals were to blame. That hostility has lasted to the present day.

When CIO learned of an in-house rebellion within ZANU, they took the opportunity to assassinate Herbert Chitepo, Chairman of ZANU in Zambia. President Kaunda arrested the whole of ZANLA's High Command in Zambia as murder suspects and expelled the organisation from the country. This set back ZANLA's military operations in Rhodesia by a full 18 months. Peter Stiff says: 'Such is the bitter fruit of division and distrust.'

ZAPU, ZANU, the OAU and the British Commonwealth demanded that Britain get rid of UDI, by force if necessary. Britain, however, was not prepared to use force against its kith and kin. It would have been a very unpopular move amongst whites in Britain and could well have cost Harold Wilson's Labour Government substantial support. There was a belief among black nationalists that the Rhodesian problem could best be solved by talks. The leaders shared this opinion with their soldiers and a lot of them believed there was little point in fighting and getting killed if a political settlement was in the offing only six months down the road .

The MK soldiers, on the other hand, knew only too well that South Africa would only be freed after a long and bitter war. The National Party government paid absolutely no attention to the world-wide abhorrence of apartheid, for one thing. For another, while Western countries verbally condemned apartheid, in practice they supported the regime. America denounced the ANC's and PAC's intention to overthrow the apartheid regime by force. Instead they advocated evolution and not revolution — whatever that might mean. I suppose the reason was that South Africa was also anti-communist and the situation there didn't threaten America's economic interests.

We in the MK were well aware that Afrikaners are doughty fighters and the only language they would listen to was the language of the gun. Speeches, petitions and peaceful protests would not serve to move them one iota. That had already been tried and it had failed. The apartheid police had responded violently to peaceful protests — the most spectacular being Sharpeville in 1960. The 1976 Student Revolt still lay in the future but the response would be the same — more killings.

Finally MK resolved to go to war in Rhodesia alongside ZIPRA. Joshua Nkomo's men were confident the fighting would only last six months or so and after a few bursts of machine-gun fire in the bush, a political settlement would result.

History proved this thinking to be flawed in the extreme. The Rhodesian War lasted from 1966 to 1979. In the end ZANU took power and not ZAPU, as the ANC had so confidently predicted.

We learned later that the decision at HQ to send MK to fight had not been unanimous. Some said the ANC leadership wouldn't be able to justify the deaths of MK soldiers there to the people of South Africa after liberation. The most controversial part of the decision, for my part, was that no senior leader, either political or military, went along with the men.

'If things go badly in Rhodesia', Chris Hani is said to have argued, 'how would we escape the charge that we sent in our guys and stayed behind ourselves because we had a good idea what would happen to them?'

Chris and the then MK Chief of Staff, Mjojo Mxwaku (later Major-General Lennox Tjali in the SANDF), however, volunteered to go with the men. Chris was appointed Chief Political Commissar of the joint ZIPRA/MK force. Mjojo would lead a group of MK men who would first deploy into Rhodesia and later attempt to penetrate South Africa.

One would have expected that an army going into battle for the first time would have been led by ZIPRA's and MK's most senior commanders. They had a need to establish a reputation of leading from the front, but they missed the opportunity. Field commanders who send their men into battle and stay behind themselves will never be respected by their men. The soldiers rightfully concluded that their senior officers were afraid to fight. The MK men used to joke about their commanders' whiskers which they called bedroom beards. They compared them derisively to those worn by Cuban revolutionaries like Castro and Che Guevara.

'Castro and the others had beards because they lived and fought in the bush. There's no time to shave out there and nobody has a razor anyway', Duncan Khoza said, roaring with laughter. 'With our top commanders sleeping in city bedrooms with their girlfriends, what excuse do they have for not shaving?'

Whether it is a commercial or a military organisation, a leader should lead. Mandela was appointed Volunteer-in-Chief when MK was formed. This made him its first commander-in-chief. So what did he do? He left the country for military training and afterwards returned to South Africa to mobilise MK, before he was betrayed and arrested. He set a precedent and anybody who aspired to step into his shoes should have followed his example: train outside the country and then return to fight. But the NEC had rather different ideas. How could we respect a leadership that led from the rear?

Chris Hani volunteered to leave his post at defence headquarters and go with us. That's the kind of officer we were willing to follow — a man amongst men. The commanders who remained behind and didn't go to war were the ones who caused problems for the ANC. Throughout the struggle they never participated in a single battle, but when they returned to South Africa in the 1990s many were made generals. Joe Modise became Defence Minister, no less.

Months before the proposed infiltration we were told that an advance reconnaissance group had penetrated Rhodesia to make contact with the people. This was vital so we would know how to locate those who were ready to join and support us once we were in the country. The man who led this so-called recce group was Joe Modise himself. His group disappeared and a week later reappeared with their uniforms and boots heavily coated with dirt and mud. We of the MK rank and file gave Joe the nickname *Nyawo Zinodaka* (the man with muddy boots) — for none of us believed that he and his colleagues had actually conducted an in-depth reconnaissance. He gave Oliver Tambo a full report which said they had made contact with people inside Rhodesia who were ready to welcome and help us.

Because of the oil embargo that Britain and the United Nations had imposed on Rhodesia, ZIPRA's intelligence people maintained that Ian Smith had only enough oil supplies to last for six months. This meant he wouldn't be able to fight for long because oil is a vital component of any war machine.

Another story they concocted to cheer us up was that General Sam Putterill, the Rhodesian Army commander, had ZAPU sympathies and that once the fighting started he would issue conflicting orders to create confusion. The ZIPRA contingent was even issued with impressed medallions showing the face of Joshua Nkomo to hand to people once we crossed the Zambezi River so they would recognise the face of the man who would soon be taking over the leadership of the country. Some would carry pamphlets in their packs for distribution that optimistically told the people that they must support ZAPU because it would soon be taking over the country.

Events proved this to be wishful thinking.

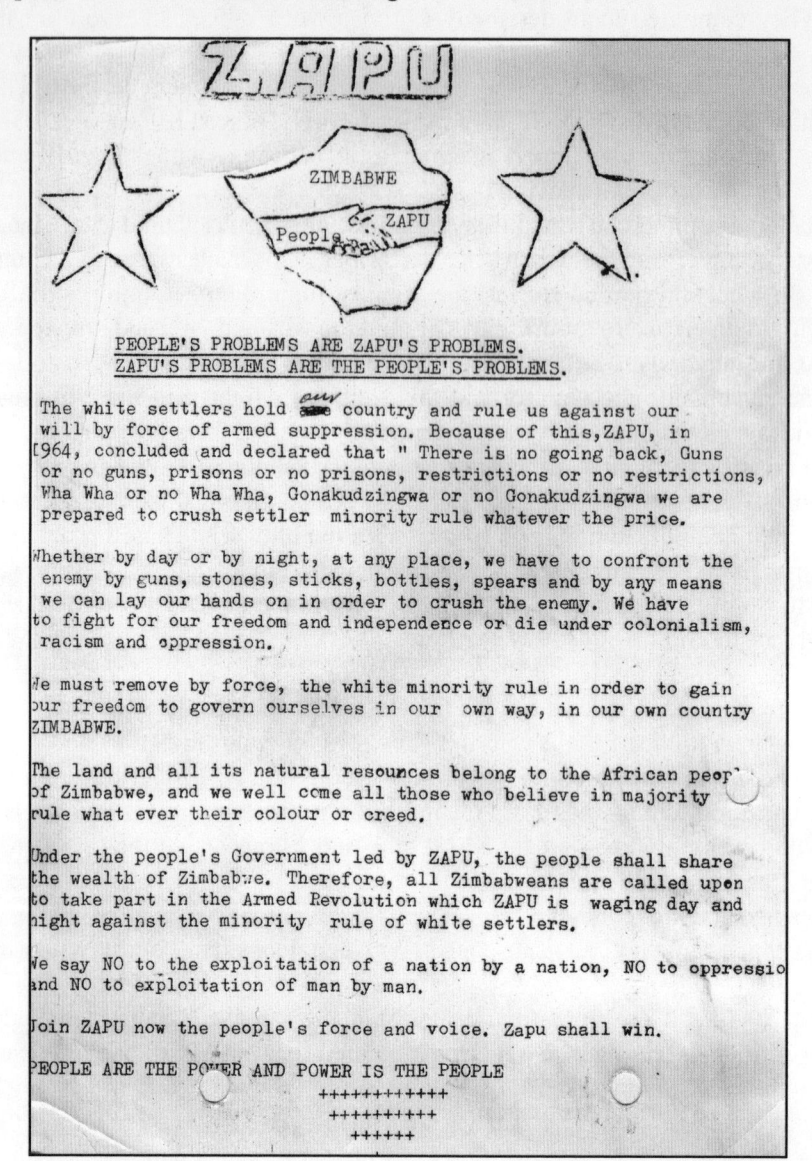

> **ZAPU**
>
> **PEOPLE'S PROBLEMS ARE ZAPU'S PROBLEMS.**
> **ZAPU'S PROBLEMS ARE THE PEOPLE'S PROBLEMS.**
>
> The white settlers hold our country and rule us against our will by force of armed suppression. Because of this, ZAPU, in 1964, concluded and declared that " There is no going back, Guns or no guns, prisons or no prisons, restrictions or no restrictions, Wha Wha or no Wha Wha, Gonakudzingwa or no Gonakudzingwa we are prepared to crush settler minority rule whatever the price.
>
> Whether by day or by night, at any place, we have to confront the enemy by guns, stones, sticks, bottles, spears and by any means we can lay our hands on in order to crush the enemy. We have to fight for our freedom and independence or die under colonialism, racism and oppression.
>
> We must remove by force, the white minority rule in order to gain our freedom to govern ourselves in our own way, in our own country ZIMBABWE.
>
> The land and all its natural resources belong to the African people of Zimbabwe, and we well come all those who believe in majority rule what ever their colour or creed.
>
> Under the people's Government led by ZAPU, the people shall share the wealth of Zimbabwe. Therefore, all Zimbabweans are called upon to take part in the Armed Revolution which ZAPU is waging day and night against the minority rule of white settlers.
>
> We say NO to the exploitation of a nation by a nation, NO to oppression and NO to exploitation of man by man.
>
> Join ZAPU now the people's force and voice. Zapu shall win.
>
> PEOPLE ARE THE POWER AND POWER IS THE PEOPLE

A ZIPRA leaflet calling on people to fight the white minority

MK moved us from Tanzania to a place called Kaluwa Base in Zambia. At the Morogoro Camp en route there, Joe Modise found me on duty cooking breakfast for comrades. He ordered me to fill a tub with hot water so he could have his morning bath. I bit my tongue instead of telling him to do it himself. I poured a container of water into the tub, then filled another and put it on the fire to heat up. When that was ready I poured the hot water into the tub and resumed cooking. Meanwhile Joe spent half an hour talking to some men, obviously forgetting about his bath. When he found the water was only lukewarm, he came charging over.

'Comrade Thula, where's the hot water I told you to put in the tub?'

'It's there in the bath tub, Comrade Joe', I replied, seething with anger.

'But the water has gone cold. Why didn't you tell me my bath was ready?'

'Because I'm not your wife or servant', I replied. 'I left South Africa to fight as a soldier and not to fill baths and be your domestic servant.'

The commander-in-chief turned and left without saying another word.

At Kaluwa we sensed that it wouldn't be long before we were sent to fight and we prepared ourselves feverishly. For two hours each morning we worked really hard helping to build a road that led through hills, swamps and forests. After that we spent the rest of the morning doing physical exercise. We became very fit.

One day when running back to camp I found that a small pebble in my right boot had caused an angry red sore just above my ankle. I reported to Doreen, the medical officer, who gave me an antibiotic injection and told me not to lace my boot as it would irritate the sore. At midday we paraded to observe one minute's silence for Chief Albert Luthuli. News of his death had just reached us.

Jeqe, the base commander, ordered me to lace up my boot. I explained that I had been instructed not to do so by the medical officer.

'I'm ordering you to tie that boot, Comrade Thula!' he shouted.

I explained that if I did so it would irritate the sore and my foot would swell.

'That's an order!'

'Stuff your order', I shouted back. 'I need this foot to march and I'm not going to make it worse because of a stupid order.'

He took me to a tent where Joe Modise was seated at a table. He entered first and explained what had happened. He then called me in and Comrade Joe asked if it was true that I had defied the camp commander's order.

I confirmed it was true.

'Now, *I'm* ordering you to lace up your boot up, Comrade Thula', he said.

'Stuff your order, Comrade C-in-C', I replied.

Joe just sat at the table and stared.

At last he responded by asking if I hoped to join the new army after we had freed South Africa.

I shook my head and told him I wanted nothing to do with his new army.

'If that new army is officered by people like you and Jeqe who issue stupid orders, Comrade Joe, you can keep it. I'll fight until liberation day, then decide where I'll go and what I'll do.'

'Maybe you don't realise it, Comrade Thula, but you are being insubordinate. I can charge you with mutiny and even have you shot.'

'Maybe you have forgotten that we are volunteers and not mercenaries, Comrade Joe. We're not paid a brass cent to be here. If you think you can treat us like mercenaries, I'll go to President Tambo and resign from MK. I believe you'll be sending us into battle soon. As a guerrilla I will be marching and when I fight it will be on foot. For that I must have healthy feet. Is that so difficult for you and Comrade Jeqe to understand?'

9

When we return

The MK men of the Luthuli Detachment — as Oliver Tambo had named them — were about to find out whether they were really soldiers or just a bunch of trained and angry armed Africans.

With our ZIPRA comrades we were singing a deeply moving song as we dismounted from the trucks that had transported us to within five kilometres of the Zambezi River.

'Ngamhla sibuyayo kothula kuthi du' (On that day, when we return to fight, there shall be a great silence of wonder). It continued: *'Kokhala uVorster, kokhala u Verwoerd, kokhala imbayimbayi phezulu kwentaba'* (The only sounds to be heard will be the weeping of Vorster and Verwoerd when they hear the guns roaring in the mountains).

The singing was deep, harmonious and infused with emotion. The time had come to put into practice what we were singing about.

Oliver Tambo marched with us. Next to him was the young and light-complexioned Chris Hani. Chris laughed a lot. He was almost unknown at that time either within or outside the ANC, but he would one day make his mark on history. At the time he was little different from the rest of the men marching with their president.

'Comrade Chris', OR asked, 'are your men ready for the tasks that lie ahead?'

'Their morale is high and physically they are in excellent shape, Comrade President. It's their equipment that makes me unhappy.'

'What's the matter with it?'

'Each soldier has only one magazine and they have no grenades. When their magazines are empty and the enemy is charging at them, how long do you think it'll take them to reload and resume firing? If they had grenades they could at least keep the enemy at bay while reloading.'

Tambo pondered a moment but before he could reply, Mjojo Mxwaku, commander of the Lethuli contingent, spoke up.

'Comrade President, Chris is right. The men are not adequately equipped. We raised this point with Commander-in-Chief Comrade Joe Modise, but he told us that these were the only weapons that MK could afford. Because of that we decided not to pursue the point.'

Tambo halted the march, called an urgent meeting of section commanders and asked bluntly: 'Are your men properly equipped for the task ahead?'

They answered emphatically in the negative. Tambo despatched Joe Modise to get more magazines and a supply of grenades.

We were armed with a variety of weapons mostly originating from the Communist Bloc, although some emanated from Europe and even America. Weapons for the liberation movements were sourced, presumably to best advantage, by the Liberation Committee of the OAU. The most common personal weapons in the MK and ZIPRA detachments were the Simonov semi-automatic carbine (SKS) and the AK47. For 9mm pistols we had either the Tokarev or the Makarov. While the various models of all those weapons were almost identical in design they were manufactured in a great variety of Eastern Bloc countries including the Soviet Union, Hungary, Yugoslavia, North Korea, China and East Germany.

Joe returned the next day with his truck packed with magazines, ammunition and grenades. It was offloaded and the section commanders lined up their men. Each soldier was given an additional magazine, one grenade and 300 rounds of ammunition.

'*Viva* Comrade Tambo. *Viva*!' we shouted.

After a three-hour march through the Zambian bush we came to one of a series of deep gorges on the Zambezi River below the Victoria Falls. We stared across at the country we were about to infiltrate. Down below us the rushing river made a thunderous noise and for hundreds of metres the waters ran almost milky white with foam. We had to shout at the top of our voices to make ourselves heard. The Rhodesian side was an area of mopani trees, dry grass and rocks. There was no sign of life, but somehow the presence of the enemy could be felt.

'Will the commander-in-chief be going into Rhodesia with us?' Robert Baloyi asked President Tambo slyly.

We all smiled, knowing the answer in advance.

'Comrade Joe won't be crossing with you', OR replied. 'He will remain in Zambia directing operations and control the deployment of reinforcements into Rhodesia when they are needed.'

'How will he direct operations when we are engaging the enemy if he is at the rear?' Robert persisted.

'Comrade Chris will direct operations inside Rhodesia. When some of you cross into South Africa Comrade Mjojo Mxwaku will assume command. That's what the Military HQ has decided.'

'It's strange, Comrade Tambo, that our own commander-in-chief, Akim Ndlovu, is also not prepared to lead us against Smith's soldiers', Kayeni Dube, a ZIPRA guerrilla, interrupted. 'He says that if he is killed, ZIPRA won't mount any further operations. Do you accept that reasoning, Comrade OR? Do you believe that if one man is killed — say either Comrades Joe or Akim — then both organisations will collapse?'

I interrupted and said: 'Fidel Castro led his men into the Sierra Maestra and Samora Machel, even as we speak, is directing and leading his men from the front in Mozambique. It seems to me that we have a strange leadership philosophy in both ZIPRA and MK where the military leaders refuse to lead their soldiers on operations.'

OR looked exhausted. The men were gathered in a large group around him and he peered at their faces in the gathering darkness. 'Although I am your supreme commander, I am a civilian and not a soldier. I will raise the questions you have asked at the next Military HQ meeting and ask its leaders for an answer.

'Today we are taking the first steps in the long journey home to rejoin those we left behind after promising them we will return.' We will see our task through to the end. The enemy is strong and we mustn't underestimate them. But you are also strong. You are well-trained and will meet their bullets with your own.

'Tonight you will cross into enemy territory and begin the work of freeing our people from oppression. They are relying on us to reverse the gains of colonialism on our continent. Don't fail them. Fight valiantly like your forefathers did before you. Remember the heroes of Africa . . . Makana, Dingane, Bambatha and Sekhukhune. Remember the great Mzilikazi and Lobengula. Remember the great Chaminuka and Nehanda who gave their lives in defence of the freedom of the African people.

'*Amandla*!'

The guerrillas raised their rifles in salute and roared: '*Ngawethu*!'

There was a sudden silence. It was a hot African night. Crickets began their usual chirruping and in the distance a hyena could be heard greeting the advent of the night, perhaps in anticipation of the battles that would follow and the bodies of the dead they would feed on afterwards. A night owl hooted in the distance, but the sounds were faint over the overpowering roar of the river below.

Suddenly a short burst of gunfire shattered the silence.

'Who did that?' Chris barked. 'No order has been given even to load, let alone open fire. Who fired those shots?'

He disappeared into the darkness to investigate. He returned a few minutes later and had a short whispered conference with OR. Tambo nodded.

'We can no longer cross here', he announced. 'The enemy might have heard those shots that a comrade fired accidentally. If they did they might be waiting in ambush when you cross.'

We returned to the trucks and mounted quietly. At 22:00 the vehicles stopped on a dirt road and the order was again given to dismount. We marched through the bush accompanied by OR until just after midnight when we reached another of the Zambezi's gorges. It was the Batoka Gorge some 35 kilometres downstream of Victoria Falls as the crow flies — but as the fish swim down the mighty Zambezi River it was much farther.

Spikes were hammered into cracks in the rock and using ropes, we descended slowly into the gorge. Torches were not allowed so we had to seek footholds in the pitch darkness. Absolute silence was demanded except for whispers when real problems developed. Occasionally rocks broke loose beneath our feet and tumbled down the rocky precipice. Those nearing the bottom heard them coming and clung to the cliff face with eyes closed, praying that the rocks would miss them. In the end we were lucky and only a few minor injuries were suffered during the descent.

The first men down inflated the Russian-supplied rubber boats. The best swimmers, Boston and Guluva, jumped in and swam for the Rhodesian bank with ropes tied around them. They made landfall a considerable way downstream because of the pull of the current but they scrambled up the bank and walked back. They tied the ropes to trees to steady the boats during the crossings. After that they scrambled back along the ropes to the Zambian shore and helped to load men into the boats. Although the current was powerful, with the help of the ropes, the boatloads of men made it safely across.

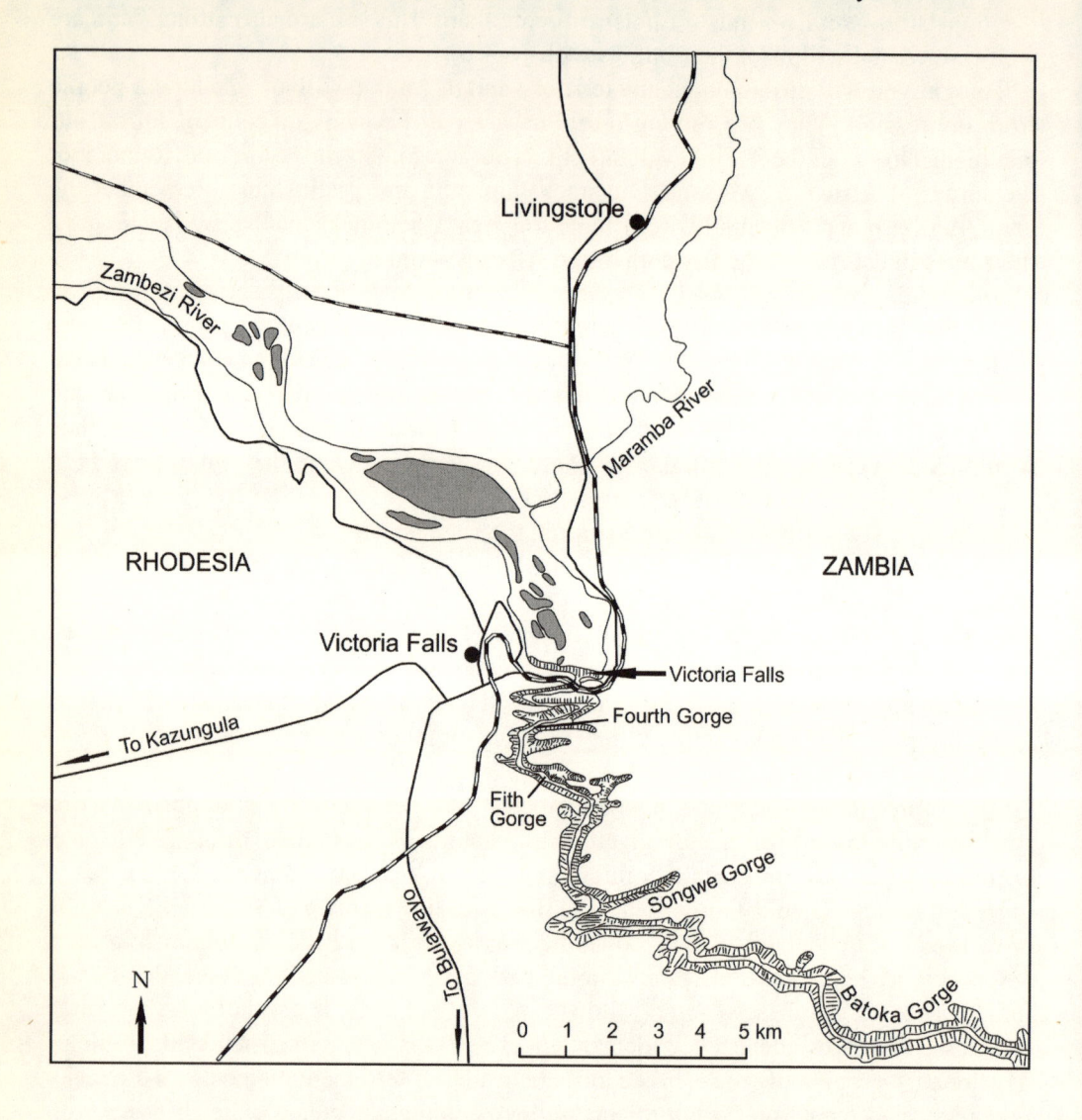

The Zambezi River and a few of its gorges downstream from Victoria Falls. Bakota Gorge was where the Luthuli Detachment crossed.

By 07:00 the next morning we were all in Rhodesia. It was 2 August 1967. We looked across at the Zambian bank and raised our rifles in a salute to our supreme commander. Only those around him heard his words as he waved back. He said: 'If I was just ten years younger I would have marched at the head of those boys myself.'

We lay in the shade of the mopani trees and waited for nightfall. At 18:00 we began our fateful march. Chris set a blistering pace. We were fit, well fed and fresh so there were no laggards. We came to a strip of cleared and swept ground about 30 metres wide. We knew its purpose was to allow the Security Forces to detect people who had crossed into the country. It was patrolled daily by a motorised military unit. We didn't know much about tracking or backtracking in those days and took no precautions. We just walked across it, and afterwards changed direction several times to create confusion. In the event, they picked up our spoor and by the next day the hunt was on. Our boots were Cuban-made and the soles left a recognisable figure of eight print on the ground. We marched throughout the night and rested at 06:00 the following morning.

After two nights of foot slogging we reached a clinic in the Dett area and three ZIPRA soldiers went in to speak to the people. They returned with food, bread, tinned meat and medicines. This was the only contact we had as a group with civilians inside Rhodesia. After that the march resumed at a furious pace.

After a week a combined force of ZIPRA and MK men hived off and headed for Lupane to open the Eastern Front. I think there were 23 men in all. They were attacked and all but wiped out sometime around 13 August. Those who lived to tell the tale were captured.

When ANC people talk about our participation in the Rhodesian War of Liberation, this group is rarely mentioned. They refer only to our group which entered the Wankie Game Reserve and fought around the Tjolotjo and Sibasa areas. I can remember only a few of the South Africans who died there. There was Gandhi Hlekani from Cradock, Jacques Goniwe, my friend Alfred Sharp (real name Templeton Mzondeni) from Chume near East London, Delmas Sibanyoni, Melane and James Masimini. Those captured were Freddy Mninzi, George Mothusi, George Tau, Jonathan Moyo and Bethuel Tamana.

The first battle between them and the Rhodesian Security Forces took place on the banks of the Nyatuwe River between Wankie and Dett and it lasted for ten hours. They had stopped for a rest in a dry river bed and their commander gave orders for them to be fed and watered.

At 07:00 sentries reported seeing spotter planes flying low over the area. The commander, David Madzimbamuto (alias Jonathan Moyo), didn't think the report significant.

At 08:30 the silence of the morning was broken by an outbreak of gunfire and a spotter plane with sky-shout facilities flying overhead. Its loudspeakers boomed out: 'Surrender terrorists! You're surrounded!'

David bawled back that they would never surrender.

After that the main business of the day began. For a short time there was confusion and panic amongst the guerrillas, but they soon rallied and returned fire. The commissar, James Masimini, shouted that he would shoot anybody who tried to run. When we later asked survivors why Masimini had found it necessary to make such a threat, they said it was because most of our ZIPRA allies had shown little stomach for fighting. Some had already openly said that they intended to desert at the first sign of trouble.

During the battle some ZIPRA men hid in the grass and didn't even try to fight, but others resisted bravely. The battle raged well into the afternoon. The Security Forces decided that it would be suicidal to try and dislodge such a determined group by frontal assault, so they called in helicopters to machine-gun them from the air.

MK's machine gunners like Delmas 'Nsimbi Kayigobi' Sibanyoni and Gandhi Hlekani held the enemy at bay. It was a hopeless fight from the outset because the group had been attacked before it could establish bases within the country and link up with the local people. Guerrillas cannot survive in the way a stand-alone regular army does. They derive their support from the people they are seeking to liberate. They have to merge with the population to the point where the enemy cannot distinguish between the locals and the guerrillas. The Lupane group, like ourselves, didn't get the opportunity to merge with the people, so they were unable to survive.

That night some guerrillas managed to slip through the Security Forces' dragnet, leaving four of their number dead on the battlefield. A fifth, James Masimini, also stayed behind. He volunteered to cover the retreat of his comrades and the next morning died in a gun battle with the enemy.

The Security Forces dropped leaflets from the sky urging the guerrillas to save themselves by surrendering. They promised amnesty, but the Lupane fighters ignored the offer and fought on.

The pamphlet strategy had previously persuaded a group of ZIPRA fighters who had entered the country in 1966 to surrender. We found them in prison serving ten-year sentences. They tried to play commissar to us, thinking we had no idea how cowardly they had behaved in battle.

Meanwhile, we continued our march. Then things began to happen. Mambazo (Patrick Mathanjana) was reported missing. He should never have been deployed across the border because he suffered from bunions which made marching agonising. Unable to keep up with the blistering pace set by Chris Hani, he soon he fell behind. He followed the railway line south at his own pace but was soon captured. John Dube, the ZIPRA commander, sent Rashidi (Goodman Mhlauli) and Wilson Msweli (later Major-General Wilson Nqose of the SANDF) to look for him while the detachment marched on. It was night-time and the searchers hadn't been told where to rendezvous with us.

We marched from sunset to near sunrise for about a fortnight, but after that the pace and the consequent distance covered decreased dramatically each night. We were short of food and water. Chris found himself marching at the head of an army of severely malnourished men. He did his best to motivate us but we had scarcely eaten for almost a week. Our energy had faded and only sheer determination drove us on. We were in the centre of the Wankie Game Reserve and there were no locals around who could provide us with food and fresh water. They say an army marches on its stomach, but ours marched on grim determination.

Peter Tladi reported leaving his AK47 at a place where we had rested during the night.

He was ordered to return and find it. He turned around and walked away, but we never saw him again. He was later captured and ended up on Robben Island.

And so we marched on. Men began to straggle and those of us in front had to slow the pace to allow them to catch up. Men spoke only in whispers because of the lack of food and a shortage of potable water.

We lost count of the days and reached a stage where we didn't care anyway. What did it matter if it was a Sunday or a Tuesday? Each day became the same as the one before and everything lost meaning. We just marched. We looked like scarecrows, our uniforms torn to shreds as we pushed our way through the thick thorn bushes during the hours of darkness. We still marched during the night, but rested more frequently than before. We wondered if we would ever find a waterhole. Then one morning we saw a dam about 900 metres away. We could actually smell the water and that is no exaggeration. You smell water if you have been thirsty for a long time.

Perhaps we should have taken the precaution of waiting until nightfall before approaching the dam, but we were desperate. Chris Mampuru and Ernest Modulo were sent to reconnoitre the area for an enemy presence and to see if the water was fit to drink. Ten minutes later a convoy of military vehicles passed close by. Then we saw a single-engined spotter plane flying overhead, clearly looking for something on the ground. There was a long burst of automatic fire over by the dam followed by silence. Chris and Ernest had been ambushed and killed.

We lay unmoving under the short mopane trees wondering if the spotter plane would discover us. The aircraft gradually widened its circle of search and moved farther and farther away from us until it finally flew off. We lay in concealment and waited for nightfall. When it was dark I was summoned to the HQ, ordered to select ten men and told to go to the dam to see what had happened. We walked in single file with rifles held at waist level. We reached the dam safely, but there was no sign of our two comrades. The soldiers had obviously removed their bodies. I returned and reported that there was water in the dam and that it seemed okay. The decision was taken, however, that we wouldn't drink the water in case the enemy had poisoned it.

The next night at 02:30 we smelt water again. Then there it was — a great sheet of silver shimmering in the moonlight. Water! We ran or stumbled towards it.

'Halt!' Chris shouted. 'It's not running water, comrades, so it might have been poisoned. We must hide in the bushes and wait for animals to come down to drink at first light. If it's poisoned, they won't drink. If they do drink then we'll know it's okay.'

At first light the animals came. The impalas and other buck drank tidily, but the buffalo drank and urinated in the water. Elephants appeared and after slurping in leisurely fashion for some time, they wallowed in the dam and turned it into a mud hole. When they moved off, it was our turn. I have never tasted anything so delicious. We put mud in our water bottles followed by water, then shook the bottles and drank. The mud served to fill our stomachs as if it was food. The smell of buffalo urine was strong, but with our almost terminal thirst, it didn't bother us. We filled our water bottles and left at nightfall.

Some men grumbled that we should have shot an animal for meat and that it was foolish of Chris to pass up the opportunity.

Chris pointed out that firing a shot might give our position away to the enemy.

'We'll die of hunger if we don't get something to eat, Comrade Chris. If the enemy attacks us in our present physical state I wouldn't have the energy to lift my rifle,' Reuben 'the Kulak' Nhlabathi argued.

The men laughed because Reuben still had his big stomach even after weeks of semi-starvation. He had been nicknamed Kulak, which is Russian for a petty-bourgeoisie, because of it.

Chris agreed to put it to the vote and the majority agreed by a show of hands that an animal should be shot. John Dube, being the commander, should have made the decision but Chris was closer to the men.

He left the camp with a hunting party of ten men including myself. We walked through the bush for an hour without seeing anything except a squirrel and two rabbits. That was hardly enough meat to feed us, nor worth taking the risk of giving away our location to the enemy. An hour later Chris called a halt while he scanned the bush ahead with binoculars. He eventually focussed on one spot, lowered the glasses and turned to me.

'Have a look. See the top of that hillock to the left.'

I took the binoculars and sighted them. The head of an animal filled the lenses.

'It looks like a zebra, Comrade Chris. The range is about 500 metres which is extreme so it will be a difficult shot.'

Commanders are not always the best shots in their groups. There was also the danger of risking his reputation if he shot and missed. Chris was fully aware of this.

'Where's Daluxolo?' he asked.

He was the best marksman but he was with the main group. That left Chris to do the job. He knelt and took aim. The SKS rifle seemed to explode in his hands and the animal vanished from sight behind the hillock. We didn't know if he had hit or missed it. We doubled forward and halfway down the reverse slope of the hillock found a very fat and very dead zebra.

'You'll be a good shot before the war ends, Comrade Commissar', someone joked.

The legs were removed and carried back to camp. We skinned them and ate the meat raw. Seventy hungry men can devour a lot of meat. We couldn't risk a fire or the smell of smoke. For the next three days we had plenty of meat and water and felt much better as we resumed our march.

We were later told that a platoon of Rhodesian African Rifles (RAR) soldiers had been shadowing us from the moment we had entered the country. I don't know how true this was but the story went that their informant in ZIPRA — or maybe he was in MK — had told the Security Forces we were a suicide squad who would fight like men possessed and that we didn't care if we lived or died. He said they should not attack until our food and water ran out and we were too weak to defend ourselves.

The platoon of 42 men was commanded by Lieutenant John Smith and his deputy was Sergeant Major Timitiya. We were told they were never more than six hours behind us. It was said they measured the distance we covered and radioed this to Security Force HQ, noticing that the distance we were covering nightly was diminishing and concluding correctly that we were tiring.

Lieutenant John Smith called Major Willar on the radio and said he intended to attack the next day. Willar was camped at Siwuwo Pools with 100 men and we were unwittingly moving towards him. After receiving Smith's message the major took 50 men and moved in our direction. Smith and his 42 men were behind us and Willar was ahead of us.

We were trapped like the meat in a sandwich, but we didn't know it.

10

Dead men don't need the time

Our detachment was made up of sections of six men. By then we were down from 35 to 30 men or so. In each section three men were armed with AK47s or PPSH sub-machine-guns; two had SKS rifles and the sixth man an RPG2 or RPG7 rocket launcher or a light machine gun. In addition each soldier had an F1 fragmentation grenade. All rifles were fitted with bayonets.

The first action we became involved in was the result of the indiscipline of a particular group. They had threatened to shoot their commander. The men had a legitimate grievance but their noisy behaviour was very dangerous in enemy territory. When their commander attempted to correct their behaviour they answered: 'You were given permission by the commander-in-chief [Joe Modise] to shoot anyone if they caused problems, so go ahead and shoot us and stop talking so much.'

Joe probably hadn't meant the order literally, but in any case how do you shoot armed men when you are outnumbered? The commander adopted the wisest course and fled, which was when the political commissar, Charles Sishuba, took over. Feeling flushed with their victory over their commander, the group became absolutely uncontrollable.

On that fateful day, Lieutenant John Smith and his RAR platoon heard their talking and shouting and attacked. A fragmentation grenade was lobbed amongst them and Smith fired a long burst with his FN on automatic. The grenade tore them apart. It also distorted Robert Baloyi's light machine gun, rendering it useless. Charles Sishuba, Robert Baloyi and Barry Masipa died instantly and Sparks Moloi was seriously wounded.

A fifth man, Peter Mhlongo, was shot through his upper arms and thighs. He couldn't move and had to be carried, but at least he was alive. I doubt that section even got a chance to return fire because they were caught completely by surprise. A breakdown in authority led to unruly behaviour and this cost lives. But the Luthuli Detachment was by no means crushed.

There was another onslaught of gunfire and this time I was in the thick of it. For the next five minutes we couldn't even lift our heads to determine where the fire was coming from. About 80 metres away and standing right in front of us was a huge RAR soldier. He was leaning against a tree and spraying bullets just above our heads with a Bren gun. It was fed from an ammunition belt draped over his shoulder. We buried our noses in the dust and didn't move a muscle. He couldn't see us, but he knew we were there. He was firing into every bush around us and yelling threats continuously. This was Sergeant-Major Timitiya of the RAR and he was as mad as a snake.

Lieutenant Smith, meanwhile, was shouting and laying down a wicked concentration of fire to his left and to his right.

'Destroy the enemy! Show them what we're made of! Defend your comrades!'

The soldiers ran towards us firing wildly. They dropped their heavy backpacks and knelt in a long line in front of us, shooting at an enemy they still couldn't see, but whose presence they felt. The bullets were thudding in the dirt around us and we had to make a countermove.

In the midst of all the firing there was a sudden shocked silence. The machine gun slipped from Sergeant-Major Timitiya's hands and he fell face down to the ground. The RAR men paused instinctively, not believing the evidence of their eyes. They had thought their sergeant major was indestructible. Then Lieutenant Smith flung his FN in the air and fell to his knees clutching his chest. Bullets struck his face and he spun around and fell flat on his back.

With their commanders dead the platoon continued firing, but they were losing cohesion. Should they advance or stay where they were? Should they withdraw? They hesitated in the face of the accurate return fire they were being subjected to from our positions.

Chris Hani jumped up and circled his SKS above his head.

'*Mawabethwe lamakhwenkwe bafondini, yintoni maan?*' (Let's thrash these guys. What's the matter with you?)

We leaped from cover and surged forward. The RAR men were only 30 metres to our front, kneeling and shooting. Our sudden appearance took them by surprise and they lost their courage. Our machine gunners moved forward pouring bursts into them. They broke and ran. We stopped, knelt and fired at their retreating backs. The ground was flat and there was nothing that provided cover, so they just ran.

There were two air force helicopters circling wildly overhead. We picked up a radio pack dropped by a retreating soldier and heard someone in the chopper calling the ground force.

'Do you read me? Can we drop you more ammunition? Indicate your position with a flare.'

We dared not respond on the captured radio as this would have given away our position and revealed that a radio was in enemy hands. That would probably have brought down a blistering attack from the air. The helicopter crews couldn't tell who were friends and who were 'terrorists'. They could only see armed blacks dodging around amongst the trees. We stared at the radio, wanting to speak into it.

Some RAR soldiers whom we thought had fled with the rest suddenly appeared and shouted that they wanted to surrender. Chris told us to cease firing and called on them to advance. They still had their weapons, but this seemed to have escaped Chris' notice. Nobody is perfect, especially if it's your first contact and things are happening quickly.

I sprang over to him and told him to order the enemy to throw down their weapons. The soldiers immediately raised their rifles and fired wildly at us, but to little effect, even though they were only 40 metres away. We all hit the ground and returned fire. By then some of us were using captured FN rifles and there was a lot of FN ammunition lying around. It allowed us to conserve our Soviet ammunition which was running short.

The soldiers broke and ran leaving Chris beside himself with rage. The political game he had wanted to play had backfired. He'd intended to let the RAR soldiers surrender because they were black Africans. He was going to explain to them that he and his men had entered the country to free the black people. After that he would have released them in the hope they would return to their unit and say to their black comrades: 'Those guys don't want to kill black soldiers. It's not our war. It's a white man's war. Let's refuse to fight. Let the white man do his own fighting. Those men want to free us. We know the whites oppress us. We can either refuse to fight, or go and join our black brothers in the bush.'

His 'black brothers', however, had let him down. We told Chris not to put our lives on the line like that again. Chris knew that black soldiers in the Rhodesian Army were underlings. That they were paid a salary to fight in defence of the Rhodesian state, but were not treated as equals. At that time there were no black commissioned officers in the Rhodesian Army, even in a unit like the RAR. They had to have a white commanding officer. That's why Lieutenant John Smith was commanding the platoon. The highest ranking officer after him was Sergeant-Major Timitiya, a warrant officer. He was the induna and he controlled the men on behalf of his white superiors — just like the indunas did with black workers on the Rand mines.

RAR soldiers earned less money than whites of equal rank and Chris knew it. He also knew they were called names and abused by white soldiers, but they hung in there to get their salaries at the end of the month. If they died in service, shot by other Africans like themselves, their families didn't get the same financial benefits as the families of white soldiers — even when they were killed in the same battle. Chris had gambled that while RAR soldiers, being oppressed Africans, would accept employment in a colonial force without considering themselves traitors. But when their fellow Africans rose up in arms against the colonialists, he had expected them to defect and fight on our side.

Instead, in a crowning indignity, they had fired at us. We might have been killed just because Chris had decided to be philosophical. Soldiers don't appreciate things like that and we told him so.

'From now on, comrades', he promised, 'a Rhodesian soldier is neither black nor white. He's just a soldier. If he wears a different uniform to ours we'll shoot him on sight.'

There were RAR soldiers lying around, some dead and some wounded, but we had no time to worry about them. Instead we took their packs and rummaged for goodies. Oh, and goodies there were. Biscuits, chocolate, corned beef, tinned fish, condensed milk in toothpaste-like tubes, tea, coffee, sugar and even snuff. To crown it all there were several water bags. We gulped down ice-cold water and most of us were sick. We opened cans of fish and wolfed down the contents. We squeezed condensed milk down our throats and chased it with tinned beef. It was an orgy until Mjojo called us to order.

'Comrades, some of our comrades have been killed. We must find them and pay our last respects. After that we can return and carry on looting the enemy's stuff.'

We returned to where the 'unruly group' had been wiped out. We laid them next to each other, covered them with leaves and branches, saluted and left. There was no time for burials. Sparks Moloi, their young commissar, sat leaning against a tree. He had taken most of Lieutenant John Smith's long burst in his stomach and was bleeding profusely. It was obvious he was finished.

'Comrade Thula, you'll see freedom day', he called to me hoarsely. 'When South Africa is free tell the people what happened outside their country.' He continued with difficulty. 'I was Joe Modise's spy — a sort of James Bond. But I only agreed to spy on my comrades because Comrade Joe convinced me I was defending the ANC. I reported everything the comrades said about him personally and about the leadership generally.'

He died where he sat, a disillusioned young man. Poor Sparks. I didn't bother to tell him that with the trouble we were in, none of us was expecting to see Freedom Day. It looked like there was an interminable number of years of fighting ahead of us before we could even think of such a thing. But somehow Sparks knew that I would survive. And here I am telling his story.

We returned to the dead soldiers and continued cleaning out their knapsacks. I looked down at Sergeant-Major Timitiya. A bullet had penetrated his head. There was a thin trickle of blood running down his temple and huge clots in both nostrils. He was wearing a lovely watch — and I didn't have one. I unstrapped it from his wrist.

Daluxolo was watching. He caught my eye and shrugged.

'Dead men don't need the time, Daluxolo', I said defensively.

The detachment regrouped and we resumed our march. We carried Peter Mhlongo on a stretcher made from poles and a blanket. He moaned with pain continually as we marched into the gathering darkness.

It had been an eventful day.

11

Fighting continues

We crept away from the battlefield and moved in a south-easterly direction. We had been marching south-west before the battle.

At around 22:00 we heard a battle raging far away to our right. The detachment marched on. Our progress was slow because we were handicapped by carrying Peter Mhlongo. We marched ten kilometres less that night than we normally covered and that saved our lives.

Lieutenant John Smith had calculated our progress quite accurately in his signals to his tactical headquarters. They predicted where we would most likely be the next morning and sent Hawker Hunter strike jets to bomb the vicinity. Fortunately, we were ten kilometres away from the bombing at the time.

We watched the Hunters screaming in and heard the bombs howling down and striking home. It went on for about 15 minutes. We lay quietly in the bush wondering what it was all about. About an hour later we heard human voices and dogs barking close by, but we couldn't see anything. Some began to advance theories.

'It's probably people who've come to us for protection. They're bombing civilians because of what we did to them yesterday', a theorist suggested.

'Perhaps we should go and welcome them', someone else threw in.

John Dube decided to investigate. He was wearing an RAR green beret, a Rhodesian Army camouflage jacket and was carrying an FN rifle. A few of us had exchanged our rags for Rhodesian uniforms and our guns for theirs.

Dube should have taken some men with him, but he went alone. Who knows what he was thinking? He reported later that after walking about 200 metres in the direction of the voices, he suddenly found himself in an enemy bush camp. There were many white soldiers there, some preparing breakfast or sipping tea and standing around talking in small groups. He fired a burst at them with his FN and ran.

We heard the firing and John shouting: 'They're here comrades. The enemy is here!'

He hurtled from the bush gibbering with fright.

It seems the soldiers — we thought they were Rhodesian Light Infantry but they could have been any white soldiers or policemen — had mistaken John for an RAR soldier and had paid no attention to him until he opened fire. We ran towards them firing short bursts.

We caught them in the open where they had been waiting until the strike jets had finished their work. When they saw they were under attack they grabbed their weapons and returned fire.

There were men all around in the bushes and firing became intense. Shuda Makhasi shouted that Jack Simelane had been killed. Back in Lusaka, Comrade Jack had been one of those who strongly believed that an enemy should be given a chance to surrender so he could be captured and politicised.

'We must remember that we are fighting a just war', he had said. 'These poor soldiers are not just capitalist pawns, they are also the fathers of children and husbands of wives. If they surrender we mustn't kill them. They should be captured and given political lectures. I'm sure that some will even join us.'

'Do you really believe that hardened racists who you call pawns of capitalists will surrender, Comrade Jack? Do you believe that a few political lectures will change racial attitudes that have been drilled into them since childhood?' Kenneth Malinga wanted to know.

The debate had often recurred but Comrade Jack always stuck to his ground. He was a member of the Communist Party of South Africa and believed we were fighting a class war, not a race war. Maybe he was right — but we didn't know. What we did know was that we intended to kill every enemy soldier we saw, especially after Chris' experience the previous day.

Jack had apparently approached a white soldier from behind. Instead of shooting him Jack called on him to surrender. The soldier turned and in one flowing movement shot him between the eyes. Jack's beliefs had cost him his life at the hands of the 'pawns of capitalism'. We were sorry to lose him because he was a good soldier and comrade.

I ran past a soldier who was trying to wriggle from a sleeping bag to get at his gun. I fired a short burst at him.

'That sleeping bag is mine!' I shouted to no one in particular as we ran on past.

Comrade Nicholas Donda who had been running next to me fell to his knees and clutched his chest. I stopped as he fell on his face. I wanted to help him but he was breathing with difficulty and red froth was coming from his mouth. He had been shot through the lungs and was sinking fast. I tried to lift him to carry him to the rear, but he shook his head and waved me away. He tried to speak but died before he could say anything. I ran back and reported to our section commander, Reuben Nhlabathi, that Donda was gone. We went to get him and carried him to the rear. Mjojo suddenly appeared and told us the enemy had retreated to a patch of bush about 300 metres away.

'We cannot leave them there. We need to wipe them out, comrades', Mjojo shouted. 'Bring your section, Comrade Kulak, we need your light machine-gunner.'

We left Donda where he lay and with Mjojo ran towards the enemy. Chris was pointing out their positions to about 15 of our comrades. There was an open space of about 70 metres between us and where the enemy was regrouping. While we crouched down figuring out the best way to attack, George Driver, a coloured comrade from Cape Town, acted.

He charged across the open grass patch towards the enemy, firing his sub-machine gun as he went. For whatever reason he had a white cloth tied around his head. Halfway across, his gun fell silent. He had emptied his magazine, maybe hitting some of the enemy, but we couldn't tell. While he fumbled to get a fresh magazine, a soldier stood up and began firing at him. At 40 metres he wasn't a difficult target.

'Crawl back, Comrade George, crawl back!' Mjojo shouted.

As George complied we stood up and fired over his head to divert the enemy's attention. It worked and George made it back to our position. Mjojo climbed into him, calling him every name under the sun. By then George was a very frightened soldier and was shaking like a leaf.

A legend was born from our two stupid actions of that day. After I was captured, Detective Inspector Ronald Stanley Peters, Homicide Chief in Bulawayo, asked me a strange question.

'Who was that terrorist who walked into the soldiers' camp, calmly greeted them and opened fire?'

I couldn't for the life of me remember the incident. I cudgelled my brains in an effort to recall but couldn't.

'He was wearing an RAR uniform, a green beret and was carrying an FN rifle', said Peters to jog my memory.

Then it struck me. What we had perceived as a very stupid act by John Dube was seen by the enemy to be a cool and well-planned act of bravery. They thought he had done it deliberately. I suppressed my laughter with great difficulty and told Peters that we had been trained to occasionally do such things to put the fear of God into our enemies.

'Apparently your ruse worked, because the soldiers involved couldn't stop repeating what that friend of yours did. Another thing. What about the Chinese guy with a white bandana around his head who charged the RAR firing at point-blank range? They say you had Chinese soldiers in your group.'

That was George Driver. They had mistaken him for a Chinese kamikaze. He had actually caused panic in the enemy ranks by behaving totally irresponsibly. The Rhodesians knew that some of us had been trained in China, so they jumped to the conclusion that Chinese soldiers had volunteered to fight alongside us. That's how legends are created.

After Comrade George found his way back to safety a policeman, Patrol Officer Thomas, and his attack/tracker dog popped up in our sights. We fired at the dog and missed, but Thomas was killed. His dog ran away but we heard that it was found several months later.

We brought in our dead — Nicholas Donda, Jack Simelane and Peter Mhlongo, the stretcher case. Mhlongo had not participated in the fighting because of his injuries, but had been lying under a tree while the battle raged around him. He was killed by a stray bullet.

I noticed that the MK men were standing to one side while the ZIPRA men were a few paces away.

'This isn't right', Mbijana was saying to Chris. 'When the fighting starts these ZIPRA cowards run and hide and we end up doing all the fighting. They only reappear after the battle to participate in the looting. They are just bloody scavengers. That's why only South Africans have died in the battles we have fought. Not a single ZIPRA has even been wounded. We cannot continue dying for them, Chris.'

John Dube was standing nearby and heard everything, but he didn't say a word because he knew it was true. Neither he nor his men had the stomach to fight. Without the MK soldiers they would have been lost.

'I'm taking my MK men to South Africa tomorrow', Mjojo said to Chris.

Chris shrugged and said nothing. We had volunteered to help the Rhodesians free their country, but it was difficult helping people who wouldn't help themselves. We South Africans found it difficult to understand why trained men melted into the bushes once the fighting started, only to reappear after we foreigners had killed their enemies.

We got ready to move. There were wounded men and we needed water badly. Chris selected 12 men and left in search of water. He somehow got lost and didn't rejoin the detachment. They later crossed into Botswana.

Darkness was falling and the rest of us prepared to leave. I picked up my pack and AK47 and jumped down into a dry river bed. I saw Daluxolo just ahead of me.

'Let's go Daluxolo', I said. 'The detachment is moving out.'

'I'm not coming', he replied. 'I can't leave Derek here to die alone merely because the dogs he volunteered to fight for have deserted him.'

'What's the matter with him?'

'He's had a serious attack of ulcers. He says he can't even sit up, let alone march. The ZIPRA guys have left him and rejoined the detachment. I can't do that. What would I tell my aunt, his mother? How could I say that I had abandoned him in the bush?'

'What will you do — carry him over your shoulder and shoot with the other hand if you run into the enemy? Don't be stupid, Daluxolo, let's go. You know the rule: if a comrade is unable to march and the enemy is in pursuit, we shoot him and run. Maybe we don't have to shoot Derek, but you can't stay here alone with him. Come on, let's go!'

'You can go. I'm not going anywhere unless Derek goes with me', he said with finality.

'Well, if you're not going', I heard myself say, 'then I'll stay, too. Derek is also my friend.'

I couldn't believe I had said such a thing. My mind told me I should leave both of them behind, even though they were my friends. Not all things are decided by the mind, I suppose; some are decided by the heart and maybe that's not a bad thing.

Despite Derek being a friend, something indefinable warned me not to be too sure of him. I was unable to put a finger on it, but the feeling was there. He had been offered the position of chief-of-staff of the Luthuli group to fight in Rhodesia. Now he was lying helpless on the ground.

I took his water bottle, squeezed a tube of condensed milk into it and shook it vigorously. I made him drink, then he lay down and slept. After about an hour he sat up.

'I'm feeling much better. Where are the others?'

'They left an hour ago', Daluxolo replied.

I said nothing.

Derek got to his feet and began pacing up and down, slowly at first, then with greater confidence and energy.

'I think I can walk again. We should get away from this place because the soldiers will be here at daybreak.

We began our march, no longer with the detachment, but just as determined to get to South Africa.

12

Guerrillas are to people what fish are to water

We marched the whole night in the hope of catching up with the detachment. At times we thought we heard them ahead of us, but after listening for a few minutes we couldn't be sure.

We tried to follow the Southern Cross, that constellation of stars in the form of a cross that indicates where south is. But when dawn came we were shocked to discover we were right back where we had started the previous night. We had gone round in a circle. Navigating by the stars obviously wasn't our forte. By then we realised that all hopes of catching up with the detachment had faded.

As daylight flooded over the horizon, we heard helicopters landing not two kilometres away from us.

'They are sweeping the battlefield for weapons and bodies', Derek said. 'If they catch us we'll be as good as dead. We'd better get out of here.'

We ran non-stop for about four hours. Occasionally a helicopter would pass high overhead, reminding us that danger was ever present. We crouched under trees or hid in bushes until they had passed and then continued running. At about 11:30 we stopped to rest and concealed ourselves in thick, tall grass not far from a dry riverbed.

I opened my eyes with a start to see two herd boys standing over us. One was probably about 12 and the other a couple of years younger. I had no idea how long they had been there.

'We won't tell the white people we saw you', the elder one said. 'The whites are not our relatives.' He spoke in Sindebele, a language very similar to Zulu.

'Who are you related to then?' I asked.

'You', they said in unison.

Our talking awakened the other two and they sat there listening.

'We are very thirsty. We need water to drink', I told them.

They turned, jumped, into the dry river bed and began to dig with their hands. Within ten minutes they had a metre deep hole. We watched as clean, cold and fresh water began filtering in at the bottom. We drank and drank, then filled our bottles and thanked our new friends. It was obvious that MK should have added bush survival to our training curriculum!

'What area is this?' I asked. 'How do we get to the nearest village?'

'Travel with the sun at your backs until you reach a road. Be careful as army trucks use that road a lot these days. We have no idea why there are so many soldiers around but we heard there has been fighting and that many of them have died. At home they tell us not to talk about it.'

'They're right, you shouldn't talk about it', I cautioned.

'This is the Tjolotjo area and the road will take you to the village of Gulakabili. The people there can be trusted because they don't like white people. We come from there.'

We thanked the little fellows again and left. By then it was about 17:00. We had slept for a full six hours. After that we didn't talk, we just marched. Two hours later we reached the road the boys had told us about. It was almost dark, but there was still a need for caution. We walked on the grass verge to avoid making boot prints. We didn't see anybody but we could hear a dog barking in the distance. The barking became louder and we felt sure we were approaching a village. We decided to hide in the bush until daybreak so we could scout the area and work out our next move.

We chose an area of thick brush and the three of us lay down under one blanket and slept. At about 22:00 I awoke with a feeling that I was in extreme danger. I opened my eyes, but could see nothing. When my eyes became accustomed to the darkness, I saw what looked like a tennis ball hanging from a thick string. The string was to my front and the tennis ball to my right. The ball suddenly moved farther right and the string with it. I then realised what it was.

The tennis ball was the testicles of a lion and the string its tail. I moved my eyes to the right without making any body movement and saw the huge beast was sniffing at Daluxolo's head. It seemed to have passed Derek who was sleeping between us. Then it decided to move on. It walked very deliberately until it was about 20 metres away, stopped and turned. It stood there looking at us, perhaps trying to make up its mind exactly what we were.

I put my hand on Derek's mouth and he opened his eyes.

'Lion', I whispered, indicating the direction with my eyes. 'Wake Daluxolo.'

He did so in exactly the way I had awakened him. Our rifles were under the blanket. We threw it off and grabbed our weapons. We rolled away from each other and aimed at the lion. For a moment I thought it was going to charge, but nothing happened. The village dogs were barking furiously, obviously having sensed the lion's presence. The great cat seemed undecided what to do, but then it loped off into the bushes. The barking of the dogs had annoyed it, and maybe saved our lives. Needless to say, we didn't sleep again for the rest of the night. At first light we found we were close to a cluster of huts. A young woman came towards us past a cattle kraal. She stopped about ten metres away, dug a hole in the ground with her hoe and squatted. She finished her business and stood up, muttering something to herself that we couldn't catch. She scraped soil in the hole, shouldered her hoe and walked back to the huts.

We decided to stay away from the village for the time being and withdrew into the safety of the bush. While pushing our way through the undergrowth we discovered a cave with clear running water. It was fresh and very cold. We drank deeply and filled our bottles in case we needed to leave in a hurry. We settled down but this time we didn't sleep. We had been caught napping once too often; first by the herd boys, then by that lion.

We stayed in the cave for a week, resting. During the first night we took a walk to the village. We passed some people but in the dark it was impossible for them to identify us. I saw a light in the distance and we walked over to it. It was coming through the open window of a small shop and we could see a young man inside counting money. He was alone and after a brief consultation with my companions, I decided to go in and buy something.

The fellow was about 20 and I greeted him in what I believed was passable Sindebele. He was startled but collected himself.

'My father will talk to you', he said and disappeared through a door at the back. He returned shortly afterwards with a man of about 50.

'I'm Sithole', he said in a friendly tone. 'My son tells me that you speak Zulu. Don't worry — everyone in this village supports ZAPU, so no one will betray you. Come to the house at the back of the store so we can talk. The shop is open so people might come in to buy cigarettes.'

I accompanied him to the back, leaving my comrades in hiding but on guard outside.

'We have heard that there has been much fighting in the Tjolotjo area near the Umzingwane River. They say that many bodies of black and white soldiers have been taken to the Wankie and Nyamandhlovu police stations. You boys have done a great job. My eldest son was arrested and detained last year, so when I see young men like you it gives me hope that I will be seeing him again one fine day.

'Bester, close the shop', he called to his son. 'Are you alone?' he asked me.

'Other comrades are on guard outside. I must talk to them before we continue.'

'I see you are real soldiers', he said smiling. 'You don't just blunder around like a herd of goats.'

I went outside to consult the others.

'Can we trust him?' Derek wanted to know. 'We saw you go into the house. How did you know he wasn't leading you into an ambush?'

'When those two herd boys said they wouldn't betray us, how did we know whether to trust them or not? Don't ask me whether we can trust Mr Sithole. I really don't know. Do you have any suggestions?'

'What does your instinct tell you, Thula?' Daluxolo asked quietly.

'My instinct tells me we can trust him, but I can't be sure. We're all taking a chance. But if we don't trust anyone maybe we should return to Lusaka and report to the leaders that we can't operate.'

'I hate this!' Derek burst out. 'Trusting my very life to people I don't know! It seems downright stupidity. I think we should get out of here immediately. We have exposed ourselves enough already.'

'Wait a bit Derek', Daluxolo broke in. ' I trust Thula's instinct. Let's work with the old man.'

Derek stood there in a quandary.

'Derek, a guerrilla is to the people what a fish is to water', I quoted. 'Fighting our war without the cooperation of the people will be impossible. If we can't trust them with our lives we should abandon the fight right now. We will always be faced with situations like this, both here in Rhodesia and in South Africa. Daluxolo and I will go in and talk to Sithole.'

'All right', Derek conceded. 'But I think you should go in alone. Daluxolo and I will stay outside on guard.'

'That sounds okay to me', Daluxolo agreed.

I went back inside and the old man looked at me inquisitively.

'What are your friends saying, young man? Are they wondering if I can be trusted? They're right not to be too trusting, but in my case they are wrong because I am like one of you. If I betrayed you, I would be betraying myself. The whites support the soldiers who fight for them. We support you for the same reason.'

The old man told his son to call his wife.

Bester disappeared and returned with a beautiful and dignified woman of about 40. She knelt in front of the old man as was the custom.

'I am here, *Baba*', she said quietly.

'Young men are here tonight. They're hungry so prepare a huge meal for them with lots of meat. Warriors don't eat vegetables like your son Bester here.'

Bester smiled.

'It shall be done, *Baba*', MaMpofu promised and left the room.

The old man addressed me again. 'We are Zulus like you. War runs in our veins. When I see warriors I yearn for my youth and wish I could join you in fighting these whites.'

'Yes, we are warriors, *Baba* Sithole, but we're helpless if the people don't assist us. We are a people's army and we fight for the lost freedom of the African people.'

By then I felt confident that the old man could be trusted.

'We were told by a policeman stationed at Wankie police station, who is one of us, that you killed black soldiers. May I ask why you did this, my son?'

'We want them to know that it's time to join the rest of the African people and stop eating crumbs falling from the white man's table. In the first battle our commander gave them the opportunity to approach us and surrender. But when they were close they opened fire on us. For that they deserved to die. African soldiers must openly identify with us. The white man must go into the bush alone to defend his power. He must stop using black people.'

'You are very young, but you speak with the authority of an old man', said Sithole laughing.

We had a great meal that night. I ate first, then went out and stood guard while the other two went in to eat. It was after midnight when we left for our cave. During the daylight hours we lay low, discussed things and slept. At 21:00 each evening we returned to Sithole's house for hot baths and well-cooked food.

Finally, on the third night, Derek relented and agreed that Sithole was no traitor. After that no guards were posted and we all went in and ate food together.

Sithole had endless questions and wanted to know everything.

'Are your weapons superior to those of the Rhodesian soldiers? We have been told that you have weapons from Russia, the people who have sent a man into space. Is that why you are able to kill so many of the enemy?'

Even Derek joined in the conversation.

'*Baba*, our weapons are first rate, but the Rhodesians also have good weapons. The reason why we are able to beat them is because they are visible and we are in hiding. They frequently have to shoot at an enemy they can't see, while we see their approach from a long way off. We wait until they are close enough for us to see the whites of their eyes before we open fire.'

Mr Sithole in his happiness even invited his three wives to sit in and listen to our nightly conversations. The women listened and shook their heads, remarking that we were far too young to die.

'Do your mothers know you are engaged in such dangerous work?' MaKhumalo asked. She was the youngest wife and in her late 20s. We laughed.

'Mothers are never told what warriors do', replied Sithole, scandalised. 'We would never have an army if you women were told anything. To you they are sons, but to us fathers they become warriors. We have to forget they are our sons when wars are to be fought. You women can never do that, which is why you are never told anything. You would kill us with your tears.'

We didn't just talk and eat, but looked ahead and planned. Where were we going from there? Bus drivers who travelled between Bulawayo and Nyamandhlovu gave Sithole information about Security Forces' roadblocks. They also brought newspapers which we read at Sithole's home at night and in our cave during the day. We devised a plan.

I got pen and paper from Mr Sithole and wrote to Vusumuzi, my eldest brother, telling him where we were and asking him to drive to Gulakabili to collect us. He could take us to within a few kilometres of a roadblock, drop us off to walk into the bush and around the obstacle, then pick us up on the far side. A bus with all its passengers would be unlikely to oblige us like that.

When we visited Mr Sithole on the Friday night he was restless and disturbed.

'It seems the authorities have gained wind of your presence. Two detectives came to Gulakabili and asked if three Zulu-speaking boys had been spotted in the vicinity. Everybody they spoke to denied it, but as soon as the detectives left they told me. What shall we do, boys?'

'We'll leave first thing in the morning', I said. 'We can't bring danger to a family that has been caring for us so well.'

My two comrades agreed.

'What will I tell your brother when he gets here?' Sithole asked.

'Tell him our plans have changed. We will contact him when we reach Bulawayo.'

Sithole was a crafty old man. He suggested we dress in school uniforms from his shop and travel in the guise of schoolboys. We thought it was an excellent idea, but when we tried to pay him for the uniforms he refused to take the money. I will never forget what he said.

'You want me to take money for pieces of cloth when you are risking your very lives for nothing? I'm not a dog, although I'm not rich. I come from the clan of the Sitholes, the Jobes, sons of Matshana who in his time was a great warrior in Zululand and also served the great King Lobengula. Go well, boys, and may the god of Africa protect you.'

13

Guerrillas in school uniform

Well before dawn we got ready to catch the bus which passed Gulakabili at about 04:30. Derek and I were dressed in school uniforms and carrying our school bags. We had hidden our AKs in the cave but were carrying Tokarev pistols under our blazers and had two grenades each in our school bags. We waited by the side of the road and wondered what was keeping Daluxolo. He suddenly came striding from the cave and to my astonishment I saw he was carrying his light machine gun.

'You don't intend to get on the bus with that?' I asked half in jest.

'Of course. Do you think I would go anywhere without her?'

'So you intend to get on the bus disguised as a schoolboy but toting an LMG?'

I couldn't believe that I had heard right.

'Oh, yes. What else did you think I was going to do? Throw my LMG away as easily as I see you two have got rid of your AKs? Not me, I'm sorry. The Russians told me I would free South Africa with this gun, so I'm not about to throw it away in Rhodesia or anywhere else.'

'Daluxolo, you're not thinking straight', I remonstrated. 'What's the point of wearing a school uniform if you're carrying an LMG? Be sensible. Be a good chap. There's no time to argue as the bus gets here in about ten minutes. Give me that gun.'

'Nobody is taking it from me. If you don't like it, leave without me. I'll hide in the cave for another night and take the bus tomorrow. But when I do, I will have my LMG with me.'

Derek and I tried reasoning with him, but it was useless. I had never realised he could be so stubborn and unreasonable. We pleaded, we argued, we threatened, but he wouldn't budge. As we talked, we edged closer to him, step by step. When we judged we were both within range, we pounced on him. He found himself on his back and I had the LMG.

'Yes, you can jump me and take my weapon away. But when the enemy attacks, you'll have to defend yourselves with only pistols. You are just damned fools', he yelled.

'We're not going to listen to your nonsense, Daluxolo. Even if we have to smack you around to make you see sense', I shot back.

I went and dumped his LMG in the cave. When I got back the bus was just coming round the bend. We boarded in silence. Daluxolo sat at the back and Derek halfway down. I sat on the front seat so that I could see what lay ahead. It was still dark and the headlights were on. We sat there apprehensively as the bus sped towards Bulawayo, not knowing what awaited us there, or if we would get there at all.

It was cold and most of the passengers huddled in blankets and slept. When it got light we could see that our surroundings were mostly ranch and farmland. It was a strange sensation to be amongst civilians and travelling on a bus. We were in enemy territory heading for Bulawayo — Rhodesia's second city — while the enemy furiously searched the bush for us. I felt like yelling about how crazy it was.

The other passengers began to wake up and talk. Some discussed ordinary affairs and how they were going to Bulawayo and returning at the weekend. There was some talk about the recent fighting.

'They say the terrorists have come not only to kill the whites but all of us. What do you think Masuku?' one passenger asked.

'Who told you that? You shouldn't listen to ignorant people. Haven't you heard that these boys want to remove Smith from power and install Joshua Nkomo as president?'

'If they are fighting Smith why did they kill black soldiers?' the man persisted.

'Those black soldiers have only themselves to blame', Masuku countered. 'If the war against the white people has started, why are they still serving in the white man's army?'

We just listened, pretending we were not interested. I noticed though, that the driver and the bus conductor had been conversing for some time. I had the feeling they were discussing us because the conductor kept glancing over his shoulder in my direction. I wondered what it was all about, but finally he came and sat next to me.

'There's a roadblock manned by soldiers ahead at Nyamandhlovu', he whispered. 'The driver passed it this morning on the way to Gulakabili. He says that you and your friends shouldn't worry because we'll protect you. Before he reaches the roadblock he will stop for you to get off. Go eastward through the bush. Once you are certain you have passed Nyamandhlovu, return to the road and catch another bus.'

'Very well', I said, 'and say thanks to the driver.'

I left my seat and explained to Derek what the conductor had told me. He was concerned and wondered how they had identified us as guerrillas.

'We probably don't look like the locals. I'm sure you could identify a stranger in your own area. Tell Daluxolo to be ready to get off the bus when the driver signals.'

So a roadblock lay ahead. Maybe the driver was lying, intending to divert us in the direction of the enemy, I pondered. But why would he let on in the first place? Many thoughts go through one's head at such times and this was no exception. It was simply a question of whether we could trust these people. I knew that Derek would demand I vouch for them, but how could I? The truth was that we had no choice. We had to trust them.

We came to an experimental farm on our right. The driver stopped and nodded that we should alight. The three of us got off without a word. We crossed the road in front of the bus, waved at the driver and walked towards the farm. The bus went on its way. We found a large patch of bush on the farm where we lay low. We waited for the sun to set before emerging from the hideout. We walked along several tracks until we thought we were outside the farm.

We came to a dirt road and met a woman walking alone. She appeared to have had a few drinks and was staggering slightly. We greeted her in Sindebele:

'*Litshone njani mama*?' (Did you have a good day, Mother?).

She returned our greeting and continued on her way.

We learned later that when she got home she told her husband that she had met three boys who spoke to her in Zulu. He immediately ran to the police station and reported it. This resulted in Patrol Officer Maycock and about 20 black policemen mounting a hunt, but they never found us.

We walked all night and rested in the bush the next morning. We left our hide around midday and got on a Bulawayo-bound bus at Redbank. The roadblock was far behind us. Again Daluxolo sat at the back, Derek in the middle and I in the front seat.

Passengers were again discussing the fighting. According to one man, the papers reported that some terrorists had been captured at a roadblock at Nyamandhlovu. So the first driver and conductor had been telling the truth after all.

Daluxolo moved down the aisle to Derek and told him that an army jeep was following the bus. Behind it were two trucks packed with soldiers. The look on Daluxolo's face said it all.

Now boys, things are about to get lively. Do you remember beating me up and taking my LMG? Here are two truck-loads of soldiers we must fight only with pistols. He actually looked triumphant. His whole attitude said: I warned you, you idiots, so what now?

The jeep suddenly accelerated, turned in front of the bus and slowed down bringing it to a halt. A white officer stepped down and walked to the driver's window.

'Good afternoon, driver. Have you seen or picked up any suspicious-looking characters anywhere along this road?'

'No, sir, I have only picked up some schoolboys. The soldiers searched my bus when we passed through the roadblock at Nyamandhlovu.'

'That's okay, driver, drive on. Notify the police if you spot anyone suspicious.'

He waved the bus on and the conversation turned to 'the boys'.

'You see, I told you the government has no idea how to catch them. If they come to my place I'll give them anything they need and hide them.'

They've come to free us', agreed one commuter.

'You must be careful about saying things like that. There might be police informers amongst us', cautioned another.

'Well if sell-outs are amongst us, maybe the boys are here too', laughed another.

We got to Bulawayo just after 18:00 and alighted just below Mpilo Hospital in Barbourfields Township. The house we were looking for was Elliot Dhlula's. He was a teacher and a close friend of my family. When we reached there, however, new tenants told us that Dhlula had moved and they had no idea where he was. I suggested to the others that our best option was to go to the Happy Valley Hotel which was close by. It was owned by a Mr Vera.

We got there at around 19:00. Loud dance music was coming from somewhere in the hotel. The bar was at one end and the dining room at the other. We went to the reception desk and booked in under fictitious names. We told the receptionist we were students from

Botswana who were enrolling at the University of Rhodesia. I had been told that passports were not required when moving between Rhodesia and Botswana in those days so our story stood. We ordered food — sadza, vegetables and meat — and settled down to eat. We hadn't had a decent meal since we left Mr Sithole's house at Gulakabili.

A township smart-aleck came over to our table. He looked at our school uniforms and decided that we could provide him with some entertainment. He picked up a table knife and made as if he was going to stab me with it. I ignored him and continued eating. He lost interest in me and moved over to Daluxolo and started playfully twisting his nose. Daluxolo's chest heaved in anger and I knew that if I didn't intervene he would pull out his pistol and shoot the bastard, right then and there. I stood up and walked over to the receptionist.

'That *tsotsis* (criminal) is attacking us. Look what he's doing to my friend', I bellowed in a pretence of fright.

'Hey, you good-for-nothing scumbag, leave that boy alone!' the receptionist shouted.

She marched determinedly to where the trouble was. The little thug stopped his game and fled from the dining room.

'If I ever see your face again, you won't reach middle age, you little swine!' she yelled.

She comforted us and assured us we were safe under her protection.

We thanked her profusely and said we were going to our room.

'Of course, dear children, don't you want something to drink? A beer maybe?'

'Of course Mama, we would very much like a beer or two, but can it be sent to our room? It would disgrace our school if we went in the bar in school uniform . . . There are also too many *tsotsis* around for us to feel safe', I glibly lied.

'Give me the money and I'll have your drinks sent up.'

I ordered four quarts of Castle beer and a litre of Schweppes lemonade and gave her the money.

Life was improving. It was not so long ago that we were drinking water tasting of buffalo urine!

We had earned the little celebration we had in our room. Daluxolo drank the Schweppes as he was a teetotaller then.

My brother Vusumuzi drove to Gulakabili to be told by Mr Sithole that 'my boys' had left by the morning bus to Bulawayo. He drove home to Umtali (now Mutare) on the other side of the country where he lived and taught at the Teacher Training College. We were lying low at the hotel updating ourselves from newspapers.

One of the best things for us about Rhodesian democracy was that the government was obliged to publish what it had been doing. Maybe this was an effort to reassure the white public that 'the terrorist incursions' were under control. At any rate, the Security Forces announced that they had established roadblocks in southern Matabeleland from Bulawayo to the Plumtree border with Botswana. If we hadn't read that in the newspaper, we would have headed straight for Botswana. Instead we decided it was safer to travel north-east to Salisbury (now Harare).

We took the evening train from Bulawayo and arrived in Salisbury the following morning. The train was packed with soldiers from the Wankie area returning to their barracks. It seemed the worst was over in Wankie. The 'terrorist army' had vanished, some killed, others captured and the rest on the run. We were still wearing school uniforms so the soldiers and policemen in plain clothes didn't give us a second glance. The only attention we got on the journey was from a drunken white soldier I passed in the corridor.

'Hello, sonny boy, how are you?' he asked swaying against the window.

'I'm fine sir, thanks very much.'

'He's a bright youngster this one, don't you think?' he asked, seeking an opinion from one of his drunken friends.

'Bright and well mannered', his mate replied.

'What work do you want to do when you finish school, sonny?'

'I want to be an economist, sir, so that Rhodesia can have a strong and healthy economy. That'll be good for the country don't you think, sir?' I said, playing his game.

'You're damned right, son. Just don't go getting involved in terrorism, do you hear? We have just killed a lot of terrs and now we're going home. You can rest safely because the country is under the protection of the Rhodesian army, okay?'

'Oh, yes, sir', I responded, 'I'll stick to my books. No politics for me, sir.'

'Good youngster that, eh', I heard him say as I squeezed past him into our compartment.

Fortunately he hadn't seen the slight bulge of my Tokarev pistol snug against my waist. Very good youngster, my arse!

Plainclothes policemen were all over the platform in Salisbury looking for suspicious characters. We shouldered our school bags and walked past them. Perhaps in their training manuals a terrorist was described as a huge, muscular, red-eyed black with long untidy hair. Well, there was no such black getting off the train that day.

We took a taxi to the University of Rhodesia and knocked on Professor Selby Ngcobo's door. His daughter, Pamela, let us in and gave us breakfast. The Ngcobos were family friends and Pamela and I had a romance in 1963 when I was first in Rhodesia. It was nothing serious, but I felt sure I could trust her. I called my brother Vusumuzi on the phone and asked him to pick us up.

14

To Mozambique and back

My brother immediately agreed to come and fetch us. We wanted to avoid the use of public transport, even though our luck had been fantastic so far. When we got to Vusumuzi's house Derek suffered another serious attack of ulcers. My brother talked to a friendly doctor in the Umtali township. He medicated Derek very well and within three days he was fit enough to travel. We gave my brother money and he bought us cheap but serviceable clothing and canvas shoes for daily use.

We also visited my father at Chikore Mission where he was teaching at the secondary school. It was our first meeting since 1964 when I had been forced to leave Rhodesia. He didn't ask any questions, but I knew he had a very good idea of what was happening. He slaughtered a goat to jointly thank Almighty God and the departed Bopelas for looking after me and to wish us safety in the future. We learned in conversation that posters were appearing on public buildings like post offices and on railway stations offering rich rewards for information leading to the arrest of 'terrorists' or the capture of communist weapons.

'What do you plan to do from here son?' he asked as we sat talking.

'Our aim is to enter South Africa, but we are not sure how we are going to do it.'

'Maybe the best person to ask is Oscar 'Mash' Mashengele. Do you remember him?'

'Yes I do, Dad. He was a very nice person.'

'He's now headmaster of a school in Chisumbanje, not far from here. He's a member of ZAPU and will know much more about such things than I do. I'm sure he'll be able to give you valuable advice.'

'Yes', agreed Vusumuzi, 'Mash will certainly make a useful contribution.'

We drove to see Mashengele the next day. He was a tall, stout man with a round face. He laughed a lot and when he did, his eyes narrowed into slits of delight. He introduced us to his wife, MaSengwayo, and to his children. While MaSengwayo was preparing food, Mashengele demanded to know everything about the fighting.

He screamed with delight when we told him how we had sent the RAR packing in Tjolotjo.

After we had eaten he said that his wife had prepared sleeping places for us and he wished us a restful night. As a nightcap he poured double brandies into my and Derek's glasses. We drank to the revolution and that night we slept well.

We woke up at around 09:00 the next morning to a cheerful greeting and tea in bed. Such simple pleasures had been banished from our lives for a very long time. We yawned, got up slowly and wandered into the lounge where Mr Mashengele was drinking tea.

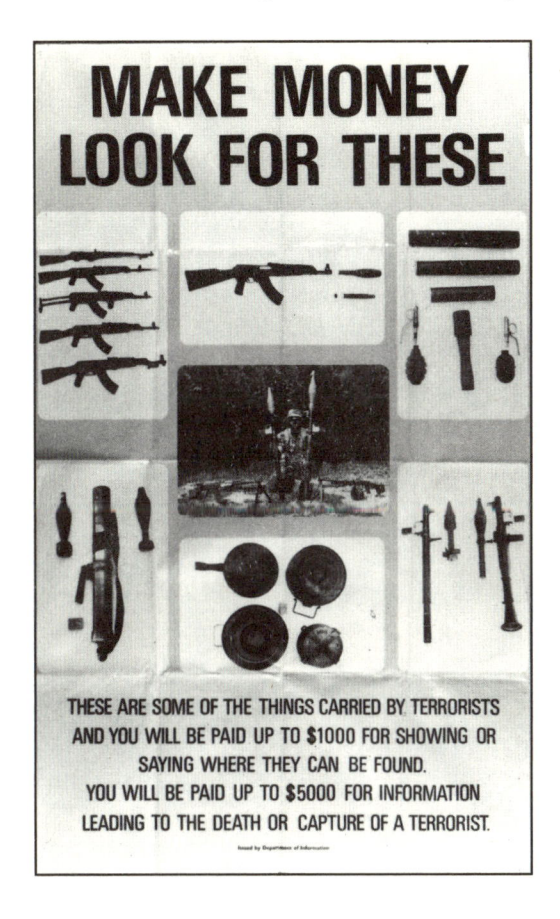

MAKE MONEY LOOK FOR THESE

THESE ARE SOME OF THE THINGS CARRIED BY TERRORISTS AND YOU WILL BE PAID UP TO $1000 FOR SHOWING OR SAYING WHERE THEY CAN BE FOUND.
YOU WILL BE PAID UP TO $5000 FOR INFORMATION LEADING TO THE DEATH OR CAPTURE OF A TERRORIST.

Rewards offered for information leading to the death or capture of 'terrorists' and for the location of 'terrorist' weapons

'As far as I can see, you guys have three options', he said. 'The first is to return to Lusaka and plan a new approach. The second is to travel to Botswana and enter South Africa that way. The third is to cross into Mozambique and infiltrate South Africa as migrant workers.'

'We're not going back to Lusaka, Bro Mash', Derek said firmly. That would mean starting the march from scratch. I think we can only consider the Botswana and the Mozambique options. What do you say, guys?'

'Botswana is the most risky, because the Rhodesians are deployed in force along that border', Daluxolo said.

I agreed. 'But before we can consider the Mozambique option I need more information. How does one become a Mozambican migrant worker and get into South Africa? If there's a good answer to that, then I'm sure that's the way to go.'

'There's a place in Mozambique called Massangena where recruiters go to hire labourers for the mines on the Witwatersrand. The recruiters are fully aware that not everyone looking for work at Massangena is Mozambican but they don't care. They just want miners', Mashengele explained.

'So you say that if we get to Massangena , Bro Mash, we'll be on our way to South Africa as miners?' I checked.

'Look, you'll have to answer a few questions, like which area in Mozambique you come from . . . who your local chief is and the river you fetch water from. Those answers are easy to find in advance. If you pass that test the Portuguese will give you a Mozambican permit to work in South Africa for a contract period of between 18 months and two years. It's as simple as that.'

We looked at each other happily because we had found an infiltration route. Once on the mines it would be easy to make our way to the mountains or the townships. When we had re-established contact with Lusaka we would be able to start working underground.

The next morning found us tense and anxious to move. Mr Mashengele and his family had been wonderful to us, but it was time to go. It was a Wednesday and by 08:00 we had washed and finished breakfast. We thanked MaSengwayo who wiped her eyes with her pinafore, maybe sensing the hard times that lay ahead for us. Women, they say, have an intuitive knowledge of such things.

Mr Mashengele took us to a village hotel, a kind of bed-and-breakfast place where a stranger passing through Chisumbanje could spend the night. We waited there for the truck that had been arranged to take us to the Mozambican border. We had given our weapons to Mashengele to hide for the day when he could arm other young men who would follow in our footsteps.

'The revolution will spread, Bro Mash', I said to him. 'Leaving our weapons with you is not like throwing them away — they will do duty in the future. But cache them far from your house so the police can never link them to you if they are discovered.'

'*Hambani kahle Mkhonto*' (Go well, men of the Spear), he replied.

We had gone to a shop next to the hotel the previous day to buy pots, mugs, soap and cheap blankets. A pretty girl served us. She smiled particularly at Daluxolo and he blushed profusely in embarrassment.

'That girl likes you, Daluxolo', Mashengele joked after we left the shop.

'She must be mad', Daluxolo said angrily.

Later on she saw us again and waved at Daluxolo. He surreptitiously waved back thinking we hadn't noticed. She probably hoped to see him again, but that hope was doomed. Women who fall in love with revolutionaries end up causing themselves a lot of heartache.

The truck finally arrived. We jumped aboard and waved to Mashengele as it drove noisily away. He stood there, a lone figure getting smaller and smaller as the distance increased. We drove through very thickly bushed areas, but the road was fine so we made good speed. Rhodesia's Eastern District was blessed with thick forests, unlike the western parts where we had been fighting. ZANU guerrillas who would later infiltrate from Mozambique would use these forests to great advantage.

At midday we reached the Sabi River which was the boundary between the two countries. We got down, paid the owner of the truck and forded the river into Mozambique. It was that simple. We walked to the general dealer's store on the hillock above the river and joined about 30 other men who were also on their way to Massangena. At 14:00 a huge truck drove into the yard of the store. The waiting men jumped and whistled and ran around the truck like small boys. We joined them, not understanding what it was all about but not wanting to appear different from the rest.

The truck had come from the seaport of Beira bringing trade goods for the store. The waiting men assisted with the offloading and carried the goods into the shop without expecting payment. We helped too, adjusting to the local situation quickly. When the truck was empty we jumped aboard with our personal goods and the truck started for Massangena.

We reached there at about 18:30 and the whole lot of us jumped off. The driver continued on to Beira without asking us to pay for the trip. I guess it was the quid pro quo for offloading the truck at the store.

Massangena was part of a wide network of recruitment centres belonging to an agency called The Employment Bureau of Africa (TEBA). TEBA's role was to facilitate the supply of cheap black labour to the South African gold mines. Miners came from as far afield as Angola, Mozambique, Lesotho and Swaziland. A recruitment centre like Massangena had a black agent who checked applicants' suitability and health and sent them along the chain to the TEBA offices in the urban centre. At Massangena the recruitment agent was a Mr Masango.

Masango greeted us in Shangaan, the language most widely spoken in Mozambique and along the eastern border of Rhodesia. We couldn't respond so he asked what language we spoke. We told him it was Sindebele.

'That'll cause a problem if I send you over to see the Portuguese. They're well aware that we recruit people from Rhodesia because of the shortage of labour on the mines, but if they discovered that you are Ndebeles they'll probably do very bad things to you. My advice is that you leave here and return to Rhodesia.'

'Why would they do bad things to us?' I asked.

'They hate Joshua Nkomo, your Ndebele leader. They say he incites black people against whites and they'll assume you are his supporters. They might even shoot you.'

'Thank you, Mr Masango, we'll take your advice', Derek said.

We picked up our things and walked out of Massangena. Masango suggested we return to where the truck had dropped us and wait for it to return. It was due at about 10:00 the following morning.

It was a terrible blow to our plan for getting to South Africa. Everything had been thought out except the language issue. Damn! We couldn't blame Mashengele because he hadn't actually been to Massangena to see the recruitment procedures for himself.

We spent the night perched in trees because of the danger of being attacked by wild animals. We chose our own trees but only dozed. If we'd gone to sleep we might have fallen to the ground like ripe fruit.

The next morning we heard the truck approaching when it was still a good distance away. We made our way to the road and flagged it down. We jumped aboard and got back to the border sometime after midday and re-crossed the Sabi River. For some hours we wandered around the bush until we found three old and abandoned grass and mud huts. We checked them out for snakes and decided to sleep there. The barking of dogs told us we were not far from an occupied village. We dined on the contents of a can of corned beef and slept well.

The next morning we were awakened by the sounds of somebody moving cautiously outside. We remained still wondering who it was. Before we could move, a man appeared in the doorway.

'At last I've found you', he said triumphantly.

We just stared at him.

'Two detectives from Umtali spent the night at Chief Mahenye's place. They said they had come to warn the chief about the possible presence of freedom fighters in the area. They called them terrorists, but we call them freedom fighters. They gave the chief a radio transmitter and told him to report the presence of any strangers to the police.'

'Why would you call terrorists freedom fighters, sir?' I ventured.

'We don't like it because it suggests that freedom-fighters are criminals.'

'When you say *we* who are you referring to?'

'We are the ZANU underground committee in the next village. I'm a teacher at the school. We have heard on the radio that there has been heavy fighting in Matabeleland and the government forces have suffered many casualties. It seems the freedom fighters are now on the run because the people in Matabeleland haven't given them support. News reports say that some have been captured. We've formed an underground committee to assist any of them who come here.'

Who was this fellow really? we wondered. Was he truly a supporter or a clever police agent? Again we didn't know what to think.

'Are *you* freedom-fighters?' he asked suddenly.

We were not ready for that question, but there was no time to hold a meeting. We looked at each other and exchanged views silently. I cleared my throat.

'So if such people do come here needing assistance, will you help them?'

'Oh, yes, and we will provide information about enemy movements. But we will do a lot more than that.'

We were again face-to-face with the situation that had confronted us at Tsholotsho — having to trust our lives to people we didn't know.

'I believe you are freedom fighters', the man said bluntly. 'You are not from these parts, which is why I'm speaking to you in English. If I could speak Sindebele I would do so because I know you come from Matabeleland.'

So there it was. Who said that people from rural areas are dumb and stupid?

'Yes, you're right. We are freedom fighters', Derek said. 'We have to get back to Chisumbanje, but we don't have the means to travel. We do, however, have money to pay someone to take us there.'

'There's a truck owned by a chap called Mazorotse that comes here now and then,' the ZANU man said. 'In fact he's due today.' His face fell. 'But those detectives from Umtali will definitely want to use it. They came by bicycle but they will want a ride back on the truck. That will cause problems for you.'

'Yes, they are bound to ask questions', Daluxolo said.

We kept it to ourselves that we already knew Mazorotse.

I decided we needed time to discuss things privately before we made a decision. I told the man to leave us alone for ten minutes and he withdrew.

'You see, guys, it's dangerous to hang around here for too long. We need to get back to Chisumbanje and the truck is the answer. I think we should brazen it out. If those detectives ask, we'll tell them we're Botswana citizens registered at the University of Rhodesia. We'll say we came to choose a picnic site where we intend to bring a group of students once the university opens. What do you think?'

'It worked when we told that story in the hotel in Bulawayo', Daluxolo remarked.

'Yes, but these are policemen — not hotel receptionists', Derek pointed out.

'I'll give them my real name', I told them and saw surprise register on their faces. 'They're Umtali detectives so they will know my father. Now a terrorist wouldn't tell you his real name, would he? That should disarm them and remove their suspicions. But don't you guys try to pretend that you come from Rhodesia, let alone Umtali.'

We agreed we would get a lift on Mazorotse's truck, lie to the detectives and get back to Chisumbanje as soon as possible. We would go to Mashengele and ask him for help to get to Botswana.

We called the ZANU man back in. We lied that we had decided not to chance the truck, but would make our way through the bush to Chisumbanje on foot.

'I'm sorry you will be leaving so soon after I found you, comrades. There is a great task ahead of us to free Zimbabwe. God be with you, comrades', the visitor said and left as quickly and quietly as he had come.

We went to where the truck had dropped us when we first arrived and hid in the bushes close to the road. It was not long before we heard the familiar sound of the truck approaching.

'I thought you lads were going to get work on the mines. What happened?' Mazorotse greeted us.

'They only took 20 men and said we should return after two weeks, so we decided to come back', was the cover story Derek gave.

'Okay then, let's go', said Mazorotse indifferently.

We got to Chief Mahenye's place and saw the two detectives get up and take leave of the chief. We alighted from the truck, got hold of their bicycles which were leaning against a large tree and wheeled them to the vehicle. Black policemen in rural areas are treated with great respect and they encourage it.

'What's your name?' the stouter of the two asked.

He spoke Chindawu, a local version of Shona. During the few months I had spent in the Chipinga district in 1963 I had learned Chindawu. I answered him in that tongue.

'I'm Thula Bopela and I speak only a little Chindawu.'

'Bopela, you said? Are you related to Mr Bopela, the teacher at Chikore?' he asked in English.

'That's my father.'

I lifted his bicycle onto the truck and hauled myself up.

'Thank you, Bopela', he said and got into the front passenger seat.

Daluxolo was speaking to the other policeman in English.

'Where do you come from in Umtali?' the policeman asked.

'The township', Daluxolo replied.

'I heard you the first time, but where in Umtali?'

'Just Umtali', Daluxolo replied flatly.

He climbed aboard while the policeman looked at him inquisitively. The intense gaze then shifted to Derek and myself. Then he stepped into the front seat next to his colleague. The truck moved off and I saw the detectives talking quietly to each other. The stout one turned and glanced back at us. There was a puzzled and suspicious expression on his face.

'Why did you tell him you're from Umtali?' Derek growled to Daluxolo from the corner of his mouth.

'What did you expect me to say? We spent a few days in Umtali so I thought it was okay to tell him I come from there. Thula told the other one his real name and that caused no problem.'

'We all agreed what we would say', Derek reminded him.

'You two always make the decisions and expect me to go along with them. Frankly, I'm tired of it', Daluxolo grunted.

So that was it. Daluxolo wanted to assert himself, but what a time to choose! This had obviously been building up since Gulakabili when we roughed him up and took his LMG. I thought about this for some time. The sun set, darkness fell and the truck droned on towards Chisumbanje.

When Daluxolo decided that he was remaining behind to care for Derek after the second battle, it had been his own independent decision. But after the three of us became separated from the detachment, he lost this independence. The decisions had been taken at either my suggestion or Derek's. We had been treating Daluxolo as a subordinate and he didn't like it.

So now we're in trouble, I thought and wondered what to do.

'Arguing won't change the situation now', I said at last. 'We've lost the initiative and the next move will come from the policemen. Let's see what they do but we must be prepared to act quickly. There won't be time to discuss it.

We reached Chisumbanje at around 19:00. The truck stopped at the village hotel where we had boarded it on the outward journey. The detectives got down quickly and walked to the back of the truck.

'Get down, you chaps. We want to ask you a few questions', the stout one said.

'We jumped down and they pushed us into a hotel room and locked the door from the outside. We heard them walk down the passage and start phoning.

There was a window so we opened it, leapt out into the darkness and sped off. We ran full tilt for about 15 minutes to put maximum distance between ourselves and the hotel. After that we reduced speed and ran at a fast jog. We could still see the lights of the hotel winking through the trees. We headed towards Mashengele's place. We heard the sound of the truck coming in our direction. It was some way off.

'This place will be lousy with policemen and soldiers by tomorrow morning. We'd better be far away from here by then', Derek remarked to nobody in particular.

'You're right, Derek', I agreed. 'Maybe that's the policemen coming after us now in Mazorotse's truck. On the other hand it could just be Mazorotse returning home alone to Fort Victoria. If he is and we get a lift from him, we'll be in Fort Victoria by morning and far away from this place.'

'It's one hell of a risk', Daluxolo warned.

'Yes, but perhaps we can find out if the cops are aboard or not', I replied.

'What do you suggest?' Derek asked doubtfully.

'I'll stand in the road to the right and wave it down. If those detectives are in there they'll have to get out on the left hand side, which will give us the chance to escape. We are young and fit and they won't stand a chance of catching us in the dark once we get moving, especially that fat one. Remember, this is the BSAP (British South Africa Police) and not the South African Police so they're not armed for normal duties. I think it's worth taking a chance.'

'I think it's bloody madness!' Derek exploded. 'We've got this far and they have no idea which way we went. Do you want them to find us again? It's insane!'

'No, I'm not mad', I responded calmly. 'You pointed out yourself that this area will be lousy with police and soldiers by tomorrow. Getting away on foot is not much of an option. They'll hunt us down in no time at all.'

'Anyway, Derek, we can't be sure the cops are on the truck. They probably had to go somewhere to report our escape', Daluxolo said. 'If it's only Mazorotse going home as Thula suggests and we let him pass by, then we'll have to run the whole night.'

'We can go to Mashengele's place and hide', Derek retorted.

'If they find us there, he and his family will be in big trouble', Daluxolo came back. 'I see nothing wrong with Thula's suggestion. It's the only sensible option.'

'That's because you got us into all this trouble in the first place', Derek shot back.

'The truck's almost here, guys', I intervened. ' Let's stop arguing.'

I walked into the road as the truck came round the bend. Derek and Daluxolo stood back. The truck changed gear as its headlights found me in the darkness waving it down. It halted a mere ten metres away.

The passenger door burst open and two familiar figures tumbled out. I turned and ran like a rabbit.

Derek was several metres ahead of me and he was flying. I didn't hear any footsteps behind me, so I glanced over my shoulder. Daluxolo was struggling with the two policemen.

'Derek! Derek! We must rescue Daluxolo!'

Derek didn't react and he soon disappeared from sight.

I ran back to the road. Daluxolo was kicking, elbowing, butting the policemen who were obstinately hanging on to him. One was trying to snap handcuffs on his flailing wrists. I took my time and aimed a kick at the stout detective's face. He shrieked with pain and released Daluxolo who ran off with the other policeman in pursuit. The one I had kicked came from behind and locked his arms around me. The other one caught Daluxolo, but was thrown over his shoulder. Daluxolo ran for his life into the bush.

I viciously elbowed the fat one in the face, but he just hung in there. We fell on the road in front of the truck. The other cop returned and joined the melee and we became a pile of flailing legs and arms illuminated by the glare of the headlights. I think it was a good fight. In court later the fat policeman wanted to relate to the judge how he and his colleague had been brutally punched, kicked and elbowed. The judge merely accepted that I had resisted arrest, but wasn't interested in the gory details.

I felt a sudden sharp pain in my head and lost consciousness.

When I came to I was handcuffed to the seat of a vehicle. I opened my eyes and the first person I saw was the girl who had taken a liking to Daluxolo.

'Yes, he's one of the boys who were with Mr Mashengele.'

I had been identified and linked to Mashengele. Now he would be in trouble.

The fat policeman lunged out and punched me in the face.

'You're in the custody of the British South Africa Police', he informed me punctuating his conversation with another array of punches. 'We'll show you what happens to people who resist arrest!'

'Leave him alone', his companion said. 'People are watching and they might report us.' He pulled the fat policeman away from me. I didn't feel any pain and it seemed strange.

15

Thula arrested

I was put in the back of an open police truck. There were six armed policemen guarding me, despite the fact that I was handcuffed and leg-ironed. We sped off into the night. I suddenly remembered that I was wearing the late Sergeant-Major Timitiya's wristwatch. It provided a direct link between myself and the dead soldier and that was enough to hang me. Somehow I had to get rid of the watch. Fortunately my hands were handcuffed behind me and I managed to unbuckle the strap. I clasped the watch in my hand and waited for the right moment to dump it. We hit a large pothole and the truck lurched. I grabbed the opportunity to flick the watch over the side.

'What are you doing?' asked a constable suspiciously, noticing my convulsive movement.

'I was making the sign of the cross. This truck could overturn at the speed we're travelling.'

'Oh, so we've got ourselves a bloody Catholic', he remarked.

'More like a Catholic communist terrorist', another constable added.

Some time later the truck drove into the yard of a police station. A large board had the words 'British South Africa Police: Chibuwe'.

Chibuwe meant nothing to me and I had absolutely no idea where I was. I was taken from the truck and led into the charge office where a black police sergeant was standing behind the counter. One of my escorts took the sergeant aside and began whispering to him. The sergeant returned, opened a large book and started writing. I couldn't read it from where I was, except for a bold 'Suspected terrorist' against my name. That explained the whispering.

The sergeant finished writing and closed the book.

'I'm Sergeant Makumbe and I want a statement from you. You will write down everything about yourself — name, surname, age and where you were born. More importantly, you will write down the names of your friends and explain what you were doing around Chief Mahenye's place, okay?'

'Okay, sergeant, but I would prefer to make a statement after I have been charged. My friends and I were attacked by two criminals who claimed they were policemen. I don't see them here. They should be answering your questions.'

'Listen you! You will make a statement and you will make it now. Do you hear me?'
'Sergeant, I have a right to remain silent. Don't you know that?'
The sergeant looked at me in astonishment.
'Don't you know there is a state of emergency in this country? Since you know the law so well, you must know that policemen have special powers. We can detain you for an indefinite period without charging you. You can also disappear from the face of the earth without anybody having to explain it. Do you understand, my barrack room lawyer friend?'

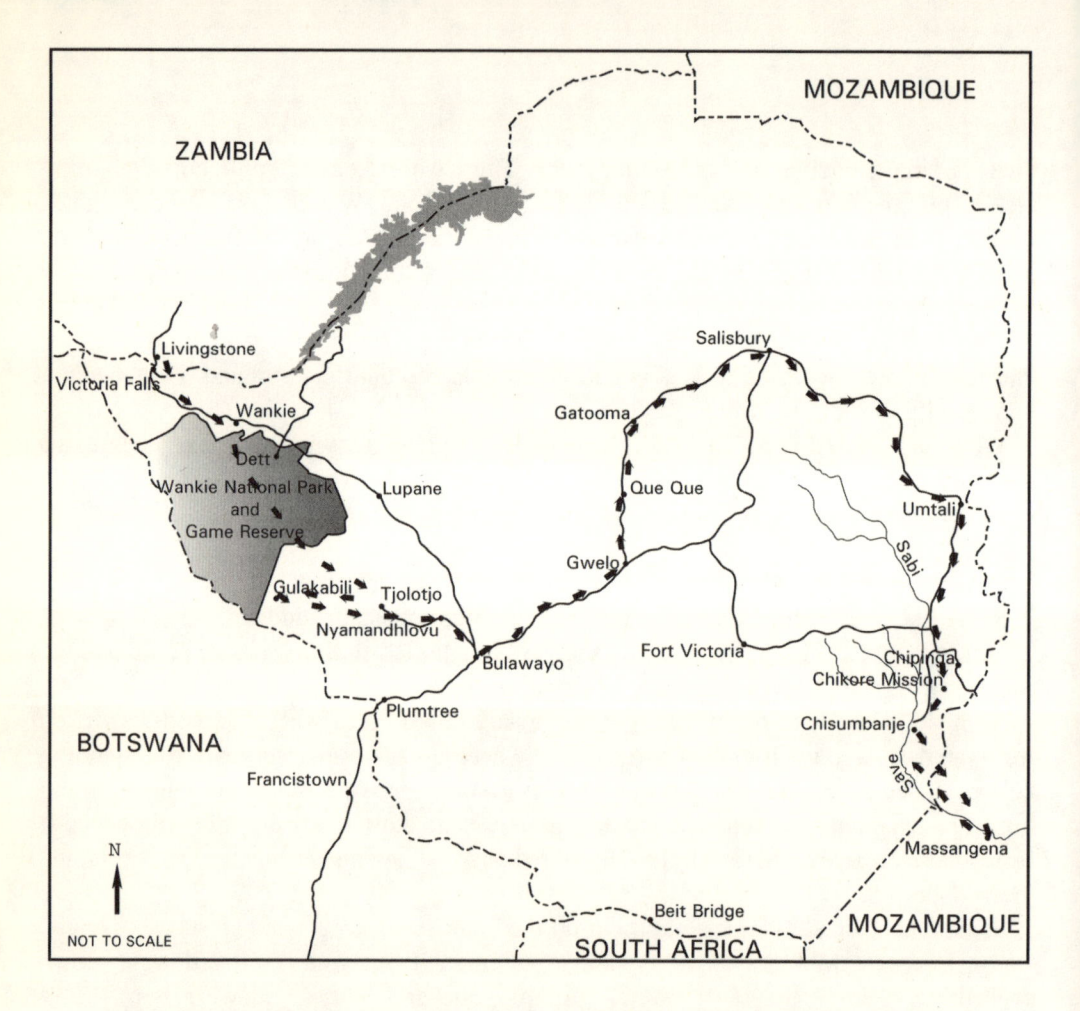

Map showing Thula's and Daluxolo's movements until the former's capture

'If you say so sergeant, I will make a statement', I said as a sudden thought came to me: these African policemen always try to be the boss when their white masters are not around. Show this one that he's not as clever as he thinks. He wants you to make a statement so he can run to his master in the morning and say: 'Look boss, I made that bloody terrorist confess.' He thinks he will get a medal.

He brought me a writing pad and a ballpoint pen and I sat down on a chair in the corner of the room. He glared at me as I began to write. I filled three pages and signed them with a flourish.

'I've finished, sergeant', I told him.

He came over, took the papers and stood reading them. When he was through, he looked at me.

'Good. I'll take you to your cell where you can sleep. Don't worry. Everything will be all right.'

I was locked up in a cell at the rear of the police station and leg irons chained me to a ring set in the concrete floor. The blankets were filthy and stank of urine. There was a bucket nearby and the smell emanating from it announced its purpose. It suddenly struck me that I had never been under arrest before.

For somebody who has never had to deal with policemen, you are doing okay, Thula Bopela, I told myself. I thought about the statement I wrote. I had put down my correct name and address in South Africa. I told the truth about coming to Rhodesia in 1963 to study and that I had been thrown out in 1964. After that, I said, I had made my way to Uganda where I studied economics and completed a BA degree. I had made my way back to Rhodesia, this time without the knowledge of my father and brother. My friends and I were seeking a way to get to Swaziland to look for employment when I was arrested. My friends ran away when we were attacked.

I dozed off towards morning and woke up startled when a heavy key opened the door.

'Rise and shine, my friend, rise and shine.'

It was Sergeant Makumbe and he seemed pleased with himself.

'Did you sleep well?'

'Not badly at all, sir, considering the circumstances.'

'Come, you are wanted at the charge office.'

He walked in front and although hindered by my leg-irons I did my best to keep up with him. I saw Mr Mashengele sitting on a bench outside the charge office but he didn't look at me. I felt despair. So they had Bro Mash.

I was more worried about him than myself. I was ushered into an office off the charge office. A white man in civvies stood at the window looking out and puffing at his pipe. A sweet aroma filled the room, a welcome change from the smell of my cell. He turned when he heard my clanking leg irons and moved towards me. He put down his pipe.

'I'm Detective Inspector Dancer, CID Homicide Chief, Umtali, which covers Chipinga District.'

'Good morning, Inspector', I replied quietly.

'Did you sleep well Mr Bopela?'

'I didn't, sir. I'm not used to sleeping chained to the floor, particularly as I don't know why I have been arrested.'

'Your statement to Sergeant Makumbe last night clearly says that you were sent out of the country in 1964 and that you have returned illegally. You could be charged for that, Mr Bopela.'

'That statement is a pack of lies, sir', I told him.

Inspector Dancer stared at me.

'Did you say a pack of lies, Mr Bopela?'

'Yes Inspector, a pack of lies', I said beginning to enjoy myself.

'Don't you know, Mr Bopela, that making a false statement to a police officer is a criminal offence?'

'I know that, Inspector.'

'Then why did you do it, may I ask?'

I glanced briefly at my friend Sergeant Makumbe. He seemed to be pleading with his eyes. I decided to crush him.

'When I got here last night, Inspector, I was handed over to your Sergeant Makumbe. When he had finished making entries in his book he demanded that I make a statement. I told him I was under the impression that I had the right to remain silent.' I paused, enjoying the sergeant's obvious pain. 'He said there was a state of emergency in Rhodesia — which I hadn't known about. He said that under a state of emergency, policemen like himself — maybe even yourself, Inspector — have special powers that allow you to detain suspects indefinitely — even murder them without anybody knowing about it.'

'Under those circumstances, Inspector, I thought it wise to cooperate with the Sergeant, so I wrote the statement.'

'And you say that statement is a pack of lies, Mr Bopela?'

'It certainly is, sir. It's the sort of statement anyone would make when threatened by people like Sergeant Makumbe. I knew that eventually I'd get the chance to tell a magistrate the truth. You must understand my predicament. I was in the hands of a power-drunk policeman who might have murdered me for all I know.'

Inspector Dancer picked up his pipe, lit it and returned to the window. He looked outside and said nothing. He contemplated the scenery.

'He's lying, sir', shouted Sergeant Makumbe.

'Does a suspect normally make a statement, sign it, then voluntarily tell you that it's false, Sergeant Makumbe?' the Inspector asked. 'So tell me sergeant, which is the truth which are lies?' Is it the statement he made to you or is he lying to me now?'

Sergeant Makumbe made no attempt to reply.

'How many times have I told you not to threaten suspects?' Inspector Dancer asked angrily. 'You keep looking for quick and easy solutions by forcing suspects to confess. When we get to court their statements are challenged and they turn out to be worthless. When are you going to stop being a thug and start being a policeman?'

Sergeant Makumbe was speechless. I began to like Detective Inspector Dancer. He was a good policeman.

'We have to rely on good police work, investigation and analysis to solve cases. It's hard work, I know, but it's the only way', the inspector continued. 'Now get out of my office. I'll talk to you later.'

'But, sir…'

'Don't "but sir" me. Get out, I said!'

I winked at the sergeant as he left. I have never seen so much hatred packed into a single glance.

Inspector Dancer removed my leg-irons and handcuffs and gestured for me to sit down.

'Do you smoke, Mr Bopela?'

'I do, Inspector.'

He opened a drawer.

'I can only offer you these', he said producing a packet of 30 Peter Stuyvesant. 'I don't smoke cigarettes myself. I keep them for occasions like this.'

'Thank you, Inspector.'

He returned to the window and stood there while I smoked.

'Mr Bopela, have you eaten since you were taken into custody last night?'

'No, sir', I replied simply and truthfully.

He made noises of disgust and marched to the door.

'Sergeant Makumbe. Come in here!'

The sergeant appeared as if by magic and stood by the desk, trembling.

'The suspect says he hasn't been fed since last night. Is that true, Sergeant Makumbe?'

'Yes, sir, but . . .'

'Make sure he's fed, okay?'

'Yes, sir.'

Makumbe saluted and left.

Dancer sat down again.

'I was going to take you to court tomorrow and charge you with illegally entering the country and apply for your deportation. But having revealed that your statement is false changes things.'

'Sergeant Makumbe needed a lesson, Inspector.'

'Mr Bopela, that's not how we work in Rhodesia. Anyway, I have been wondering what the real truth is about you. I'm going to conduct investigations of my own.'

'I don't have anything to hide Inspector. Because you have treated me well, I will make a statement freely and voluntarily.'

'That's fine, Mr Bopela. Sergeant Makumbe is arranging a good meal for you. When you have eaten he will give you pen and paper and you can make that free and voluntary statement.'

'Thanks, Inspector, I will keep my word.'

I ate like a pig while Sergeant Makumbe sat nearby glaring malevolently.

When I returned to the charge office Mr Mashengele was still where I had seen him earlier. I had been thinking hard while I was eating and had devised a plan to get him off the hook. But to be successful I had to be extra nice to Inspector Dancer. He needed a statement and a statement he was going to get.

I wrote the truth about myself until the point where I returned to Zambia from Uganda with my two friends. I invented a story that I had been approached by men who said they wanted to find out if it was possible for three or four people at a time to enter Rhodesia hidden in a truck. They offered us money, a lot of money, to test the run. We accepted and were concealed in a custom-built compartment in a long distance truck. We crossed the border safely at Chirundu. The driver dropped us off in Salisbury and continued on to South Africa. We phoned the men in Lusaka to let them know we had arrived in Salisbury safely. I wrote the phone number of the ANC's offices in Lusaka.

We then caught a bus and travelled to Umtali where we got on a Blue Line Mercedes bus that took us to Chisumbanje. We slept at Mr Mashengele's place and left the next day to make our way to Swaziland. But we got lost and landed up on the Mozambican border. On our way we ran into two policemen. I repeated that they had attacked us and arrested me while my friends fled. I wrote that the statement was made freely and voluntarily and signed it.

Inspector Dancer read the statement after lunch and appeared satisfied. He said he was going to Chipinga and would return the next morning. He instructed Sergeant Makumbe to give me clean blankets and feed me before locking me up for the night.

'Inspector', I said, 'please understand. When we came to Mr Mashengele's house we didn't say we had entered the country illegally. He was a former colleague of my father, so he had an obligation to put us up at his house. He's innocent Inspector. I'm just sorry that I took advantage of his respect for my father.'

'Okay, we'll see. I need a photograph of you first.'

He brought out a camera and snapped me in the light from the window.'

Mr Mashengele was released that afternoon and I slept the sleep of the innocent that night.

At 07:30 the next morning, the key turned with a grinding noise and the cell door was flung open. When my eyes got used to the light I saw Sergeant Makumbe framed in the doorway. He was smiling broadly and I sensed that something had gone seriously wrong while I was sleeping.

'Your friend Inspector Dancer wants you in his office', he shouted. 'He's in an ugly mood. I think we've got you this time.'

He yanked me to my feet and literally dragged me to the inspector's office. He shoved me in front of his desk. Dancer was again at the window looking outside, but this time his pipe was belching smoke.

'Here's the suspect, sir', Makumbe said, giving me a shove.

Dancer turned and looked at me, his face white. He almost exploded.

'Bullshit! Bullshit! You gave me bullshit.'

I asked what was the matter and what was bullshit. He sat behind his desk.

'Sit down Sergeant Makumbe. Let me tell you about this clever monkey.'

'He entered Rhodesia with a group of South African and Rhodesian terrorists on 10 August. They walked right across the Wankie Game Reserve until they reached Tsholotsho. Do you know where Tsholotsho is, Sergeant Makumbe?'

'No, sir, I don't', admitted the sergeant.

'Tsholotsho is in western Matabeleland. They were in a scrap with our Security Forces there and some of our men were murdered.'

'No, Inspector, it wasn't murder, it was war!' I heard myself saying.

'Maybe, Mr Bopela', he replied, his voice ice-cold voice. 'But it will be murder when you're before the High Court in Salisbury. Bopela and his friends managed to escape the dragnet and reached the Eastern Districts where they were seen crossing into Mozambique. 'He's wanted in Bulawayo for multiple counts of murder. He'll be leaving under escort for Bulawayo this morning.'

So, the game's up, I thought. Your little game with Detective Inspector Dancer is over. Now you're going to face the music!

'Why did you lie to me? Mr Bopela. You said you lied to Sergeant Makumbe because he threatened you. I didn't threaten you, but you still lied to me. That's what I cannot understand.'

'You're a policeman and I'm a guerrilla.'

'Ah, you're right. I'd almost forgotten that you're not just another man like me. You're a bloody terr!'

'I'm a soldier of my people, Inspector', I responded. 'We are fighting to free our people and you are fighting to continue the oppression that your grandfathers began. I don't expect you to understand.'

'Sergeant Makumbe, he says he is your soldier and he is fighting to free you. Do you agree? Are you oppressed by white people in this country, sergeant?'

'No, sir. He's not our soldier, sir. He's a terr.'

'If I gave you a free hand what would you do to him?'

'I would cut his throat, sir!'

'You see Mr Bopela, your own people would like to kill you. Yet you say they are oppressed.'

'Such is the power of gold, Inspector. It has turned Africans like him into dogs grateful to eat the crumbs that fall from your table. We are a different kind of African. Our numbers will grow until we take our land back. It's happening all over Africa. The white people have run from Kenya, Uganda, Tanzania and Zambia into Rhodesia. When they get to South Africa they'll come face to face with reality.'

'What reality, Mr Bopela?'

'That Africa belongs to Africans.'

'Africa used to belong to the Africans, Mr Bopela — not anymore', he said smiling.

'How did you find out about me and my friends, Inspector?' I asked changing the subject. I really wanted to know.

'You were identified by efficient police work. Everybody arrested nowadays is photographed and a copy sent to headquarters. When yours got there your comrades already in custody identified you. The rest I have told you. As Sherlock Holmes would have said, it was elementary. Have you heard of Sherlock Holmes?'

'Yes, I have.'

'You see Sergeant Makumbe. You'll never catch men like this by threatening them. They have been trained to lie and mislead. They all have well-planned cover stories. Rely on basic police work — investigation and analysis. That way you'll succeed.'

Four white policemen in camouflage uniforms pulled up in an open Land-Rover. A sergeant with a Sterling sub-machine gun came into the office.

'Ah, your escort.' Inspector Dancer turned to me and smiled.

'And remember what I said about Africa no longer belonging to the Africans.'

16

Interrogation

During my trip from Chibuwe to Bulawayo I experienced a change of mood. Until my arrest I had been confronting physical challenges — long marches, thirst, hunger and the discomfort of sleeping rough. I think I coped well. Physical discomfort doesn't bother me too much. At one point, though, I found myself more in need of emotional and spiritual resources than physical comfort. Once I was in custody I didn't give a damn about where I had to sleep or the lousy food I was given to eat. Sometimes I didn't even get food, but it did not take long to get used to that.

I complained to the member-in-charge of police at Umtali that I hadn't been given food the whole day.

'Bopela, please try and bear with us. We have food for consumption by human beings but we have run out of dog food. We'll try to get you some.'

After that I didn't complain. The key to survival in bad situations is to be mentally prepared for the worst possible treatment at the hands of the enemy. Anything better becomes a pleasure. So I wasn't expecting any favours or good treatment.

Being locked up, however, changed my outlook. It was a completely new experience. My freedom of movement was taken away. I was frequently left alone. I knew that if anyone was put in a cell with me, he couldn't be trusted and I dared not talk freely. We arrived at Bulawayo Central Police Station as I was turning these things over in my mind.

I met a charming policeman, Detective Inspector Ronald Stanley Peters — the CID Homicide Chief for Matabeleland. He was a tall Englishman with big ears and a keen brain. He also turned out to be polite, tactful and very shrewd. Many senior police officers in Rhodesia had been given Scotland Yard training, as had Dancer. They fought you with their brains and their police skills — unlike many South African Police officers who believed in brute force and torture. The BSAP types were skilled listeners and interrogators and some had law degrees. They were a dangerous breed to pit one's wits against.

'Mr Bopela, good morning, sir', Peters greeted me when I was taken to him the day following my arrival. Here was a policeman who called his prisoner 'sir'. A South African policeman was more likely to have called me 'kaffir' and slapped my face in greeting.

'Good morning, Inspector', I responded. I was very alert as I was getting to know this variety of policeman. Inspector Dancer had probably discussed me over the phone.

'Sit down, relax. It's a lovely morning, wouldn't you agree?'

'It is indeed, Inspector', I responded.

'Come on, cheer up. I'm not going to torture you, but we still have a long day ahead. Do you smoke Mr Bopela?'

'I do, but I don't want to trouble you.'

'No trouble at all. I keep various brands of cigarettes here to cater for different tastes. I have a packet of 50 Gold Dollar, 30 Peter Stuyvesant, 30 Life. You choose.'

'Gold Dollar will be fine, Inspector, thank you.'

He sat opposite me and got straight to the point.

'I hear you've been making many statements in Chipinga, Mr Bopela. Men have died here — our men — and we are in no mood for trifling. Tell me, Mr Bopela, why did you become a terrorist?

'Must I answer that question, Inspector?

'It would help if you did. I've been studying your family background. I have even spoken to your father and brother on the phone. You come from a middle-class background, not the usual breeding ground of a terrorist.'

'They say one person's terrorist is another's freedom fighter', I replied. 'Your government was responsible for me being recruited into what you call a terrorist organisation. Had the Rhodesian government allowed me to remain in Rhodesia and study law, I would have ended up as a barrister — definitely not what you call a terrorist. The white man has never been famous for acknowledging that he may be the cause of the problem. In my experience, Inspector, the whites always blame the victims of their actions. It's true to say that the South African and Rhodesian governments between them sent me straight into the ranks of MK.'

'You look like a university professor to me, Inspector', I continued. 'Why did you chose to be a policeman instead of an academic? I think that being an academic would have suited you better.'

'I take your point Mr Bopela. People are never what they should be in life', he laughed.

He became serious again and told me that he had numerous statements from my captured comrades that fully implicated me.

'I don't even need a statement from you, Mr Bopela. My investigation is complete and the dockets are ready to be submitted to the Attorney-General in Salisbury. On the basis of the evidence I am placing before him he will prefer charges against all of you. The evidence is sufficient to convict you all of murder. And for that you will doubtless hang.'

'You mean they intend to try and convict me on hearsay evidence, Inspector', I probed. 'Is that how your law works? You listen to what one prisoner says about another and then prefer charges? Is that the only lousy evidence you have?'

'It's not quite as simple as that, Mr Bopela. You obviously haven't hear about the law of common purpose. This stipulates that if a group of people come together and agree on a course of criminal action and that action is carried out, then they are all guilty to an equal degree. If you get together and agree to kill someone and you go to his house for that purpose, it doesn't matter who fires the fatal shot. You would all be equally guilty of murder.'

I lapsed into silence. This was serious. I had been expecting them to ask me where I had hidden my AK47 and pistols. I would have said I had thrown them in the bush and couldn't remember where. Now Peters was saying he wasn't even interested in the weapons.

'This law of common purpose is very convenient for when you don't have much evidence, isn't it?'

'On the contrary, my dear fellow, I have plenty of evidence, concrete evidence to ensure this law works for me. I'll prove that each of you is a member of an unlawful organisation, whether it is ZIPRA or MK. I'll show that you received extensive military training in various countries. I'll prove too that the ANC and ZAPU have a military alliance and that you were part of a group that crossed into Rhodesia on a particular date and at a particular place. I will also be able to place you on the battlefield when fighting took place and our men were killed.'

He paused and looked at me. He was really warming to his subject.

'To defend yourself, Mr Bopela, you will have to convince the court that while your comrades were carrying guns during the battles at which you were present, you fought only with your bare fists. I can't imagine the court will take that seriously.'

'You say you got all this information from my comrades, Inspector. Who are they and how can you prove this?'

'Oh, we can establish they are your comrades all right. Let me tell you something. ZIPRA started infiltrating this country in 1966. We've never had much of a problem with them. As soon as we heard they were out in the bush we just flew an aircraft overhead and called on them to surrender. In most instances they did. If you escape the gallows — which I don't think you will — you'll find them in our prisons, mostly serving ten-year sentences.

We were utterly surprised when we were fired on at Tsholotsho. We were not expecting that. It was only after ZIPRA prisoners told us they had South Africans with them that we realised what had happened. They said you were the guys killing our soldiers and not them. We know its true for other reasons as well.'

'What reasons, Inspector?'

'Because the South African Police have identified all the enemy dead we found as South African citizens. Not a single ZIPRA soldier was killed. Men only die when they're involved in battle.'

What could I say to that? Here was a policeman confirming ZIPRA's cowardice.

'Oh, don't worry Mr Bopela, you won't hang alone. As I have explained, the law of common purpose will see to it that all your friends join you, even if some claim they didn't fight. I must say you're excellent guerrilla fighters, but you won't win.'

'Inspector, if we're good fighters, and we are, we'll most certainly win. Why do you believe you can beat us?'

'Because we're always aware of your operational activities long before you launch them.

We get our information from the highest levels of ZAPU and the ANC.' He paused. 'I can see you don't believe me.'

'Inspector, you need to remember that I'm a very well trained terrorist, as you call me. When somebody like me is captured, the first thing the enemy does is to try and break their morale. The simplest way to do that is to suggest that their leaders are betraying them. You should be able to do better than that, Inspector.'

'So you think I'm bullshitting, Mr Bopela?'

'With the greatest of respect, Inspector, I know you are.'

'Very well then. We need to make you realise that you are fighting for a lost cause. Patrol Officer Maycock, come in here', he called.

A young blonde white man walked into the room. He wore a sky-blue cotton shirt, a striped tie and a navy-blue blazer.

'Sir', he reported.

'Get me that file from the safe. This is one of the fellows you were pursuing from Nyamandhlovu to Redbank after that woman reported meeting three Zulu-speaking lads.'

Maycock looked at me with narrowed eyes.

'If I'd caught up with you that night, I would have shot you', he said bluntly.

'If you had caught up with us, you wouldn't be talking such nonsense. You'd be in the mortuary or the cemetery', I replied heatedly.

Maycock went to the safe and pulled out a huge black book marked 'Top Secret' in red letters.

'Pass it to him, Maycock. He thinks we're bullshitting when we say his leaders are betraying him.' 'I don't think it we should show him classified information, sir. He's a terrorist!'

'Maycock, the poor fellow is going to be hanged. So why worry about what he sees. Dead men tell no tales, hey, Maycock?'

Maycock virtually threw the heavy book at me.

Inspector Peters took his coat and went to the door.

'Mr Bopela, we're going to lunch and we'll return in an hour. Look through the book and tell us your thoughts when we get back. Have fun.'

They closed and locked the door behind them.

I was handcuffed and leg-ironed which meant I could forget about escaping. I took a cigarette from the donated packet of Gold Dollar, lit up and inhaled. I opened the book but at first didn't fully grasp what I was looking at. When I did I realised it was a South African Security Branch book containing names, photos from identity documents and brief information about people who had gone into exile. It also showed the organisation the person belonged to and where he had been trained. My photo, name and nom de guerre were there and so were Daluxolo's, Derek's and hundreds of others. I knew many of them, but a lot were strangers. What made my hair stand on end were the copies of the United Nations High Commission for Refugees (UNHCR) documents that we had used for travelling abroad. There were also photocopies of passports used by people when travelling outside the country. There were PAC people as well as those from the

Rhodesian political organisations, ZAPU and ZANU.

How did those bastards get all this? I asked myself.

It was very clear. The South African Security Branch and the Rhodesian Special Branch were working hand-in-hand and exchanging information. Much of what I was looking at could only have originated from very senior people in our organisations. So my 'friend' Inspector Peters hadn't been talking through his hat when he told me that such people were in their pay and passing on information.

I chain-smoked one cigarette after another while I thought. What was I going to say to Inspector Peters when he returned? Was I going to tell him I believed that some of our leaders were traitors? Not a chance! If you admit such a thing, Thula Bopela, you will have to also admit that you are fighting a losing battle. From there it will only be a very short step away from agreeing to work for the Security Branch.

I had finished going through the book for the third time when the key turned in the lock and the inspector came in. He hung his jacket on a coat hanger behind the door, walked over to the window and looked out.

'Come over here, Mr Bopela, I want to show you something.'

I hobbled clanking to the window and stood next to him. He pointed to a sleek black sedan parked outside. It was fitted with TJ (Johannesburg) registration plates.

'It belongs to South African policemen who are here helping us. They are somewhat disappointed with the calibre of the MK people we have arrested so far. They were hoping we had caught some big fish. But they are still keen to talk to little sardines like you. That is, if you agree.'

'What would they want with a small fish like me, Inspector?'

'They have some interesting ideas, those guys. But as I said it's only if you agree to talk to them.'

'Inspector, are you suggesting I should work for the South African Security Branch?'

'I am not suggesting any such thing', Inspector Peters replied innocently. 'But there might well be advantages to consider before rejecting their offer.'

'Advantages, Inspector?'

'Yes. Like if we charge you with murder in Rhodesia you'll be sentenced to death and hanged. If they charge you under the terrorism laws in South Africa, the maximum sentence is ten years. That's something you must decide yourself.'

He went back to his desk and I hobbled over and sat opposite him.

'What do you think of our big black book? Interesting, hmm?' he asked looking me straight in the eyes.

'Inspector, why did you classify it as top secret?'

'That's what it is', he replied obviously puzzled.

'I think you are incompetent, Inspector Peters. If I was your boss, I'd fire you.'

'That's a curious thing to say considering your position', he said glancing at my handcuffed wrists.

'You collect photographs, names and addresses, compile them in a big book, call it top secret and leave it at that'.

'And what would my KGB friend have done if he was in my place?' he asked sarcastically.

'I would have been seriously engaged in trying to discover what military plans were in place to attack and overthrow your government. I wouldn't have been wasting my time collecting names, photos and addresses. Do you have ZAPU's and ZANU's military plans anywhere? If you don't you should stop calling yourself a policeman!'

We sat there looking at each other, the policeman and his prisoner. I had forgotten I was dealing with a Rhodesian police officer. A South African police colonel would probably have punched me, blustered, sworn and revealed his insecurity. Not Ronald Stanley Peters. He just laughed.

'You call me a terrorist, Inspector. What is a terrorist?' I asked.

'A terrorist is someone who sets out to kill innocent people without good reason and claims to be doing it to bring about liberation.'

'We have not killed innocent people. We have only killed soldiers and policemen, members of your Security Forces who came into the bush to attack us. Who are these innocent people you say we have killed?'

'I have no intention of engaging in a political debate with you, my dear fellow. You have your view of who and what you are and we have ours. To us you are a terrorist and a murderer. We will try you in the High Court for your crimes and you and your comrades will be convicted and executed.'

'We don't care what you call us, Inspector', I replied calmly. 'We know that if you were a black African, oppressed by European colonialists, you would also fight to regain your lost freedom. Just because you happen to be the oppressor, doesn't make us evil. And labelling us as terrorists or whatever won't alter our image in the eyes of oppressed black people. To them we are still freedom fighters. You whites have lost your right to define reality for the black people. We can do that for ourselves. You will execute us, you say? Very well, but if you think you can execute the truth, then you are more foolish than we imagined. Our deaths will only bring thousands more fighters to the freedom banner.'

'Okay, okay, to hell with your communist propaganda. Tell me, Thula — if I can call you that — why did you become a terrorist? Your father and eldest brother are teachers. That makes them middle-class and financially comfortable. What's all this nonsense about oppression? You don't come from the ranks of the poor and uneducated, so why are you feeling oppressed.'

'It's not personal oppression we fight Inspector, it's national oppression. We are oppressed as a nation. You say my father and brother are financially comfortable. That's true, but you must understand that oppression can't be defined in monetary terms only. Imagine a rich man who has no freedom of thought or speech, or movement or freedom of association . . . who can't choose how he is governed and by whom. Would such a person feel free simply because he has millions in the bank?'

'I see the Russians taught you the art of political propaganda well. But there's nothing in my book which explains why you should have joined a terrorists organisation.'

Then he seemed to lose interest in the subject. 'It's been a long day for us both, Mr

Bopela. I propose we stop sparring and have a rest. Tomorrow you will be taken to Mpopoma Police Station where you and your comrades will appear before a magistrate.'

'I thought you said we would be charged in the High Court, Inspector?'

'Not tomorrow. You have to be formally arraigned, but you won't be asked to plead. It's just another of our ways of putting the fear of God into you. After that you'll be taken to Her Majesty's Khami Maximum Security Prison where we will detain you until you and your comrades have to appear at the High Court in Salisbury. We won't see each other again until then.'

He stood up to his full height and stretched out his hand. I found myself shaking it. Apart from that he didn't lay a hand on me and never threatened me. Inspector Ronald Stanley Peters was no fool. He was courteous but deadly. A typical British policeman. He even called you 'sir' while arranging the noose around your neck.

Another policeman who interrogated me was Detective Inspector Mac McGuinness. He was of the same cut as Peters. He asked me:

'Why didn't you lot cross at the spot originally planned by Oliver Tambo? What changed your minds?'

'Inspector, how did you know we were supposed to cross at that particular place? And how did you know Comrade Oliver Tambo was with us?'

'Never mind, just answer me. We have sources in your organisations that I'm hardly going to identify for you.'

'A soldier accidentally discharged his weapon, so Comrade Tambo decided we should move elsewhere just in case your people had been alerted by the shots.'

Inspector McGuinness almost exploded.

'That was months of careful planning and intelligence gathering ruined by a damn fool terr having an accidental discharge just as I was about to spring the trap. Beelzebub! I could have had the whole lot of you bastards — including your communist boss, Comrade Tambo. Damn your pagan gods!'

'You're saying, Inspector, that you knew in advance that we would be crossing into Rhodesia at a particular spot and at a particular time? And that Comrade OR would be with us?'

'You're damned right', the Inspector fumed. 'I had a large reception committee ready for you on our side of the river. We had planned a really good party.' He shook his head. 'You bastards were just lucky, really lucky.'

17

Death Row
The legion of the doomed

Things went pretty much as Inspector Peters had said they would. We appeared before the magistrate at Mpopoma Police Station and were formally arraigned. Afterwards we were bundled into police vans and taken under heavy escort to Khami Maximum Security Prison.

I met the comrades Peters had spoken about. The MK guys were William Motau and myself. The rest were ZIPRA soldiers I had last seen at Tsholotsho. There was Kayeni Dube — a loud-mouthed coward — Abel Moyo, Tennis 'Nkonkoni' Khumalo, Morris Ncube and Harry Hadebe. I learned that Harry had identified me to the police which led to Detective Inspector Dancer realising the statement I had made to him was false. I felt no bitterness. Harry explained that he thought I was dead and the policemen were merely asking him to identify me. But none of that mattered now. What mattered was what lay ahead of us.

Nkonkoni had also identified me as having been present. He explained to me that he fled when the battle started, but had ran straight into the muzzles of the RAR rifles. He was lucky not to be shot. They took him prisoner and demanded to know how many we were, who our commander was, what weapons we carried and what our objectives were.

'You can find the information in my grave', he told them bravely.

His captors were not charmed and they took him to a temporary base close to the battlefield. They explained to Special Branch policemen there that he was being difficult.

One SB man got particularly annoyed with him.

'Let's see just how tough you are Nkonkoni. I promise that after what I am going to do to you, you'll tell us everything we want to know.'

They bundled him into an air force helicopter. They tied a rope around his leg and once airborne they kicked him through the doorway and left him dangling in space. He went absolutely hysterical. The helicopter climbed to about 3 000 metres and Nkonkoni could see trees far below rushing past like a green smudge. The white SB officer appeared in the doorway above him brandishing a large knife. To Nkonkoni's horror he began to saw through the rope until eventually his life was literally hanging by a thread..

'I started screaming, Thula', he said. 'I bawled out that I would tell him everything he wanted to know.

'Then talk', said the officer.

'I literally screamed out answers to every one of his questions.'

'Didn't it occur to you that you were betraying us, Nkonkoni?' I asked, laughing uncontrollably in spite of myself at the mental picture of his predicament.

'I didn't care. I felt to hell with everyone. Do you really think I would have let that white man cut the rope and let me plunge to my death just to save your skins? No, my friend, saving my own life was far more important. After liberation you guys can try me and shoot me for giving information to the enemy. I wouldn't hold it against you. When it comes to the push you save your own life first. I could already see myself falling through empty space and crashing down on the rocks and trees below.'

I could see his point.

The Sheriff of Bulawayo arrived at the prison one morning and all seven of us were taken from our cells and brought to the prison administration block. The sheriff trembled as he read the charges that each one of us would face and he handed us copies of the charge sheet. We were all charged with murder as Inspector Peters had predicted — five counts of murder.

'The charges you are facing are grave', the Sheriff said. 'I am not the person who framed the charges against you. They come straight from the office of Attorney General Theron Bosman in Salisbury. My duty is to read the charges to you and serve charge sheets on you.'

When we returned to our cells, other ZIPRA men asked what we had been charged with. We told them it was murder. They said that was nothing. We were heroes and even if they found us guilty we wouldn't be hanged because the Smith government was illegal. The United Nations, the British government, the Commonwealth and the OAU wouldn't allow it to happen.

It was such men that Inspector Peters had told me about. They had been trained in various countries — Egypt, Algeria, China, Cuba and Yugoslavia — and had progressively infiltrated Rhodesia since 1966. The difference between us and them was that they had surrendered without firing a shot. They were serving ten-year terms and were telling us we wouldn't be hanged because the world would protest vigorously! If they were so sure of that, why hadn't they opened fire on the Rhodesian Security Forces? We were listening to a pep talk given by cowards.

We were transported to Salisbury at the beginning of November and detained in Her Majesty's Maximum Security Prison. The officer in charge was Superintendent Barker and the prison chaplain was Rev Clarke. Two days later a pro-deo lawyer, a Mr T. P. Hathorn, came to see us. A pro-deo lawyer is one appointed and paid by the government to represent defendants without means appearing in the High Court. It's not legal for a person to appear on charges as grave as murder or treason without legal representation. The question we asked ourselves was why ZAPU or the ANC didn't hire a lawyer for us.

As Inspector Peters put it, we were 'small fish.' Too small to waste money on. Joshua Nkomo, the President of ZAPU, would definitely have had the best legal representation if he had been on trial for his life. The Rev Ndabaningi Sithole, President of ZANU, would later also have the best legal representation.

It seems there are always inequalities in organisations that claim to fight for equality. The external leadership of the ANC certainly didn't live under the same conditions as the common fighting soldiers. They enjoyed all the facilities of city life while we just existed far away in the bush. Even the military commanders — with the exception of Samora Machel of FRELIMO — didn't stay in the camps with us. Their food was certainly not the same as ours. When sick they were flown overseas for the best medical treatment, while in the camps we were treated by half-trained medical orderlies. We went for military training. They didn't and nor did their children. And now that we had been captured and faced death sentences, there was no quality legal representation.

People will suggest we are complaining . . . denouncing our organisations . . . attacking our leaders. No, we are merely stating facts — the reality of the circumstances in which some of us fought for freedom. The inequality of treatment made us spiritually strong. Now, after liberation, when our leaders see many of our comrades clothed in rags and living in shacks, we know they feel ashamed. We saw the glaring inequalities even before we left home to fight, but that didn't cause us to falter. Most revolutionaries are not prominent people who make eloquent speeches; they are ordinary men and women who are prepared to make enormous sacrifices — and who rarely get a mention when freedom comes.

In South Africa we were lucky to have a Nelson Mandela, a Walter Sisulu, a Govan Mbeki, who went to prison for 27 years. They suffered greatly and we honour them as heroes. But even there the inequality is unmistakable. Tourists who go to Robben Island are shown Mandela's cell, Walter Sisulu's cell and where Ahmad Kathrada slept and worked. No one demands to see the cells of Daluxolo and others whom Inspector Ronald Peters would have classified as 'sardines'.

We accepted our fate and in November we appeared before Justice Lewis and two assessors at the Salisbury High Court. We were represented by a white man whose only interest in us was the fee the government was paying him and he told us so. The prosecutor was Advocate B J Treacy, a hoarse-voiced British-trained Queens Counsel. Opposing him on our side was our pro-deo lawyer, T P Hathorn. We didn't stand a chance and we knew it. We were about to be railroaded to the gallows.

We sat and listened as the white man's justice ran its course. Firstly the murder charges. All those killed in the battles we had fought were either soldiers of the Rhodesian African Rifles or members of the British South Africa Police. They were armed and trained professionals and it was war. In the end, though, we were charged with murder. It might have been law, but it was certainly not justice — it was an expression of power.

After two weeks of tedious testimony we were found guilty on all counts.

The court was adjourned until the next day for sentencing. There was much melodrama in the High Court relating to the death sentence.

'Silence in court!' the registrar bawled.

The judge and his assessors entered and took their seats, one assessor on either side of the judge.

The registrar of the High Court seemed to go berserk.

'Hear ye! Hear ye! This honourable court is about to pass sentence.'

Everyone including we accused stood up.

The judge began to intone in a deep and sombre voice. I wondered later if judges rehearsed such moments by standing in front of mirrors in their chambers.

'This Court, after careful consideration of all the facts relevant to this case has found you guilty as charged. You are hereby sentenced to death by hanging. You will henceforth be taken from this court to a place of waiting. On an appointed date you will be taken thence to a place of execution where you will be hanged by your necks until you are dead. May God have mercy on your souls!'

From the day you enter the white man's court, God is involved in the proceedings. Witnesses raise their hands and swear on the Bible to tell the whole truth and nothing but the truth, so help them God. Yet when they open their mouths they lie. And when they sentence you to die, they invoke God's mercy on your soul!

So where is God's role in the matter? The white man's God in court turns out to be the God of Lies. Why didn't they just get on with the business of sentencing you to death and leave God's name out of it? But the white man in Africa always carried a burden of guilt when he administered what he called justice to the 'natives'. He had to portray himself as the instrument of God meting out justice in His name. Everything he did had to be cloaked in God's robes, otherwise it would be laid bare as the action of lusty, murderous and hypocritical men who were intent on oppressing the natives. As if we on death row cared whether they did what they did on God's command or not!

To cope with the trauma of being sentenced to death, and maybe hanged, the crucial factor was to see things from the correct perspective. We had to have complete faith in our cause and consider things from that standpoint. If what happens to one is not seen from the perspective of one's own beliefs and principles, the interpretation of what is happening would be flawed. How does one handle the fact that the law of the land does not take into consideration that you are human beings who want to be ruled by your own elected representatives? If you rebel against the injustice of being ruled by people you have not elected, you are labelled a terrorist, hunted down and shot or hanged. It is the lot of the freedom fighter to be condemned by the ruling regime.

Ian Smith rebelled against the British government and he saw it as a just act. Our rebellion against his regime, as Africans, was regarded by him as terrorism. Were we supposed to regard Ian Smith and his Rhodesia Front as a legitimate government? Why was it right and justifiable for him to rebel against Great Britain while our rebellion against him was regarded as criminal? Through Mr Justice Lewis they had the temerity to cloak the entire proceedings in the guise of 'civilisation and Christianity'.

This is the perspective that a freedom fighter needs to see the situation from, in order to cope with the trauma of being sentenced to death. He needs to know and understand that these people are hypocrites who have no moral right to pronounce his fate. By doing so he places himself in a position to deal with his predicament.

There was a group of about 110 men in B Hall, all charged with murder. We were a motley crew. The majority were common criminals who had killed while committing robbery or rape or who just wanted to get rid of somebody. Those of us who had killed to free a nation were in the minority. Of the so-called 'politicals' most had murdered political opponents. There were ZAPU men who had murdered ZANU men and vice versa. Even amongst the seven of us who had gone through the rigours of the Wankie Campaign, there were men who had run away and hadn't fired a shot. According to the law of common purpose, as explained by Inspector Ronald Stanley Peters, they were in the same predicament as those who had killed, killed and killed again. The hangman was waiting in the shadows for us all.

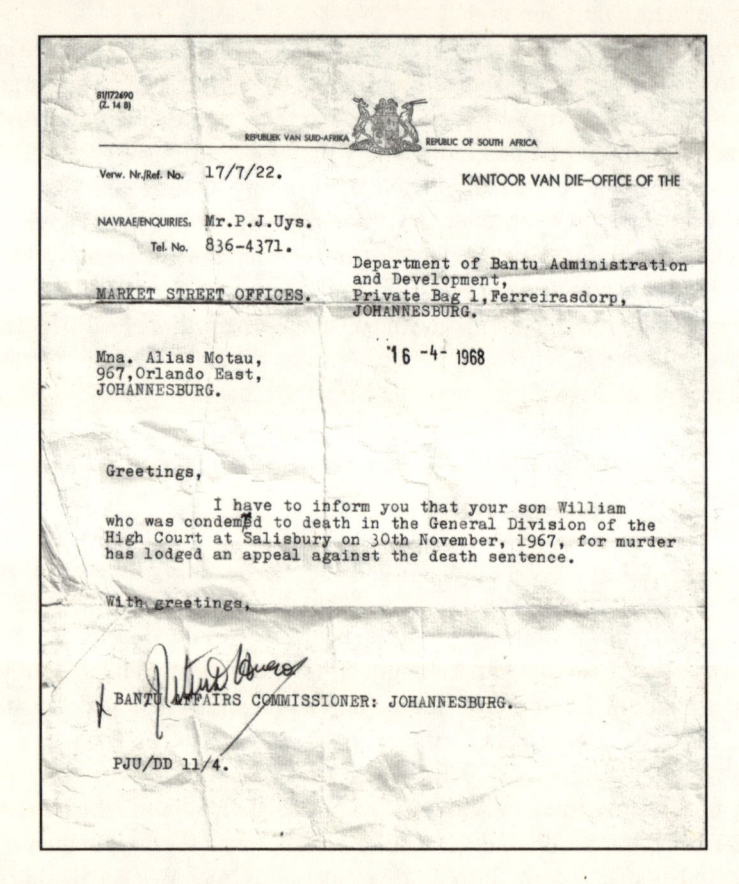

Letter from the Bantu Affairs Commissioner, Johannesburg, to the father of MK prisoner William Motau, advising that he had lodged an appeal against the death sentence imposed on him in Salisbury

The question was: could we respond to the same fate in the same fashion? Surely a ZAPU man who had murdered a ZANU opponent couldn't approach his end in the same way as one who had shot and killed members of the Security Forces? Could one of those who had run away at Tjolotjo without firing a shot face his destiny in the same way as one who had experienced the satisfaction of seeing men fall at the command of his trigger finger? While we were all condemned to meet the same end, our mental paths to that point were very different.

We arrived on Death Row in November of 1967. It was summer and hot. The red flannel shirts issued to all condemned prisoners were being boycotted. The prisoners were walking around wearing only shorts. We didn't ask why, but assumed it was because of the hot weather.

In the evening after lock-up time somebody would invariably shout in Shona: '*Ngatinamateyi madzishe*' (Gentlemen, let us pray).

A rhythmic clapping of hands would follow and that would last for a long time. While this was going on somebody in his cell (all Death Row prisoners slept in single cells) would get 'an inspiration' and call on the ancestors to look favourably on him. He would appeal for protection against the 'overwhelming power of the white man'. He would invoke Chaminuka, the Shona's rain god and Mbuya Nehanda (a spirit medium who had been hanged in Salisbury Prison after her capture during the Mashonaland Rebellion of 1896). Not once during my entire sojourn on Death Row did I hear anybody invoke the name of Jesus of Nazareth. It would have seemed abominable even if many of the prisoners were Christians. They were black men praying to their ancestors to intervene on their behalf and Jesus was tacitly seen as a white deity from a different spirit world.

There seemed to be a weakness to this entire spiritual exercise. How could those common ancestors handle prayers made by people who belonged to both ZAPU and ZANU? How could African ancestors handle political division among Africans who murdered each other instead of attacking the real oppressors, Ian Smith and his white supporters?

I used to lie in my cell and listen to the clapping, wondering what it meant. I was not a religious person at the time. I had been raised in a Christian home, but I was not a Christian. My father had seen to it that I was baptised and had given me several so-called Christian names. Before retiring for the night my father or my mother would pray. At school I attended morning and evening prayers, but it was merely in conformance with the wishes of those controlling my life. As for African ancestral belief, I knew next to nothing about it so I couldn't meaningfully participate in its worship or expression.

Even in the freedom movements, conformity was required. Take the issue of the red flannel shirts. The Red Cross paid a visit and found Death Row prisoners using blankets to cover their shoulders, or nothing at all. They demanded that Superintendent Barker explain why he didn't provide shirts for the inmates to wear.

'The moment prisoners step into Death Row they are issued with red flannel shirts', he told them. However, the prisoners believe that red is taboo. They think that if they wear red shirts it'll annoy their ancestors who'll ensure they end up being hanged. Red is the colour of blood and it signifies death.'

The Red Cross officials didn't believe this story. It was too farfetched for sophisticated people from the snow-covered mountains of Switzerland that were so far from Africa to believe that sort of rubbish. Yet it was the truth. After the visitors left, Superintendent Barker told the prisoners they would be compelled to wear their red shirts.

'Those who refuse, will not be allowed to leave their cells to take part in the 35 minute exercise period in the prison yard.'

Despite the threat, the prisoners chose to remain in their cells and forgo their twice daily exercise breaks.

I asked a ZAPU political commissar, Skhosana, to explain the taboo. If I was to show solidarity with the rest by forfeiting my exercise periods for an indefinite period, then at least I wanted to know what it was all about.

'We believe that the colour red is offensive to our ancestors', he confirmed. 'We are under our ancestors' protection while on Death Row and the last thing we want to do is offend them. That's why we won't wear the shirts.'

I found myself face-to-face with behaviour motivated by a belief that I didn't share, yet I was being pressured to conform. If it had been a minor matter I would probably have gone along with it just to keep the peace. But to give up an activity that helped to keep one sane was not, in my view, a small matter. I decided to assert my independence.

'I don't believe such nonsense, Comrade Skhosana', I told him. 'If you guys think that wearing a red shirt will make a difference to whether you are hanged or not, it's your funeral and not mine. I'm going to wear that shirt and go out for exercise.'

'You can't, Comrade Thula', he replied. 'You will be jeopardising the lives of everybody here. Remember this — if the ancestors become angry and some of us are hanged because you have gone against custom — you will be held responsible'.

'Hold me responsible by all means if you want to', I replied. 'If what you say is true the ancestors will take revenge against me and get me hanged. They will certainly not harm innocents like you who haven't been wearing their red shirts.'

'The ancestors mete out group punishments', Skhosana said sharply. 'Maybe you don't care what happens with your life, but we care about how your actions may effect the lives of others.'

'Let me speak plainly, Comrade Skhosana. I'm a Zulu. My people have fought many great wars and died in large numbers. My ancestors are warrior ancestors and they understand what happens in wartime. They're not going to turn their backs on me because I've put on a shirt that I'm forced to wear because I'm a prisoner. The colour red means nothing to us Zulus.'

'We've told you it's taboo to us and our ancestors', Skhosana replied quietly.

'Mbuya Nehanda was a spirit medium and they hanged her in this very prison, Comrade Skhosana. Did that happen to her because she wore red? I doubt that, because as a spirit medium she knew far more about her ancestors than a city-born chap like you.'

'I can see that nothing I can say will persuade you. Wear the damned shirt and we'll blame you for whatever might happen to us here', Skhosana told me.

He left to speak to the rest and tell them there was a rebel in the camp.

The guards came to ask if any prisoners were willing to don their red shirts and go out for exercise. I replied that I would and I was joined by two other MK men, Willie Motau and Bothwell Tamana. That day we were allowed morning and afternoon exercise periods far in excess of the mandated 35 minutes. This was because there were only a few of us and it took little effort on the part of the guards to supervise us.

The other prisoners accused us of being sell-outs and traitors. They also accused us of behaving undemocratically by going against the voice of the majority. They were very hostile. We didn't bother to argue because we knew it would have been an exercise in futility. The opinion formulators there were old men who claimed to know everything about African religion. They played on inbred superstitions to exert their authority and control the behaviour of the rest. They felt very bitter because we had challenged their abilities to direct everybody's behaviour to their liking. We merely pointed out to those who asked why we were wearing our red shirts that we were soldiers. We had no intention of allowing ourselves to be ordered around by old men who lived by dreams and taboos.

This type of problem is rampant in black organisations that claim to be democratic, but the fact is they are controlled by people who use undemocratic methods of decision making. Skhosana and the rest had never been elected to leadership in Death Row. They had never even asked the other prisoners if they believed in the red shirt taboo or not. Most people like to conform, so nobody challenged them until we came along. Now we were sell-outs and traitors!

In Africa, religions beliefs are not universal. They change according to area and tribe. There are Africans who have converted to Christianity and have nothing whatsoever to do with ancestor worship. Then there are communist and atheist Africans who believe that all religions are pie in the sky. All these people were represented in political organisations during the freedom struggle. Nobody could, or wanted to say what form of religion should be dominant. The ANC, for one, has never bound its members to any particular belief system. You can be whatever you like and no one will give you problems.

At Salisbury Maximum Security Prison the old men imposing the taboos and rituals well knew only too well that many of the men who belonged to ZAPU and ZANU were Christians. This alone should have warned them against trying to impose their taboos on everyone. The Shonas were not the only tribespeople who belonged to those organisations. Most members of ZAPU were Ndebele — Mzilikazi's people — and Shona taboos were different to Ndebele ones. This led to serious division among them in the prison.

One day we were joined in the exercise yard by an Ndebele chap — he with the rope around his leg in the chopper — Nkonkoni Khumalo. He had also decided to defy the ban on red shirts and the ritual prayers chanted every night.

'The Shona only invoke the spirits of their own ancestors like Chaminuka and Nehanda', he said. 'They say nothing about Mzilikazi and Lobengula, despite them being more powerful than the spirits of the people they are invoking. I've had enough. Red has no spiritual significance to the Ndebele people so I'm not going to be part of their nonsense. I'm out of it.'

We explained that the ANC kept religion out of the organisation because our leaders knew it could cause division. We asked if there was anything in ZAPU law that demanded people should pray to ancestors. He said there wasn't. So we asked how come we were being called 'traitors' and 'sell-outs' because we had chosen to wear the red shirts and take our exercise?

'You see Bopela, there are people here who have their own private religious beliefs. Their problem is that they expect everybody to believe what they believe and do what they do. It's a sort of dictatorship.'

'But most of you ZAPU guys obey them. If they are private beliefs how come everybody is refusing to wear their shirts and are willing to sacrifice something precious like exercise?'

'Bopela, I know our people', Nkonkoni replied. 'The majority conform because they don't want to be the ones spoiling unity. They are also afraid of being called sell-outs and perhaps secretly afraid that the red curse might get them hanged. Not many people have independent minds like you guys.'

They labelled Nkonkoni a 'tribalist' but he didn't care. He just wore his red shirt and exercised with us. Others who were like-minded were afraid to say so and suffered in silence. The fear to differ can be paralysing. The ridiculous thing was that our organisations were demanding freedom of speech from our oppressors but didn't allow it amongst their own members. It was a problem that continued to plague us even after we had survived Death Row. People were always dreaming up 'policies' and making people conform to them. Such people set themselves up as leaders in the absence of the true ones.

18

No 'thank you' for Daluxolo

Daluxolo and Derek had fled separately into the bush when the two policemen had tried to arrest us. Neither knew where the other was. Both independently concluded that the only man capable of helping them was Oscar Mashengele. When Daluxolo got there that morning he discovered that Derek had already been and left. Mashengele told each of them it was dangerous to be there during daytime because the police were probably watching the house. He said they should return that night.

After Daluxolo left Mashengele was arrested and taken to Chibuwe Police Station for questioning, but was released that afternoon. When Daluxolo and Derek turned up again he told them that I was in custody. He suggested they come back two nights later by which time he hoped to have worked out where to send them. At least they were together again and they spent the next two days hiding and surviving as best they could. When they returned, Mashengele told them to go to my father at Chikore. Having been there before they had no problem finding the place, but it took them two days of walking.

My father was very disturbed when he saw them.

'Where is my son Thula?'

'I'm sorry, *Baba*, but Thula has been arrested.'

'When and where did this happen? How did you two manage to escape?'

They described how I had been arrested four days earlier at Chisumbanje. Explaining how they had managed to evade capture must have been difficult. Derek omitted to say that as soon as he saw the two policemen getting out of the truck, he fled without bothering to check if his comrades were safe. Nor did he mention that he heard me shouting that Daluxolo was in trouble but just continued running. Daluxolo for his part 'forgot' to tell my father that I returned to rescue him, but that he abandoned me and fled the scene.

My father told me many years later that he had felt inclined to tell them both to get lost.

'They had abandoned my son, their comrade, and were asking me for help. But I decided against sending them away because they looked so helpless.'

My father shared his secret with Mlotshwa, a teacher at Chikore Mission. They agreed to hide and feed the boys until the hue and cry died down, after which they would decide what to do. Other teachers who were not even members of ZAPU also lent a hand. They

121

explained that they belonged to ZANU, but were assisting because the struggle was against Ian Smith and not ZAPU. My father was not politically active and only became involved because I was.

Meanwhile, the two boys remained in hiding. By December it was considered safe to move them from Chikore to Bulawayo. Mashengele had been released and he made the arrangements. He had a contact in Bulawayo and he borrowed a car to take them there.

Bitter animosity was developing between Derek and Daluxolo. Each blamed the other for the trouble they were in.

'Thula returned to rescue me and you never even looked back', Daluxolo said accusingly.

'You're the last person to point a finger at me', Derek stormed back. 'When we were in Chief Mahenye's area we agreed that if the detectives asked, we would tell them we were university students from Botswana. Thula distinctly warned us that nobody should claim they came from Umtali. Yet that's exactly what you did but you couldn't say where in Umtali. It was your stupidity that got us into this.'

'Maybe I did make a mistake', said Daluxolo humbled. 'Remember, though, your ambition for a senior position was the only reason you volunteered to fight in Rhodesia. If you hadn't been offered the position of chief-of-staff you wouldn't have gone. That means you wouldn't have been left behind because you could no longer march. I was stupid to tell Thula I intended to stay behind and guard you. I know now that if our positions had been reversed you would have left me there to die.'

This led to a fight and they were separated by the teachers hiding them.

They promised not to fight again, but their mutual animosity didn't diminish.

Once in Bulawayo, Mashengele left them in the hands of his contact man and returned home. Many years later, Mashengele told me how Detective Chief Inspector Dancer (he had been promoted) had visited him at the school.

'My wife made tea and we discussed the weather, the school and education in general for a full 20 minutes. I couldn't even guess why he had come.'

Then Dancer told him.

'Mr Mashengele, since we last met, new evidence has come to light and this time I intend to get to the bottom of the matter. One of those three men is now cooperating with our Security Branch counterparts in South Africa. [The man was Derek who by then was a detective sergeant with the SAP's Security Branch.] He has revealed that even after the arrest of Thula Bopela, you still continued to assist the other two. He also revealed how you took them to Bulawayo and left them with your friend. He is willing to return to Rhodesia to testify if you deny the role you played.

Dancer arrested him and took him to Chibuwe Police Station. Mashengele was afterwards sent for preventative detention where he remained until all detainees were freed just prior to the internal settlement in March 1978.

My father also had a visit from the police at the behest of Derek. He said that while I might be a terrorist to them, as my father he obviously had a different view. He told them that he could never have shut his door in the face of his son when he was asking for help.

Amazingly he wasn't arrested.

The contact person in Bulawayo advised Daluxolo and Derek to make their way to Francistown in Botswana and report to the ANC office there. That night they set off on foot for the border. They travelled only at night and hid in the bush during the hours of daylight. One afternoon when they were close to the Botswana border, Daluxolo woke up and found that Derek had gone. He waited for him for the whole night and the next night crossed the border into Botswana.

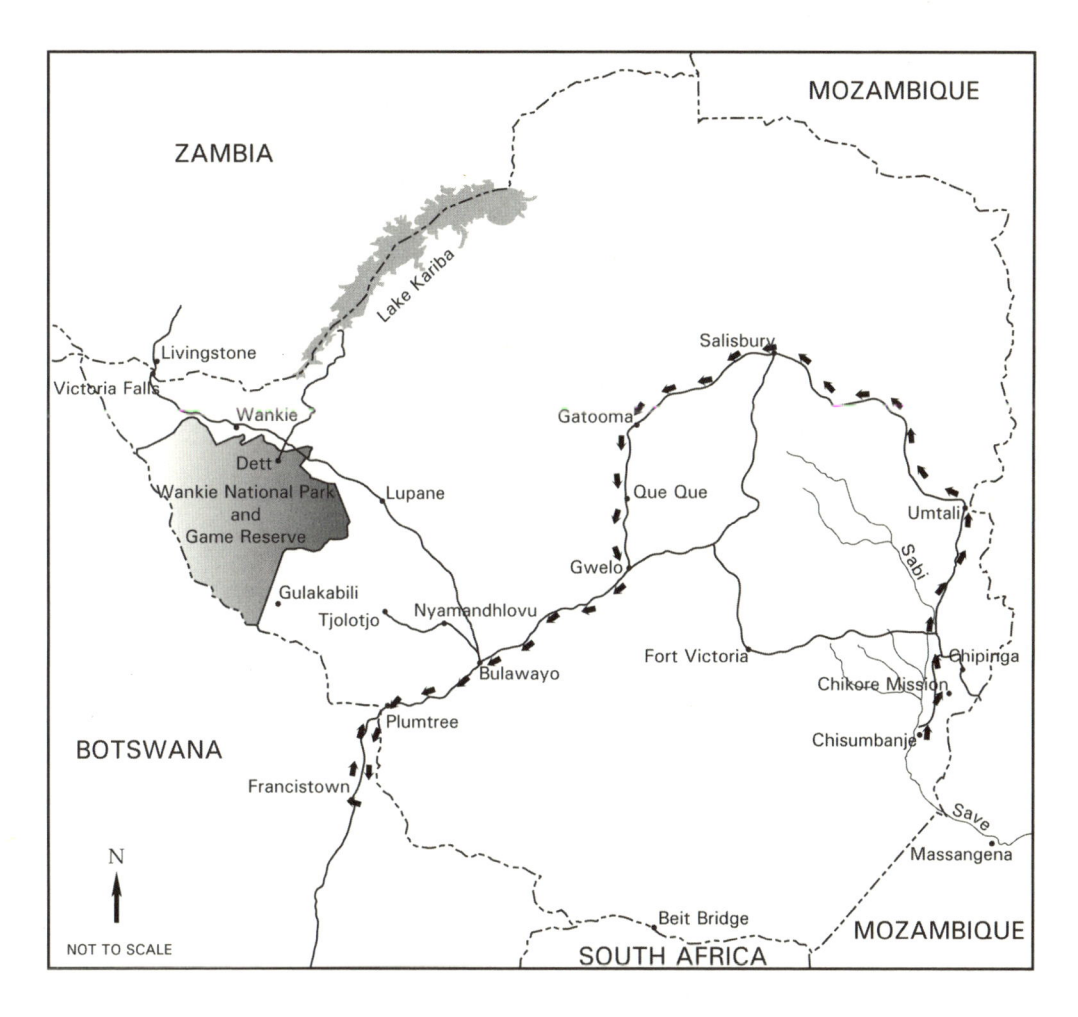

Map showing Daluxolo's movements subsequent to Thula's arrest

At the ANC office at Francistown one of the staff told him that Derek had already been there. He had left a message for Daluxolo asking to meet him three days later at a spot on the Rhodesian side of the border, which was also close to South African territory. From there, he said, they would cross into South Africa together.

Daluxolo was surprised by the mysterious note but nevertheless kept the rendezvous. No one was there and he dozed off and fell asleep. He woke up to find himself surrounded by Rhodesian policemen.

Derek had set him up.

It takes hard thinking to even begin to understand people like Derek. When they joined organisations like MK it was assumed they did so because they were committed to the struggle to free their people. It was only much later after their true colours were revealed that people realised that they had only been seeking their personal fortunes. They owed allegiance to nobody but themselves and would betray anybody anytime if an opportunity arose to feather their nests. There were a lot of such people in the liberation movements.

It was some time before the ANC learned that Derek had become a South African Security Branch policeman. From Durban he had contacted the ANC in Lusaka and claimed he was underground. He asked for information on arms caches inside the country and this was given to him. They also gave him the names of contact people inside the country that would be useful to him. Needless to say, he passed this information to his new comrades in the Security Police. Many people were arrested and numerous arms caches uncovered. His actions caused a serious setback to the struggle.

But Derek got his comeuppance. At about 22:00 one evening in 1975 a car stopped outside the house where he lived with his family. Some men got out, entered the yard and went to the window of the bedroom where Derek and his wife were sleeping.

They opened fire through the window.

'I know the sound of those guns. They're ours', he told his wife before he died from gunshot wounds.

19

Call me *Baas*, you bastard

Daluxolo was taken to Beit Bridge. The Rhodesians escorted him to the centre of the bridge and handed him over to the waiting Major 'Rooi Rus' (Red Russian) Swanepoel of the Security Branch. He was accompanied by Captain van Rensburg and Lieutenant Ferreira. Rooi Rus was later promoted to colonel and became notorious for his no-holds-barred methods of extracting information from suspects. It was he who ordered the shooting of the students in Soweto in 1976.

I have portrayed the behaviour of the white senior British South Africa Police officers of Rhodesia as accurately as possible. Apart from my personal dealings with them, comrades like myself who were captured in Rhodesia, related similar experiences while in their hands. The police officers there who used violence against us were mostly junior men. The black policemen were particularly brutal. I believe they felt the need to be harsh and violent towards us to prove to their white masters that they had no sympathy for our cause. The senior officers I encountered never laid a hand on me.

But from the moment Daluxolo fell into the hands of the SAP he was violently assaulted. They beat him continually during the long drive from Beit Bridge to the Compol Building on the corner of Pretorius and Paul Kruger Streets in Pretoria where he was detained. They handcuffed him to a steel beam that went from one side of the room to the other and he was left hanging there with his toes barely touching the ground.

They didn't try to extract any important information from him. Most of their questions were posed in Afrikaans. Although he grew up in Natal, he never acquired a working knowledge of Afrikaans, so he was at a distinct disadvantage. He was savagely assaulted for this failure too.

'*Hy is 'n swart Engelsman, hierdie kêrel* . . .'(This chap's a black Englishman).

There was serious competition between Afrikaans-speaking and English-speaking South Africans to get black people to speak their language. In Afrikaans-speaking areas like the Free State and the former Transvaal, a black would often be abused or even assaulted for failing to answer or make conversation in Afrikaans. This would never happen to a white English speaker. If a black spoke excellent Afrikaans no one labelled him '*n swart Afrikaner* (a black Afrikaner). It was only when he spoke English that he became *'n swart Engelsman*.

Daluxolo suffered heavily for his lack of language skills. Most Afrikaners are emotional about their language, almost to the point of insanity, it seems to me. The reason lies in history. After their defeat at the hands of the English in the Anglo-Boer War of 1899-1902, the British High Commissioner, Lord Milner, went out of his way to crush the Boer language and culture. At school, English was the one and only medium and a Boer child caught speaking Dutch was made to wear a board on which appeared the words 'I am a Donkey. I spoke Dutch'. Afrikaans evolved from Dutch and it only became an official language in 1924. Afrikaners have been very protectionist about *Die Taal* ever since.

Another thing that got Daluxolo a few extra backhanders was addressing his captors as 'sir.' A black person addressing an Afrikaner male in those days was expected to say '*Baas*', with or without his name. If he was addressing an Afrikaner female the correct form of address was 'Missus' or 'Madam'. Any form of deviation, like using a first name, would have the female complaining to her man: 'That black is cheeky', and he'd be for the high jump. A cheeky black was one who didn't openly demonstrate his subservience to whites. Poor Daluxolo had no idea of this and thought that when he called his police captors 'Sir' he was just being polite.

He was left suspended from the bar for many days and nights. When he needed the toilet he had no option but to do it in his pants instead. He was given no food. It was not long before he was just a horrible-smelling piece of human flesh. The policemen used to come singly or in pairs several times a day to assault him as he hung there. After that entertainment they would light cigarettes and stand chatting about other things. They did not even ask him specific questions about his activities for the ANC.

It seems to be an entrenched culture even to the present day for many South African policemen to use violence against those arrested, especially if they are black. Even the Police Commissioner, Jackie Selebi, himself a black, has admitted the scale of the problem. But according to him it's the job of the prosecutors, not his office, to deal with violent policemen. If that's the case, the violence will continue, because for the complaint to get to the prosecutor's desk the police must take it there. And how many policemen will rat on their colleagues?

South African policemen, it has been suggested, should receive training in human rights. I believe they know human rights very well — but only white human rights. That's why both black and white policemen rarely ill-treat a white suspect. They respect his human rights. When a white cop is violent towards a black suspect it is an issue of racism. When a black policemen uses violence on a black suspect the issue is sycophancy — a desire to please one's masters.

One day Daluxolo heard Matome, a black police informer who was cleaning the floor outside the cell, talking to no one in particular but loud enough for him to hear.

'Why', he asked, 'do ANC people get themselves killed by refusing to address white policemen as *baas*? What's wrong with calling them *baas*? Is it so important? I really cannot understand you ANC people.'

As a cleaner, Motome was well placed to be an informer in both directions. He had seen how viciously Daluxolo had been tortured and he knew it was because he hadn't addressed Rooi Rus Swanepoel and Piet Ferreira as *baas*. What Matome didn't realise was that Daluxolo had no idea the solution to his problem was so simple. But suddenly he saw the light.

He waited until Piet Ferreira came into the room where he was hanging from the beam.

'*Baas* Piet, May I have some water. Please, *Baas* Piet.'

Piet Ferreira became almost berserk with happiness. He ran back through the door and shouted to Swanepoel at the top of his voice:

'Rooi Rus, *kom hoor, kom hoor. Die Zoeloetjie kom nou reg*!' (Come and listen. The little Zulu is starting to come right!)

Rooi Rus came thundering into the room and Daluxolo greeted him.

'Good morning, *Baas*.'

Daluxolo looked at the two idiots with contempt as they almost danced for joy.

'Unlock him Piet, unlock him. The little Zulu is all right now. *Die baklei is uit*' (His fighting is finished).

Daluxolo was uncuffed and he collapsed in a heap on the floor. They called for Matome and told him to give him a hot bath, clean clothing and food. While he had spoken to them in English he had used the magic word *baas*, so all was forgiven. To think they might have beaten him to death over it!

After this episode Daluxolo was transferred to Pretoria Central Prison. Rooi Rus Swanepoel remained the Security Branch officer investigating the charges against him, but he was no longer violent having won the battle of the '*Baas*'. He concentrated on demonstrating to Daluxolo how well informed he was about the ANC and MK.

Daluxolo was still indignant when he told me the story. 'Thula, he wasn't interested in getting information from me. Instead he was telling me things I didn't know about the ANC and MK. It became very clear to me that the Security Branch was getting its information from very highly placed sources in the ANC. He boasted that he could tell me anything I wanted to know about MK. It was frightening.'

Rooi Rus told him what had been discussed by the OAU's Liberation Committee and the National Executive Committee of the ANC.

'We have people in African governments, Daluxolo, highly placed people who denounce apartheid during the day and then fly to Pretoria at night to ask for money. Do you believe that those kaffirs sitting at the OAU's HQ cannot be bribed to tell us what African heads of state are planning against us? We even have people in the communist states where you go for training. We have other people who sit in OR Tambo's meetings and report to us. We could kill your Tambo just like that [he clicked his fingers in imitation of a gunshot] if we wanted to. But that wouldn't solve the problem. The ANC would only appoint someone else in his place and trouble would continue. We find it better to leave him where he is and get a constant flow of information about the latest plans he is hatching against us. They can send you for training anywhere in the world and we'll know about it. Then when they send you back to South Africa they'll tell us so we can wait for you and blow you to bits.'

Daluxolo found himself listening to Swanepoel, fascinated. He told Swanepoel virtually nothing except where he was trained and when. He didn't have to say more.

'You don't have any information to give us, Zoeloetjie, but do you know why? It's because we know everything about you and your organisation. When you crossed into Rhodesia we knew exactly when and where it was going to happen. Then for no good reason that damned Tambo changed his plans. Without that we could have destroyed the whole lot of you including him.'

Daluxolo spent the whole of 1968 in Pretoria Central Prison. Derek visited him in an attempt to persuade him to become a turncoat like him. Daluxolo refused. Derek insisted that the struggle had failed and that the best solution was to join the winning side. Daluxolo told him to go to hell. In the end Derek gave up and stopped visiting him.

(Above) Thula's grandfather Blanjan Mhlathini ...opela. He instilled Thula with the glories of ...ulu history.

(Above) Thula when he joined MK as a young man.

(Left) Rev Japhta Skumbuzo Luthuli, Daluxolo's father. He sent him into exile to join MK when he was only 15.

(Above and right) Grainy photographs showing MK cadres undergoing training in an external country.

(Left) Zolile Nqose, a member of the Luthuli Detachment, shown as a major-general in the SANDF.

(Above) Oliver Tambo. President of the ANC at the time of the Wankie Campaign.

(Above) MK's Chief of Staff, Lennox Tjali (nom de guerre Mjojo Mxwaku) who volunteered to fight with the Luthuli Detachment. Shown here as a major-general in the SANDF.

(Below) Joe Modise, MK's commander-in-chief.

(Below) Chris Hani volunteered for the Luthuli Detachment and became the chief political commissar of the combined MK/ZIPRA force.

(Above) AK47 with scabbard and bayonet. This and the SKS this were the most common weapons carried by the Luthuli Detachment.

(Right) RPG2 rocket launcher with rocket and booster.

(Right) Carry-pack for RPG2 rockets.

Top left) Tokarev pistols. Soviet, Hungarian, North Korean, Chinese and Yugoslavian models.

Top right) Various types of water bottles

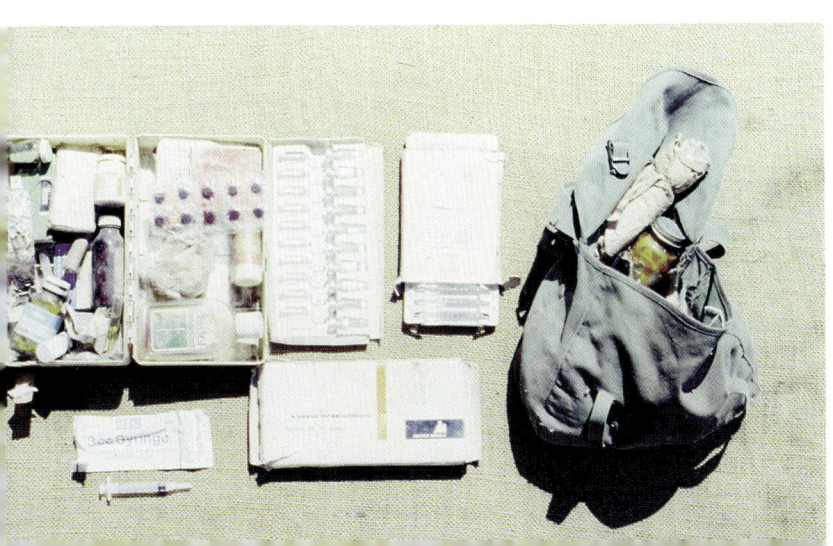

(Above) Simonov (SKS) semi-automatic carbine. Top to bottom Chinese type 56, Soviet model and Chicom T56 with handmade stock.

(Left) Medical kit.

(Above) The mighty Zambezi River's third gorge below the Victoria Falls illustrates the hazards of the crossing.

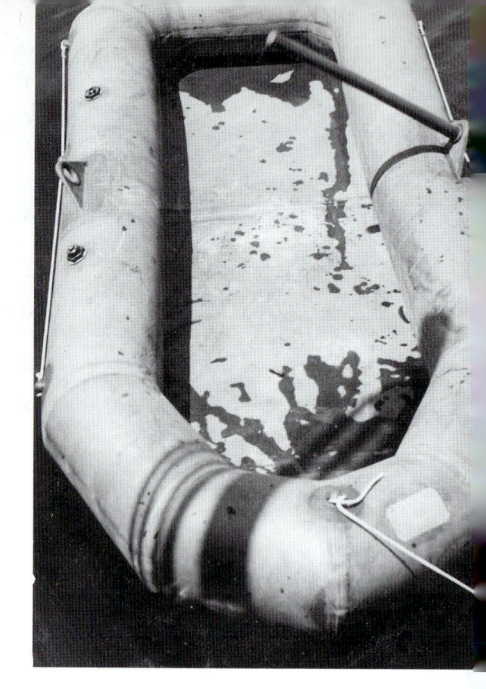

(Above) Soviet-supplied rubber boats used to cross the Zambezi River.

(Below) The Victoria Falls and some of its gorges seen from the air.

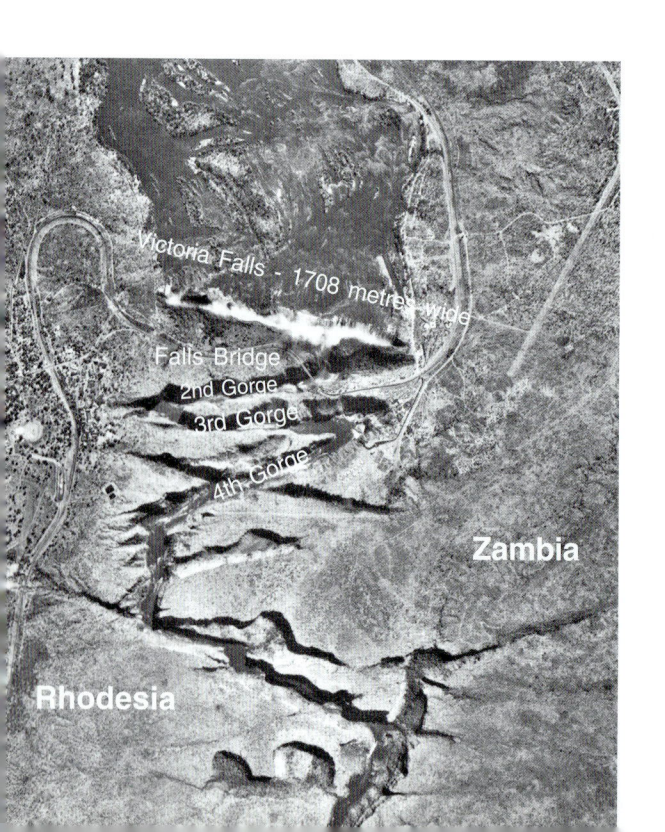

(Below) Joshua Nkomo medallions carried by ZIPRA guerrillas.

(Right) A selection of boots worn by MK and ZIPRA Wankie campaigners. The Rhodesian Security Forces found the Cuban boots (centre) with their figure of 8 sole pattern the easiest to track.

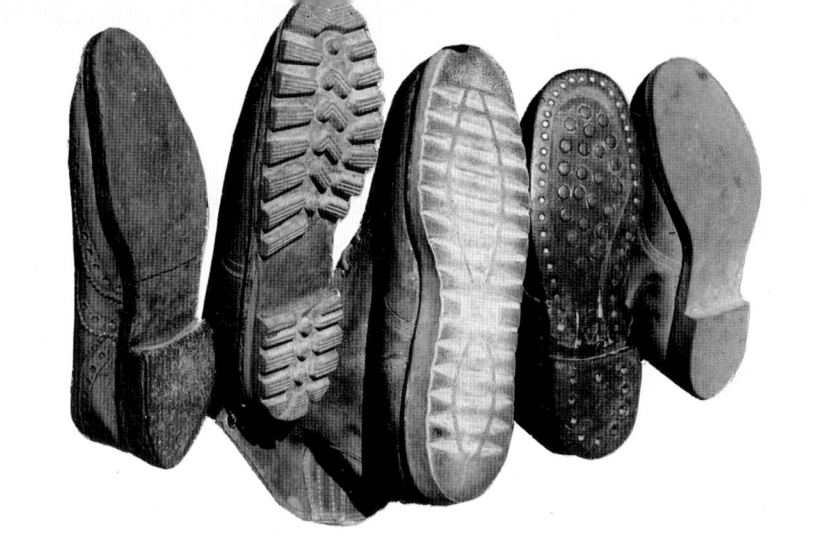

(Left and below) British South Africa Police photographs of captured MK and ZIPRA kit and equipment.

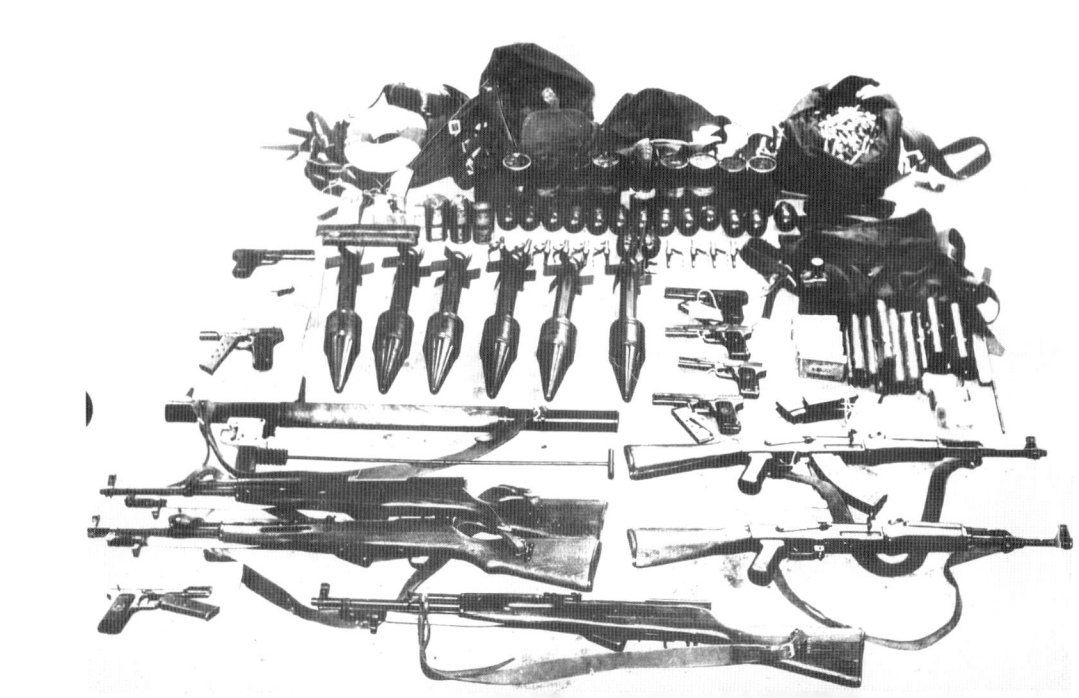

(Above BSAP photographs). (Left) Model wearing captured uniform with AK47 and pack. (Right) Model wearing Soviet Army pattern uniform with SKS carbine.

(Below) Thula's father Simo Bopela (left) and Oscar 'Mash' Mashengele (2nd right middle row) in group photograph of teachers at Chikore Mission. Both assisted Thula and Daluxolo is their attempts to escape from Rhodesia.

In the 80s and 90s a state of war existed between the ANC aligned United Democratic Front (UDF) and the Inkatha Freedom Party (IFP). The army was frequently committed to keep the peace.

(Above) A young UDF comrade carrying a tyre during disturbances in KwaMashu. It was the UDF's necklacing tactics that disgusted Daluxolo and prompted him to switch his support to the IFP.

(Above) Daluxolo (centre in dinner jacket) at his wedding in 1992. The guests were members of the IFP's Caprivi-trained hit squads of which he was chief political commissar and commander-in-chief.

(Left) Daluxolo on his release from prison on Robben Island, 1980.

(Above) Natal and KwaZulu were torn apart by riots and revolts caused by black political dissatisfaction.

(Left) Mrs Christobel Nhlumayo and her son — refugees after armed attackers torched their home at Nkapini near Margate.

(Below) A country store torched because the owner supported the 'wrong' party.

(Above) A member of the SAP's Internal Stability Unit holds the remains of a petrol bomb that gutted a house in KwaMashu.

(Below) Police officers investigate the scene of kangaroo court lynchings at Bhambayi.

(Above) A fireman looks on as smoke pours from the windows of Glebelands Hostel in Umlazi after it was torched.

(Left) Thandazile Khomo demonstrates how she saved herself from armed attackers by hiding behind a headboard.

(Below) Peace parade. People of all factions became sick of the killings. Thousands of factory workers line Sea Cow Lake Road waving as cars with headlights on drive past.

(Top left) IFP Minister Dr Frank Mdialose talks to Chief Everson Xolo at the Mvutshini massacre scene.

(Above) Nompululelo Shozi (14) (centre) was lucky to be alive after her brother and his girlfriend were murdered in an armed attack. Neighbours keep vigil at her home.

(Left) Utter despair written on the face of a KwaMashu resident who lost everything after an armed attack.

(Above) The National Party government allowed Zulus, but no other tribesmen, to carry traditional weapons in public.

(Left) Everyone hits the deck when gunfire erupts outside a stadium where an election rally was in progress.

(Right) Medics treat the wounded. When Zulus armed with traditional weapons marched on the ANC's HQ at Shell House in Johannesburg there was an armed confrontation. 11 Zulus were shot dead and many others wounded.

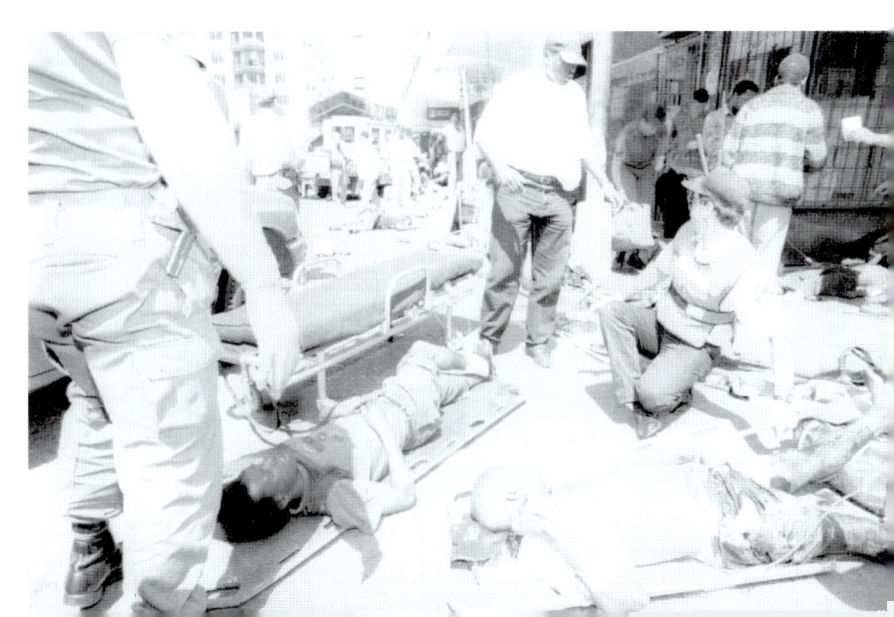

(Left) Thula, who had cut his ties with MK, is seen here with Cherry at a formal Eskom dinner. Daluxolo sought him out and requested he act as a go-between with the ANC to negotiate the withdrawal of his hit squads from the IFP/UDF struggle.

(Above left). Thula arranged for Daluxolo to see the ANC's Intelligence Chief in Natal, Jacob Zuma.

(Above right). President FW de Klerk and Nelson Mandela during the CODESA negotiations. Zuma arranged for Daluxolo to meet Nelson Mandela and the withdrawal of the IFP hit squads was negotiated.

(Left) Lt Col Daluxolo Luthuli, SANDF, receiving medals from Army Chief Lt-Gen Romano — also ex-MK — 2003.

20

Letter from the gallows

There's a distinct difference between a soldier dying in the heat of battle and one dying within the stark walls of the hangman's execution chamber. Dying in battle is sudden, unexpected and frequently without pain, but dying by the hangman's noose is another story.

Here's how the system worked in Rhodesia. After sentence had been passed, there was a waiting period while your case automatically went to the Appellate Division where it was examined and discussed by senior judges in the land. It could be months before you learned from your lawyer that your appeal had been allowed or dismissed. From that point on you knew that without doubt you were going to die. Nobody told you exactly when it would happen — it could be any day. But what did you do in the meantime?

A condemned prisoner lives with death each. He thinks and worries about it. He has to face the fact that one fine day his life will be snuffed out. He enters into a lonely state of mind because dying is a very lonely and personal business. Every person dies alone and reacts to the act of dying in his own way. One person might wake up one day and say to himself: What the hell! What if I die? No big deal. Everybody dies sooner or later.

But not everybody can be that philosophical about ceasing to exist. Most people fear death. It is a mystery and nobody knows what it's like to die and what happens afterwards — if anything. The fear of the unknown becomes overwhelming. One tries to cling to life, hoping that somehow it's just a bad dream. Refusing to accept that he is going to die is the worst thing a Death Row prisoner can do. It has nothing to do with being brave or cowardly. It's simply a necessity to accept the inevitable. No one has said that it's easy, but that's the key to the whole matter — accepting the inevitable.

Christians believe that when they die they will go to a beautiful place called heaven. They should find it easy to die because they have eternal life to look forward to. Yet even Christians tremble and cringe when death looms up in front of them. And what about a man who has no religion? What does he have to look forward to beyond the grave? I was such a man.

I heard that my appeal against the death sentence had been dismissed and that the next government official who would deal with me was the hangman. I was 23 years old and it's not easy to die at that age. Having no religious beliefs made the prospect even grimmer because I had no hereafter to comfort me. Somehow I had to come to terms with reality.

Many friends have asked me to describe what it's like to be on Death Row knowing that the end is nigh. The story does not begin when one is about to face the hangman. For me it started a long time before that when I volunteered to be an MK soldier. A soldier going into battle knows that he can die at any moment. He must come to terms with that reality. If he doesn't he will run away from the battlefield when the bullets begin zinging around him. When the bombs begin to fall and mines explode beneath his feet, he will drop his gun and flee.

A soldier doesn't go into battle expecting to die — he expects to kill his enemy and survive. He is a fool, though, if the thought of death doesn't enter his head. He has to deal with it by minimising the importance of his life and maximising the cause he is fighting for. He needs to accept that there is a more important goal out there than his life. He must convince himself that his death will mean freedom to a nation that's oppressed. He balances his life against the many lives of those he will free from tyranny. At that point the possibility of losing one's own life becomes bearable. That gives him the courage to sing his battle song and march into combat with a firm step.

In battle, though, one is armed and able to shoot at and kill those trying to take one's life. If one is a guerrilla in Africa, there is probably thick bush to duck into if the enemy seems overwhelming. In Death Row, however, there are no AK47s and SKS rifles to defend oneself. There is nothing to strike back with except one's spirit. Death is certain and the spirit is what needs to be prepared and strengthened for the ordeal that lies ahead. If one can achieve that, the hangman will hear a song of freedom in his execution chamber and not the whimpers of men crying in terror and begging for mercy.

The situation I found in the MK camps had not convinced me that our revolution would triumph. I had seen tribalism fuelled by high-ranking people in the organisation rear its ugly head amongst the soldiers. Our military leaders had not shared the hardships of the camps, nor had they led us into battle. After becoming a prisoner in enemy hands I had seen evidence that the revolution was being betrayed by senior members of the ANC. A policeman had told me that although we were excellent fighters, we wouldn't win because they were aware of our operations long before they commenced.

I sat with these thoughts mulling through my mind at the most crucial time of my life. I had no certainty that my people would be freed. The ANC slogans proclaimed that 'Victory is certain', but was it? I needed to convince myself before I could begin the process of steeling myself to face the hangman. There was even division of opinion in prison and there were power-mongers and traitors among us. There was not a single leader on Death Row who I could turn to for strength. But I needed to find that strength and find it fast.

I remembered Nelson Mandela's speech when he and the other leaders were on trial for their lives. It was prefaced: *Why I am Prepared to Die*. I had read the speech in Dar-es-Salaam and when I thought about it now, I suddenly felt powerful emotions inside me. I began to feel strong, but I still needed something infinitely more powerful than that. I recalled Fidel Castro's speech, *History Will Absolve Me*, when he stood trial in Havana after the failure of the raid on Moncada Barracks. I looked for more strength, and at last I found it.

I remembered the stories my grandfather, Mhlathini ka Dambuza ka Batshazwayo had told us when we were young. I remembered how the great Zulu regiments had rolled across the plains in their charge towards Blood River. In my mind's eye I could picture the 16 000 war shields, assegais and battle clubs of the impis. I could hear the roar of the cannon and the crack of rifles as the enemy fired into their ranks. The warriors fell but a louder cry deafened my ears as I pictured the battle in my mind. It was the cry: '*Uyadela wena osulapho*' (We envy you who have fallen), shouted by the warriors who were still charging as the river turned red with blood. Yes, and that great general, Ndlela ka Sompisi, led the charge from the front and not from the rear.

I saw that outstanding 70-year-old general, Ntshingwayo ka Mahole ka Khoza, leading the impis in 1879 as they rolled across the hills towards Isandlwana straight into the mouths of the British cannon and the massed rifles. I saw the Zulu army waver as the British fire reached a crescendo. Then a British officer, Lieutenant-Colonel Pulleine, seeing the Zulu army pause, called on them to surrender.

The commander of uKhandampemvu regiment, Mkhosana kaMvundlana of the Biyela people stood tall and rallied his men: '*OkaNdaba akashongo njalo*!' (The king didn't send us here to negotiate with the British).

The men raised their war-shields and resumed their charge.

The rest is history.

I sprang to my feet in my lonely cell, my mind on fire with mental pictures of my ancestors stabbing and dying in the maelstrom of battle. I began to laugh at myself. Thula, how could you even begin to worry about death when your grandfather spent so much time preparing you for this moment? I sat down and lit a cigarette. I was ready. I reminded myself that I came from a people who knew how to kill their enemies — a people who knew how to die.

I had won my battle with fear, the fear of dying. Greater men than me, men like King Cetshwayo '*Uzulu laduma obala lakungemunga kungemtholo* (The thunder that crashed above Isandlwana hill), had died. Who was Thula Bopela in this larger scheme of things? Shaka Zulu and other extraordinary men of valour — Nozishada ka Maqhoboza, Mkhosana ka Mvundlana of the uKhandampemvu and the victor of Isandlwana, Ntshingwayo ka Mahole — had died for their beliefs.

A ZAPU man, Chirisa Chimsoro, had been sentenced to death for killing an African chief who was collaborating with the government. He and his friend Jeremiah had blasted the chief with a shotgun. Chimsoro along with Jeremiah and four others were taken from B-Hall. They were to be hanged at A-Hall on the Monday morning. Before the time came to surrender himself to the hangman he wrote a letter to his comrades.

> Dear Comrades,
> It's Monday at three in the morning. It's the last day. I will see sunrise, but I shall not see the sun set. No matter, what must be must be. We go to face the hangman at nine today.
> I want to leave you hope, comrades, because people in our circumstances need hope.

We need to see beyond the terrible valley of death to the hills beyond. I have seen the hills beyond, even before descending into the valley of darkness today. My creator and my ancestors have come to me and have shown me the beauty that lies beyond. I want to share it with you, so that you also might have courage and hope.

I went to sleep last night at ten in the evening. I had a dream. I dreamt I was running on a meadow, a meadow of lush green grass. There were no trees and the ground was as flat as a plate. I ran gathering speed and began to rise in the same way that an aeroplane rises when it takes off. I flew straight into the blue sky.

I saw white clouds above me and I rose towards them. Before I got into clouds, a thought occurred to me, that if I went into the clouds and beyond I might not return to Earth. I decided to turn back and fly back to Earth. Then a strange thing happened.

An old woman, very, very, old, came through the clouds and spoke to me. She had snow-white hair and could have been a thousand years old. Yet there were no wrinkles on her face. She had the face of a very beautiful young woman. She spoke to me.

Chirisa, don't turn back. Come through the clouds and go with me, because the land to where you are about to go is a beautiful land. It's a land such as you have never seen before. It's the land of the spirits. I have been sent by your great-great-great parents to lead you to that world. It's the world that people on Earth speak about, but have no idea what it looks like. Christians call it heaven. Africans call it the Land of the Ancestors, but nobody knows what it looks like. Before I lead you there, you have a right to know what it looks like.

In the land you are about to enter there are no white, black or yellow men. They are all spirits, human beings with spiritual bodies. Their bodies are like the one you see on me. The bodies we have don't feel hunger, pain or fatigue. They cannot be stopped by material obstacles like walls and glass. They are spiritual bodies.

The quality of the spirit is what determines one's status in the world I come from. The quality is derived from the kind of person you were when on Earth. Everything is based on quality. The Supreme Spirit, the Spirit that rules this Land is a pure Spirit. No other spirits are pure, only the Supreme Spirit. The Christians call this Spirit God, the Muslims call It Allah. The Red Indians call It Manitou, the Zulus call It Nkulunkulu (the Great Great One), the BaSotho call It Modimo, and you Shonas call It Mwari. The Kikuyu of Kenya call it Ngai, and the Hindus call It Shiva. Different nations call this Spirit by different names, but they are referring to the same one. This Spirit is the Source of all life, and all life returns to It in the end.

This Spirit sends human spirits out to work out their quality on Earth to determine what they shall be at the end of their days on Earth. The Spirit puts its Law into the spirit that it sends to Earth and when that spirit returns, the Great Spirit will assess and classify the quality of the spirit it has called back to Itself.

Chirisa, you have been tried and condemned by the rulers of the Earth, and they have found you guilty of killing a chief and labelled you a murderer. No matter, the Great Spirit has passed judgement on you and that judgement is favourable. That's why I'm here, because in the eyes of the Spirit you are innocent. You have been judged by the rules of men who came to our land and raped it and set themselves up as the government and made laws. These laws, in the eyes of the Great Spirit have no validity, because the people who have made them are thieves of the land and murderers. A criminal cannot pass judgement. If it does, the judgement will be invalid in the eyes of the Great Spirit.

The great in the land you are about to enter are those who obeyed the laws the Great

Spirit placed inside them when It sent them into the World and not earthly laws made by powerful men. It does not count in this world that you are white or black. The white man may be great on Earth, and even call his race God's chosen. But the Supreme Spirit has not chosen any race above others. All men and women are equal in the eyes of the Supreme Spirit. He judges them according to the degree to which they have adhered to His law while they were on Earth.

Your people, the black people will also fall under the same curse, for their hearts will be seduced by power and wealth. Today you are an oppressed people, so you think the white people are evil. Yes, the white people have done evil things in the eyes of the Supreme Spirit. But when you get your freedom, you will be oppressed by a black ruler. For people are neither black nor white, they either adhere to the law of the Supreme Spirit or they won't. Only after you have had a black ruler and he has oppressed you, even worse than the white man, will you understand that seeking justice on Earth is a futile business.

Justice, Love, and Law are properties of the Supreme Spirit. You will never find these things in the World. They find expression only in the quality of the Supreme Spirit, who rules the World where I shall now lead you to, my child. Come, Chirisa, it's getting late. Let us go to the World of the Supreme Spirit. Turn your back away from the Earth. You will lose nothing thereby.

Comrades, I have told you the vision that has been given to me before I cross the Dark Valley of Death. I am strong enough to face the hangman and die, because I have been shown what is to happen to me hereafter. When your time to cross the Dark Valley comes, remember what I have said. It's better where you go than where you come from.
Yours in the struggle,
Chirisa.

At 07:30 Chirisa and the others about to be hanged were taken from their cells and escorted to a small chapel where Father Clarke, the prison chaplain, invited them to make their last confessions.

'The world has condemned your bodies to death, gentlemen. If you confess your sins before God and receive absolution, you shall enter into eternal rest for your sins will have been wiped away. Your bodies will die, but your spirits shall live. Claim the inheritance that's yours through the Blood of Jesus Christ, who died on the Cross to remove all sins and give pardon to those who invoke His Name!'

'Father Clarke, let us proceed to the place of execution. Don't detain us. You represent an iniquitous system and you cannot arbitrate between us and the Supreme Being. Only He qualifies to hear our sins, for He, only He, has the capacity to judge. Let us through', Chirisa said speaking for all the condemned men.

Father Clarke stood aside and the men marched on to the execution chamber. The hangman stood at the door of the gallows and welcomed them.

'My name is Cyril Thomson. I am your hangman. I am not the one who arrested you, neither am I the one who tried and sentenced you to death. I am the one who executes the decision that has been made by others. There is nothing personal between us. I am just doing my job. I trust you will face your ordeal like men.'

The six men entered the chamber and the prison guards began preparing them for execution. The condemned men began to sing. Chirisa led them in songs that are only sung on occasions like this. Their voices soared and the chamber filled with beautiful sounds that one didn't expect from the throats of men about to die. They had conquered fear, the fear of death, and there was nothing left to intimidate them anymore. Death is the final weapon of the oppressor. If you overcome the fear of death, then, and only then, do you become truly free.

The men were made to sit down. Their arms were handcuffed behind their backs. Leg irons were clamped around their ankles. Canvas bags of iron filings were strapped to each foot. Their weight equalled the weight of the man. Black hoods were slipped over their heads to conceal their agonies as they died. Nooses dropped from the roof of the execution chamber and were looped around their necks. They were ready for execution.

They sang loud and lustily. It was the last thing they would do before they entered eternity. At this grave moment, their response was that of men who truly wanted to be free. The preciousness of freedom is not properly understood by those who have never offered their lives in the fight for it. There were many who made brilliant speeches about freedom, but it was at no risk to their lives. There were others who sent men to fight for their mutual freedom while they remained safely in the rear. Freedom comes cheaply to such people so they cannot measure its true value.

But people who have trembled on the brink of death in the freedom fight have a standard by which to measure. To them freedom is more precious than life itself. After our liberation many people who were not involved in the struggle for freedom came to power. It's the way of the world that those who take no risks end up controlling those who do. And how do they use that power? Too often they abuse it and use it as a tool to enslave and impoverish those for whom the freedom fighters fought and gave their lives. If Chirisa and Jeremiah could only see what has become of their beloved Zimbabwe since liberation — the Zimbabwe they gave their lives for — they would indeed be very sorry men. They did their job and freed the people of Zimbabwe from white control at the cost of their lives. Those who remain behind have a duty to nurture that hard-earned freedom. But will they when they have never risked their lives to obtain it?

At 08:50 the phone in the prison superintendent's office rang. It was the President's office. His Excellency Clifford Dupont had granted four of the six prisoners a temporary stay of execution. The nooses were removed from their necks, the bags of iron filings unstrapped from their legs and they were taken from the execution chamber.

At 09:00 the trapdoor beneath the remaining two unfortunates opened and they dropped into empty space.

And so Chirisa and Jeremiah passed on to the land of the Supreme Spirit.

21

New Lock Prison, Pretoria

In 1969 Daluxolo was transferred to Natal where he and 11 other MK men were to stand trial in the Pietermaritzburg Supreme Court. Others charged with him for various offences were Linus Dlamini, Amos Lengisi, Matthews Ngcobo, Lawrence Phokanoka, Johannes Seleka (otherwise known as Mabhalane), Patrick Mathanjana, Silas Mogotsi, Ezra Sigwela, Thwalimfene Joyi and Donald Mathengele.

A pro-deo lawyer, a certain Mr Manger, was assigned to defend Daluxolo and his fellow accused. They had no confidence in this lawyer, however, and put an end to his services. The ANC made arrangements for an attorney, a Mr Bhagwandas, to represent them. Bhagwandas was paid through a London based company which enabled him to brief two QCs, Advocates Muller and Wilson, to represent the accused.

It's difficult to understand why it was thought necessary to retain the services of two QCs when it was obvious that such trials were usually mere formalities. Much has been said about the independence of the South African judiciary in those days. Yet, if we remind ourselves that judges were drawn from a section of the population that supported apartheid, the ideological orientation of the judges becomes an issue. It is likely that many of the judges, because they were appointed by a racist government, were racist themselves. Yet we still listen to arguments that the South African judiciary was independent in the days of apartheid.

Derek was the state's star witness. His real name, Leonard Mandla Nkosi, was revealed at the trial. He knew all the accused and was regarded as an expert witness on guerrilla warfare and MK activities.

Daluxolo was found guilty and sentenced to ten years hard labour — the maximum sentence under the Terrorism Act. The others were given varying terms depending on the circumstances of their cases. Matthews Ngcobo was sentenced to 20 years hard labour.

At last it was all over — the marching, starving, hiding and the tension of living in fear of being captured. The ordeal Daluxolo faced as a convicted freedom fighter was hard labour on Robben Island for ten years. Robben Island! The very name struck fear into the hearts of the toughest MK men. Now it is a World Heritage Site and tourists go there to enjoy themselves and walk over the ground where Nelson Mandela spent most of his 27 years of imprisonment.

The men expected to be sent to Robben Island almost immediately. Instead, they were taken to New Lock Prison, otherwise known as Pretoria Central. New Lock was where Death Row prisoners were kept while awaiting the outcomes of their appeals and where executions were carried out. Why it was necessary to incarcerate prisoners serving ten year sentences in such a prison is not really a mystery. It just demonstrates the inhumanity of the people who ran the South African legal system.

At New Lock a certain Colonel Aucamp came to listen to any complaints the prisoners might have. They soon learned, though, that immediately after lodging a complaint, their treatment became harsher. Yet they continued to complain. At mealtime the cell of a complaining convict would be opened and a plate tossed inside. A cursory examination of the plate showed signs of fresh food. It had obviously been emptied in the dustbin. The message was clear: we have food here, but you won't get any. Complain and you'll starve.

Daluxolo and his comrades were kept in a separate section used for political prisoners. Condemned prisoners, of which there were three categories, were kept in another section. There were those who had lost their appeals and who would be hanged any day; those whose appeals were still being considered; and those who had been condemned to death but who had not yet submitted their appeals. The prisoners whose appeals had been dismissed could be distinguished by their behaviour and they sang Christian songs day and night. They knew they would soon die.

Daluxolo was frequently removed from his cell and lined up outside the execution chamber along with Death Row inmates. There was a roll call of the men due for execution that day. When all the names had been read, a warder would brusquely tell Daluxolo that his name was not on the list for hanging. He would then be returned to his cell. This mental torture was meted out repeatedly to all the prisoners who had been given gaol sentences for 'terrorism' at Pietermaritzburg.

I asked him why they had been taken to a 'hanging prison' in the first place.

'Thula, have you forgotten how savage these Boers can be? It was their idea of fun and an expression of their opinion that we should have been sentenced to death.'

'Did you believe that they might have executed you?' I asked him. 'You knew your sentence was ten-years imprisonment so how could anyone bluff you that you might be hanged?'

'Those Boers had the power of life and death over black people. Maybe they would have hanged us and claimed later that there had been a mistake. Who could have stopped them? Or they might have hanged us, disposed of our bodies and claimed we had escaped. Who knows? They could have done anything to us in those days. You have no idea how nerve-wracking it was.'

'So each time they took you to the gallows you thought you were about to die?'

'Yes. From the day I was taken to Compol Building and found out how Rooi Rus Swanepoel and his friends treated me, I had resigned myself to death. After my father came to see me at Compol, I told myself it didn't matter what they did to me. I had talked to my father so he knew that I had carried out his instruction and fought for the cause. By the time I came to New Lock I was sure they'd kill me one way or the other.'

'Did your father visit you after you were taken to New Lock?'

'Yes, he came to see me at both places. At Compol he shouted my praise names which made me feel very strong.'

'I didn't know you had praise names, Daluxolo.'

'I have. He said: '*Inkunzi engqukuva abayikhuze ukuhlaba ingakahlabi*' (The young bullock they accused of goring other bullocks long before horns appeared on its head).

'Did the guards know what he was saying?'

'They couldn't understand his words, but they read the situation accurately. They brought my father there with the intention of intimidating me, but instead they heard him reciting poetry. Rooi Rus saw me smile at my father's words and realised he had made a mistake bringing him there. Why are you surprised that I have praise names? Don't you have them yourself?'

'I do.'

'What are they?'

'They call me: '*UmaBhunu bambuka ngamafelikiki kwelaseRhodesia*' (The one the Boers saw through their binoculars in Rhodesia).'

We both laughed, and looked at each other with renewed respect.

22

Robben Island

Daluxolo and his comrades were transported by Colonel Aucamp to Cape Town in private vans to avoid the danger of someone intercepting and freeing them. From Cape Town they crossed to Robben Island by boat.

A new structure called the *Sink Tronk* (Zinc Prison) had been recently built there and that's where they were taken. The political prisoners had been separated into three groups. B-Block was where Nelson Mandela and the other leaders were kept. The political prisoners called B-Block *Makhuluspan* (Big team). Then there was the General Section where political prisoners like Harry Gwala, Steve Tshwete and so on were kept. *Sink Tronk* became the third section.

Sink Tronk was constructed from corrugated iron and was just a huge open hall where the prisoners slept on the floor. There were no separate cells and no privacy. At one end of the hall was a shower and a toilet. A prisoner using the toilet did so in full view of the rest of the prisoners. You could say that these men got to know each other intimately!

On arrival each prisoner was issued three blankets, a sisal mat, soap, toothbrush, toothpaste and a face towel and was given a haircut. A prison haircut is standard and has nothing to do with style, choice or the prisoner's personality — they were simply shaved bald. They were given prison numbers which became their official names. Daluxolo's number was 6/70 — meaning he was the sixth prisoner detained on Robben Island in 1970. Clothing comprised khaki shirts and shorts. They were given no footwear and summer and winter they went barefooted. In winter they were issued with khaki jackets which were withdrawn with the onset of summer.

A normal day began at 06:00. The prisoners had quick showers and were given a breakfast of mealie- meal porridge sweetened with brown sugar. Ground fire-blackened mealies did the job of coffee. After breakfast they were taken to the yard and issued with a four-pound hammer and a rubber ring with which to hold the rocks they had to crush. The rocks were hammered into gravel which was used to repair roads around the prison and even the prison walls. The warders, all white and mostly Afrikaans-speaking, stood guard at a distance with German Shepherd dogs.

Midday lunch consisted of mealie cobs and a whitish drink called *phuzamandla* (the drink of strength). It was so weak, though, that it gave the prisoners neither strength nor nourishment. The convicts would return to work and continue breaking rocks until 16:00. Then they would be lined up, searched and taken back to *Sink Tronk*. After washing they would get their evening meal which again would be mealie meal porridge with either chicken, fish or bean soup. The food was clearly not designed to nourish, but the prison authorities obviously believed it was the kind of food black prisoners deserved.

Lieutenant Fourie, a harsh and insensitive Afrikaner, ran the *Sink Tronk*. He never listened to complaints and always addressed prisoners in Afrikaans. Afrikaans was effectively the official language on the island. Those running the South African penal system knew only too well the kind of warder who would be harshest to black political prisoners — he was white, male and Afrikaans-speaking. It's no use arguing with us that not all Afrikaners were like that. The fact of the matter was that we never met any Afrikaners who treated black people decently and politely. We can only record what we saw, what was done to us and who did it.

A prisoner was allowed to write and receive one letter every six months and both the incoming and outgoing mail was heavily censored. The prison officials snipped off the parts of a letter that they decided were not appropriate for the prisoner to read. It was not unusual to receive a letter which showed only the salutation and the name of the person who wrote it. Cruelties of this nature tell you more about the mentality of the people carrying them out than anything else they say or do.

There were both ANC and PAC leaders on Robben Island. On the PAC side there was the organisation's president, Robert Sobukwe and other senior officials like Zeph Mothopeng, Clarence Makwetu, John Pokela and Selby Ngendane. On the ANC side were Nelson Mandela, Walter Sisulu, Govan Mbeki, Harry Gwala, Elias Motsoaledi, Ahmed Kathrada and others. The leaders of the parties spent many years together on Robben Island, but when released they were still just as divided as they had been when first imprisoned.

Many people have asked why these leaders didn't try to iron out their differences and unite the people.

Mandela says that from the day he arrived on Robben Island he believed that stretching out the hand of friendship to the PAC leadership was one of his main tasks. His approaches were rudely brushed aside. He said that their arrival on the island was seen as an 'encroachment on their territory' by the PAC leadership. They held several meetings with the PAC leaders, but men like Zeph Mothopeng regarded themselves as more militant than the ANC. Zeph believed that while on Robben Island the ANC prisoners should accept the leadership of the PAC. Some PAC leaders, Mandela said, even expressed regret that the ANC leaders hadn't been hanged!

African people are cursed with a leadership that always finds reasons for division, conflict and war. Unfortunately most African leaders see politics as an opportunity to acquire personal power and wealth. The leaders of the PAC and ANC had decades in which to patch up their differences but they didn't. Even to this day the two organisations remain divided and at loggerheads. It is difficult to predict a time when unity amongst black people will arrive because their leaders don't seem to want it.

What is an African leader anyway? It appears to us that any Tom, Dick or Harry who made political statements directed against the apartheid state was regarded by some people as a leader. It's very easy to become a 'leader' amongst African people. Then they discover that the 'leader' has become a billionaire while his followers are poorer than ever and the economy of the country is falling to pieces. Yet there is no shortage of people who still regard this 'rags-to-riches' politician as a leader. If the African people don't begin to more closely examine the characters of the people they call leaders — and stop mistaking demagogues and orators for leaders — their problems will be endless.

On Robben Island days became weeks, weeks became months and months became years. The essence of prison life is routine. The prisoner knows that for many years to come he will wake up at a specific time, in a specific place, do specific work and eat the same food. Prison officials resent anything likely to interrupt their routine. Change threatens the stability they are comfortable with. When outsiders like the Red Cross or magistrates visited the prison the prison officials became uneasy. They habitually lied to such visitors about the way they treated the prisoners. It prevented their routine from being disturbed.

Daluxolo was released in 1979 after completing his full ten years on Robben Island. Before leaving he was called aside by Curnick Ndlovu, a senior ANC leader from Natal. Curnick told him he was to join the Inkatha Freedom Party (IFP) once he got home. He explained that the IFP was a good umbrella under which to conduct MK activities. His task would be to use the IFP as a means to covertly recruit young men and women for MK for military training outside the country. He would also keep track of important IFP policy decisions and report back to the ANC. His handler would be Chris Hani who was operating clandestinely from Lesotho. Daluxolo was told the instructions had come from the island's top leadership. Linus Themba Dlamini was present during these discussions.

23

Death sentence commuted
A peep into the mind of an African leader

On 19 August 1969 my sentence was commuted to life imprisonment. I had been on Death Row for 21 months. Rev Father Clarke, the prison chaplain, broke the news to the prisoners concerned.

'Are you happy, Thula my son? Surely, this is great news?' the chaplain asked me.

'To be candid with you, Father, I'm not particularly happy', I replied truthfully.

'You amaze me. You have spent such a long time in this terrible place and have come so close to being removed from this world. How can you not be happy?'

'I have lived with the reality of death for so long Father, I have come to accept it. I'm not saying it was easy — it was very, very difficult — but I managed it. To accept death one needs to renounce life and do so genuinely and fully. When one has reached that point and then his life is suddenly tossed back to him, it is difficult to rejoice.'

'So you prepared yourself for death so well that you began to look forward to it? If we were not talking about dying, I would have said that it's academically interesting.'

'To beat the hangman Father, you have to surrender willingly what he plans to take from you by force. If you try to cling onto life and cry and beg the hangman for it, he will feel great satisfaction in hanging you. I surrendered my life completely so that I would be able to march and not crawl to the gallows. If you contemptuously fill the execution chamber with revolutionary singing, then the hangman's victory becomes a defeat. If you go to the gallows whimpering with fear and wetting your pants, your adversary will have triumphed.'

'I have seen many men go to their deaths in this prison, my son. As you have said, some sang bravely during their last minutes while others trembled and begged for mercy. Before this conversation I never understood what goes on in the minds of people about to die. Thank you and God bless you.'

We were taken to C-Hall which is next to B-Hall. There prisoners were kept in single cells. It was called solitary confinement and was supposed to play havoc with a prisoner's nerves. The warders put us in solitary as a punishment and hopefully to drive us mad. We had spent almost two years in single cells in B-Hall, so solitary had become a normal way of existence for us. We woke up at 06:00 and cleaned our cells. At 06:30 the cell doors were opened and we were counted. When that was over we went to shower and have breakfast. After that we were locked up until 10:00.

The hall was a three-storey building. At 10:00 prisoners on all floors on one side of the hall were let out to have a 30 minute spell of exercise in the prison yard. After that it would be the turn of the prisoners on the other side. In the afternoon the routine was repeated. This continued for days, weeks and months on end.

The ZAPU prisoners we had been with on Death Row said nothing about how we should behave towards ZANU prisoners. Everybody had prayed together and exchanged political views. We had all mixed easily together. On Christmas Day, for instance, food parcels brought to the prison by ZANU relatives were shared by everyone. In the two years we spent there we shared everything from cigarettes to news to food. Irrespective of affiliation, those so inclined prayed together and generally we saw ourselves as people faced by a common threat. When we came to C-Hall all that changed and suddenly the ZAPU prisoners wanted nothing to do with ZANU prisoners.

It was in this difficult political climate that I was privileged to gain an insight into the mind of one of Rhodesia's foremost nationalists — the Rev Ndabaningi Sithole, the ZANU president at the time. Not all of the Rhodesian black nationalist leaders went to gaol, although some claim nowadays that they were either 'in prison or in the bush.' What they mean is that they were in preventative detention in camps where they enjoyed all the privileges available to detainees. They could wear their own clothing, eat the food they chose or food brought to them by relatives. They had access to good medical treatment and were allowed to further their studies. Sithole was detained in such a place along with other ZANU leaders like Robert Mugabe, Edgar Tekere and Enos Nkala.

Then he got himself into trouble. The Rhodesian Special Branch arranged to have some of their men serve as prison warders to get information. A few of them got close to the reverend and whispered the slogan: '*Pamberi neZANU*' (Forward with ZANU). He was thrilled and even more so when they offered to smuggle his letters in and out of the detention centre.

'It's not right that when you write letters to your wife, *Mudara* [old man], they should be read by young white prison officers', they told him. 'Leave it to us. We'll smuggle your letters out and smuggle the replies back to you without the authorities knowing. Trust us, *Mudara*.'

Sithole trusted them because he believed they were ZANU supporters. He wrote letters to his wife, MaNxumalo, and the letters and replies were delivered safely. What he didn't know was that before his letters got to the addressee, Security Branch opened and read them, photocopied them and sent them on.

It was not long before he extended his writings to his ZANU underground people suggesting a plot. His idea was to have a bomb detonated in the cabinet room when Smith and his ministers were meeting. Sithole saw himself as some kind of African Guy Fawkes!

This correspondence fell into the hands of Special Branch. When everything was ready he wrote his final instructions about placing the bomb and when it should be detonated. This letter never reached the ZANU operatives charged with the mission. Instead, a police superintendent went to the detention centre and arrested Ndabaningi Sithole.

When he appeared in court on this charge, the prosecution literally destroyed his political career. The Director of Public Prosecutions, B J Treacy, called the police superintendent to the witness stand.

'When you told the accused you were arresting him on such a serious charge, what was his reaction?'

' M'lud, he turned the colour of khaki!'

This brought suppressed laughter from some spectators in court.

'What do you mean by "he turned the colour of khaki?"' BJ Treacy went on.

'M'lud, that's the closest a dark-skinned man like the Reverend can come to turning pale.'

'Pale, Superintendent? Do you mean pale with anger?'

'No, M'lud, pale with fright.'

'Silence in Court!' the judge barked to spectators who were laughing openly.

Worse was to come. Sithole took the witness stand and was cross-examined. It was a major mistake. He should never have allowed himself to be subjected to such expert and intensive questioning.

He was confident, though, that he could successfully hold his own against a wily lawyer like BJ Treacy.

'Reverend Sithole', Treacy began, 'you are the President of ZANU?'

'Yes, I am.'

'That position in the organisation also makes you the supreme commander of ZANLA?'

'It does, yes.'

'So as the supreme commander isn't it true that you hold the ultimate responsibility for the actions and activities of all ZANLA personnel?'

'That is correct.'

'It follows then, Reverend, that the murders of white farmers carried out by ZANLA men now awaiting execution at Salisbury Prison were your ultimate responsibility. They carried out those murders on your orders. Is that true, Reverend?'

Too late, Sithole saw the trap he had been led into. By admitting he was ZANLA's supreme commander with the ultimate authority over the actions of its men, he could be held responsible for the death of the white farmers.

'No, no, no!' he shouted. 'I didn't issue any orders to kill white farmers, my Lord!'

'This court is well aware you didn't issue the orders personally, Reverend Sithole', Treacy told him with a malicious smile. 'Your commanders issued the orders but as supreme commander the ultimate responsibility is yours.'

Reverend Ndabaningi Sithole was in serious trouble. His only way out was to condemn the killing of the white farmers, but by so doing he would denounce the actions of his own soldiers. If he did that the men awaiting execution would be reduced to the status of common murderers. But if he accepted the responsibility as supreme commander of ZANLA he might literally be placing a noose around his own neck. In a desperate attempt to save himself he denounced the killings. In doing so he destroyed his own career as a revolutionary leader.

The court understood his agony and adjourned until the following day. The newspapers went mad. The headlines screamed: '*ZANU leader denounces the actions of his own men.*' The following day the Reverend tried to repair the damage he had done to his political career. He argued that he had been confused by the speed at which the prosecution had fired the questions at him.

'Do you, then, Reverend, wish to withdraw any statement that you made to the court yesterday?' Treacy laughed at him.

'No, no. I only wish to place it on record that although I am ZANLA's Supreme Commander, I didn't issue the orders that led to those killings!'

There was no way out. He was given a six-year prison sentence, becoming the only nationalist leader to be convicted in a court of law and sent to prison.

He arrived in C-Hall just after we left Death Row. The place buzzed with the news. ZANU people were in the same hall with their president, but he had denounced their armed struggle. ZAPU was jubilant. This left their beloved Joshua Nkomo as the only credible political leader in Rhodesia. Ndabaningi had knocked himself out of the political equation. Even his followers didn't want to talk to him. We MK men were also told not to have anything to do with him because it was policy not to associate with ZANU people.

When our cells were opened in the morning for us to go for our 30 minutes exercise, we found ourselves in the same group as the reverend because he was on our side of the hall. I had seen him briefly in 1963 when I was living with my father and brother at Chipinga where the Sithole family also lived. My father had introduced me to the family along with Ndabaningi's wife MaNxumalo and her children. So I decided to approach and greet him. To my mind, you didn't visit a man's family, have a meal in his home and then behave as if you didn't know him. I wasn't going to kow-tow to a bunch of self-important nobodies simply because they believed that by not greeting a person you achieved some sort of political end.

'*Sawubona, Baba*' (Hallo father), I began.

Sithole spun around and stared at me.

'*Sawubona, mfana*' (Hallo, young man), he replied obviously puzzled. 'Who are you?'

'I'm Thula Bopela, son of Mr Bopela who teaches at Mount Selinda in Chipinga. I met you and your family in 1963.'

'Ahhh, I see. I know your father. It's good to hear oneself being greeted as *Baba*. The young men here call me *Mudara* [old man]. I feel as if I have been greeted by one of my own children. But why are you here, *mfana*?'

'I'm an MK soldier. We are military and political allies of ZAPU. We fought together in Wankie and I was captured.'

'Yes, I understand. We read about the fighting in Wankie and heard that South Africans were amongst the fighters. But what do you hope to gain by fighting in Zimbabwe?'

'The destruction of colonialism, whether it's in Zimbabwe, Namibia, Mozambique or South Africa itself.'

'Wonderful. You boys are true Africanists. But what should we do with you if ZANU — and not your ally ZAPU — comes to power?'

'It would be the correct thing if you acknowledge our role in Zimbabwe's liberation by granting us bases in the country from which we can operate against South Africa.'

My comrades, especially the ZAPU men, could have killed me with their looks for talking to the ZANU leader. They asked me afterwards what we had discussed and I told them.

'But Comrade Thula, we have all agreed not to talk to that man, so why are you doing so?' asked David Madziba, a ZAPU commissar.

'Some of you decided that we shouldn't talk to ZANU. We had no part in this decision. You just told us not talk to ZANU people', I answered.

'But comrade Thula, you are duty bound to abide by the decisions of the majority', he persisted.

'Comrade Thula, why is it you go against everything we decide to do?' Kayeni Dube added. 'At Death Row you insisted on wearing your red shirt. Now you want to fraternise with ZANU.'

'I oppose things I think are stupid. Despite wearing a red shirt they didn't execute me and here you are too. In Death Row you were friendly with ZANU people. Now that we're out of there, why should we take you seriously when you say we shouldn't have anything to do with them. When you promote sensible things I promise I'll listen.'

I continued having discussions with the Rev Sithole during exercise periods. I asked him why he broke away from ZAPU and formed ZANU.

'I concluded that ZAPU under Joshua Nkomo's leadership wasn't going to free Zimbabwe, so I decided to form an organisation that could achieve it. Nkomo is a coward. When ZAPU was banned he was out of the country. Instead of returning to mobilise the people he flew to London and created a leadership vacuum. I saw it as my duty to fill it, so I formed ZANU.'

'But *Baba* Sithole, is it right to create a split in the ranks of African nationalism on the basis of one man's weakness? ZAPU is the black people of Rhodesia who want freedom. It's not just Joshua Nkomo.'

'At that point Nkomo *was* ZAPU. Nobody dared criticise what he did and he had come to look on himself as a sort of demigod. In African politics, my boy, you cannot differ with the leader of an organisation and remain a member. The people would have killed me because they believe he is faultless. It happens all over Africa where followers see their leaders as little messiahs. And soon those leaders begin to think that they are. In Ghana they call Kwame Nkrumah *Osagyefo* — which means messiah.'

'I grant you that', I concurred. 'But you and *Baba* Nkomo have a history of division and violence amongst your followers. *Baba* Sithole, while you're in prison and *Baba* Nkomo is in detention, if another leader appeared from amongst the people and managed to unite and lead them to freedom, how would you react towards him after your release? Would you shake his hand, congratulate him on his achievement and pledge your support and loyalty to him?'

The reverend began to tremble and I thought he was going to have a seizure.

'*Mfana*, we are talking about power? '*Ubukhosi abutshelekwana, uyangizwa*' (You don't lend power to another person).

'We are talking about freedom and the liberation of the Zimbabwean people. We are not talking about political power.'

'Do you know the history of the Ndebele people, my boy?'

We discussed history. How King Mzilikazi learned that King Dingane of the Zulus had despatched a huge army under the command of General Ndlela ka Guqa ka Sompisi ka Nomasingila to engage him and his people in battle and destroy them. How Mzilikazi decided to cross the Limpopo River into Zimbabwe to save his people. How he split his people into two groups, placing his son Nkulumane in command of one group which then crossed into Zimbabwe. They met little opposition from the resident Karangas, settled down, built homes and planted crops. Mzilikazi led the other group and made his way through today's Botswana, got lost and ended up on the Zambezi River. Nkulumane's group saw their herds multiply and their crops ripen in the fields. But they couldn't begin harvesting because according to Zulu custom, a feast called *Inxwala or ukuchinsa iSelwa* (thanksgiving) had to be held before it could begin. Only the king could officiate, but he was nowhere to be found.

The *izinduna* (king's councillors) called a meeting and told the people that the king couldn't be found, after several attempts to do so. The people were told that, in the interests of national survival, it was necessary to solve the problem of succession.'

'We need to appoint somebody in the king's stead otherwise the people will starve and many will die of hunger', said an induna, General Zwangendaba. 'The king has a son, Prince Nkulumane, whom we appointed to lead us.'

The people approved and Prince Nkulumane was appointed in his father's place. But within a month King Mzilikazi reappeared.

'How can that sun rise before this one has set? How can there be two suns in the sky? It's an *umhlola*' (an abomination), were his comments when he discovered what had happened.

'And that is precisely what will be the position if another leader appears to take my place', the reverend said triumphantly. 'That's the question I would also ask if someone else became the first president of Zimbabwe while I was in prison. That would also be like having two suns in the sky. It would have been *umhlola*.'

I was amazed. He was the political leader of an African democratic organisation and here he was falling back on an monarchical analogy. Mzilikazi had the right to ask such a question because a new king could only be appointed after the old king died. Ndabaningi was no king, but clearly he saw himself as one. He accused Joshua Nkomo of believing he was a messiah while he was acting in the same way.

I pondered far into that night about the problem of power amongst African leaders. Power — not the liberation and freedom of the people — was their issue. The leaders mobilised the people to fight for freedom, but their only real concern was who got that power. Sithole would probably contest anyone else's right to rule and a civil war would result because there couldn't be 'two suns in the sky'. I trembled at the thought of what awaited the people of Zimbabwe under the leadership of such people.

I spoke to him again the next day.

'*Baba* Sithole', I asked. 'if you became the first president of a free Zimbabwe and the people realised that your policies and the way you governed were wrong, what could they do?'

'In a free Zimbabwe', he answered, 'there'll be freedom of speech and freedom of the press. Through those channels people will be able to express dissatisfaction to their president.'

'And if they did that and you still refused to listen, could they throw tomatoes and rotten eggs at you during a Freedom Day rally?'

'No, no, certainly not, *mfana*! We don't do such things to our African leaders. We respect them. In Europe, yes, such things are accepted, but not here in Africa.'

'*Baba*', we are just soldiers. If you refuse to accept protestations in the form of tomatoes or rotten eggs on your face, would you be happier with a bullet?'

'You mean people might assassinate me?'

'Yes, leaders who suppress peaceful protests don't leave people with any alternative.'

'A tomato is infinitely more preferable to a bullet', the reverend answered, clearly disturbed that such a thing might ever be contemplated against him.

Ndabaningi was consistent if nothing else. When Bishop Muzorewa became prime minister of the government of national unity in Zimbabwe-Rhodesia in 1979, Sithole refused to recognise him. Muzorewa might have been a puppet of the Rhodesia Front party, but I doubt he would have accepted anyone other than himself. By then he had been ousted by Robert Mugabe and others as the ZANU leader. The ZANU-Ndoga party he led had been reduced to a mere shadow of the party it once was, but he didn't seem to realise it.

The power struggles of African leaders pose serious problems. They cause coups d'etat, the murder of leaders and ongoing civil wars. They also bring untold suffering to the African people. The leaders claim they hate colonialism and maybe they do, but they certainly love the trappings of colonialism — state houses, limousines, titles, travelling overseas at taxpayers' expense, conferences in five-star hotels that deliver no solutions, bodyguards, executive jets and the rest. Most successful African politicians enter politics as poor township boys, but by the time they exit, most are billionaires. There is a direct relationship between power and wealth in Africa. Politics is a business and a very lucrative one. The people who vote the politicians into power, however, become progressively impoverished and dissent is ruthlessly suppressed. That's the irony of African revolutionary struggles.

24

Khami Maximum Security Prison

We were transferred from Salisbury to the Khami Maximum Security Prison near to Bulawayo in 1970. My new prison number was 895/70 which denoted that I was the 895th prisoner detained in Khami in 1970. At that time only political prisoners were kept there. Two-metre high walls surrounded the maximum security area, with towers at the corners mounted with machine guns. Guards with German Shepherd dogs patrolled the inner and outer courtyards around the clock.

We were taken through the administration block to a wide empty courtyard. We were ordered to strip and were issued with white cotton shirts and shorts. The maximum security area there was made up of A and B halls. All cells in B-Hall were single ones and that's where we were taken.

A normal day at Khami began with the arrival of the guards to take over from the night shift at 06:00. First there was a head count. Then each prisoner brought out his night pot, emptied it in the toilets, washed it and returned it to his cell. After that it was the showers. The water was always cold, summer and winter. We were not allowed face cloths or towels so we had to wash with our hands and stay wet. The time allowed for bathing was ten minutes, after which we donned our uniforms. This, of course, made them wet and in winter we shivered with cold. We walked barefoot throughout the 11 years I spent at Khami.

Breakfast was sadza — a stiff lump of cooked mealie meal that the Rhodesians loved. Burnt mealies ground into a powder did for coffee and we welcomed it because at least it was hot. At 07:00 we were lined up and searched. From there we marched to the quarry where we performed hard labour — and hard it was. A ladder was lowered and we descended to the bottom. Awaiting us were holders made of rubber to grasp the rock, mesh eye protectors, four pound hammers and a few fourteen-pound hammers. Our job was to crush rocks into tennis ball size and reduce those into gravel. It was tough and tedious work. The guards stood at the top of the quarry continually shouting at us to get on with our work and stop talking.

At about 10:00 we climbed out of the quarry leaving our tools behind. We were searched and given the midday meal. Again it was sadza, this time with rotten vegetables or a piece of meat the size of a toenail. After that we would be searched once more and locked up in our cells. The guards would go for their own lunch leaving a skeleton staff on duty. At 12:30 the other guards would return, open our cells and search us. We then returned to the quarry and continued crushing rock until 15:30 when we would again leave the quarry. At 16:00 they fed us more sadza with vegetables. After another search we were locked up for the night. By 17:00 a prisoner's day was finished. It was a soul-destroying routine.

Prisoners were issued with a sisal mat and three blankets and they slept on the floor. The condition of the blankets depended entirely on the Yards Officer. If he was a nasty and vindictive type the blankets were often threadbare. A more reasonable Yards Officer issued new and warm blankets. The blankets were manufactured on the premises, so there were always stacks available in the prison stores. Initially we were unlucky with our Yards Officer, a Mr Crater, who was an out-and-out fascist.

Crater, a former South African policeman, boasted that during his 25 years of service in the Force, he had been stationed in nearly every major city in South Africa. When talking he had the habit of clamping his jaws shut and speaking through his teeth. He had very little education, maybe a standard six, and he heartily disliked educated prisoners or those who were studying through correspondence courses. He sought ways and means to take away such study privileges and in 1972 he succeeded. All study privileges for political prisoners were stopped.

A delegation of inmates went to the Yards Office to plead to be allowed to continue their studies.

'We will be model prisoners, Mr Crater. We will work hard and behave ourselves if only you will allow us to study', the leader of the delegation told him.

'You don't understand my problem', Crater responded. 'If I allow you to study it means I will have converted Khami Prison into a university. I will be producing lawyers and economists. Word will soon spread that Khami Prison has become a university. Then all the black boys in the townships will come banging on my prison gates demanding to be let in so that they can also study. I really cannot allow that to happen.'

The matter ended there.

Crater was true to form when he was later approached by a delegation asking for an improvement in food and living conditions.

'I see your problem, Bopela, but you must appreciate mine. If I improve the food around here and give you new blankets and mattresses to sleep on, word will spread that Khami Prison has become a hotel. Then all the native boys and girls will demand to be let in so they can enjoy the good life. I really can't allow that.'

And he didn't.

The Red Cross was due to come to Khami to see for themselves how the prisoners were treated. The day before, Crater assembled the prisoners and asked if any of them had anything to complain about. They remained silent, knowing that complaining to him was pointless.

'Okay, if you have no complaints, I don't want to hear that any of you have complained to the Red Cross either. Do you understand?'

'But Mr Crater, what's the use of complaining to you?' a prisoner spoke up. 'We might as well try our luck with the Red Cross. Maybe there'll be some changes here if we speak to them.'

'Listen to me carefully', Crater said slowly and deliberately. 'I run this prison, not the Red Cross. You can complain to the Queen of England; you can write to the President of America or to Mao-Tse-tung for all I care. Only I can make things happen at Khami. But if you dare to complain to the Red Cross I will make your lives miserable after they leave.'

We went ahead and complained to the Red Cross. When they left all hell broke loose.

Crater and a squad of ten black warders went to the cell of everyone who had complained. The assaults began and it was terrible. The black warders vied to outdo each other with their brutality. Their master, the nice Mr Crater, stood there looking on while his goons beat the hell out of us.

We were stripped naked, thrown into solitary confinement cells and deluged with buckets of water. The cells were empty of any kind of furnishing and had thick double doors which, when slammed shut, left the cell in pitch darkness. The flooded bare cement floor made sleep impossible. We were put on 'spare diet' which reduced our already limited food ration by 75%.

It was Crater who refused to allow us facecloths and towels. We would come in from the pits white with rock dust, stand under the cold shower and wash ourselves with the palms of our hands. We began to purchase face cloths from non-political prisoners. They were nothing more than strips torn from old discarded mattresses. A small section of cloth cost four packets of the cigarettes that were smuggled to us.

During the numerous daily searches we managed to hide these precious pieces of cloth under our arms, in our mouths or wherever. Inevitably, they would occasionally be found, confiscated and burnt. This meant saving cigarettes until one had accumulated another four packets — an extremely difficult thing to do if one was a smoker.

During one search a large number of facecloths were found and burnt before they marched us to the quarry to work. It was a cruel deed and left those affected badly depressed. Normally we chatted together while breaking rocks but there was little conversation that day. We were stewing with anger but didn't know what to do — a state of mind familiar to black people under oppressive white control.

A guy called Du Plooy had been appointed Yards Officer in Crater's place and he stood on the edge of the quarry and looked down at us. He obviously sensed our anger.

'Is everybody happy here?' he asked.

Boniface Mzondiwa, who normally wielded the 14-pound hammer, answered him.

'You ask if we happy. You give towels to white bandits [prison slang for convict] because they are your brothers. Yet you won't give to black bandits because you think they enemy. And you ask if we happy?'

Boniface had to repeat his pidgin English a few times before Du Plooy understood. He turned to Corporal Timitiya who was in charge of the guards on that shift.

'This prisoner is saying we only give towels to white prisoners. Black prisoners don't get them. Is that true, corporal?'

'Yes, sir', the corporal answered.

'But why corporal?'

'Sir, Mr Cunningham said we mustn't give them towels and Mr Crater carried it on.'

'But Cunningham left the service five years ago?'

'Yes, sir.'

Du Plooy went to the superintendent's office to query the order.

'Superintendent, the terrorists at the quarry are very angry. It wouldn't surprise me if we had a riot one of these days. They are angry because white prisoners get towels and black prisoners don't.'

'Who gave such a stupid instruction, Du Plooy? Was it you?'

'No, not me. It was old Cunningham and it was carried on by Crater.'

'But Cunningham's been gone for five years.'

'Yes, but his instruction remained in force.'

'Change it right now, Du Plooy.'

Du Plooy went to the prison workshop where the prisoners convicted of common law crimes worked. He instructed them to cut and trim large pieces of cloth about half a metre square. When we returned from the quarry we found them in our cells. We were later issued with proper towels.

We went to thank Boniface Mzondiwa whose pidgin English had got the message home. It was well known that although his English was poor, Boniface refused to allow other prisoners to interpret for him when he spoke to white prison officers.

'The reason is simple', he said. 'You educated blacks are cowards. When I say something that you think will make a white man angry, you change the substance of my speech. I remember telling a white man where I was working before I joined the struggle that he was a liar. The black man interpreting for me merely told the white man that I didn't believe him. The white man got very angry even with that.'

'Are you calling me a liar?' he yelled

'Yes, sir, you big liar', I shouted back.

'I was fired, of course, but after that I made up my mind never to allow educated blacks to interpret for me.'

The question of relationships between ZAPU and ZANU continued to disturb me. Soon after our arrival a meeting was called by ZAPU prisoners and the MK men were asked to attend. The issue of relationships between ZAPU and ZANU prisoners was discussed.

'ZANU is the enemy of the people of Zimbabwe', George Moyo said. 'We can understand why white people hate us and treat us the way they do. But ZANU people are Zimbabweans like us. They have sold out so we must crush them.'

'ZANU are Shona-speaking people like me, but they preach tribalism and mobilise people on tribal grounds', Manzonzo chipped in. 'That's unacceptable. *Mudara* [old man] Nkomo has tried to unite the people whether they are Shonas or Ndebeles. ZANU wants a purely Shona organisation. That will sow the seeds of tribalism which will destroy us even in a free Zimbabwe. So they must be destroyed first.'

'We expect our South African comrades to support us and not fraternise with the enemy', George Moyo continued. We don't talk to ZANU people. We won't even share

167

a cigarette with them. If we find them in a place where we can attack them, we do so. Can we count on the support of our MK comrades in this?'

'I believe we MK people must meet separately and thrash this matter out. The ANC's policies with regard to how we relate to political rivals are not the same as yours', I told the meeting.

There was a hurried consultation among our ZAPU allies.

'Our MK comrades can feel free to hold their meeting. I must stress, though, that any decision reached that is friendly to ZANU will be regarded as a declaration of hostility towards ZAPU', George said.

We moved away to hold a separate meeting. I could see by their faces that some of my comrades had been intimidated by George's closing remarks. There were 15 of us and we sat in a circle. Those present were William Motau, Blackie Molefe, Aubrey Mdletshe (died in exile), Henry Nsele (died in South Africa), George Tau, Freddy Mninzi, Petros June, Bothwell Tamana (died in exile), George Mothusi (died in prison), Reginald Hlatshwayo (died in prison), Ralph Mzamo, Joe Sithole (disappeared after 1980), Marshal Forster, Isaac Mapoto and myself.

There was no one among us to whom we looked for leadership. We were just common foot soldiers. Some opted to toe the ZAPU party line so as to remain in their good books and close to those controlling that organisation. Others were for following the normal ANC policy of being friendly to all liberation movements. I could see that we were going to be split right down the middle.

'We are in Rhodesia and allies of ZAPU, so I don't see how we can go against their policy', Freddy Mninzi opened the discussion.

'ZAPU is also the biggest liberation movement in this country and they will definitely come to power. If we offend them how long will our friendship last?' Henry Nsele wanted to know.

'If you say we shouldn't fraternise with ZANU, I can reluctantly accept that. But what if these guys expect us to spill the blood of ZANU members? I'm sorry, I won't do that', William Motau observed.

'Where does this policy of non-fraternisation come from? When we asked ZAPU's leaders in Lusaka how we should react if we bumped against ZANLA in the bush, Vice-President Chikerema unequivocally told us that we shouldn't attack ZANU. Who makes ZAPU policy? Is it the leaders or the followers?' asked Blackie Molefe.

'We must remind ourselves what our leaders ordered us to do', I interrupted. 'They said we would fight the Rhodesian and South African Security Forces — not ZANU. And remember how the ZAPU guys fled when we were confronted by the Security Forces in the bush? Now they have a newfound courage — courage to kill their own fellow Zimbabweans. I want nothing to do with that.'

'How are we going to develop the relationship we have with ZAPU if we go against their wishes?' Freddy Mninzi wanted to know.

'If you're my friend, Freddy, and I find you quarrelling with your brother at your home, can I take a knife and stab him to death to promote our relationship? I asked. 'Blood is thicker than water and one day you will denounce me for killing your brother. When the day comes that ZAPU people want to mend fences with their ZANU compatriots, they'll claim that it was us who caused trouble between them. Mark my words.'

'ZAPU will come to power in this country and we'll be foolish to buck them on this issue. We should think ahead, comrades', another prisoner said.

'I think I will speak to our ZAPU comrades and tell them we are not all of the same mind. Let those who don't wish to adopt the ZAPU position do so. I will support ZAPU', Ralph Mzamo said.

Only four of us thought differently. While ZAPU was free to do what they thought best in their country, we wouldn't be part of a campaign of violence against ZANU. We were well aware that it was likely we would face a lot of hostility, perhaps even violence, because of the position we had adopted.

In the prison yard prisoners grouped according to their political affiliation. There were the two large groups of ZAPU and ZANU. Volleyball clubs were also formed on this basis. When we began to recruit prison guards to the freedom struggle, they also had to affiliate to either ZANU or ZAPU. The four of us sat alone in what we called our nuclear-free zone.

Fights sometimes broke out between the ZANU and ZAPU groups. We remained clear and stayed out of the fray. In fact we usually ran to our cells to take shelter because the prison warders would wade in with riot batons and hit anything that moved. I had never seen anything like that fighting. It was plain stupid. I used to ask myself how such people could even think of ruling a country. It was obvious that the conflict wouldn't end when they came out of prison. It might even burgeon into a long and bloody civil war.

We sometimes held discussions with the ZAPU men who sought to shift us from our neutral stance but we always refused.

'What do you hope to achieve by killing ZANU people? They don't rule the country. Even if you killed them all you would still be without power. Power lies with Ian Smith and you are afraid to attack him', I would say.

'Tribalism, Comrade Thula, is as much an enemy of Africa as colonialism', Happy Mariri said to me.

'ZANU peddles tribalism and we will crush that while we are fighting against colonialism!'

'I oppose the idea of fighting Africans while the whites who took our land are left untouched. Let's say that ZANU comes to power and not yourselves. Won't they want to take revenge on you?'

'It seems to me, Comrade Thula, that you don't believe ZAPU will take power in a free Zimbabwe. Let me make it clear — the first black president of this country will be none other than His Excellency Joshua Mqabuko Nkomo. Doubting Thomases like yourself will be shot!'

'Let's leave the future to itself, but I will remember your words, Happy.'

Prison chaplains posed another problem. Most were priests who had failed to build congregations outside of prison because they were incompetent. There was the Rev

Mapondera of the Methodist Church, Father Magava of the Anglican Church and Father Ansgar Hoffman of the Catholic Church. They tried to get us to attend their sermons, but we refused. They were trained to preach to the converted, not to people who by political orientation were hostile to Christianity. Yet we were not communists. Our aversion to Christianity came from a belief that it was a white man's doctrine used to soften the blacks into accepting colonialism. It taught that one should love one's enemies, turn the other cheek and forgive 77 times over. They also preached that the poor are blessed and would inherit the kingdom of heaven.

'Pie in the sky to look forward to when you die', the prisoners laughed and walked away when prison chaplains tried to administer to them. The priests got angry because they were not used to people ridiculing their faith. Once Rev Mapondera instructed the guards to force the prisoners to listen to his sermon. When we still refused, the guards set dogs on us and beat us with batons.

'Does Rev Mapondera believe he can get people to heaven by force?' I asked Father Crane, the resident prison chaplain, during an angry meeting.

'People come to God by grace, my son', he replied.

'Then why are prisoners assaulted and bitten by guard dogs if they refuse to become Christians?'

'That will never happen again, I promise you', Father Crane responded grimly.

After that the assaults stopped, but we still refused to attend sermons. When the priests tried to discuss matters of religion with us, they found they couldn't deal with the questions that were fired at them. We laughed at them too, and this made them really angry.

'You say God loves us all, Father Magava? Why do the white people, the ones who brought this Christian doctrine, hate us so much?' a prisoner asked.

'The white people don't hate you. They came to Africa to bring light to a lost nation that was living in darkness', the priest replied.

'If they love us so much, why are we in prison?'

'You are in prison because you broke the law!'

'Whose law? God's law?'

'God puts governments in place to rule people and it's our duty to obey these governments.'

'So it was God who appointed a white racist government in this country. Well, Father, if God did that, we can only conclude that He is also a racist. So to hell with God! Forward with Joshua Nkomo!'

'Only a communist can say things like that!'

'The communists we've met behave far better towards us than you Christians. Your problem and the problem of your white masters is hypocrisy.'

The church and the government those black priests served were white and racist. We believed they were using the priests to change our religious and political beliefs. We viewed them, at the very least, as stooges paid to preach a myth to their own people. So everything they preached we turned around and used to question the behaviour of the whites towards the blacks.

'Father Magava, you were sent to convert us to Christianity. The people who truly need to be converted to Christianity — genuine and not racist Christianity — are your white friends. Preach to them and not to us.'

'Why do you people always link politics to religion?' Father Magava asked in exasperation.

'The people who brought Christianity to Africa also colonised us', answered a prisoner. 'Those who took Christianity to Europe didn't politicise or colonise it. They didn't give the people Jewish names like Jehu and Jehosaphat. But in Africa we were given white names that were called Christian names. Issues of religion cannot be separated from politics?'

'And', another prisoner added, 'the same people who told us 'thou shalt not steal' stole our land. Those who said 'thou shall not kill' murdered our ancestors when they tried to defend their land. The one who also said 'do unto others as you would have them do unto you' captured us and sold us into slavery. Christians sold us like cattle and took our humanity away from us. As a black priest you cannot even begin to preach Christian teachings to us without explaining the appalling behaviour of whites towards blacks.'

'You might notice, Father, that we are not even saying that the Christianity of the humble Man of Judea, Jesus Christ, is wrong. Jesus practised what he preached, so it is impossible to reject his teachings. He healed the sick, opened the eyes of the blind and made the lame walk.

'If Jesus visited Rhodesia, South Africa or America, they'd label him a communist and crucify him because he'd denounce racism and call on the rich to share with the poor. If he visited Nelson Mandela on Robben Island they'd call him a terrorist. He'd try to bring about change in the lives of black people in America by peaceful means, as did Martin Luther King, and they'd shoot him too! Yet they call themselves Christians!'

I'm sure the priests who were sent to convert us found themselves at a loss. They discovered that not all freedom fighters were enemies of Christ as they had been led to believe. They had been told that all of us had received Soviet and Chinese communist indoctrination and didn't believe in the existence of God. Yet here were 'terrorists' explaining the scriptures to them!

During political struggles in any country the Church cannot remain neutral. It cannot stay silent when people are being oppressed, murdered and gaoled for disobeying unjust laws. It is their duty to protest on behalf of the downtrodden. Priests should visit, help and comfort the families of prisoners of the system. The Church acquires meaning for the people when they see it opposing oppression. The government of the day, however, puts tremendous pressure on the Church and it needs the courage and strength to defy this. It is then that the Church becomes a symbol of resistance to evil.

Most, although not all churches in southern Africa chose the safe course. They didn't oppose the racist governments of the day and argued that their mission was to preach the Gospel and not get involved in politics. In South Africa, of course, there was the Dutch Reformed Church which not only supported the government, but shaped the religious doctrine on which apartheid was built. When the ANC came to power the dominees shouted loudly that they had made a mistake and that apartheid was a sin — after all that time. They continue to preach every Sunday and one wonders what they now say to their congregants whom they indoctrinated to hate black people. Racism can be removed from the statute books, but can it be removed from the hearts of the racists?

25

Mutiny in Angola
Betrayal and abuse by one's own comrades

During the Soweto Students' Uprising in 1976 ten thousand or more young men and women marched to protest about being taught in Afrikaans. The police opened fire and hundreds were killed or wounded. The survivors and others youngsters decided their best course of action was to leave the country. Thousands crossed the borders and went into exile. Some decided to undergo military training and return to take revenge on the armed white men who had massacred their friends. They would join the liberation struggle, fight the oppressor and free themselves and their people.

When they reached the camps they were welcomed with open arms. They met older cadres who had joined the struggle in the 1960s and some who had seen action in Rhodesia. They felt at home — part of the greater movement of people who were enemies of oppression. It was a great life. They were given military courses and advanced political training. Camp life provided an opportunity for interaction with older cadres and even the leaders — to their mutual benefit.

The big camp in Angola was Novo Katenga. The South African Air Force attacked and destroyed it.

After this the top leadership decided to establish several widely separated camps. If one was attacked the rest would remain untouched. It was a sensible decision, but with camps located in different regions and different countries the feeling of togetherness that had been experienced at Novo Katenga was lost. The camps established in Angola were Quatro, Camp 13, Pango Quibaxe, Viana Transit Camp and Caculama. The leaders no longer lived with the rank and file and administrators were appointed to run the camps and ensure their security from enemy attack.

While Daluxolo and I were in prison in the late 1970s and early 1980s a situation began to unfold in the ANC camps in Angola, Uganda and Tanzania. Events took place that triggered other events. Many of the people appointed as administrators to run the camps saw themselves as demigods — the lords and masters of those young men and women who left South Africa to join the struggle. Doubtless there were some enemy agents amongst them who had been sent by Pretoria to infiltrate the ANC and MK — but most genuinely wanted to join the struggle. The problem for *Mbokodo* (the grindstone) — the ANC security department — was to separate the spies from the ordinary cadres. Unlike motor vehicles, spies have no registration numbers that serve to identify them. Mbokodo

— the grindstone of the junta authority — possessed virtually unlimited power in the camps.

Anybody with even a basic understanding of espionage and counter-espionage knows that counter-espionage people are usually more disadvantaged than the spies they are supposed to catch. In normal society when someone is suspected of being a spy, an investigation is required to established the facts. This could take a long time. In the meanwhile the spy is free to carry out sabotage, steal documents and send information to his or her handlers.

One can understand the ANC spy-catcher's dilemma at the time. He was judged by the results he produced. So some of the more desperate counter-intelligence agents resorted to torture to extract information from a suspect, even on the slightest suspicion. A confession made in such circumstances could easily have been motivated by a desire to save one's life or to put a stop to the torture. But if pronounced guilty, an innocent person could be jailed or even executed. The atrocious behaviour and methods of the Mbokodo became notorious. It turned life in the camps for new arrivals into a nightmare

One thing led to another until the cadres could take no more of it and revolted. The uprising was put down with great violence. Despite this, anger smouldered until it became downright hatred. It was a situation that could lead to another mutiny, maybe a more carefully planned and successful one the next time.

On 13 February 1984 the ANC's Working Committee (WC) of the National Executive Committee (NEC) appointed a special commission to look into the explosive situation that had developed within its ranks in Angola. It was called the Stuart Commission after its convenor, James Stuart. The other members were Sizakele Sigxashe, Mtu Jwili, Antony Mongalo and Aziz Pahad.

Their terms of reference were to investigate and report on:

- The root cause(s) of the disturbances.
- The nature and genuineness of the grievances
- Outside or enemy involvement, their aim and method of work
- Any connection in other areas
- The ringleaders and their motives.

The commission interviewed practically every ANC member in the Viana Transit Camp and the Pango, Quibaxe, Caxito and Caculama military training camps. Thirty-three cadres detained in the Luanda Maximum Security Prison were also interviewed as were members of the Military High Command, the Regional Co ANC Chief mmand and the Representative in Angola.

The commission prepared a short questionnaire to assist the cadres to answer the questions put to them. The commission accepted that the report they drew up after completing their work was not exhaustive, mainly due to time constraints.

A picture emerged that filled the commission with horror and revulsion. Things were completely out of control and the fault clearly lay with the camp administrators. It had not always been like that. Cadres remembered the spirit of a true people's army at the Novo Katenga Camp when it was run by dedicated revolutionary commanders and officials. It had a well organised logistics section and a variety of food supplies were almost always available. When shortages occurred, everybody starved, not just the rank and file. The administration people would address the cadres and explain the reason for such shortages and introduce remedies. Everyone appreciated the situation.

There was a vibrant cultural and recreational life, plus political training of a high order. Cuban military personnel, assisted by MK stalwarts, gave advanced military instruction. Those in leadership positions shared the hardships of camp life with the cadres and a spirit of genuine comradeship blossomed. Morale was always high. Disciplinary lapses were punished but in a humane and constructive way and cadres were involved in the disciplinary proceedings.

The administrators became an elite group, enjoying separate housing, cooking, dining and other facilities. Imagine an elite group emerging from the ranks of oppressed South Africans! They established separate logistics arrangements to ensure they always had good food. They slaughtered chickens, pigs and ducks for their tables while the common folk never saw meat at all.

One is reminded of the reply the Bishop of Nottingham was reputed to have given Robin Hood after taking him prisoner for hunting in the king's forest. Robin wanted to know why the Bishop planned to hang him for killing a buck which he had done just to keep body and soul together.

'Venison, Robin', the holy man had retorted, 'was created by Providence [God] for the satisfaction of privileged palates, not for the base hunger of unqualified knaves like you.'

No doubt the administrators of the camps in Angola would have responded similarly if challenged.

For long periods cigarettes were unavailable to the cadres, but the administrators always ensured they had ample supplies. They had plenty of liquor to enjoy, but the mere possession by ordinary cadres merited severe punishment. They threw regular parties to which female cadres were invited and they used their senior positions to seduce them. There were cases where husbands or boyfriends were transferred to other camps to make their partners more sexually available. One trainee was reported to have attempted suicide because his girlfriend was taken away from him.

Women who granted sexual favours to the administrators were given preferential treatment. This so affected discipline that such women began to reject the authority of their immediate officers. Attractive women in the camps became sex objects rather than soldiers under training. Cadres were forced to perform household chores — fetching bath water, cleaning rooms, washing and ironing clothes for members of the administration.

Understandably, resentment against these officials skyrocketed but there was not much the cadres could do. Any criticism or complaint was immediately labelled 'anti-authority', 'lack of confidence in the leadership', 'work of enemy agents' and so on. When cadres tried to get messages to the top leadership about the state of affairs in the camps, the messages were intercepted and destroyed or doctored to reflect well on the administrators.

The victimisation of those daring to complain or criticise was widespread.

All these grievances were tabled before the Stuart Commission and included in the *Report of the ANC Commission of Inquiry* dated 14 March 1984. This is not anti-ANC propaganda. They are matters included in the ANC's own report, which it must be concluded, is the truth.

At the Kabwe National Consultative Conference in 1985 the ANC adopted a Code of Conduct. Its purpose was to lay out a policy regarding human rights within the organisation. There was an outright rejection by delegates that information should be suppressed to defend the integrity of the ANC. It was put on record that people didn't surrender their basic human rights when they joined the organisation — significantly adding that 'justice and respect for life must exist within our ranks'.

The post of Officer for Justice under section B of the Code of Conduct was established. This officer, in collaboration with the office of the President and under the overall supervision of the NEC, was charged to do the following:

- Maintain the principles of legality within the organisation.
- Supervise investigations when they reach the stage where charges are being contemplated against members.
- Ensure that no person in the custody of or under investigation by officers of the organisation is treated in a cruel, inhuman or degrading way.
- Make regular inspections of the manner in which people deprived of their liberty are treated, with a view to ensuring that the purposes of re-education rather than vengeance are fulfilled.
- See to it that no undue delay takes place between completion of investigations and the date of the trial.
- Take all necessary steps to minimise the period of waiting.

It was also stated that no force was to be used against persons in confinement. The policy of relying on the two 'Ts' (tips and torture) for information was firmly rejected.

So with all these good policies in place, how then could the situation in the camps reach a stage where people were tortured and even killed?

What did the Stuart Commission report say about Mbokodo? On page 13 it said that there was a unanimous affirmative response in all camps when asked if the security department was exceeding its duties by taking on the task of disciplining offenders. Such duties were at times assumed without consultation with or approval from camp administration officials. Mbokodo was said to be 'an army within an army' with unlimited powers and immune from punishment. The report continued that harsh methods of enforcing discipline by some security comrades had made it 'the most notorious and infamous department in the camps and perhaps in the whole movement'.

Complainants and witnesses gave evidence that security comrades had tortured and killed many cadres. 'And if they kill us who is going to fight inside the country?' an interviewee added. 'Some of the things they have done would shock our people and turn them against the movement.' Flogging scars were seen on the backs of cadres at Caculama Camp.

The security department had created open disunity within the camps. Comrades believed that Mbokodo was not working in the interests of the general membership nor of the movement. They relied on rumours passed on by unreliable informants and were incapable of proper investigations to find information for themselves. Their behaviour had exposed them as cynics and sadists.

It was said that those who joined Mbokodo ignored their former friends and acquaintances because of their newly achieved high status. In confirmation it was said that the National Commissar called the security comrades 'his boys, the red ants'.

To the surprise of the cadres, this violence, harshness and brutality against them continued despite an order by the then regional commander, Comrade Mashigo, prohibiting it. It seems there was no punishment for defying his orders.

It's not our intention to write a detailed story of the happenings in Angola. We merely wish to indicate that there was a major crisis in the organisation in the late 1970s and 1980s. Certainly there were spies and some confessed or were exposed. It seems likely, however, that many of those who suffered or were killed for being spies were nothing of the sort. Yet members of Mbokodo responsible for such atrocities escaped justice completely.

At that time a situation prevailed in the ANC where the 'policemen' also became the judges, juries and executioners rolled into one. It was ironic that this was happening within a political organisation that was waging a liberation struggle to stop this very form of behaviour in South Africa where apartheid policemen held the power of life and death over black people. Why didn't the decision to kill or release comrades suspected of spying rest with the National Executive, with the President being the final appeal authority?

Who gave orders for people to be tortured, maimed or killed? Where did they get this awesome authority from? People fled South Africa to fight for freedom from oppression, yet ended up being oppressed by their own. To this day the ANC — and that includes all of us who belong to this great organisation — still have the blood of innocents on our hands.

Oppression and the abuse of power that triggered the mutiny in Angola already existed in my own time in the camps. Although it was a fight for freedom, one couldn't always expect freedom within the ANC. It was a case of resisting white oppression with all your might, but tamely submitting when the ANC oppressed you in turn.

All I can say is that in my case they were sadly disappointed.

26

Planting seeds of mutual destruction

Outside the country in the mid-1970s, a ZAPU leader, Jason Moyo, was moving mountains in an effort to get ZIPRA and ZANLA to amalgamate into one organisation that could launch joint operations against Rhodesia. He succeeded to the extent that a new force called ZIPA (Zimbabwe People's Army) was formed. Meanwhile, in prison, ZAPU foot soldiers were making our lives a misery because we refused to make war on ZANU. Clearly there was a big problem in ZAPU: the leaders said one thing, and the followers another. We were caught in the middle. The South African nationalist movements were lucky in a way because their leaders were all jailed together on Robben Island. If the ANC people there had attacked PAC elements, Mandela and the others would have put a stop to it. There were no leaders in Rhodesian prisons, however — they were all in detention centres. This created a power vacuum that was filled by people motivated by passion, not by reason. Despite being politically backward, they somehow managed to impose their will on the rest.

ZANU itself was having serious problems outside the country. In 1975 Rhodesian Intelligence picked up information that a ZANLA commander, Thomas Nhari, was leading an in-house rebellion. What he was rebelling against was unknown. Apparently he and his followers had taken over ZANLA's main base at Chifombo in Mozambique and had killed a large number of people who opposed them, including two senior ZANLA commanders, Lovemore Chikadaya and Peter Ngwenya. Nhari's rebels even drove to Lusaka in an attempt to arrest Josiah Tongogara, the ZANLA commander-in-chief, but they failed. Tongogara counterattacked and finally rounded them up at Chifombo, put them through a trial of sorts and executed them.

Rhodesian Intelligence decided to take advantage of these internal squabbles and assassinate Herbert Chitepo, ZANU's director of operations in Zambia. They knew that if they killed him, suspicion would fall on ZAPU or dissidents within ZANU itself. It was important that it should not appear as if the Rhodesians were implicated.

They succeeded brilliantly. After the assassination, President Kaunda arrested the whole of ZANLA's high command in Zambia for murder. This seriously disrupted ZANLA's military operations for 18 months. Peter Stiff in his *See You in November*: *The story of an SAS assassin*, says that the Rhodesians used the opportunity created to strike many blows against ZANLA and ZIPRA in Zambia, giving the impression that it was internecine fighting between the two movements.

Long before our arrest in 1967 talks had taken place regarding the future of Rhodesia. The British government had been at pains to point out to the white settlers that if independence was granted, it would have to be on the basis of majority rule. The white settlers had no intention of accepting that and talks collapsed. This led to Ian Smith's UDI (Unilateral Declaration of Independence) on 11 November 1965.

In 1969 another attempt to resolve the issue was made, but without success. The OAU was calling for armed force to be used against the rebel colony. However, I am sure the African leaders knew in their heart of hearts that it was somewhat farfetched to expect the British to attack their own kith and kin over a bunch of natives. The United Nations had already imposed sanctions and the white government voiced antagonism saying they would harm the African people more than the whites. Indirectly, it was a confession that there were two societies in Rhodesia, one white and wealthy and the other black and poor. Otherwise, why would economic sanctions harm one section of the population more than the other?

The bush war was raging, but because newspapers were rarely available to us in prison, we couldn't tell how well the struggle was going. The newspapers we did see published the outcomes of cross-border raids into neighbouring states and the heavy casualties suffered by the liberation forces. The casualties suffered by the Rhodesian Security Forces were either non-existent or very few. These selected newspapers were given to us so we could understand that we were losing the war. What the prison authorities didn't know was that we had our own sources of information. With the passing years we had learned the wisdom of not antagonising the African guards by calling them sell-outs or Smith's dogs. We began to befriend them and even win their sympathy for our cause. It was they who regularly smuggled newspapers, magazines and periodicals to us and we read them with a hungry fervour.

Whenever there were talks about talks our spirits rose, expecting that such talks would be successful and we would be freed. When talks failed, our hopes were dashed and we returned to our gloom. We never despaired, though, because as some wise person remarked: 'Hope springs eternal in the human breast'. There were, for instance, the Victoria Falls talks at which South African Prime Minister B J Vorster featured along with President Kaunda of Zambia, but nothing came of it.

'I wish I had the power to collect all those politicians and lock them up in one house and tell them that they would only be released once they reached a settlement. We would be out of this place within 48 hours', a prisoner said after the collapse of those talks.

'They hold their meetings in five-star hotels, sipping ice cold beer and eating buffet. Do you think they are in a hurry to settle?' his cell mate added. ' Do you believe our leaders still remember that they have people in Rhodesian prisons? I somehow doubt it.'

'Why do you say that? Are you suggesting that because you want to get out of prison our leaders should just agree to anything and sign?' a prisoner asked.

'You'll get a high rank in the future army if the leaders hear you talking like that. People who know how to make excuses for the leadership are usually very handsomely rewarded. Carry on like that, my boy, and you'll be a general when you're forty', said the prisoner who was convinced the leaders held their talks in five-star hotels.

'Comrades, comrades, we are depressed because the talks have failed. Let us not fight about it', another prisoner put in.

After this the venue shifted to Geneva in Switzerland, but nothing came of those talks either.

We calculated that after the failure of each round of talks it would take another two years of bargaining and arm-twisting to get the parties back to the negotiating table. The to-ing and fro-ing went on throughout the 1970s and our hopes rose and fell.

We shouldn't forget the Africans who involved themselves in counter-guerrilla activities in Rhodesia, Mozambique, Namibia, Angola and South Africa — purely, I believe, for the love of money. They joined counter-insurgency units like the Selous Scouts in Rhodesia, RENAMO in Mozambique, the Inkatha Freedom Party, the Witdoekies, Ama-Afrika, Iliso Lomzi and the African Democratic Movement in South Africa. In Rhodesia the Selous Scouts, with their large complement of black operators, killed numerous guerrillas and their civilian supporters. The black members wore ZANLA uniforms and carried AK47s. They learned ZANU slogans and songs and enticed people to attend meetings — only to be killed or arrested as ZANU supporters.

Those who joined the freedom fight should have understood the kind of people they were putting their lives on the line for. They made war among themselves even as their white enemy was making war on them all. ZANLA and ZIPRA fought each other and the Rhodesian Security Forces fought both. For example, in 1979 towards the end of the Rhodesian War, a curious situation developed because of fighting between ZANLA and ZIPRA. Three companies of MK soldiers were infiltrated into southern Matabeleland from Zambia to stiffen ZIPRA's effort against ZANLA which had moved into what was regarded as prime ZIPRA territory.

Peter Stiff in his book *The Silent War: South African Recce Operations 1969-1994* explains how South African Special Forces operating in Mozambique from Rhodesia's eastern border were engaging mixed units of ZANLA and FRELIMO infiltrating Rhodesia and giving them a hard time. Those who got past the Recces into southern Matabeland were often engaged and finished off by MK soldiers fighting alongside ZIPRA. MK, of course, never realised that effectively they were fighting on the same side as the SADF.

The ANC had always preached that we should never view the PAC or any other liberation force as a military target. Now MK was in southern Matabeleland fighting against ZANLA and FRELIMO forces. It must have been humiliating indeed for OR Tambo to go and eat humble pie before Robert Mugabe when ZANU and not ZAPU came into political power.

During late 1979 at the height of the Lancaster House negotiations in London, the ANC in Lusaka did begin to sense that ZANU and not ZAPU would come to power in Zimbabwe. Many splits had occurred in the ranks of the black nationalists. FROLIZI (Front for the Liberation of Zimbabwe) led by James Chikerema had split from ZAPU but it died in its political infancy. UDengezi was a ZAPU faction led by J Z Moyo. ZANU by then was led by Robert Mugabe and there was Muzorewa's United African National Council. Ndabaningi Sithole was leading a small faction that had split from ZANU called ZANU-Ndoga. There were many suns in Zimbabwe's political sky.

We heard news that the Lancaster House talks had eventually resulted in an agreement for free and fair elections to be held in which all Zimbabweans, black and white, would take part. In the interim Lord Soames had been appointed as the British governor.

Everybody started talking about what they would do when they left prison, despite much uncertainty.

'I joined the struggle when I was 23', one prisoner remarked, 'and I have never been employed in my life. Where am I going to find a job when I come out?'

'If ZAPU fails to win power I'm doomed because I don't even have an O level certificate', another lamented. 'We were told the revolution should come first and education later. But how can I go back to school at my age? If we get into power, though, I'm sure our leaders will give me a job in government regardless of my lack of education. They can't just turn their backs on us.'

'I have a feeling that we will all be abandoned. I don't know why but that worry is there all the time', Mdletshe, a far-seeing prisoner, remarked.

'Why are you so quiet Comrade Thula? Why don't you tell us what your plans are when you leave prison?' I was asked.

'My feeling is that within ten years South Africa will be free. I'll spend that time studying and when my country is free I'll return and make some contribution, even if it's small.'

'Do you believe what Comrade Mdletshe says? Do you think our leaders will forget us in our old age when they come to power?'

'Frankly, I do', I replied.

'But surely comrade, the ANC owes us a debt, don't you think?'

'Of course they do, but debts are not always repaid. I also have a feeling that this one won't be.'

'You're mistaken. Just you wait and see', said Marshall Forster. 'There'll be a huge crowd of people waiting to greet us when we're released. I can hear the cheering in my mind. We'll be heroes and our leaders will welcome us back with open arms. They'll publicly thank us for the enormous sacrifices we have made.'

'I wouldn't count on a heroes' welcome if I were you, Marshal', I said. 'There are no leaders among us here. We are just common foot soldiers. Do you honestly believe that political organisations honour foot soldiers? In Britain they recruited millions of young men to go and fight the Germans in the trenches during World War I. The recruiting slogan was *Dulce et decorum est, pro patria mori* (It's sweet to die for one's Motherland). Yet when that terrible war was over, the British government turned its back on them. So, Comrade Marshal, take a lesson from history and be wary about promising yourself a heroes' welcome.'

'The lowest rank that ZAPU can give me when it forms the first black government in a free Zimbabwe is colonel. But after 12 years in prison I expect I'll be made a general', Moffat Hadebe, a brave and resourceful fighter, was heard to say. He had been in prison since 1968 counting the years as they had slowly passed by.

In the real world outside of prison, the ANC had begun to lend support to Mugabe as well as Nkomo.

We were on tenterhooks during the run-up to the election. Then news came that Robert Mugabe's ZANU-PF had won an overwhelming victory. They would be forming the first majority government. The ZAPU prisoners were stunned.

It shouldn't really have mattered which party came into power and it didn't to me. I had joined the struggle to free the oppressed black people of Zimbabwe and South Africa. Majority rule had come at last and the country would in future be under black rule. Wasn't this what all the fighting, killing and dying had been about? So why were so many of my black fellow prisoners unhappy now that the freedom struggle had been won? Some prisoners were prancing around and running wild in celebration, while others were crying.

What was wrong with these people? Ndabaningi Sithole's followers mourned visibly. ZAPU people said openly that the election had been rigged and the result was fraudulent. How could they know that when they were in prison at the time? Some suggested the British had cooked the election results to help Mugabe win. The problem was that none could explain why they would do such a thing.

The British didn't like Mugabe; that was plain. They were more comfortable with Joshua Nkomo than Mugabe. In fact, one reads in Peter Stiff's *See you in November: The story of an SAS Assassin* that the road Mugabe habitually used when visiting the British Governor Lord Soames at Government House, had been mined by Rhodesian Intelligence. The same crowd also pursued Mugabe right to London during the Lancaster House Conference in an effort to assassinate him. According to Stiff, a claymore anti-personnel mine inside a briefcase had even been planted in the foyer of the hotel where he was staying. This mission was called off at the very last minute. Mugabe was seen as a communist and the British had been fighting such people since the end of World War II. Was this a man the British would rig an election for? The arguments still continue to rage.

There were mutterings from ZAPU about 'going back to the bush' — the bush they had fled when we needed them to fight Ian Smith's soldiers! I was an outsider and I knew that if ZAPU had won, ZANU people would have claimed the elections were rigged: they would have been the ones talking about returning to the bush. I suddenly saw clearly that the issue was not freedom for the people of Zimbabwe. It was which tribal grouping would take power.

Moffat Hadebe wept bitterly and openly. His dreams of becoming a general had slipped away. It was no consolation to him that he had contributed to the liberation of his people. He was downcast and resentful on the eve of his country's liberation.

It was a strange atmosphere to be in. I felt some malicious pleasure at seeing the disappointment of my former tormentors. They — both ZAPU and ANC men — had staked their futures on the blind belief that ZAPU would win power and their personal fortunes would be made. Now they were sitting in the debris of their hopes, too stunned to do anything but weep like wives who had lost their husbands. For months they had been confidently referring to ZAPU as the government-in-waiting. Anybody who had questioned this belief was regarded as a traitor — a doubting Thomas, as Mariri had put it. I felt only contempt for them. The Zimbabwean people had voted for the first time and chosen the man they wanted to rule them. They should have been ecstatic, not lamenting. I learned something that day about African nationalism.

I was over the moon, of course. I had lived long enough to see Rhodesia freed in a struggle that on many occasions had almost cost me my life. I had come through a war and I still had four limbs, both eyes and a brain that was still functioning okay — despite 12 years of continuous stress in prison. I was still sane even after the harrowing experiences of Death Row and many years of solitary confinement.

Soon I would walk out of prison, go somewhere and have my first hot bath in 13 years. The last hot bath I had enjoyed was at Mr Mashengele's home in Chisumbanje in 1967. I had a 13-year-old thirst for a cold Castle beer and I knew I would soon assuage that. There were beautiful women out there and I had almost forgotten what a woman was. It would be so nice to ride in a bus and a train again. I wanted to watch a good football match again. I had missed that so much while in prison. I was looking forward to once more going to a public library to choose a book, any book, and read it.

I was happy because I was going to again see members of my family, not once a year at Christmas, but whenever I wanted to. I was happy that I would be free to walk around at any time of the day or night without a prison guard restricting my movements. It was 1980 and I looked forward to again making decisions about my life and deciding the direction it would take instead of being told what to do.

We expected to be released from prison immediately now the election had come and gone and we were in a free country. ZANU prisoners were promptly released and the ZAPU ones followed shortly afterwards. But not us. Eventually we MK prisoners were moved from Khami Maximum Security Prison to Grey Street Prison in central Bulawayo. But nothing was said about our release. Depression set in.

We heard that independence celebrations would be held in Salisbury on 17 April. The Rev Canaan Banana would become president and Robert Mugabe would be sworn in as prime minister of the new State of Zimbabwe.

We heard that world leaders would be coming to Zimbabwe to celebrate its independence from colonial rule. We read in newspapers the prison guards allowed us that the ANC leaders were coming from Lusaka to join in the celebrations.

Independence Day came and went. None of the ANC leaders even visited us before flying back to Lusaka, although they well knew we were there. I have never been offered an apology or even an explanation or for this extraordinary behaviour.

And so we continued to sit in prison.

Eventually on 8 May 1980 the superintendent told us we were being released that day on the orders of His Excellency President Canaan Banana. We were the last political prisoners to be freed.

Most of us were handed old ex-government khaki clothing that had been given to us after our arrest in 1967. We expected the ANC to send us some decent clothes, but nothing was forthcoming.

There was no ceremony on our release. The guards merely opened the heavy front door of the prison and we stepped out into Grey Street as free men.

I was right about a welcoming committee. There wasn't one. Not a soul was there to meet us in this foreign country which the ANC had sent us to assist in its liberation. We were the forgotten men of the revolution. I'm sure that if we had been leaders in our organisation, great publicity would have accompanied our release. Elaborate arrangements would have made to accommodate us in a top Bulawayo hotel. Instead we stood in Grey Street shifting our feet and wondering where to go. We didn't have enough coins in our pockets to buy a decent meal. Such is the gratitude of princes.

Passers by stared curiously at us as we stood there looking lost. It was a wonderful feeling being out, but suddenly we didn't know what to do with our new-found freedom. The day we had been looking forward to all those years had come at last. We were a bunch of abandoned combat veterans who had been dumped.

'Maybe the ANC didn't know we were being released today. That would explain why they're not here', Mapoto said in a loyal attempt to cover for the organisation.

'They were here to celebrate Zimbabwean Independence on April 17, so why didn't they come to see us in prison. I'll tell you why. It's because we have become a liability to them', I said.

'What if that isn't true, Comrade Thula? Are you not making a harsh judgement on the organisation?'

'Well they're not here and that won't change. The ANC is a very lucky organisation. The people it treats shoddily are the very ones who make excuses for it.'

'Comrade Thula is right', Willie Motau stated resignedly. 'How long are we going to cover up for the ANC? The truth is we're in a strange city and we have no idea where to go. When we get hungry what will we do for food? Where are we going to sleep tonight? We are destitute. We are nothing.'

'We say in Zulu: '*Umbeki wenkosi akabusi nayo*' (The one who helps the king to ascend the throne does not sit next to him once he is on it), I said.

An Alfa Romeo sedan drew up next to us. A woman in a nursing sister's uniform was behind the wheel. She lowered the driver's window and called out.

'Which one of you is Thula?'

'That's me.'

'Your brother has sent me to fetch you. Get in the car.'

I had never seen her but I soon learned that she was Professor Ngcobo's daughter, Nomsa. The professor was a family friend. I glanced at my comrades and felt a tug at my heartstrings. Nomsa was going to take me somewhere. I didn't know where, but at least I was no longer alone. I would have somewhere to sleep tonight and something to eat. But what about my comrades?

Aubrey Mdletshe sensed my turmoil and walked up to the car. He introduced himself.

'Look after our comrade well, sister', he said. 'Don't worry about the rest of us. We have a plan and we will survive. Thula, enjoy your good fortune and don't be embarrassed by it because you are leaving us. We will look back on this one day and remember how we began our first day of freedom like beggars in the street after so many years of imprisonment.'

I saluted and they returned my salute. Nomsa drove off.

27

Daluxolo
Double agent

Daluxolo was taken from Robben Island by members of the Security Branch. They escorted him to his home at Georgedale in KwaZulu and released him to his family. It was an emotional homecoming with laughter, tears and prayers of thanksgiving. His mother, Nomthandazo, had last seen her son when he left home in 1963 at the age of 15. Now he was a man of 31 who had spent half his life away. She had prayed every night for his safe return and could scarcely believe that he was back in the bosom of his family.

Daluxolo had never seen anybody as happy as his mother was that day. She cried and tried to smile between her tears. She kept repeating: 'My child! My child!' That night she read the parable of the Prodigal Son from the Scriptures. When she came to where the father says: 'This my son was dead, and is alive again; he was lost and is found', her voice became almost angelic. It was her way of chiding his father for lying to her about sending him to an African healer to be cured of sores.

There was much catching up to be done and they talked until dawn. He told them about his days in MK and the terrible ten years on Robben Island. In those days few people who hadn't been imprisoned there knew what Robben Island looked like. It was certainly not a World Heritage Site and a tourist destination then. It was bleak and isolated.

His parents for their part told how the police had come looking for him after he left the country. His father told them he didn't know where he was. It was only later that his mother learned the truth about his absence.

'I sent the boy out of the country with other young men to learn modern warfare so that they could come back and free the country', his father told her.

'Why was I not told, *Baba*?' she asked. 'Didn't it matter that I had carried that boy inside me for nine painful months?'

'You see, my girl', his father had said. 'I didn't think it right to recruit other people's sons to send to war and allow my own son to stay safely at home.'

Catching up on the news was fun, great fun. What had happened to this person and that person? Young girls he had known had families of their own. This person had died and that person had left the area.

The following day an ox was slaughtered to thank God and the ancestors for preserving the young man through all kinds of perils and for bringing him home safe and sound. The people of Georgedale came to feast and see the celebrity they had heard so much about. And here he was right before their very eyes, he who had gone to the Soviet Union, fought in Rhodesia and been incarcerated on Robben Island. Such adventures! Was this the same quiet boy they used to see running around in Georgedale only 16 years ago? It couldn't be. It seemed unbelievable.

They were wonderful days for the family. The only person not at home was his sister Nonkululeko. She had married an engineer, Fakes Nkosi, and they lived in Swaziland. Daluxolo spoke about visiting them one of these fine days.

The days passed and he began to think of what lay ahead.

'What are you going to do, my son, now you're free?' his father Japhta asked him.

'Why? Are you bored with having me at home after so long? Do you want to send me on another mission already?' he asked laughing.

'No, my boy, I'm happy to have you at home and I would like to keep you with me', the old man responded. 'But I know that someone like you will not settle down and forget everything he has done. There is activity all around us, political activity and police activity. Always remember that the eyes of the state have not left you since the Security Police dropped you here a fortnight ago. Be careful whom you talk to about your future intentions. There is no harm in talking freely about the past, because the authorities know all that already.'

'I have decided to become a member of the IFP, father', Daluxolo blurted out.

'You're ANC and so am I. I'll die ANC. Why do you want to join the IFP?'

'I'll continue to work for the ANC while I'm a member of IFP.'

His father listened quietly while his son explained the instructions he had been given before he left Robben Island. He shrugged.

'Then that's different. In fact, even I have an IFP membership card', his father admitted. 'Everybody belongs to the IFP nowadays because it is politic to do so. But my work is for the ANC. It's the only way to continue the struggle and stay out of police hands. As I said, I'll be ANC until I die, but it suits me to be IFP as well. Fortunately the IFP colours are the same as ours, as is the clenched fist salute and everything. It was a clever move by the ANC when it supported the formation of the IFP.'

'Have you stopped recruiting young men for MK?' Daluxolo asked.

'Why should I stop? I can be IFP during the day and denounce armed struggle. But at night I continue to make arrangements to send young men and women out of the country to continue it.'

'I have the same mission, *Baba*. How do I join the IFP?'

'Tomorrow I'll put you in touch with people who will get you registered as an IFP member. Remember the police will be watching what you do. If they think you have gone back to your MK ways, they'll kill you and not just capture you next time. But if they see you at IFP rallies they'll think that Robben Island softened you up. You have no idea how stupid these Boers can be.'

'At the Compol Building in Pretoria they nearly killed me because I didn't know I was supposed to address them as '*Baas*.' When I started calling them that they became overwhelmed with happiness. It didn't occur to them that I was just faking the marks of respect.'

'That's why we'll beat them in the end', his father observed. 'They only believe in force. They think that having a powerful army will keep them in power forever.'

'Surely there must be some reasonable men amongst them who know better? There must be wise as well as stupid men in any nation.'

'Oh, yes, but they don't listen to sense. When an Afrikaner says it's impossible to keep a people under oppression indefinitely they denounce him as soft on blacks — a *kaffirboetie*.'

His father put him in contact with Gideon Mdletshe, a member of MK who had also joined IFP. Gideon took him to Ulundi to meet the great man himself, Chief Mangosuthu Gatsha Buthelezi, IFP President and Chief Minister of KwaZulu. He was introduced as a former MK soldier who had seen action in Rhodesia and had just completed a ten-year prison sentence on Robben Island. Dr Buthelezi was gracious and welcomed him to the Inkatha Freedom Party and the struggle for liberation under the IFP banner. He said that many Zulus from the ANC had already switched their allegiance to the IFP. He was also introduced to MZ Khumalo, Dr Buthelezi's personal assistant and probably the most powerful man in the IFP after Buthelezi.

Daluxolo and his father travelled through Umtata in the Transkei and as far as the Fish River. On their return trip Daluxolo recalled that an ex-Robben Islander and co-accused of his at Pietermaritzburg Supreme Court, Ezra Sigwela, worked in Umtata for the Transkei Council of Churches and he looked him up. Ezra was happy to see his old comrade-in-suffering, but he was also pleased for another reason. He had already made plans to travel to Georgedale to tell Daluxolo that Chris Hani wanted to see him in Lesotho.

Ezra asked Daluxolo to return some time later so he could give him money, directions and the name of a contact man in Lesotho who would put him in touch with Chris Hani. This was duly arranged and Daluxolo made his way to Maseru, the capital and only place of any size in Lesotho. His contact, Mogalake Sello, immediately took him to Chris.

Chris had last seen Daluxolo at Wankie in 1967, a long 13 years before. Chris wanted to know what his old comrade was doing with himself. Was he enjoying his new-found freedom? Daluxolo explained the instructions given to him and said he was anxious to get started.

'Great', Chris said. 'That's exactly what I had in mind. Your membership of the IFP will reassure the Security Branch and they will stop watching you. Pretoria will regard it as a move away from the ANC's strategy of violence towards the IFP's policy of non-violence. The IFP will keep the people politically alert by denouncing apartheid while we mobilise for war. There's a need to infiltrate all homeland-based organisations so we can steer them in the correct political direction.'

'Yes, Comrade Chris, *aluta continua* [the war continues] as we say. The IFP will give me perfect cover while I perform my tasks.'

'MK needs to train more people and flood the entire country with combatants, who in turn will train others', Chris said. The MK army must grow within the country so we can escalate operations and be more effective. We cannot strike a serious blow with our army in Tanzania, Zambia and Angola. That's why I'm here.'

'Good, Comrade Chris, very good. You remember how frustrated we were in those camps? We all wanted to return to the country but none of our leaders were willing to come with us on operations.'

'Do you still remember our slogan: If the mission is difficult, what shall we do?'

'We'll do it!' Daluxolo bawled in response.

'If the mission is impossible, what shall we do?' Chris shouted.

'We'll attempt it!' Daluxolo yelled back.

They both laughed, remembering their Wankie days.

'I'll give you money and a gun, Comrade Daluxolo. The money will allow you to buy a vehicle in sound mechanical condition. With this you will be able to travel anywhere in the country at short notice. Many operations have failed because no transport was available when a cadre had to move. I don't need to tell you what the gun is for. I'll get the stuff to you in South Africa. When you go back use the Qacha's Nek immigration post to exit Lesotho. You know as well as I do that guerilla never uses the same route twice.'

'Absolutely', Daluxolo confirmed.

It was great being with Chris. He was a soldier's soldier. He could be very humourous and had a ready laugh. Living with ever-present danger had made him more serious than he used to be, but he still loved a joke. He told Daluxolo what he had been doing since his release from imprisonment in Botswana after the Wankie campaign. They talked until late in the night.

Chris had walked into South Africa from Botswana in 1974 with orders to establish a political infrastructure for the ANC in the Cape. For some time he based himself in Johannesburg and organised underground units and a communications system. He had worked out numerous infiltration routes into South Africa.

Chris then moved to Maseru and remained there for eight years. Chief Leabua Jonathan was showing himself to be friendly towards the ANC and allowed them to establish a presence there, albeit unofficially, but they were not permitted to open offices or carry arms. Chris' function was to use Lesotho as the transit route to bring MK cadres into South Africa and build up the ANC/SACTU/ SACP alliance in the Free State and the Cape.

There had been little real military activity since Wankie. Chris had come out of that one with an enhanced reputation as a fearless fighter, willing to go where others feared to tread. He had now ventured right into the lion's den to organise resistance under the very nose of the enemy. He was a man loved and respected by the common soldiers as well as by other MK commanders.

Then the Soweto uprising erupted. What had been a trickle of recruits leaving the country became a flood. MK officers based in Lesotho, Botswana and Swaziland made contact with the students and urged them to join Umkhonto we Sizwe. By 1977 about 4

000 angry students had jumped the border and people like Chris were kept very busy.

The Security Branch became aware of him and began to plan his demise. There were two recorded attempts on his life — both involving the use of explosives to blow up his vehicle — but there were several others unrecorded. In the first attempt, the Security Branch persuaded a certain Tumelo Ramatolo to plant a device in Chris' car at Maseru. Ramatolo belonged to the Lesotho Youth Organisation and was a close confidant of Chris. He mishandled the bomb, however, and it exploded and injured him severely. He fled to South Africa after obtaining bail.

The next morning Daluxolo left for South Africa via the border post at Qacha's Nek. After he cleared immigration a man appeared seemingly from nowhere, gave him a bag and disappeared. When he got the chance to examine it he found it contained money and a Makarov pistol. There were also some nice clothes with the compliments of Chris Hani.

When he got back to Georgedale, Daluxolo gave the money to his father who bought him a secondhand Mercedes 280S in excellent condition. He was ready for operations.

The ANC asked him to go to Swaziland after his first visit to Maseru. There he met Maphumulo, Khuzwayo and Osborne Mathenjwa. They told him that Moses Mabhida, MK's chief political commissar, wanted to meet him in Mozambique. He decided, however, that this might be unwise as it could jeopardise his chances of returning to South Africa. Instead he sent a message that he had made contact with Chris Hani in Lesotho who was his handler. If Mabhida had a specific task for him he could tell Hani. He heard nothing further on that score.

Meanwhile, the South Africans were planning a major operation to disrupt ANC and MK operations in Lesotho and kill Chris Hani. They dubbed it *Operation Lebanta*. According to Peter Stiff in his book *The Silent War: South African Recce Operations 1969-1994*, during their preparations for the raid the South Africans sent intelligence agents in the guise of businessmen to establish ANC targets in Maseru. One of them, a particularly deadly operator named Grey Branfield — a former detective inspector in Rhodesia's BSAP — got so close to Chris that they went jogging together in the mornings. Chris was lucky because no killings were to take place before the raid. Peter Stiff also details in his *Cry Zimbabwe: Independence Twenty Years On*, how in 1981 Branfield (nom de guerre Major Brian) led a South African Special Forces team into Zimbabwe and succeeded in assassinating Joe Gqabi, the ANC's and MK's chief representative there. Branfield was killed while working for a security company in Iraq in 2005.

The *Operation Lebanta* raid eventually took place in December 1982 against targets pinpointed long in advance. Twenty-seven people were killed in this attack. They were accorded a semi-state funeral by the Lesotho Government and their coffins were draped in the gold, black and green colours of the ANC.

Chris and his family had a narrow escape. When they didn't find his body amongst the dead, the soldiers launched a massive manhunt, but he eluded them and got safely back to Lusaka.

After this Daluxolo lost contact with the ANC for a while.

28

Inkatha and students go to war

In June 1976 Soweto had erupted and students took to the streets to protest the compulsory use of Afrikaans as the language of instruction. The police opened fire and hundreds died. Strikes, work stay-aways and consumer boycotts followed. The tide of opposition to apartheid rose to a point where it became clear that the state had lost control of the townships. When the police and the army tried to restore order, the international community denounced the Pretoria government for oppressing blacks. The government decided that the solution was to organise a clandestine force of black people who would attack UDF (United Democratic Front) activists without it being blamed on the state.

In September 1976 a stay-away was called by the youth in Soweto and Zulu hostel dwellers at Mzimhlophe went along with it. When a second stay-away was called, they disagreed and went to work. On their way back to the hostel, they were attacked. They launched a counter-attack and several youths died. The hostel dwellers had a sound argument: they needed the wages and had families to support. But in the climate of the time they were seen to be collaborating with 'the system'. They were also Inkatha supporters and therefore targetable.

Chief Buthelezi had been calling Inkatha a liberation organisation, but with the UDF rising against the state, the time for 'talking liberation' was over. What action would the IFP take in these circumstances? In April 1980 students in the KwaMashu and Umlazi townships in Natal became part of a nationwide school boycott. IFP rejected the boycott and Buthelezi demanded that the students return to school. An Inkatha programme to teach pupils discipline had been introduced throughout Natal. It was a compulsory course, taught for an hour a week at all levels. Students were told to keep away from activities like strikes and boycotts. Now 36 schools in Natal had joined the protest and Buthelezi was incensed.

At the IFP Conference in June 1980, Buthelezi complained that the teachers had failed to instil into learners the right attitude towards the struggle as waged by the IFP, calling the strikes 'protest politics'. The *Daily News* reported him as saying that he would train an army that would be responsible for keeping order, preventing the destruction of schools and controlling student riots. His vision was that every Inkatha region should have a paramilitary force committed to restoring order in black politics.

The Natal students proved to be as politically active as those in the rest of the country. In 1980 black pupils launched a nation-wide strike against their sub-standard Bantu education. A call went out to boycott classes and the students in all major urban centres responded. Over 6 000 learners in KwaMashu and Umlazi townships took part. The Minister of National Education threatened to fire teachers who supported the boycott. But it persisted and grew by the day. By April of 1980, barely two months after its launch, the number of students participating had swelled to 100 000. In several instances, the police responded by firing teargas and using firearms. The crisis deepened and Prime Minister P W Botha decided to hold talks with the Union of Teachers Association. He conceded that the students had justifiable grievances and promised to institute an inquiry into the feasibility of having a single education system for all races.

At the height of the school boycotts in KwaMashu and Umlazi — the two Durban townships under IFP administration — Inkatha supporters organised themselves into armed impis and attacked students with spears, sjamboks, sticks and knobkerries. Dr Oscar Dhlomo, Secretary-General of the IFP, warned that 'we must not be blamed if we [the IFP] lose patience'. Chief Buthelezi himself charged that 'evil forces' were at work and that this could lead to vigilante groups being formed who would 'shoot to kill' those found interfering with school buildings.

According to Mzala in his *Gatsha Buthelezi: Chief with a Double Agenda*, by the mid-1980s clashes between Inkatha warriors and students had become daily occurrences with the latter being attacked indiscriminately in the streets. In various subsequent court cases, students described how they were abducted, beaten, handcuffed by prominent Inkatha officials and taken to Ulundi, KwaZulu's capital. Some women signed affidavits that Inkatha members had beaten them in their homes while many students complained that their homes had been torched.

The students in Natal came to the conclusion that Buthelezi held the same view towards them and their grievances as the apartheid regime. They organised and opened branches of the Congress of South African Students (COSAS). COSAS launched a campaign against the indoctrination of students via the Inkatha 'syllabus'. This meant that the Youth Brigade would fade away as the voice of students in Natal. COSAS became the recognised mouthpiece. Then the Youth Brigade revealed their true colours.

Mzala said:

> Instead of joining the student campaign, the Inkatha Youth Brigade set about establishing ties with right-wing Afrikaner parties and organisations. They met with the SRC of the Stellenbosch University and attended the annual congress of the *Afrikaanse Studentebond* (ASB) in Potchefstroom. Before this there was a meeting between the executive of the ASB and the Inkatha Central Committee. Responding to the growth of COSAS in KwaZulu, Chief Buthelezi told the KwaZulu Legislative Assembly in October 1980 that 'it was formed as a front organisation for the ANC mission-in-exile'. Chief Buthelezi must have known that this allegation could well lead to the detention of COSAS members by the Security Police. Inevitably the students took this to mean that Chief Buthelezi, far from fighting oppression, was assisting the very regime which the people were opposing.

During this period unrest had also flared up at the University of Zululand, popularly known as Ngoye. With a graduation ceremony pending, a student body meeting adopted a resolution calling on Chief Buthelezi, in his capacity as the Chancellor, to restrain Inkatha warriors from attending the ceremony in their uniforms and that both the university administration and Chief Buthelezi should not allow the graduation ceremony to be turned into an Inkatha rally.

On graduation day (23 May 1983) students attempted to prevent armed Inkatha warriors from entering the campus. Police were called by the university authorities to disperse students assembled at the entrance gates. Shots were fired by the police and teargas as well as dogs used to disperse the students. Fifteen students were arrested before a large armed Inkatha regiment arrived in a massive show of force.

Very early on Saturday 29 October 1983 an impi of about 500 armed warriors arrived. Mzala said:

> The early morning mist had hardly lifted when Zulu warriors armed with spears, cowhide shields, kerries and battle-axes slipped on to the campus, chanting and singing. Unaware of the impending terror, students were eating leisurely Saturday breakfasts when the still mist was shattered by the pounding of sticks and shields and war cries as the Impis swept through the campus.

Five students died in the melee and this took the antagonism between the students and the IFP to a new height. From then on it was all-out war. Whether it was the UDF or Inkatha that hurled the first stone, struck the first blow or fired the first shot is academic. The political stance taken by the IFP in national politics meant that a confrontation between itself and the UDF was inevitable. With the latter vowing to make apartheid South Africa ungovernable and the IFP seeking to force black people to accept the unacceptable, there could only be one outcome.

The Zulus in Natal were now divided between those who were working to bring down the apartheid state and those who had taken the opposite position. The students led the charge while workers staged industrial actions and called for disinvestment. The IFP and other organisations in the homelands were opposed to boycotts and disinvestment. The strategy of the National Party to divide and rule by making blacks fight blacks in defence of apartheid was working well — at least for the time being.

29

Daluxolo
UWUSA organiser

Daluxolo didn't immediately become active in the IFP after he joined, but he met people, attended meetings and gathered information on how the IFP worked. He also became a member of the United Workers Union of South Africa (UWUSA) and was appointed as an organiser. UWUSA was a trade union formed by the IFP with government financial assistance to combat COSATU's calls for foreign businesses to disinvest. The IFP suddenly began to show signs of being an organisation that opposed everything the ANC stood for. They continued their policy of non-violence as a strategy for bringing about political change. The ANC had abandoned this policy in 1960 after 48 years of fruitless protest.

The ANC, of course, opposed the Bantustan system, but various chiefs supported it because it enhanced their power, status and pockets. The government touted these chiefs both at home and abroad as the true leaders of the African people. The ANC and PAC were dubbed 'terrorist organisations' and their leaders labelled as communists; the chiefs became 'moderate, reasonable, Christian African leaders'. When the ANC called for economic sanctions and disinvestment as a strategy to weaken the apartheid regime, the leaders of the Bantustans and the IFP opposed it.

Government policy was consistent in the way it introduced the concept of Bantustans to the blacks. If they opposed the plan, the government got traditional leaders to support it to ward off accusations that it was a racist system. If COSATU claimed it was the desire of black workers, UWUSA sang the National Party Government's tune to nullify their voice.

Daluxolo immersed himself in UWUSA and IFP policy and began to think and act like an UWUSA shop steward.

'Didn't you worry that you might end up believing what you said?' I asked him. 'At some point you became a true IFP follower and not a double agent of the ANC. Why did you stop sending information to the ANC after Chris Hani left Lesotho?'

'The ANC called me to Swaziland and I went and gave them all the information I had. Later, when I was appointed a member of the central committee and commander-in-chief of IFP, the ANC maintained that it wasn't my mission to become a senior IFP official. I questioned whether I could have refused those appointments without causing suspicion and they had no answer. I also pointed out that the really top grade information the ANC wanted could be better obtained by somebody on the central committee. They had no answer for that either.'

'They called me to Swaziland for a third time, but I didn't go because somebody whose name I will not reveal warned me that comrades in Swaziland were going to kill me. This made me furious and I think it was at this point that I committed myself to the IFP.'

It's necessary at this stage to give a brief description of the labour relations as they were in the Bantustans and in KwaZulu in particular — this will assist in giving background to the formation and ideology of UWUSA and helps to explain why the IFP sought to build an Inkatha-based union movement.

The structural position of every Bantustan in the political economy of South Africa was that of being a reservoir of cheap labour and provider of a stable workforce. The development strategy for the Bantustans, therefore, was necessarily based on the attraction of investment. Employers in the Bantustans were guaranteed the right to pay low wages and the workers were effectively prevented from achieving wages and working conditions commensurate with the rest of South Africa. The only incentive for industrialists to invest in these Bantustans — which were far from the seaports and markets — was the low wage bill.

In the 1960s it became the policy of the South African government to encourage investment in the border areas to stem the influx of Africans from the rural areas into the cities. If the strategy could be seen to be job-creative, it would also give the Bantustans some degree of legitimacy. To this end, a series of labour proclamations were issued, effectively excluding workers in the Bantustans from the provisions of the Labour Relations Act. This meant that the minimum wage and conditions applicable to black workers in the rest of South Africa no longer applied. By this measure, black workers in the Bantustans were left at the mercy of employers, with predictable results.

In 1984 the workers in the clothing industry in the Bantustans worked a 45-hour week, whereas those in the rest of South Africa worked a 40-hour week. At the Isithebe Henred Freuhauf plant at Mandini, the minimum hourly wage was 80c compared to R1.80 in the company's other plants outside KwaZulu. When the Metal and Allied Workers Union (MAWU) began organising at various plants, the employers made it known that they would be willing to recognise MAWU provided it didn't mobilise for wage parity with plants outside KwaZulu.

It was inevitable, therefore, that trade unions which campaigned for the protection of the black workers in the Bantustans against exploitation would come into conflict with the authorities throughout the homelands. The unions were harassed with security legislation or banned altogether and a number of their leaders were detained. In Bophuthatswana a trade union could function legally, conditional upon it recognising that Bophuthatswana was 'independent'. In Kaiser Matanzima's Transkei, all trade unions were banned and strike activity made illegal. The Ciskei had similar restrictions and hundreds of trade union officials were detained.

Until that time, KwaZulu had been the only one that permitted selected trade union activity. When it gained self-governing status, it replaced South African industrial laws with its own. This permitted the legalisation of trade unions and the establishment of an industrial court. Actually though, no trade union has ever been established in KwaZulu, nor an industrial court set up. In 1984 a union called the National Sugar Refining and Allied Industries Employees became the first union to affiliate to the IFP. This, under KwaZulu labour law, was permitted, including permission for unions to join a political party, give it financial aid, influence its members to join the political party, and assist that party in any other way.

At the start of this relationship Chief Minister Buthelezi didn't reveal his bias towards capitalism and seemed to believe that his organisation could straddle two horses running in opposite directions. He needed the trade unions to bolster the membership of Inkatha, but he also didn't dare offend the industrialists. The industrialists wanted him to provide a cheap and docile workforce while the trade unions wanted a climate where they could mobilise to get better wages and working conditions for their members. Something had to give.

The true attitude of the KwaZulu authorities was revealed in 1982 during two strikes of workers at the Bata Shoe Company at Loskop. Bata's wage bill inside KwaZulu was about a third of what they paid outside the territory. The first strike centred around refusal by management to deal with the National Union of Textile Workers (NUTW) as well as demands for the reinstatement of fired union members. The union appealed to the KwaZulu administration to intervene.

In a subsequent press statement NUTW recorded its bitter frustration at the attitude of the KwaZulu officials. They didn't know then that Inkatha had a company called Khulani Holdings (Pty) Ltd which had a financial relationship with Bata and that the KwaZulu government owned shares in it. The workers clearly didn't stand a chance. 250 workers were fired and the strike was broken.

In 1984 a second strike occurred at Loskop. Bata workers again appealed to the KwaZulu government to intervene and the company met the relevant KwaZulu minister. However, workers were then subjected to intimidation, arrest and assault by the KwaZulu police. During 1986 NUTW members were forcibly prevented from attending union meetings and were attacked by Inkatha vigilantes at Hambanathi Township.

Objectively, it was impossible for the IFP to come down on the workers' side because it had to support investors. The promise to uphold workers' rights in KwaZulu was merely a ploy to get them to support Inkatha.

When Chief Buthelezi launched his UWUSA before an audience of 50 000 at King's Park Stadium in 1986 his chosen theme was foreign investment. Mzala reported in his book *Gatsha Buthelezi: Chief with a Double Agenda*:

> In his speech, Chief Buthelezi said to the crowd: 'I would like to know whether, in fact, it's your wish that disinvestment and sanctions should be imposed in South Africa? Shall I tell those overseas that you are now ready to suffer even more deprivations than you are suffering already?'

There were cries of 'No' from many in the audience. The theme was selected by Buthelezi because — according to an Inkatha pamphlet announcing the launch of UWUSA — Elijah Barayi, the COSATU president, had attacked Buthelezi by declaring COSATU's support for economic sanctions against South Africa. The pamphlet claimed that Inkatha did not support disinvestment because 'it believes the free enterprise system is the most powerful system man has devised which is capable of fostering sustained economic growth'.

Buthelezi was also quoted in this pamphlet as saying that Inkatha would 'not stand by . . . when the African National Congress Mission in Exile and the United Democratic Front move in to usurp the function of those trade unions which are so deeply valued in all Western Industrial societies . . .' He added that Inkatha was faced with a situation where crosscutting membership between it and COSATU could become a problem and warned that Inkatha would, if necessary, enter 'the field of labour relations'. Trade unions that put politics before employees' rights would prey on the benefits of workers and contribute to the poverty of those who had no viable unions to fight for their rights, he said. Inkatha would not sit back when COSATU 'politically poached' members and tried to hijack the South African trade union movement.

At its launch, UWUSA elected its office bearers. They were senior company executives and not one was a worker. What manner of trade union is it that is headed by non workers — indeed, by capitalists and aspiring capitalists? On its policy standpoint, it stated:

> UWUSA believes that political issues should be resolved through negotiation rather than violence...UWUSA's attitude towards COSATU is not intended to be confrontational. Instead, UWUSA believes COSATU's standpoint on various socio-political issues is non-productive, self-destructive and negative...UWUSA shares the views of the President of Inkatha, Chief Buthelezi, concerning the future dispensation of South Africa . . .

The major reason why UWUSA came into existence was to oppose COSATU. COSATU mobilised workers at a national level and was a powerful ally of the liberation struggle. It also supported disinvestment and could mobilise national strikes to harm employers who exploited the workers. COSATU was a thorn in flesh of employers and foreign investors who sought to make huge profits by using cheap black labour. UWUSA opposed virtually everything that COSATU held dear, so conflict was inevitable.

Daluxolo was put to work to help mobilise workers around Durban and get them to cancel their membership of COSATU.

'All Zulu-speaking workers were required to leave COSATU and become members of UWUSA. One couldn't be a Zulu and not support Inkatha and one couldn't belong to Inkatha and support COSATU', Daluxolo explained.

'But Daluxolo', I asked, 'was UWUSA prepared to confront employers who paid Inkatha members miserable wages? Was a single strike or stay-away organised by UWUSA to improve the working conditions or wages of its members?'

'That wasn't UWUSA's purpose. It existed to mobilise workers along tribal lines and force them to relinquish their COSATU memberships. UWUSA's enemy was COSATU, not the employers.'

'But surely, Daluxolo, as UWUSA shop stewards you still had to give workers a reasonable explanation as to why COSATU was so bad. You couldn't just tell them to withdraw without giving them good reasons.'

'Oh yes, we gave them reasons, but whether they were good ones is another matter. We used to say that COSATU, like the ANC, was dominated by communists. I don't think many workers really knew what a communist was, but just the word "communist" spelled trouble with the government. COSATU, we told workers, was controlled by the Russians in Moscow and by the Chinese in Beijing. We explained that COSATU would loot the gold, diamonds and all mineral wealth and hand it to their Russian and Chinese friends if the ANC assumed power. We also told them that by calling for disinvestment the ANC/COSATU alliance wanted to take away their jobs and let their families starve.'

'And did they believe this rubbish, Daluxolo?'

'Not really, I must say. We were not talking to children. These people had been members of COSATU-affiliated unions for years and they trusted their leaders. It was difficult to discredit people like Elijah Barayi, Cyril Ramaphosa, Gwede Mantashe and John Gomomo. So we resorted to intimidation and terror tactics instead.'

Daluxolo's admission was supported by two cases that occurred in 1986. In the first, Phineas Sibiya, Simon Ngubane and Filomena Mnikathi were accosted and murdered on the road between Mpophomeni Township and Lions River by Inkatha members. The killers were wearing Inkatha Youth Brigade T-shirts, Inkatha uniforms or lapel badges showing a picture of their leader, Chief Buthelezi. Those murdered were members of MAWU. The killers were arrested but no prosecutions materialised.

In the second incident an NUM official, John Bhekuyise Ntshangase, was attacked and bludgeoned to death by UWUSA members at Vryheid Coronation Colliery in 1987. Zulu speakers like Ntshangase who supported NUM were told that it was a Xhosa union and that they should withdraw their membership. They reported the high level of intimidation by UWUSA members to management but no preventive steps were ever taken. Other NUM members left the mine, fearing for their lives. Mzala reported:

> In February 1987 a caucus meeting of the underground workers' representatives was held as a result of which representatives met a Mr R Westermeyer, the Industrial Relations officer. At this meeting, P Mhlungu, an UWUSA employee representative and chairperson of the underground workers' caucus, said that certain workers in other sections of the mine were troublesome, as they were Xhosa employees, and that if management wouldn't deal with them, he (Mhlungu) should be empowered to do so. After this meeting, rumours circulated that there would be attacks on Xhosa-speaking mine workers. As a result, Nxitywa and others met with management to complain about these threats.

In another incident an acting section hostel manager and known UWUSA member, Andries Mbata, went to Abion Mavuso's house armed with a knobkerrie and told him he had come to kill him because he was a Zulu who lived with and supported Xhosas. His other 'crime' was that he recruited members for NUM.

UWUSA disappeared after the 1994 elections.

30

The Caprivi two hundred

With the relationship between the IFP and ANC souring because of the UDF's policy of making the country ungovernable, armed confrontations between the IFP and UDF began to occur with increasing frequency from 1983 onwards.

Students boycotted classes and the IFP sent armed impis to beat and stab them back to the classrooms. The students and other members of the UDF stoned and burned the houses of councillors in the townships around KwaZulu. Guns began to appear on both sides, but at first they were crude weapons like shotguns, homemade pistols and obsolete rifles. It was not long, though, before AK47s, R1s and R4s were brought out. Casualties on both sides increased. The chosen weapon of the UDF members was the necklace — a petrol-filled car tyre that was hung around the neck of a victim and set alight. Victims would horribly burn to death while the UDF comrades sang, chanted and danced around the rubbery funeral pyre. It was barbaric.

There was escalating anger and animosity in the black community. Chiefs in the rural and peri-urban areas were targeted and shot and their houses or businesses burnt. The spiral of violence seemed to grow by the day. The turning point in what had become a low intensity civil war came, according to Peter Stiff in his book *Warfare by Other Means: South Africa in the 1980s and 1990s* when:

> The Director of Military Intelligence, General Tienie Groenewald, saw Buthelezi at Ulundi on 25 November 1985 at the latter's request. Groenewald told him and the acting KwaZulu Police Commissioner, General Sipho Mathe, that MK was training a specialist unit in Mozambique to assassinate him (Buthelezi), KwaZulu cabinet ministers, their deputies, various government officials and other VIPs. They also planned to destroy KwaZulu government buildings. If true this was an extraordinary volte-face for the ANC, who until then had believed that killing Buthelezi would make him a martyr. Chief Buthelezi confirmed that he had received information to this effect.
>
> ... Thabo Mbeki denied to the Truth and Reconciliation Commission in September 1996 that the ANC ever considered such a plan. He contended the story was a plot by senior military officers of the former regime to get Buthelezi on their side. Chief Buthelezi refuted this. The Rev Londa Shembe, leader of one of the largest independent churches in South Africa, had maintained covert links with the ANC and MK. Shembe had heard

that the ANC had assigned Terrence Tyrone, an MK operative, to assassinate him. Shembe's family rejected the plan. He was, they said, totally loyal to the ANC and he would not have betrayed their plans. Chief Buthelezi, however, produced a warning letter from the Rev Shembe and a file of secret intelligence reports confirming the assassination plots.

The authors of the reports don't deny the possibility that such an assassination plot designed to get rid of Buthelezi existed, but why was he the only target and not the rest of the homeland leaders? What had he done to deserve being singled out for special attention? But those providing the information were white officers of the apartheid regime which had its own agenda of divide and rule.

It appears significant that the decision to support Inkatha militarily against the ANC was code-named *Operation Marion*. Was this short for marionette — a puppet controlled by strings pulled by Military Intelligence?

According to Peter Stiff:

> Chief Buthelezi asked the SADF to provide him with close protection as he did not trust his existing SAP-trained bodyguards. On a broader plain, he required an intelligence service, a defence force and his own State Security Council for KwaZulu with which to facilitate and coordinate counter-insurgency actions. In addition he asked that a battalion of Zulu troops be based at Jozini.
>
> Groenewald briefed the Chief of Staff Intelligence, Vice-Admiral Dries Putter, on his discussions with the Chief Minister. He recommended the SADF meet Buthelezi's needs by secretly training a defensive unit of between 50 and 100 men and an offensive unit of ten to 20 men. In turn Vice-Admiral Putter spoke to SADF chief, General Jannie Geldenhuys, on 27 November and suggested that either he or Defence Minister Magnus Malan seek an urgent meeting with Buthelezi to capitalise on the new spirit of goodwill and cooperation he was displaying.
>
> The next day an extraordinary meeting of the State Security Council (SSC) was convened at Tuynhuys, Cape Town, and Chief Buthelezi's requirements were discussed. The council mandated Defence Minister Malan, Constitutional Development and Planning Minister Chris Heunis and Law and Order Minister Louis le Grange to help Buthelezi create a security force for KwaZulu. A special interdepartmental committee was appointed to implement decisions. In turn, this committee set up a sub-committee to investigate Buthelezi's special needs, including a paramilitary unit and the power to issue firearms licences . . .
>
> The top secret Liebenberg Report (named after Army Chief General Kat Liebenberg), which was handed to SADF Chief Jannie Geldenhuys, said the unit was required to 'neutralise' the UDF. It would have the capacity to mobilise people of 'Zulu culture' and would include about 30 men to operate covertly against the UDF. They would form the basis for a future KwaZulu defence force. The SADF would benefit because it would make it more effective against the UDF. If successful, it would pave the way for similar projects in other national states.

After this there was no going back for Chief Buthelezi and the IFP. They had placed themselves firmly on the side of the apartheid regime and were totally controlled by the SADF. They were effectively a surrogate force no different to RENAMO.

Daluxolo was staying at the Prince Mshiyeni hospital with many other IFP people. They were heavily engaged with UWUSA activities, drawing Inkatha supporters away from COSATU. With Zulus who didn't belong to the IFP they used the tactic of labelling both the ANC and COSATU as Xhosa-dominated organisations. Sometimes it worked, sometimes it didn't.

In early April 1986 he was approached by Melchizedeck Zakhele 'MZ' Khumalo — personal assistant to Dr Buthelezi, Siegfried Bhengu — an ex-MK fighter and an IFP Central Committee member, and Mangaqa Mncwango — another Central Committee member. They told him the IFP had decided to form an armed wing and were appointing him as the unit's Chief Political Commissar. He accepted the appointment. They cautioned him not to breathe a word of what had been discussed.

On 16 April he was called to attend an urgent meeting at Nhlungwane Camp near Ulundi. He arrived there at about 15:00 and found 50 young men who had been there for several days. Members of the IFP's leadership who welcomed him to the camp were MZ Khumalo, Musa Zondi (national chairman of the IFP Youth Brigade), Mangaqa Mncwango (executive committee member of the Youth Brigade) and Ntwe Mafole (publicity secretary of the Youth Brigade).

Daluxolo was told that the young men at the camp would be the first group to go for military training and that he would be going with them. He also learned that they would be departing immediately and there wouldn't even be time for him to return home to pack a suitcase. He had to go in the clothes he was wearing. He had no idea how long they would be away, nor their destination. He didn't even get the opportunity to tell his fiancee, Miss Sibongile Mthembu, that he was leaving. It was not the first time he had been involved in such a situation. It had been the same when he joined MK in 1963 — complete secrecy, an unknown destination and duration of absence.

A furniture removal truck appeared at 17:00 and Daluxolo and the other young men piled in. They were driven to Louis Botha Airport (now Durban International) where they boarded an SAAF C130 transport aircraft. They took off at about 22:00 and flew for five hours. A rumour did the rounds that they were going to be trained by the Israelis — Mossad (Israeli Intelligence) to be exact. No one had any idea how far Israel was from South Africa, so when the plane touched down everyone believed they were in Israel. Daluxolo only discovered much later that they had landed at the Immelmann airstrip in the Caprivi.

The runway was illuminated by torches to guide the aircraft, but these were extinguished as the plane touched down. The trainees disembarked in complete darkness. They were led to military trucks and driven through the early morning darkness. When they eventually stopped, they were ordered to debus.

'This is your camp', they were told.

Dawn revealed bush, nothing but bush. They seemed to be in the middle of nowhere. The only living quarters were four thatched huts in which the white instructors were going to live. They were lined up and addressed by a white man.

'I'm JJ and I'm the commander of the instructors here. We work for a company that the IFP has contracted to give you six months military training.'

He was actually Major Jake 'JJ' Jacobs, an experienced Recce operator and RENAMO specialist.

One of the whites was called Steve and another was the 'sergeant-major' who was in charge of logistics. He never gave his name.

The trainees were set to work to build a camp from scratch. This involved bush clearing, levelling the parade ground, digging latrines and constructing thatched houses for themselves. There was much to be done. They had no idea where they were and nicknamed the base Capernaum, in case they were in Israel after all.

It was actually Hippo Base on the Kwando River and part of Military Intelligence's San Michelle guerrilla training base in the Caprivi. Other guerrilla forces like RENAMO and particularly UNITA were also being trained there. It had been dubbed San Michelle — the patron saint of paratroopers — by its overall commander, Colonel Jan Breytenbach — the founder of the Recces and 44-Parachute Brigade. He was known by the Zulu name of *Mehlwensimbi* (eyes of steel).

Before that first group had finished building the base, another group of 50 arrived and by the end of the week a third group of 50 commanded by Thompson Xesibe joined them. A final group brought the number to 200 men.

They were divided into four platoons of 50 men — Alpha, Bravo, Charlie and Delta — and told to choose their own commanders. A white instructor was allocated to each platoon to provide specialist training.

The training operation was the overall responsibility of Colonel Cor van Niekerk, assistant to General Neels van Tonder, who was accountable to the Chief of Staff Intelligence (CSI) for *Operation Marion*. Colonel van Niekerk was CSI's Director of Special Tasks and responsible for the training and equipping of surrogate forces. The recruits were never told their instructors' real names, but knew them only by noms de guerre. However, they discovered that JJ was Major Jacobs and JP was Captain Opperman. A Sergeant Cloete was also an instructor there.

Each man was issued with a G3 and an AK47 rifle as well as live ammunition. They were told their camp was situated in an area where UNITA, MPLA and SWAPO were active and the need to defend themselves might arise. The instructors preferred the AK47 to the G3 which was KwaZulu Government issue. Because it was heavy it was used only for training and the men kept their AKs with them at all times. Instruction commenced with a six week course in basic discipline, drill, physical training and political indoctrination.

Officers' meetings attended by Daluxolo took place each evening. The day's training and events were discussed and plans were made for the following day's programme. It was during these meetings that Daluxolo became certain they were being trained by SADF personnel and not by employees of a private company. It made no difference to the eventual result, so he just got on with it. After the meetings he would have discussions with the trainees, find out their views on the training and what problems they were experiencing and solve them if he could.

He was introduced to officers from UNITA and RENAMO. The instructors said they were all resistance forces deployed to combat communist incursions in the southern African sub-region. The communists, they were told, were MPLA in Angola, FRELIMO in Mozambique and the ANC Alliance in South Africa. It became obvious that when they were properly trained and equipped, they would all be deployed to support the SADF in a fight against the liberation movements. Effectively they would be SADF surrogate forces pursuing their own agenda, but also defending white power and privilege. The trainees were not allowed to visit the camps of the other surrogate forces.

At the end of each month MZ Khumalo came to the camp to pay salaries. He was always accompanied by either Colonel Swart or Colonel van Niekerk. Daluxolo got a salary of about R500 per month and the trainees about R300. CSI laundered this money through Military Intelligence to Armscor who paid the money into a variety of Inkatha accounts to give the impression it came from donations made by Inkatha supporters.

After basics, the recruits spent the next eight weeks on weapons training. They were instructed in the use of the AK47, the G3 rifle, the RPG7 rocket launcher, the Uzi sub-machine gun, hand grenades, anti-tank and anti-personnel mines, the 9mm Browning pistol, Makarov and Tokarev pistols and various explosives. They were taught how to lay ambushes, how to abduct people and how to rescue those who had been abducted. They laid landmines and learnt how to blow up buildings and vehicles. Much time was spent instructing them on every aspect of guerrilla and counter-guerrilla warfare. Daluxolo didn't train the men himself, but interpreted where necessary, helped to explain things, motivated the men and demonstrated what the instructors wanted done.

Brigadier Mathe came with MZ Khumalo on one occasion and told the men they would later be integrated into the KwaZulu police force. He expressed great satisfaction with the progress.

The final phase of the training involved separating the 200 men into four groups, each of which was given different forms of specialised training. Daluxolo helped Colonel Jacobs and the other officers select men for the various groups. Each man was assessed, analysed and allocated to a group according to his personal traits, character and skills. They had to match the characteristics required for the roles they were required to play. Afterwards they were given additional group-specific training.

The largest group, made up of 100 men, was the Contra-Mobilisation group and its leader was Joyful Mthethwa. They were trained as IFP field organisers and taught how to expand Inkatha's support base and promote its image as a liberation organisation. They were also charged with identifying and recruiting suitable field organisers. They would identify 'trouble-makers' and people who denounced the IFP and opposed its growth and popularity. In particular, they were to pinpoint UDF field organisers and relay their details to the Defensive Group. They were given extensive lectures on propaganda, raising political awareness, the compiling and distribution of pamphlets, how to infiltrate opposition organisations, the art of public speaking and so on. Many lectures for this group were conducted by a Dr L Pasques and four of his associates.

The Defensive Group's prime task was intelligence gathering. There were 30 of them and they were led by Sitwell Mkhwanazi and Phumlani Mshengu. This function required people of above-average intelligence who were good communicators. They had to gather their own information, cultivate independent sources and utilise intelligence passed to them by the Contra-Mobilisation Group. They were trained to record information, analyse it and convert it into proper intelligence. They were taught that information could come in the form of rumours, hearsay and even disinformation circulated by the enemy. They had to verify rumours, follow-up on hearsay and double check and verify every item of information. They were trained in the use of dead letter boxes, shadowing people, the use of listening devices, cameras and other technical aspects of intelligence work.

The Defensive Group was probably the most important in the organisation because they were its eyes, ears and brain. A lack of information or wrong information could lead to bad decision-making by the commanders. The officer in charge of training this group was Captain Opperman, alias JP.

Members of the Offensive Group were naturally aggressive people, hard men who would kill without asking questions or feeling remorse. They came to be known as *oTheleweni* (ruthless killers). They had to be top performers in all facets of their training in arms, explosives and physical work. The *oTheleweni* were men who placed a low premium on life and would eliminate the party's enemies without batting an eyelid.

They numbered 40 men in all and were led by Leslie Mkhulisi and Peter Msane — the hardest and most ruthless of the lot. They were trained in house penetration, ambushing people travelling in motor vehicles, setting booby-traps, and the abduction of targeted individuals. They would stop at nothing to further IFP objectives and aims. Their white trainers were Jerry, Kloppies and Sergeant Cloete. Cloete was a top marksman who had represented South Africa in international rifle competitions.

The 32 men in the VIP Protection Unit were led by Bheki Zikalala. They were selected for their proficiency in the use of handguns, the Uzi sub-machine gun and driving vehicles in unusual and difficult conditions. They were excellent marksmen. They would become the personal aides of cabinet ministers and VIPs. Their work was completely legal and aboveboard because it was known and accepted that VIPs needed bodyguards. New instructors for this group were brought in, including a man who was in charge of security for Ciskei strongman, Brigadier Oupa Gqozo.

Towards the end of the six months training, Daluxolo flew to Ulundi via Pretoria with Colonel Swart and JJ Retief. Discussions took place with top IFP officials relating to the progress of training and how and where the recruits should be deployed on their return. It had already been decided they would be absorbed into the structures of the KwaZulu Police, but they wouldn't be involved in normal police work. Instead they would remain the IFP's armed wing and carry out the tasks they had been trained for under its umbrella.

They returned to the training camp by the same route and it was only then that Daluxolo discovered they had been in the Caprivi all along. Henceforth they came to be referred to as the Caprivians. Everything about the training operation was treated as top secret. The men were warned time and time again never to disclose anything about their training, their duties, operations and the persons they were involved with to anyone. It was made plain that a breach of this code could result in the guilty party 'taking the first bus' — a euphemism for being killed. They were allowed to write letters home while undergoing training, but the letters were scrutinised and censored. Those considered revealing were destroyed.

On completion of their six months training, a passing out parade was held. Those present were MZ Khumalo, Brigadier Cor van Niekerk, Colonel Swart and Colonel Jan *Mehlwensimbi* Breytenbach. After the formalities of an inspection and drill had been completed, the groups were given the opportunity to demonstrate the skills they had learned. They conducted mock battles, a house-clearing demonstration, abductions, firing and handling of different weapons including RPG7 rocket launchers. It was an impressive display and all officers present agreed that the trainees had been turned into fine soldiers. The parade was videotaped by Jerry who gave the tape to MZ Khumalo. MZ told Daluxolo later that he had handed it to Chief Minister Buthelezi.

At the end of the proceedings, the contingent boarded a C130 Hercules aircraft and flew back to Louis Botha Airport from where they returned to Nhlungwane Camp.

They arrived to a welcome-home celebration. Chief Buthelezi personally thanked them for volunteering to defend the IFP. It was the first time the Caprivians, other than Daluxolo, had met the Chief Minister. MZ Khumalo was also there as were KwaZulu Police officers including Brigadier Mathe, Captain Hlengwa, Captain Dunge and others. An ox was slaughtered and the Chief Minister dedicated it to the trainees. Then the feasting began.

After the celebrations members of the Offensive and Contra-Mobilisation groups went to Cape Town for a further six week course. Everyone was given a month's leave to allow them to spend time with their families.

Chief Buthelezi now finds it embarrassing to acknowledge his Caprivians and the acts carried out on behalf of the IFP. The IFP's position these days is that Minister Buthelezi knew nothing about the Caprivians — despite him having asked the South African Government for a para-military group. When the South African Government approved *Operation Marion* and agreed to train and provide weapons for the unit, who were they doing it for? To believe that Minister Buthelezi knew nothing about the Caprivians is the same as Alphonse Dhlakama denying that he knew anything about RENAMO and its operations against FRELIMO.

There is no reason to doubt General Tienie Groenewald's story that the IFP was being randomly attacked by the UDF, that chiefs and headmen were being killed and that Chief Minister Buthelezi's own life was threatened. But when the chickens came home to roost and the Caprivians were being arrested, it became politically inconvenient to acknowledge them. Yet Daluxolo and his men were risking their lives to protect people who now dismiss them as common criminals and murderers. The same happened to Colonel Eugene de Kock. The old apartheid regime has labelled him a mass murderer who ran amok killing black people without orders. The men who trained him, provided him with resources and braai'd meat with him and his men at Vlakplaas all ran for cover. They preferred to profess astonishment at what Vlakplaas had been up to. But merely because they decided to surround themselves with a bodyguard of lies shouldn't prevent anyone else from telling the truth.

Peter Stiff reports in his book *Warfare by Other Means*, that shortly after the Caprivians returned, Colonels Cor van Niekerk and John More visited Chief Buthelezi and presented him with a bulletproof vest. Buthulezi expressed his gratitude to them for training the 206 men 'which he regarded as a boost to his safety'.

Buthelezi talks of having had only a small police force to defend himself and his IFP cabinet colleagues. When his name was mentioned later in court documents relating to the hit-squad activities of the Caprivians, he called it 'the biggest poppycock I have ever heard'.

Stiff quoted Chief Buthelezi as saying:

> When the violence started in 1985 I had a duty not only to see to my own protection but the protection of other people . . . so we selected the 200 young people for training. Where they were trained and how they were trained — I was not involved in that. Now if some of the people decided then to break the law and do what they did, then that's a matter for them, because that's a matter of law, which needs to be resolved in court. To try to drag in my name merely because I did that . . . there was nothing sinister about that. I have a very clear conscience about it. I was threatened, people were dying and they were asking what we were doing about that. With only a small police force, the acting commissioner at the time, decided we should approach the military.

Daluxolo was allocated an office in the IFP headquarters at Ulundi. He operated from there travelling extensively throughout KwaZulu Natal. He also assisted Colonel Luthuli in the compilation of KwaZulu Police appointment certificates for trainees. The certificates described the holders as detective constables and were signed by Brigadier Mathe. They were issued to the Caprivians.

While the Caprivians were on their one month's leave, MZ Khumalo called Daluxolo to accompany him to a meeting at the headquarters of the SADF's 121-(Zulu) Battalion at Mtubatuba. They were joined by Major Louis Botha of the Security Branch, Cor van Niekerk by then a brigadier, Captain Opperman, 'Jerry' and others whom Daluxolo couldn't recall. It was decided that those present would become a planning committee and would control the deployments and activities of the Caprivians.

The VIP Protection Unit had already been absorbed into the KwaZulu Police (KZP) without undergoing police training. They were issued with four new Toyota Cressidas and two Toyota Kombis. They moved to the Police College at Ulundi where they fell under Captain Dunge.

The Offensive Group was placed under the command of Captain Opperman and Jerry and posted to Port Durnford. They were also issued with new vehicles, arms and ammunition under strict control.

The Contra-Mobilisation Group was placed under Daluxolo's command. They were issued with four new Kombis, two white, one red and one cream. The members of this group were deployed to their home areas for duty. They were mainly involved with political work and intelligence gathering and it was felt they would be more successful if they were known to the people they were dealing with.

Daluxolo raised a concern when driving home with MZ after the meeting. He asked why the white people who trained them in Caprivi had rejoined them in Natal. Were they going to direct operations and select targets? If that was so, how would the Caprivians be able to escape the reality that they were being commanded by SADF officers? Had the IFP become a surrogate organisation of the Boers? If it had, was Chief Minister Buthelezi aware of this and did he approve?

'Yes, commissar, they will be directing our operations and the Chief Minister has approved it. They are giving us the money and weapons that enable us to fight, so we can't just brush them aside now that the training is over', MZ told him.

'But that will put us in a position where they can blackmail us into attacking and killing MK freedom fighters and not just those who want to attack Inkatha. If that happens, how can we still call ourselves a liberation movement? My understanding of our role was that we aim to remove the apartheid regime by peaceful means and that we won't be deployed against MK as long as they don't attack our people.'

MZ didn't reveal any disquiet at Daluxolo's questions, but promised to raise the matter with the Chief Minister and give him feedback. But he never did. After this Daluxolo was often excluded from meetings of the Planning Committee without explanation. MZ had probably told them he was asking awkward questions. With *Operation Marion* commanded by white SADF officers, the IFP had indeed become a buffer to protect white power from the liberation movements.

In late 1986 MZ approached Captain Opperman and told him the trainees 'wanted to strike back . . . they were trained and sitting idle'. Opperman allegedly approached Colonel John More and asked permission to launch an operation targeting 'persons whose death would have a positive impact on the IFP'. Colonel More later denied that such an approach had been made.

However, Captain Opperman instructed Daluxolo to select four targets 'whose death would have a positive impact on Inkatha'. Daluxolo nominated four members of the Defensive Group, including Bhekisisa Alex Khumalo, to compile target dossiers. When these were passed back to Opperman, he asked Military Intelligence and the Security Police to check the names to ensure none were informers. They were apparently all in the clear and the hits were approved.

Bhekisisa's recommended target was Victor Ntuli who lived in KwaMakutha. Ntuli, the dossier said, was an UDF activist and the paymaster for operations directed against Inkatha. He was also a trained MK operator. What it failed to mention was that the target house reconnoitred by Bhekisisa belonged to Rev Willie Ntuli. Victor was only an occasional lodger.

According to Opperman, Colonel More gave him the final go-ahead and arranged for the issue of AK47s and ammunition from Ferntree — a secret military base close to the

Drakensberg Mountains — by a Colonel Dan Griesel. Opperman said it was planned to take the weapons to Pretoria after the hit for destruction in a furnace at Iscor (the state-owned Iron and Steel Corporation). Griesel later admitted his role in the operation, but More denied his.

On 20 January 1987 Captain Opperman, Sergeant Cloete and MZ Khumalo rendezvoused with a 12-man hit squad in a dry river bed near Ulundi. Daluxolo and Bhekisisa Khumalo were among them. Weapons were issued and torches taped to rifle barrels to illuminate targets. The layout of the Ntuli house was sketched in the sand and the squad members were given a final briefing. They were also allowed time to practise and test weapons.

Sergeant Cloete had been responsible for the preliminary training. He said that Captain Opperman had ordered him to train a squad to penetrate the house and 'kill all the occupants' — including the women and children. He thought it was a lawful order because the attack had been authorised by Pretoria, but ventured the opinion that Opperman was 'mad'. He also said it was the most outrageous order he had ever been given.

Captain Opperman and Sergeant Cloete travelled to the Malibu Hotel in Durban where they met Major Louis Botha, the Security Police's liaison officer for the operation. His job was to divert normal police patrols and 'sweep' the scene for incriminating evidence before the police got there. Botha later also denied involvement.

In *Warfare by Other Means* Peter Stiff described the carnage that ensued during the attack:

> Victor Ntuli had been in hiding for a month and was away. His brother, Rev Willie Ntuli, however, was at home. A lot of women and children were staying the night because of a late night prayer meeting.
>
> Anna Khumalo was asleep when she was awakened by a bang on the door and a fusillade of shots. She quickly grabbed her toddler and tried to get out of the house, but so many people were asleep on the floor that she could not get past them. So she ducked into a wardrobe, her baby in her arms, and cowered down. She heard a frightening crescendo of gunfire and screams.
>
> Meanwhile, Bhekisisa Alex Khumalo, the guide, waited in the Combi while the ten-man offensive team smashed its way inside and sprayed shots at the unfortunates there.
>
> Neighbours alerted by the shooting came out, but they were driven back into the safety of their homes by the gunfire. Thembinkosi Mkhize, an Inkatha member, saw a minibus arrive at the Ntuli house at about 02:00. 'Three or four men got out. When I saw they were armed with firearms I hid under the bed. I was afraid.' He did not leave his house again until the police arrived.
>
> Silence eventually returned, but Anna Khumalo was petrified and she remained with her baby in the doubtful safety of the wardrobe. Several hours later she plucked up enough courage to leave it and was confronted by a charnel house of 12 bodies, including five children under the age of ten.
>
> Rev Willie Ntuli and his three children aged six, 16, and 19 were amongst the dead. His wife, Ethel Ntuli survived as did her one-year-old granddaughter, Nomvula. They were

saved because a body fell and covered them. A church elder, Ernest Thusini, his wife Faith and their children Nomfundo (10), Phumzile (8), Vukile (7), twins Mbuso and Nombuso (6) and Sanele (4) were asleep when the room was sprayed with bullets. Ernest, Faith and Nombuso survived. Nomfundo became the 13th fatal casualty when she was declared brain dead after more than a week on a life support machine. Ten-year-old Ernest Ntuzhini, whose four siblings were less fortunate, also escaped with his life after hiding in a wardrobe.

Ironically, although he survived that attack, Victor Ntuli was shot dead at a political rally in 1990. No one was arrested for his murder.

No arrests were made because the Security Police did everything they could to destroy evidence and to obstruct the policemen investigating the case. The murders would later come back to haunt those involved in the planning of the attack.

Shortly afterwards MZ told Daluxolo that he had been promoted to commander-in-chief, making him the senior military commander in the IFP's armed wing. It is probable that Chief Minister Buthelezi approved the appointment because, as the supreme commander and president of IFP, it seems unlikely he would have been bypassed at such a time.

Daluxolo later applied to the Truth and Reconciliation Commission for amnesty and described the role of the Caprivi trainees in Mpumalanga (KwaZulu):

> During the day the Caprivians worked as police, go out of the police station, do their raids. However, in the evening they have to take off their uniforms and get involved in the struggle. When I refer to the 'struggle' I mean it was getting themselves to do what they were trained to do in Caprivi.
>
> During this period, there were literally hundreds of incidents where attacks were launched against UDF people, property and homes. It is impossible for me to record the extent of these attacks. The comrades responded by attacking us with equal vigour. A state of war existed between us. I often played a command role in directing our attacks. I did the following: arranged for arms and ammunition; gathered fighting men; chose people who would lead the attacks and different aspects of the attacks; decided on the strategy of an attack; and decided on the target or areas to be attacked.
>
> After the attack, I arranged for injured persons to be medically treated by sending them to clinics or hospitals; collected firearms and ammunition and stored them safely; arranged our defensive structures and strategies; reported back to the planning committee through MZ Khumalo.

Daluxolo told the TRC about an attack on a UDF meeting of about 300 people at a house named 'Summertime' in Unit 1, South Mpumalanga on 18 January 1988. He did not personally participate but sent a group led by Phumalani Xolani Mshengu and including Sbu Bhengu, members of the Inkatha Youth Brigade and other Caprivians. He said that Mshenu and Bhengu were:

> ... armed with two of our AK47 rifles. The Inkatha Youth members were also armed with whatever arms we were able to lay our hands on. The group approached the house and commenced firing on the people who were there. From there they went on and attacked

other houses and killed about nine people.

Daluxolo told me which way his thoughts were going when we were still openly comrades in MK. The longer he had remained with the ANC, he said, the more convinced he became that a tribal power struggle existed. He had witnessed tribal faction fights at Kongwa Camp and had seen Joe Modise exposed as a tribalist mobilising people on tribal lines. He observed that certain people in the ANC had a problem with Zulu history. He believed they were plotting to stifle the struggle in Natal because they feared another Isandlawana. He couldn't help remembering those who had frankly said they were tired of reading about Zulus every time they opened a South African history book.

He became really angry when attacks by the UDF on IFP members took place. The Zulu blood in him began to boil. As had happened when they were in exile, the Zulus were again under attack. What political outcome did the ANC hope to achieve through their surrogate UDF by killing IFP people? he wondered. Who ruled South Africa — was it the IFP or the National Party? Did they think they could free South Africa by killing IFP members? There were plenty of other Bantustan leaders in South Africa like Kaizer Matanzima of Transkei, Lennox Sebe of Ciskei and Lucas Mangope of Bophuthatswana. Why didn't the ANC attack and kill their people?

Then it dawned on him. It was because certain people in the ANC and UDF were out to settle old scores with the Zulus. We had heard them pressing the Russians to agree that Shaka's wars were unjust wars. They never asked about Moshoeshoe's wars to unite the BaSotho, despite both leaders having used the same methods.

Before joining MK Daluxolo hadn't seen himself as a Zulu in the liberation struggle. He considered himself just another South African black oppressed by apartheid. In the MK, though, he had seen and heard things that made him realise that although he might not regard himself as fighting in the struggle with a Zulu agenda, those of other tribes did. With the UDF attacks on IFP people, the killings, the necklacings, the shootings and the knifings, his Zuluness rose to the surface. He saw their attacks on the IFP as attacks against Zulus, no matter who was doing it.

In 1988 Daluxolo was arrested for firearms offences. In his book *Warfare by Others Means* Peter Stiff wrote about what happened next:

> A signal dated 31 August 1988 from the office of Minister of Defence, General Magnus Malan, to the Chief of the SADF, General Jannie Geldenhuys, said there was a need to 'temporarily remove' a member of the *Marion* group. Senior military officers and the Commissioner of Police, General Johan van der Merwe and his deputy, General Basie Smit met to make arrangements.
>
> Captain Opperman testified that '[Major] Louis Botha told me [Daluxolo] Luthuli had been arrested and was telling everyone' in the cells who cared to listen about *Operation Marion*. 'They tried to convince us Luthuli was going to blow *Operation Marion* wide open', he said. 'The security threat to the country would have been immense. General Buchner [the KwaZulu Police Commissioner] suggested we kill Luthuli. If it should have come out, the Defence Force would have taken a helluva knock, the National Party would

have taken a helluva knock and Inkatha would have gone down the drain.'

Both he [Buchner] and Major Botha were in favour of the idea, Opperman said. 'We [Military Intelligence] told Botha we would not carry it out without a specific written order from the police.' The embryo plan, Captain Opperman testified, was finally sunk after a meeting with MZ Khumalo. 'Khumalo was shocked and was definitely not keen for such a thing [the murder] to take place.'

Eventually Daluxolo was released on bail and he laid low in Mkhuze Camp until the hue and cry died down. He continued his duties as commander-in-chief. He had no idea that the Security Police had recommended having him bumped off while he was in detention.

In 1991 Daluxolo summoned Caprivian, Gcina Brian Mkhizi, who was with the KwaZulu Police's Esikhawini Riot Unit, to a meeting at Ulundi. Various IFP notables were also present. Mkhizi was told that the time had arrived to use the skills he had acquired at Caprivi. The plan was for him to work with the Inkatha Youth Brigade and direct attacks on ANC-dominated areas.

The hit squads mounted raids with increasing frequency and between 1991 and August 1993 they killed an unknown number of people in the Sundumbili/Nyoni, Mandini and Eshowe areas. Prominent Inkatha-aligned officials gave them ongoing direction and logistical support in the way of weapons, ammunition, vehicles, accommodation and finance. A number of hit lists were compiled at meetings with IFP leaders. The targets were ANC officials, members and sympathisers. In addition to targeting particular individuals, the hit squads carried out dozens of random attacks on shebeens, bus stops, buses and streets where ANC supporters were known to gather. On some nights they conducted two or three attacks on different targets. Sometimes they would just roam around a section of a township known to be an ANC stronghold, looking for people to attack. After each hit Mkhizi would report back with the results.

Over the same period 422 Inkatha/IFP office bearers were assassinated by the UDF.

31

Zimbabwe
Bitter fruits of division

I once asked Robert Mpofu of ZAPU the reason for that organisation's existence. For a moment he looked at me as if I was out of my mind. When you ask people questions like that where the answers appear obvious to them, they suspect that your brain has gone a little soft.

'ZAPU is there to liberate the black people of Zimbabwe from colonial oppression', he told me condescendingly.

In 1980 Robert Mugabe's ZANU-PF won by a landslide and Mugabe became the first black prime minister of Zimbabwe. ZAPU loyalists continued to murmur angrily that it was a rigged election. But how could they know that for sure?

In fact contingency plans to rig the elections had been put in place — but they were to become operative only if it looked like ZANU-PF was heading for victory. The white Rhodesians believed that neither Nkomo nor Muzorewa would obtain a clear majority, in which case they would form a coalition government. Mugabe, it was thought, would win a mere handful of seats and become a weak opposition.

It was wishful thinking. Nkomo was seen as a 'reasonable terrorist leader', which meant that he wouldn't treat the whites too harshly if he got into power. Muzorewa was their man and if the two leaders formed a joint government, the future and the wealth of white Rhodesians would be secure. Mugabe, on the other hand, was feared by them to the extent that an elaborate plan had been put in place to assassinate him at the Lancaster House conference. As we have noted, this plan reached trigger stage, but was called off at the last minute for reasons unknown. Whoever did so was a very wise person because if the plan had gone ahead, civil war would have immediately broken out and many lives would have been lost.

Why then was the plan to rig the elections called off and by whom? Peter Stiff in his book *Cry Zimbabwe: Independence Twenty Years On* had this to say:

> The Rhodesians had contingency plans in the event of ZANU-PF winning the elections, thanks to its blatant intimidation of the electorate. This entailed manipulating the results by substituting ballot boxes. The final decision to go ahead lay with the CIO Chief, Ken Flower. However, in the final 48 hours before the results were announced, it became clear to him that a ZANU-PF victory was inevitable. To have any marked effect, substitution

would have to be on such a large scale that it would raise serious suspicions. He called it off.

Stiff says that even though the CIO Chief called off the planned rigging of results against ZANU-PF, substitution did occur in Bindura. He believed the local Special Branch commander ordered it, but ' it made no difference to the results', which were announced on 4 March 1980. Of the 80 seats in contention, ZANU-PF won 57 while ZAPU finished with a miserable 20. Those in the ZAPU camps were devastated. Nkomo and his lieutenants believed they had been cheated, but apparently decided to swallow the bitter pill.

What would have happened if ZAPU had won the elections instead? It would have been ZANU-PF's turn to claim they had been cheated and threaten to resume the struggle. A lot of people seemed to have missed the point that for the first time black people had the vote and had exercised it to bring in a majority government. Instead of appreciating that as the greatest event in local political history, they instead switched to squabbling over who was going to rule and who had power. This is the worrying thing about black politics. It starts as a movement to free black people — as Robert Mpofu explained — but after that it becomes a struggle for power amongst the black people themselves.

Ndabaningi Sithole typified the thinking of black leaders when he told me he wouldn't accept a democratic outcome if he didn't become the first prime minister of Zimbabwe. Elsewhere in Africa black people are dying by the million because there are too many people vying to rule. Power is an end in itself among African leaders, rather than the freedom of the people from colonisation or creating a viable economy. Raw power is the name of the game.

If the real issue in Zimbabwe was to free the black people from white oppression, why couldn't ZAPU merge with ZANU-PF to bring unity to the country? It was because ZAPU had come to believe that they were destined to rule and nobody else. In prison ZAPU members had openly referred to themselves as 'the government-in-waiting' and when the results were published they wept openly. I found this behaviour hypocritical in the extreme. You fight to free your country and when it is free you weep because your organisation has lost the election.

The trouble is that black people lack a sense of nationhood. Their political consciousness stops at tribal or political party level. Even organisations like the Pan Africanist Congress of Azania (PAC) who claim to be Africanists have been devastated by internal power struggles and tribalism. The ANC itself is not immune to internal tussles and even tribalism. They manage to keep such destructive impulses under control, which is why the ANC remains in power.

It had been agreed that after the elections both ZANLA and ZIPRA would surrender their weapons to a new national army and become amalgamated within it. ZANLA complied immediately, which is easy to understand because their political parent had become the government. ZIPRA had no intention of paying more than lip service to the agreement. ZIPRA had an impressive armoury of weapons in Zambia including recoilless rifles, 82mm mortars, surface-to-air missile launchers (SAM7s), 57mm anti-tank guns, 122mm rockets and much more. They boasted a motorised infantry brigade and some Soviet T53 tanks. Much of these armaments were brought into Zimbabwe, but were not surrendered and remained firmly under ZIPRA control.

Extensive dissident activity by ZIPRA elements broke out in several parts of the country. This worried the new government greatly. In February 1980, before we had even been released from prison, the newspapers reported that about 200 ZIPRA guerrillas were mobilising in the north-west of the country where the party had its power base. Mugabe, the new prime minister, outlining his policy of reconciliation said:

> If those who have suffered defeat adopt the unfortunate and indefensible attitude that defies and rejects the verdict of the people, then reconciliation between the victor and the vanquished is impossible.

This is not the place to relate every incident that occurred between the two political rivals. The intention is to show that after Zimbabwe had been freed from white oppression, the black nationalists found other reasons to fight — this time amongst themselves. ZIPRA actually sought military assistance from their once sworn enemy — the apartheid regime in South Africa.

Peter Stiff in his book *Cry Zimbabwe* outlines how ZANLA and ZIPRA occupied separate but adjacent camps in the Bulawayo township of Ntumbane. Whoever chose to place two hostile forces so close to each other must have had rocks in his head. The problems started when Enos Nkala, ZANU-PF's Minister of Finance, addressed a ZANU-PF rally in Bulawayo on 8 November 1980. He launched a vitriolic attack on ZAPU and on Nkomo personally. At the White City stadium the following day he became even more belligerent against ZAPU. Meanwhile, unknown and unnoticed by ZANU, thousands of ZAPU supporters entered the stadium and proceeded to disrupt the rally. They threw rocks at Nkala and threatened to tear him apart. The police riot unit responded with teargas and baton charged the demonstrators. They were finally ejected from the rally and order was restored.

When Nkala resumed his speech, he said: 'As from today ZAPU has become the enemy of ZANU-PF. The time has come for ZANU-PF to flex its muscles. Our supporters must now form vigilante committees for those who want to challenge us. There must be a general mobilisation of our supporters.'

Until this point only unarmed civilians on both sides had been involved. Although one person had died and others had been admitted to the nearby Mpilo Hospital with injuries, the worst of the day was still to come.

At 17:15 the real fighting began when ZANLA spotted bus loads of armed ZAPU supporters entering the ZIPRA section of the Ntumbane Camp. They grabbed guns and fighting erupted. Each side opened fire with AK47s, machine guns, mortars, rockets and grenades. Approximately 3 000 men on each side were involved. The ordinary township residents were forced to flee their homes. The civilian supporters of both parties armed themselves with knives, clubs, pangas and any other weapons they could find. They clashed violently, burning and looting each other's homes.

When ZAPU began to lose the edge, they sent a radio message to ZIPRA's Motorised Infantry Brigade at the Gwaai River Mine assembly point. Fighting continued throughout the night. Early the following morning, 10 November, a convoy of trucks and armoured vehicles arrived to stiffen ZAPU's position. The battle raged on as the two most powerful nationalist organisations in Zimbabwe fought for political superiority. In the end it was the new National Army, in the main comprising units of the old Rhodesian Army, that was instrumental in quelling the violence.

The hostility between the two parties deepened. Eventually Robert Mugabe felt the need to have a special strike force of brigade strength that he could use to deal with ZAPU. The National Army was not partisan enough for this purpose. He needed men who were ideologically and emotionally committed to the defeat and destruction of ZAPU as a political and military force. He signed a secret bilateral agreement with North Korea whereby it undertook to train and equip a new unit — 5-Brigade. Mugabe had his tool to deal with the ZAPU threat.

So what was the ZAPU threat? There were elements who refused to accept the legitimacy of the election because they had lost. They rejected ZANU-PF and its leader. They decided to return to the bush and fight to destabilise Mugabe's government. We don't know whether Joshua Nkomo himself was the instigator of this stratagem. My personal experience of ZAPU supporters was that many were quite capable of going against the policies of their leaders — and that's what began to happen.

A dissident problem developed. Armed ZAPU members attacked farmers, carried out criminal activities and even attacked elements of the new National Army. The regular ZIPRA soldiers were apparently more disciplined than their guerrilla cousins. They became integrated into the new army and accepted orders from appointed officers — some from ZANLA and others from the old Rhodesian Security Forces. Yet even apparently conforming former senior ZIPRA commanders became implicated in issues around the ZAPU arms caches.

ZAPU started to deduct Z$50 from the monthly stipend of Z$150 that the government paid to all former ZIPRA regulars and guerrillas and used it to purchase farms and businesses. ZAPU claimed the properties would be used to provide employment for those demobilised men who couldn't be integrated into the National Army.

The money initially collected amounted to Z$20 million and ZAPU donated it to Nkomo in his personal capacity. He used it to buy 152 properties including a motel and entertainment complex with a snake park, a 1 000 hectare vegetable farm, butcheries, a hotel in Bulawayo, a secretarial college, a rural health clinic, a manufacturing company, a building company, a haulage firm, a general store and a service station.

The deadline for the integration of the former guerrilla armies into the National Army was September 1981. That date came and went, but the massive armaments at ZIPRA's Gwaai River Mine Camp were not surrendered and its Motorised Infantry Brigade remained there firmly under ZIPRA control. Later, a convoy of vehicles left the mine and managed to disappear without trace. However, government searches started to unearth rich arms caches at Gwaai River, throughout Matabeleland and farther afield. Peter Stiff reports in his *Cry Zimbabwe*:

> On the 7th February 1982, Prime Minister Robert Mugabe announced that 30 arms caches had been discovered at Ascot Farm, 35km north of Bulawayo. They consisted of 3 000 AK-47s, 1,700 pistols, 75 RPG-7s, SAM-7 missiles, 20 mortars, anti-aircraft weapons and landmines. Ascot Farm belonged to Nitram (Pvt) Ltd, a ZAPU-owned company with two directors, one of them Joshua Nkomo.
>
> At Nest Egg Farm, Douglasdale, Bulawayo, the government found a fleet of 43 military vehicles parked under trees and invisible from the air. There were Soviet-supplied transporters, ambulances, fuel tankers and a complete signal maintenance unit. At Woody Glen Farm they unearthed vast stocks of medical supplies and equipment including penicillin, syringes, pain-killers, stethoscopes, gas bottles and other equipment. At Kenmaur 36 000 rounds of ammunition and 124 rockets were found. At the ZAPU-owned motel and snake park on the Bulawayo Road south of Harare, a huge quantity of AK-47s and ammunition was located.
>
> Discovery of this vast amount of buried and undeclared ZAPU weaponry convinced Mugabe that ZAPU was planning an attack and the overthrow of his government.
>
> 'The only way to deal effectively with a snake is to strike and destroy its head. How else can I describe a man we supposed was our friend?' Mugabe snarled.

On 11 March 1982, ZAPU's two most senior commanders, Lieutenant-General Lookout Masuku and Dumiso 'Black Russian' Dabengwa (ZAPU Intelligence Chief) and four ZAPU senior officials were arrested by Mugabe's CIO.

Is it reasonable to conclude that ZAPU was planning an overthrow of Mugabe's government, given their refusal to surrender their weapons? Why was so much war material buried on ZAPU farms and properties? Were they planning a sneak attack? It's our belief that ZANU-PF was justified in concluding that a detailed plan by ZAPU to attack them and hurl them from power existed. Otherwise, why didn't ZAPU surrender the weaponry?

Conversely, did the behaviour of ZAPU and the activities of its dissidents justify the draconian response of ZANU-PF — the formation and unleashing of 5-Brigade on the Ndebele people and the terrible atrocities that were carried out by this murderous force? While we believe it was correct for ZANU-PF to view ZAPU as a serious security threat, the 5-Brigade operations in Matabeleland — known as the *War of Gukurahundi* in which at least 15 000 civilian men women and children were slaughtered — can never be justified or excused.

It's not our intention in this book to record 5-Brigade's activities in detail. We merely summarise the findings of the Chihambakwe Commission which was appointed by the ZANU-PF government on 13 September 1983 as a direct result of overseas pressures.

The Catholic Commission for Justice and Peace produced 17 witnesses who had testified to the Chihambakwe Commission. They told harrowing tales of atrocities by 5-Brigade. They spoke of mass shootings, people being shut up in their huts and burned alive, wholesale beatings, mass detentions, thousands of rapes and so forth. The Zimbabwean government openly stated after the report had been handed to it that it would not be published — and it never has seen the public light of day. In a real sense it was an admission by Mugabe's government that the activities of 5-Brigade were too heinous to be made public. Despite the suppression of the report, author Peter Stiff, a former senior Rhodesian policeman, managed to get hold of a copy.

A random selection of actual acts of brutality by 5-Brigade reads like this:

- They burnt down a hut and badly beat five villagers over several days.
- They abducted a ZAPU chairman who was never seen again.
- They abducted a villager who was never seen again.
- They raped five school mistresses and a schoolgirl.
- They took 600 to 700 women and children away in trucks to an unknown destination.
- They shot ten people dead and burnt another two to death in their hut.
- They rounded up a large number of people, beat them and said they were taking them to their camp. They were never seen again.
- A man approached a 5-Brigade patrol to give his family time to flee. They shot him dead.
- They shot two men dead and decapitated a woman with an axe.
- After forcing villagers to strip naked they beat them up and raped the young girls.
- They intercepted a villager and bayoneted him to death.
- They raped four primary schoolgirls in the presence of their parents.
- They repeatedly raped 50 schoolgirls during the several months they were based near their school.
- They shot two men and ordered their wives to bury them and laugh while they did so.
- They conducted a roll-call in a village, shot dead those who stepped forward and raped the village women.

It was clear that 5-Brigade had been sent to Matabeleland to rape women, kill men and burn huts, rather than curb dissident activity. Not a single report refers to them taking action against dissidents. The trauma was ratcheted up by raping girls in front of their parents and murdering men in the presence of their wives — then forcing them to laugh while burying them. The inhumanity of this torture is indescribable. Their commander, Colonel Perence Shiri, justifiably known as 'the Butcher of Bhalagwe' was rewarded for his murderous diligence by being appointed Air Marshal of the Zimbabwean Air force.

The situation deteriorated into a well-orchestrated ethnic cleansing, with the Shona avenging themselves on the Ndebele who had colonised them under Mzilikazi. The struggle for power between Joshua Nkomo and Robert Mugabe degenerated into a bloodbath. For people who had just emerged from a liberation struggle against white colonialism, it was shameful and degrading.

The seeds of mutual destruction had always been present. Back in the 1960s when ZANU broke away from ZAPU, the latter resorted to violence against their rivals. In the bush, ZANU blood had been spilled not only by the Rhodesian Security Forces but also by their ZAPU compatriots. When some of us preached mutual tolerance between the two groups in prison, we were labelled 'ZANU collaborators'. The end was predictable. Speaking at the memorial service of the late Joshua Nkomo in 2000, Mugabe admitted that terrible things had been done in Matabeleland, and remarked:

> It was an act of madness. We killed each other and destroyed each other's property. It was wrong and both sides were to blame. We have had a quarrel. We engaged ourselves in a reckless and unprincipled fight.

The irony is that the blood-letting still continues among black Zimbabweans with ZANU-PF and the Movement for Democratic Change (MDC) continually at one another's throats — notwithstanding that the MDC has had its teeth pulled and has only words and world opinion left to fight with. When will it all end?

The saddest part for me was the discovery that ZAPU, in their eagerness to unseat ZANU-PF, teamed up with white former Rhodesian soldiers who had just joined the SADF. Joshua Nkomo, the father of Zimbabwean nationalism, ended up in the camp of his sworn enemies soliciting their help to evict a former political ally, ZANU-PF, from power. He denied it of course, but the evidence is there. We will end this sorry chapter by quoting from Peter Stiff's vast resources to reveal the total infamy to which ZIPRA had descended:

> In October 1983 two dissidents, Spar Mapula (18) and Watson Banda (16) captured by Zimbabwe Security Forces confessed to having been trained by South Africans at 'Ntabeni' near Louis Trichardt. It was apparent they were two of the 12 recruited by ZIPRA and trained on its behalf by the South Africans . . .

32

Back to basics

I left prison in May 1980 with nothing. Education for political prisoners had been stopped in 1971, so the highest qualification I had was an O level. I had no work experience except for breaking rocks, so I couldn't even begin to talk about employment history. Never having had a job I didn't even know how to go about looking for one. I had never heard of a thing called a curriculum vitae (CV) or its relevance to finding a job. I didn't even know that jobs were advertised in newspapers.

I had taken up residence with my brother Vusumuzi and his family in Highfields Township, Harare. Both he and his wife left for work early in the morning while I remained at the house listening to jazz. I hadn't done that for many years and there was a good collection of records in the house which helped to pass the time.

It concerns me now that if I had gone to Angola after my release from prison I might not have survived. I have a reputation in the organisation for speaking my mind and resisting unfair treatment. In Angola I might have had my lips sealed for good.

While in Harare I received a phone call from one of my former prison mates, Aubrey Mdletshe. He later died in Lusaka and I'm led to believe he drank himself to the devil. He told me that Joe Modise had booked into a five star hotel in Bulawayo and had called a meeting in his room.

'Where is Comrade Thula?' he wanted to know. 'Is he still one of us? Why is he staying in the ZANU-PF stronghold of Harare? Has he joined ZANU?'

Aubrey replied that I was living with my brother's family in Harare and that I was still a loyal member of the ANC. Aubrey told me I would be wise to attend the next meeting which was being held in Bulawayo in two days time. I took a train there and went to the fancy hotel. Joe was sitting cross-legged on his bed in yogi fashion like an Indian potentate. My comrades were already there sitting on the floor facing him. I went and stood by the window.

He was going on and on about how our group in prison was the most divided he had ever heard of. He didn't reveal who had told him this, but somebody amongst us must have reported it to him. Joe didn't discuss the cause of this alleged division, but just berated us for it.

When he was about to declare the meeting closed, I raised my hand.

'Comrade Joe', I said. 'I understand you asked questions about me at your first meeting. Do you mind asking them again so I can answer you directly? I understand you wanted to know why I am living in Harare and whether I am still a loyal member of MK.'

'Yes, Comrade Thula, I'd like the answer to those questions.'

'Why shouldn't I live in Harare?' I shot at him. 'Where do you want me to live? If you had wanted me to live in Bulawayo where would it have been? Is there a place in Bulawayo that the ANC prepared for us to live when we came out of gaol? On our release from Grey Street Prison, where was the ANC welcoming committee waiting to show us where to stay and to give us money for food? Only people like you have money to book yourselves into posh hotels — not lowly buggers like us. Yet the first thing you do is question my loyalty. Who the hell do you think you are? I have spent the past 13 years in prison while you were in Zambia waiting for people like me to free Zimbabwe so you can visit here without being arrested. And you dare to challenge my loyalty?'

Joe was speechless until he got his anger slightly under control.

'When I return to Lusaka I'll tell the Revolutionary Committee that I have never been so grossly insulted by a soldier.'

'Tell them everything I said', I shouted. 'Do me a favour and repeat my exact words to the Revolutionary Committee. The exact words, do you hear? Tell them you have never been so insulted by a soldier and tell them I've never heard so much bullshit coming from a general's mouth.'

I left the room and slammed the door behind me.

I went to the station and returned to Harare. On reflection I don't believe that a soldier who'd dared to talk like that to MK's Commander-in Chief would have got out of Angola alive — if I'd been stupid enough to go there.

I kept asking myself what I was going to do in the next five or ten years. I had always fancied being a lawyer and decided to give it a try. In 1980 I registered to study A-level English literature and history after which I would go to university and study law. I sent an application to the then University of Botswana, Swaziland and Lesotho (UBSL) and was accepted on the strength of my O-level certificate. But where was I going to get the funding?

Some ANC people my brother had known from his university days had come from Lusaka and we entertained them. Whisky was the favoured beverage. He asked them to rustle up a scholarship for me and they assured him it would be no problem. They insisted that as I was a veteran of the Luthuli Detachment I was now their responsibility and he could stop worrying. I was told to write to the ANC's Education Department in Lusaka as soon as I was admitted to university and a scholarship would be granted as a matter of course. My brother stopped worrying, but I didn't. I had already written to Lusaka three times without response.

I couldn't wait any longer so I moved to Bulawayo to look for a job. I found accommodation at the Young Men's Christian Association (YMCA) hostel on 9th Avenue. It was run by a Mrs Dhlula, an old friend of the family. I walked around town every day looking for work. My job-seeking modus operandi would have been amusing if my personal circumstances hadn't been so pathetic. The only thing I had was my O-level Certificate. I would enter a bank, for instance, and tell a teller I was looking for a job. He would ask if I had seen a job advertised and I would say no. I just wanted a job. The teller would smile sympathetically and say there was no job. This happened at one place after another. I would go to the reception of a firm and tell my story, only to be asked the same questions. I had thought that jobs had to be available in such a big town and all I needed to do was to let businesses know I was available. After a fortnight of tramping the streets I was still without work.

One day life smiled on me. I saw a building called Railway House with a sign outside saying that commercial clerks were needed and that applicants should apply within. I walked in and a pretty young woman at the reception greeted me with a smile and asked what she could do for me.

'I want to apply for a job', I told her.

'What qualifications do you have?'

'O-levels', I told her.

'Okay. You will need to go through an aptitude test and pass a medical. If those are satisfactory the National Railways of Zimbabwe will hire you. When will you be available to take the test, sir?'

'Now!' I said and saw surprise in her eyes.

'You could come tomorrow if you wish. It doesn't have to be now.'

'No', I said, 'I would like to do them now.'

'As you wish.'

She led me to a sort of classroom type place and waved me to a table. She explained that the test would cover my comprehension and use of the English language; as well as elementary mathematics. She passed me a question paper and provided me with an examination pad and a pen. I had an hour and a half to complete the test and she said I should begin as soon as I was ready. I could call her if I had a problem.

I read through the paper quickly and decided to start with the language and grammar section. It didn't give me too many problems. I then moved on to the comprehension and crackled that within 30 minutes. Then I turned to the maths — really only basic arithmetic. I have never been comfortable with arithmetic, so I devoted more time to it. Still with ten minutes in hand, I returned my paper and was sent for a medical. From there I went to the Tivoli Restaurant on 9th Avenue and had two very cold beers.

First thing next morning I was back at Railway House and the same young lady met me at reception. She smiled broadly and my hopes soared.

'Congratulations, Mr Bopela, you did very well in your tests and your medical showed you are in excellent health. Here are your results. Please take them to Mrs Muchemwa who'll handle everything.'

I entered another office where a plump woman of about 32 was behind a desk. She was on the phone and from what I could gather the person on the other end of the line was shouting and giving her a hard time. She was trying to get a word in edgeways but all she could manage was: 'I'm sorry, sir. Yes, sir. I understand, sir.' Finally her ordeal ended and she put down the phone. She waved me to a chair and glanced through my results.

'Mr Bopela, you're a life saver. The man I was talking to is Mr Pinchen. He's very cross because I sent him a clerk who passed his aptitude test but failed his medicals. "How do you expect me to hire a sick man, Mrs Muchemwa?" he shouted. "Find me a clerk right away who isn't dead or dying." When can you start work? How about tomorrow?'

I drew a deep breath. It was clear that Mrs Muchemwa had no idea she was talking to an ex-con. A job at last. After all those miserable years since 1964.

'I can start right now', I told her.

And that's how I landed my first job. Mrs Muchemwa became my boss and she patiently taught me everything I needed to know. I am eternally grateful to her. Pinchen also turned out to be a nice man. Part of my job was to write monthly reports about the work in progress so he could make assessments.

I studied my two A-level subjects at night so I was kept busy. On weekends, though, I used to go to Mpopoma Township where I had friends. We drank and ate lots of roasted meat. However, after the outbreak of fighting between ZANLA and ZIPRA at Entumbane, I stopped going to the townships because it was no longer safe. I didn't intend to get caught up in that sort of thing again.

There were excellent clothing shops in Bulawayo and although I wasn't earning much, I managed to buy myself some nice clothes. I found saving easy because rent and food at the YMCA were inexpensive. Towards the end of 1980 I received a letter from UBSL telling me that they were not offering law courses in 1981 because the faculty was about to be split up. It seemed there was disagreement between the three countries supporting UBSL as to whether their law graduates should continue going to Scotland for their final two years of study, as had been the case until then.

Lusaka had still not replied so I had no scholarship money anyway. Some friends told me that getting a scholarship depended on the whims of a few individuals. I had no idea what their criteria were for allocating scholarships. Experience has taught me that in any organisation there are people who infuse their own petty agendas into the operations and use available resources to further their own ends.

I never did get a scholarship from the ANC. Maybe I should have gone to Lusaka, knelt down in front of those people and licked their boots. It might have made a difference but that wasn't me. And perhaps Comrade Joe Modise had put in a bad word for me. At any rate I decided to find a scholarship for myself.

In 1982 a comrade phoned from Zambia and warned me not to go there. He said that a lot of people who were unpopular with certain commanders and leaders were being murdered in Angola. When I pressed him for details he said he couldn't mention names during an international phone call, but would explain everything when he visited Harare. In the event I left for Kenya before he came and I only caught up with him after South Africa's liberation.

'You did well to listen to me back then', he told me. They were really out to kill you.'

I travelled to Selebi-Pikwe in Botswana to visit my Aunt Zini. At her place I met a very beautiful lady called Cherry Duduzile Khoza from Durban who taught at Zwelesithembiso

Higher Primary at Umlazi in Natal. She was also visiting my aunt. By the time she left to return to South Africa and I took the train for Bulawayo, we had agreed to become man and wife.

On 28 March 1982 we were married at my father's estate in Gweru. I had resigned from the National Railways of Zimbabwe to further my studies. The World University Service had granted me a scholarship to study for a Business Administration degree in Kenya. I was supposed to begin my studies at the United States International University, Nairobi Campus, on 2 April 1982 and I flew to Nairobi on April Fools Day. I was 38 years old and had not been in a classroom for the better part of 20 years. After seeing me off at Harare Airport, Cherry returned to South Africa. She later flew to Kenya to join me.

The man who helped me get the scholarship was Walter Msimang, a tall fellow who enjoyed jokes as long as they were not at his expense. He worked for the United Nations World Food Programme in Nairobi. He had trained in the Soviet Union and specialised in radio communications. He then enrolled at the University of Zambia and completed a degree that he had begun in South Africa before leaving the country. At the International University he obtained an MBA degree. He was a very smart fellow, was Walter. He became President Tambo's Defence Secretary, if you could use that term for what a Canadian Intelligence Officer referred to as a 'broomstick army'.

I went to register for the Business Administration degree, but was told that the courses required passes in Maths 1, 2 and 3. I hurriedly backed off. I tried the Economics faculty and was told the same story. I had reason to believe I would be treated more kindly at the Sociology/Anthropology Department, but I was mistaken. They wanted me to study and pass Maths 1 and 2 as well as Statistics. I almost cried, but having no further options, I registered.

I had spent my high school years ducking and diving to avoid maths. The teachers who taught me arithmetic and elementary maths were fond of using a switch at the drop of a hat. They boasted that they taught a difficult subject which was not suitable for fools like me. So I became terrified of maths. At high school the maths master was Mr Mbuli, a veteran teacher who could make maths understandable even to mere mortals. I actually passed the subject for my Junior Certificate and went on to matric, but my old fears returned and I opted for history instead. Now here I was at university, again faced by that 'impossible' subject. I was absolutely certain I would fail the degree.

The maths curriculum was handed out after Cherry arrived in Nairobi. I took one look at it and I knew I was sunk. I went home and told her that I was going to flunk the degree because I could never master the maths. I flung my bag in the corner and got myself a beer from the fridge. I needed it.

'Show me your curriculum please, Thula', Cherry instructed.

'It's in that bag and I don't want to look at it. Not just now, anyway.'

Cherry got up, retrieved the bag and took out the syllabus. She paged through it for some 30 minutes. 'I can teach you everything you need to know and I'll guarantee you'll pass', she told me confidently.

'Really?' I asked sceptically.

She started me from scratch as if I had never heard of maths before. She taught me the sets and why the concept was important. She explained that maths was the friend of the user. It had always been drilled into my head that it was the student's enemy, a difficult subject suitable for geniuses only. She demonstrated that it was really just a language, like English or any other one. I merely had to learn the grammar and apply it in a logical fashion.

As the days and weeks passed, I listened in wonder as this woman, my dear wife, slowly, patiently and relentlessly dismantled the mental barriers that I had built in my mind. Maybe I was not such a fool after all. When maths lectures began at the university I found myself right up to speed and familiar with all the concepts that Cherry had taught me so well.

Sitting at Cherry's feet and being taught like a schoolboy brought us very close. I learned to appreciate her for what she was — an absolute expert in many fields. It transformed my attitude not only towards her but towards women in general. I came from a culture where women never got the opportunity to display their intellectual wares — it was assumed they didn't have any. Mrs Muchemwa had taught me my job at the National Railways of Zimbabwe and I respected her for that, but this was different. Cherry used to go about her chores as a housewife — washing, cleaning, ironing and cooking during the day — but at night she became the professor.

Round about this time I heard that Joe Modise had spread word in Lusaka that I was a spy and should be avoided. A certain ANC man visited Lusaka from Nairobi and when he returned he called a meeting of ANC members, but excluded me from it. Some comrades told me that a Norwegian chap mentioned that Joe said I couldn't be trusted. Fortunately, most of my friends and comrades in Nairobi knew me better than that and told the Norwegian to go to hell.

It showed how easy it was to blacklist anybody in MK. People like Joe Modise wielded a lot of power and because they didn't understand the responsibilities that went with it they abused it. Joe never learnt that, to perform to their full capacity, soldiers need high self esteem. That only comes if they are treated with respect and take pride in themselves. When soldiers are degraded and treated like dogs, they'll take the first opportunity to turn tail and desert the battle. To stand there and fight, a soldier needs to believe that cowardice is something below him. Joe also didn't understand that to get respect from subordinates one has to earn it. Although he was our commander-in-chief, most of us had little respect for him.

After freedom came, Joe was himself accused in parliament of being an apartheid spy, although no evidence was produced to support it.

Our first child, Tshitshi, an enormous baby girl, was born in 1983. I had thought it would create a problem between us if Cherry produced a girl as our first child. I wanted a boy, but when I saw Tshitshi just after her birth, I forgot her gender. She was such a beautiful baby and she was mine. It was a miracle for a one-time MK fighter and Death Row prisoner. I was now a husband and a father. I had two people I loved and had to look after. It completely energised me and I studied like a madman. At the end of three years I passed my Sociology/Anthropology degree with a distinction Cum Laude. I believe I could have obtained a Summa Cum Laude, but I made tactical mistake.

Dr Gale was our International Relations lecturer and at one lecture he was outlining American foreign policy in Africa. He covered North Africa where the emphasis of America's foreign policy revolved around manipulating Arab attitudes towards Israel. He claimed there was no real policy towards Central, East and West Africa. Regarding southern Africa, and South Africa in particular, he said that America was opposed to apartheid, but believed that evolution and not revolution would solve the problem.

Black students immediately attacked this evolution theory, especially Aggrey who came from Tanzania. Dr Gale spoke of terrorism and the perils of communist influence and gave those as the reasons why America proposed a peaceful approach to the dismantling of apartheid. I didn't join in the argument at first and was content to listen to Dr Gale's arguments, which I jotted down.

'Maybe my understanding of South African politics isn't good enough, Dr Gale, but there's a South African revolutionary here with us and maybe I should defer to him. Thula, my brother, I think you give us your opinion', Aggrey said.

'Ah, so there's a South African in my class. I didn't know you're South African, Mr Bopela. Please tell us your view of American foreign policy towards South Africa.'

Intellectually it was a seductive moment. Perhaps I should have kept my views to myself, but the temptation to put this arrogant American in his place was irresistible. I fired with both barrels.

'If we need to evaluate whether American foreign policy towards South Africa is acceptable, we should begin by analysing the history of the country making the foreign policy', I began.

'The United States of America is a country that was taken violently from native Americans by European people and they made it a British colony. When the British Government demanded they pay taxes without any representation in the British Parliament, they fought the American War of Independence and won. They conquered the Red Indians, massacred them in large numbers and took their land. They fought between themselves during the American Civil War and more than 600 000 Americans lost their lives.

That was revolution and certainly not evolution!

'More recently they participated in two wars against Germany and its allies. In World War II they became the only nation to use nuclear devices against another nation when they dropped atomic bombs on the cities of Hiroshima and Nagasaki in Japan.

'This was hardly a policy of evolution waiting for situations to resolve themselves.'

I paused and looked at the other students who were listening in fascination.

'Should I continue?' I asked them.

'Right on Thula, we are with you.'

'They fought in Korea in the 1950s and something like five million people died — mostly civilians. They sent a half million men to fight the Vietnamese people until they were eventually kicked out in 1975.

Closer to home, the Americans have shot four of their own presidents. They also killed that man of peace, Rev Martin Luther King. American westerns are about men packing large revolvers who solved all their differences by violence. There was no question of letting situations evolve in the old Wild West.

'Yet when black South Africans want to free themselves from oppression and racism, the Americans preach that we shouldn't use violence. So why should we pay attention to their so-called foreign policy as far as it relates to South Africa? It means nothing to us. The only foreign policies relevant to us are the Soviet Union's and Cuba's because they train us and provide weapons with which to free ourselves', I concluded.

Spontaneous applause broke out from the students.

Dr Gale waited for the clapping and whistling to die down before replying.

'Thank you Thula for an enlightening exposé of black South African attitudes towards our foreign policy, but somehow I doubt it is the majority view', he said icily. 'Chief Buthelezi, the leader of six million Zulus, also agrees that violence is not the right option for transforming South Africa. We believe there are other black leaders in South Africa who see the wisdom of his approach which vindicates American foreign policy.'

'I won't attack Chief Buthelezi's strategy of non-violence', I said, 'because even the ANC's armed struggle has not yet succeeded in freeing South Africa. But Buthelezi strikes me as being a person who throws raw meat to a wolf in the hope that it will convert to a vegetarian.'

The students' laughter drowned Dr Gale's remarks, whatever they might have been.

That incident cost me dearly. Until then Dr Gale had graded my essays A, but from then on he began to grade me B and B+ without any comment. A white American lady married to a Kenyan Masai, Linda ole-Moi-yoi, provided an explanation as to why my aggregate dropped. She had overheard Dr Gale discussing my attack on American foreign policy with considerable disapproval. I have no doubt that it cost me a Summa Cum Laude.

I struck up a relationship with Enock Bam. He was married to a clanswoman of mine called Bongie, a very sweet woman. They had both studied linguistics in England after which they had joined a Bible Society dedicated to the dissemination of the Christian doctrine. The society had sent them to Kenya from Holland — where they had been granted political asylum — to translate the Bible into one of the African languages. Cherry became very friendly with Bongie and the two families became inseparable.

In 1984 I sought Canadian citizenship through the Canadian embassy in Nairobi. I told them everything about myself — my MK background, my training in the USSR, the fighting in Zimbabwe and so on. I reasoned that they could easily check me out and discover whatever I had not disclosed and use that as a reason to deny me a residence permit.

I needn't have bothered because they denied us a residence permit anyway. The Intelligence officer there suggested that the Russians could use me to conduct subversive activities against the Canadian state. I asked him why the Russians would do such a thing and he told me that the Soviets encouraged communist party members to seek the citizenship of Western countries. Once they qualified they might remain a 'sleeper' for many years until they were activated for a particular mission.

It was a farfetched theory and quite nonsensical in my case. I was not and have never been a member of the communist party. I had been given accommodation in Nairobi by an admitted South African communist, Ian, who had since emigrated to Canada to teach at one of their universities. Why did they give him residence and deny it to me? What's more two of my ex-MK comrades, Walter Msimang and Zola Ngcakani, had both obtained Canadian residence in spite of having been trained in the USSR. I asked the Canadian to explain the difference between myself and my comrades.

'Mr Bopela, they are also terrorists, but the difference is that you not only trained in the Soviet Union, you also went into Rhodesia and fought. So the difference is that you are a committed terrorist.'

I had good reason to fight against the governments of Rhodesia and South Africa, but I had no motive to fight the Canadians. But it was clear that arguing wouldn't get me anywhere. I'll never know the real reason for the refusal of my application.

When I told Enock Bam this story he suggested I forget Canada and seek political asylum in Holland. Bongie had become very attached to Cherry and our little daughter, Tshitshi. She waited with baited breath while I considered the idea. When I said that we would do it, she was in her seventh heaven and couldn't stop hugging and kissing me.

Bam settled down to work out a plan for getting us into Holland. It was agreed that I would buy a return air ticket to Amsterdam on the pretext that I was only there to visit The Bams and would return to Zimbabwe after a fortnight. I would only activate this plan in 1985 once Bam and his family had settled back in Holland.

In December 1984 Cherry, Tshitshi and I returned to Zimbabwe. Living in Kenya had been a rich and enlightening experience. It was an exciting country with the potential for great economic development, but it was severely handicapped by a corrupt president and ministers.

33

The Netherlands

Early in 1985, I got a message from Bam that they were back in Holland and I should make my move. I applied for a visa and purchased a return ticket. I flew out of Zimbabwe in April. Bam fetched me from Schiphol Airport and we went by train to Woerden, a small town south of Amsterdam where they lived. Woerden is one of those little known Dutch towns — pleasant, clean and with a rural atmosphere. Nothing much happens in Woerden. If you're looking for bustle and excitement, you need to go to Amsterdam, The Hague or Rotterdam.

My first shock was discovering how different Dutch is from Afrikaans. I had assumed that because Afrikaans has its roots in Dutch, the two languages would be much the same. Nothing is further from the truth. When I began to attend Dutch lessons, the lady teaching us noticed that whenever I tried to write or speak Dutch, I ended up expressing myself in Afrikaans.

'Stop telling yourself that you can speak and write Dutch, Mr Bopela, because you can't. If you keep believing it's the same as Afrikaans you won't make any progress. The students from Turkey, Iran, Iraq, Pakistan and elsewhere in Africa are making faster progress than you because they've never heard of Afrikaans.'

I also discovered how different Dutch people are from Afrikaners. A black who grew up in South Africa expected Afrikaner people to be rude, insult you, call you names and give you dirty looks. They also tried to force you to speak Afrikaans. The Hollanders on the other hand, will try to speak to you in whatever language you understand best. They would ask: '*Spreekt mijnheer Bopela Nederlands?*' (Can you speak Dutch Mr Bopela?). If you shake your head, they'll try English, French or German. They're good linguists and almost all of them speak at least those four languages.

Intellectually I found them flexible, but they can be tightfisted. If they offer you a glass of wine they pour it and leave the bottle in the kitchen. When you finish the glass they ask if you'd like more. After the third glass you get tired of saying 'yes' and tell them you've had enough, even when you haven't. I could never understand why they didn't put the bloody bottle on the table in front of you as we do in South Africa, instead of fetching it from the kitchen glass by glass. Bongie took us to a farm where we met an old man who was a friend of hers. He offered us tea and kept the biscuits in his hand. Every time you finished a biscuit he asked if you wanted another. If you replied in the affirmative, he took one from the packet and gave it to you. And he was a very rich farmer!

I got a train from Woerden to Amsterdam, reported to the immigration police and asked for political asylum. I had to write down everything about myself and say why I merited consideration as a political refugee. I had become used to writing my life history from my days in Nairobi and I wondered whether, at the end of it, the Dutch like the Canadians would tell me to go to hell — or to any other place outside their country!

We stayed with the Bams for only a short time. While I was there I learned that Bam entertained high political ambitions and even had dreams of becoming president of South Africa. He had written to Oliver Tambo and proposed that the ANC leadership should resign and call an election outside the country. The winner would become the new president of the ANC, and later of South Africa.

Bam complained bitterly because Tambo ignored his letter.

'Can you believe his arrogance, Thula? Is that the right way for a people's leader to behave?'

'He probably wondered who you were because I don't think you are particularly well-known in ANC circles. I've met Tambo and he is a courteous man. I can only suggest that since you weren't writing as the president of an organisation, he felt there was no need to respond to you'.

It was the wrong thing to say, considering that I was living in his house. I don't think he ever forgave me.

I decided to move to Rotterdam because I had applied to the Institute of Social Studies in The Hague to study for a masters degree. I reasoned that even if the Dutch refused me political asylum, I could in the meantime acquire a higher qualification. The immigration police had told me that my application could take a while — a year or even more — to be processed because there were thousands of people applying for political asylum.

I was allowed a small sum of money which I collected from the refugee centre at the end of each month. I used it to rent a furnished room in Bellevoystraat in central Rotterdam. One day I received a call requiring me to report to Professor Ken Post, head of the Development Studies Department at the Institute of Social Studies. It was pointed out that Professor Post was leaving for North Vietnam in a day or two, so I was needed there urgently. I took a train from Rotterdam to The Hague and a tram to Scheveningen where the Institute was situated.

I went to Professor Post's office and found the door open. I walked in but no one appeared to be there. There was a huge pile of books, documents and papers on a desk. I went back to the door and knocked loudly. A voice from behind the desk responded: 'Come in!' The professor emerged from behind the pile of literature. He was a short man with a head as smooth as an ostrich egg. Thick horn-rimmed glasses showed he was shortsighted. He kept unconsciously fondling his beard.

He came from behind the mess on the table, greeted me airily, shook my hand and asked me to sit. He sat down next to me and got straight to the point.

'Mr Bopela, your CV says you left South Africa in 1963, but it is silent about your whereabouts and activities until 1982 when you went to Nairobi to study for your BA degree. What were you doing during those years?'

I dreaded having to answer a question that exposed my prison years. I could hardly produce a CV that said I was a former bush fighter and a prisoner and give it to a white man whose political sympathies were unknown. Imagine Professor Post's reaction if he was a sympathiser of the Pretoria regime.

I was quiet while working out how to reply. Eventually I decided to be true to myself and tell it the way it was.

'In 1967 I was a bush-fighter in Rhodesia, Professor. I fought in the Wankie battles as a member of MK's Luthuli Detachment. I was captured, tried in the High Court and sentenced to be hanged. This was later commuted to life imprisonment which I served until Prime Minister Mugabe declared a general amnesty in 1980.'

Professor Post said nothing and just sat there pulling his beard. It was very quiet in the office. An inner voice began to tell me: You see, blood is thicker than water and you should have known that, you idiot. This man is thinking how he can take revenge on me for killing his white cousins in Rhodesia.'

'I would be honoured to have someone in my faculty who has struck a blow against colonialism, comrade', he said. 'The snag is that we only admit people who are 35 or younger. You are above the limit by six years.'

My heart sank and I waited for him to say how much he regretted the rule but couldn't make an exception and admit me. Then it suddenly penetrated my thick skull that he had just called me 'comrade'. That had to mean something.

'You spent a total of 17 years in the struggle', the professor eventually resumed after an excruciatingly long pause. 'By deducting that 17 years from your age we find that you are really only 24 — well within the age limit. So congratulations Comrade Bopela, I'm delighted to welcome you to the faculty of Development Studies.'

I was dazed, but began to understand. Ken Post called me comrade because he supported our liberation struggle. I couldn't find the words to thank him, but I think my face told him how grateful I was. He introduced me to his secretary, Lijske Schweigman whom I came to know quite well. She was a wonderful person who always went the extra mile to find solutions to students' problems.

I began attending the Institute in September. My fellow students came from the length and breadth of the world. There were Africans, Indians, South Americans, Asians and Europeans. Most were people seconded by their governments to do postgraduate work there. I am not certain, but it appeared such students were subsidised by the Dutch government to assist developing countries acquire the skills needed for economic regeneration.

I was again funded by the World University Service (WUS), which had picked up the tab for my BA in Kenya. I had long since given up trying to get help from the ANC and decided to do things for myself. Annette Bokkenhauser, a Norwegian lady who ran the WUS Nairobi office, had stretched policy somewhat and provided the sponsorship I needed. It seemed strange that white people who knew nothing about me were only too willing to assist, while my own ANC people seemed to obstruct me at every turn.

I met Rev Auke Hofman, a magnificent Hollander and a true man of God, who was the student chaplain at ISS. Lijske explained to him my problem of getting political asylum and that my family was still in Zimbabwe. People applying for asylum were not allowed to have their families join them until asylum had actually been granted. And my family was about to expand — Cherry was expecting twins. Nandi and Nombali were born in Zimbabwe in August 1985.

Father Hofman listened to my story and asked me to pray with him. He said he would see what could be done. He emphasised that I would have to be patient. We had many discussions in his office which gave me a lot of strength.

Asylum was at last granted in 1986. Rev Hofman found money to fund air tickets for Cherry and our little. ones He drove me to Schiphol to meet them and drove us home to Rotterdam. My room at Bellevoystraat was adequate for me, but hardly satisfactory for a family of five. I found a small flat at number 207 Alsemstraat in Hoogvliet, a suburb of Rotterdam. We lived there until we returned to South Africa in 1991.

We were together as a family for the first time. Nandi and Nombali were six-month old cherubs and Tshitshi was two. Suddenly I had these little people around me and I didn't quite know what to do with them. I was getting this advanced education but none of it taught me about parenting or being a husband. There were no textbooks about that around! I suddenly felt intimidated by the responsibility of having a beautiful wife and three other lovely female creatures.

I was kept busy in 1986 writing a thesis to satisfy the conditions for obtaining a masters degree. The title was 'Migrant workers in a compound — a system of labour control'. When I eventually submitted it to Professor Post, he promptly rejected it. In his view, my methodology was flawed. I didn't panic but studied some more and improved it. I submitted it a second time and he again rejected it. Now I did panic because the submission deadline was only a month away. While Professor Post was willing to compromise on my age, he was not prepared to compromise on the quality of my work.

I worked on the paper frantically, seeking guidance from Freek Schiphorst, the junior supervisor of my thesis. He made some valuable suggestions and I was able to convince that 'wicked old man', Ken Post, that I finally had a decent thesis. The third version was thankfully accepted and I was on my way to obtaining my Masters degree in Development Studies. I thank Professor Post, Freek and Lijske for getting me there.

I played tennis in Holland when I had the time. My friend, Hans Tonino, enjoyed a game followed by cold beers at the Hoogvliet Tennis Club. There was also Nico Stenneke and his son Bart. They often quarrelled when Nico lost concentration and conceded a point. They were great fun, though, which is why I remember them. Then there was Corrie (I forget her surname) who loved her tennis. She became very solicitous towards me and my family, found lots of toys for the babies and helped Cherry with numerous other things she had to cope with. We were very happy at Hoogvliet.

After my graduation I decided to take a short rest while I worked out what to do next. I was sick and tired of living on Dutch charity. It was fine getting money every month from the Department of Social Welfare while I was busy with my studies, but I began to question whether I was raising my family or the Dutch government was doing it for me. As my children began growing up, I asked myself how I could take pride in their growth, when I hadn't earned the money to buy them food or clothing. My Zulu pride began to suffer. A man in my culture works to earn money to provide for his family. So I set out to look for a job.

I was a reasonably fluent Dutch speaker after my 18-month language course, so I went out to practise on the Rotterdammers. One guy said: '*Mijnheer spreekt zoals en parlementaris*' (Your Dutch is very parliamentarian). Maybe it wasn't colloquial, but it was good enough for me to communicate effectively. Despite this, I unsuccessfully hunted for work for two years. There were jobs in the social welfare sector, but the people in charge didn't want to employ me.

I must explain that it was not government policy to refuse me employment. It was just that certain officials decided they didn't want to give a job to a *buitelander* (foreigner). The ordinary person in the street didn't regard us as political refugees, but as black economic refugees. People from Surinam — a former Dutch colony in South America — who had left the third world to make money in Europe, were viewed in the same light. We were all tarred with the same brush because of the colour of our skins. I only wanted a job so that I could put something back into the Dutch economy that I had been a drain on for so long. This was the only instance of racism that I picked up in that otherwise wonderful country.

In 1989 I decided to study for an MBA. I applied to the Rotterdam Business School, the finest business school in Europe, and was accepted. I then went to a certain organisation and asked them to fund my studies with a bursary. They agreed and said that all they needed was a letter from the Rotterdam School of Business confirming that I had been accepted and a letter from the ANC (on an ANC letterhead) to say I was a bona fide political refugee. It never occurred to me that I would have a problem proving that.

A man called Masiphula Mbongwa (later director-general in the Ministry of Agriculture) was at the ANC office in Holland. The main ANC representative for the Benelux countries (Belgium, Netherlands and Luxembourg) was Godfrey Motsepe who was based in Belgium. He later came within an ace of being assassinated by the South African Secret Service.

I asked the organisation that had undertaken to fund me to ask Mbongwa for a letter supporting my status as a bona fide political refugee. In the meantime I joined the programme at the Rotterdam Business School. When I was two months into the programme I got a call from the registrar who said it was the school's policy that students should pay at least 50% of their annual fee before the end of the first quarter. If I didn't pay by the end of the following month I would be obliged to withdraw from the programme.

I had no idea what the problem was. I phoned the organisation that had offered the bursary and asked why my fees hadn't been paid. Their answer gave me the biggest shock of my life. Mbongwa had told them he couldn't vouch for me as a bona fide political refugee from South Africa, so they couldn't release the funds. I phoned him and asked for an explanation.

'You see, Boet Thula, I have heard from you and many others that you fought at Wankie and were in prison in Zimbabwe until 1980. But since I wasn't at Wankie nor in a Rhodesian prison I can't vouch for you.'

I asked him why he hadn't contacted Godfrey Motsepe in Belgium who would vouch for me. There was no answer. He could also have confirmed my status with Baleka Kgositsile (now Baleka Mbete, later Speaker of Parliament). Mbongwa had often boasted that he was in constant touch with the ANC's headquarters in Lusaka so he could have checked with them too, but he didn't. Instead he disregarded my plight and I was thrown off the MBA course.

I don't know what it was with Mbongwa. He had often complained that MK guys from Natal used to tease him about having a muscular body which he never intended to utilise as a soldier — only as a student — and he was very resentful about such taunts.

At any rate he refused to help an old freedom fighter to re-establish himself educationally so he could contribute to the struggle in a non-military way in post-apartheid South Africa.

Perhaps I should have personally phoned Godfrey Motsepe in Belgium. Or contacted Lusaka and asked for verification. Maybe I should have attempted to trace Zola Bona (now Zola Skweyiya, later Minister of Social Welfare) and asked for his help. I'm sure he would have come through for me because we were together at Kongwa Camp — a place that Mbongwa stayed well away from. I could also have contacted Zola Ngcakani (later Inspector-General of Intelligence). But I didn't do any of those things because I was deeply fed up with the whole business. From the day I had first asked the ANC for assistance I had been ignored.

I'm not blaming the ANC for my misfortunes and I'm not embittered. It would be easy to say: 'The ANC turned its back on me so stuff them', but that would not be true. Life has taught me it's usually the little insecure people in an organisation who do the mean and petty things to people. The ANC is an organisation of contrasts. There are rotten people in it who could drive you to a point where you denounce the organisation and leave. But there are others — and I have met many of them — who live by the cardinal principles of the ANC. The pity is that so many creeps worm their way in.

I met Masiphula Mbongwa at the Ministry of Agriculture after our return from exile, but he still didn't impress me.

The opportunity to get back on the course at the Rotterdam Business School slipped by. Nevertheless, in desperation I wrote to Mendi Msimang, the ANC representative in London (and later Treasurer-General of the ANC). I stated my case and asked for funding. He answered promptly and referred me to Nathaniel 'Nat' Masemola who ran the Luthuli Foundation in London. Nat advanced funding immediately which enabled me to enroll for an MBA course at the Webster University of Leiden . I later had the honour of meeting Nathaniel Masemola and his wife back in Johannesburg, which gave me the opportunity to personally extend my thanks.

Webster University is an American business school. To obtain an MBA there one had to pass 12 courses in one's core discipline — in my case marketing. Passes in five business courses were also required. I started in 1990 and finished the 12 courses in 1991. This gave me an MA in marketing. I then received a letter from London saying I would have to wait a year before for the funding for the other five modules would be available. Sitting around doing nothing for a year didn't appeal to me, so I decided to return to South Africa. The ANC was no longer a banned organisation and I was free to go home.

I discussed my decision with Cherry but she wasn't too happy. Fighting between the UDF and the IFP was still going on and this concerned her. I explained that we had lived on other people's money for as long as my pride could stand. I had to get a job and begin raising my children with money earned by myself. She reluctantly took my point. We agreed that she and the kids would remain in Holland for the time being. When I had a job I would find a house and arrange for them to join me.

I told my friend, Rev Auke Hofman, and he supported my decision. I applied for a passport at the South African embassy in The Hague and it was ready within a fortnight. I approached Professor Post who lent me money to buy an air ticket. At the end of 1991 I took a 12-hour nonstop flight from Brussels to Johannesburg.

At the immigration counter at Jan Smuts (now Johannesburg International) Airport, a slight drama occurred. My passport had a Belgian exit stamp, but there was nothing to indicate when I had left South Africa. The white official behind the counter looked at my passport, looked at me and I looked back at her, but I said nothing. She went to an office at the back and returned some minutes later with another white officer who had 'security' written all over his face. He looked at me, whispered something in the woman's ear and angrily waved me through. He didn't unfurl a banner saying: 'Welcome home Mr Bopela . . . we are glad to see you back Mr Bopela.' I took my passport and breezed through the airport building. I shouted: 'I'm back! I'm back!' to no one in particular and strolled through the exit with Cherry's relatives who had come to meet me.

We went to Alexandra Township and sat talking, catching up with the news. As a result I missed my connecting flight to Durban and spent the night there. The next day I boarded a mini-bus taxi and headed for Natal. It was the best thing that could have happened to me. If I'd caught my flight I wouldn't have seen anything of the South Africa I had been missing for so long. It gave me the opportunity to see the countryside, farms, small towns, filling stations and the people — particularly those chatting away in Zulu in the taxi. The taxi driver was playing township jazz — music I had not heard for many years. Being back after an absence of 27 years was intoxicating.

When we crossed the Tugela River into Natal I felt a lump in my throat. We passed Mooi River, Pietermaritzburg and Pinetown. I wanted to sing with elation, but those in the taxi would have thought I was quite mad. My eyes were glued to the window as the taxi raced towards Durban. There was Gillits, Kloof and Westville. When the taxi cleared the rise at Mariannhill and began to descend towards Durban, I felt dizzy with joy. There was the city of my boyhood, hemmed on the far side by the blue of the Indian Ocean. That picture, my first view of Durban after all those years, remains with me to this day.

34

Home in the RSA

Everybody was talking about the New South Africa. Nelson Mandela was released from prison soon after my arrival home. The country was caught in a frenzy of excitement. The man had been in prison for 27 years and now he was free! What was he going to say? Would he shout 'Kill the wizards!' like Dingane ka Senzangakhona? The country was awash with AK47s and sadly they were mostly being used by blacks against other blacks. The whites were holding their breath, not knowing what would happen next. Many were making hurried plans to emigrate to Australia.

Blacks were going into hotels, restaurants and bars where they had never been allowed before. One could see the dull resentment on the faces of whites when they saw blacks invading the places which had been their private preserves. Blacks were buying houses in formerly 'whites only' areas and the residents had no option but to reluctantly accept them as neighbours. Black children appeared in what had always been 'white schools' and sat in the same classrooms and at the same desks as the white children. The awe in which whites had been held for centuries suddenly vanished.

The problem with the New South Africa was that while much was changing, other things stayed the same. Many whites still hung on to their prejudices and resented black people. The blacks saw this and laughed openly at frightened whites, some of whom were hoping that apartheid might still return. Others accepted the inevitable and made the necessary adjustments to their lives.

For centuries South Africa had been two countries in one. The first was white, wealthy, powerful and privileged and the other was black, poor, powerless and downtrodden. Indications were that white privilege was about to be swept away and blacks would begin to share those rights. Blacks were even going to be allowed to vote, horror of horrors! Then they would rule over us, the whites concluded correctly. And even marry our daughters! Absolutely intolerable! Right wing Afrikaners in particular were heard cursing FW de Klerk, their president, as a traitor for unbanning the ANC and releasing Mandela.

I was encouraged by certain comrades to become a member of the South African National Defence Force, but I decided I couldn't serve under a defence minister like Joe Modise who had avoided killing even a mouse during his military career.

Meanwhile, the war between the blacks of the UDF and the IFP continued to rage. There were tit-for-tat revenge killings that went on and on until nobody understood why it had started or where it was going to end.

The Bantustan leaders felt besieged. The whites had capitulated to the liberation movements — the arch enemy — and they felt betrayed. These puppet leaders had staked their lives and their political reputations on the whites remaining in power forever. Something they never believed would happen was taking place right in front of their eyes. They had become rich and powerful under apartheid, but now apartheid had vanished like the morning dew. They fought on nevertheless in the vain hope of clinging to power.

My father came from Zimbabwe to visit and we both stayed with my elder brother, Mduduzi. I had last seen my father when I left Zimbabwe for Holland in early 1985. We were both over the moon with happiness. He decided to slaughter an ox as a thanksgiving to our ancestors for looking after me throughout those terrible years. We brewed African sorghum beer and bought Castle beer and brandy. It was a feast. As the youngest son in the family I did the errands, fetching and serving drinks for the guests. Columns of smoke rose from the homestead's chimney and cuts of beef were roasted over several fires in the yard. There was a huge tent where visitors sat on plastic chairs. My father addressed the guests, thanking them for coming and sharing his happiness at the safe return of his son, Thula. The people applauded and someone stood up when my father had finished his speech.

'We rejoice with you Hlomuka [clan name of the Bopelas] because you are back with us after so many years. We have heard certain things about Thula, this son of yours and we would like him to tell us in his own words where he has been and what he was doing. Some of us remember him as a young man, but others here have never seen him before. He has travelled greatly from what we have heard. He has seen peoples and lands we shall never see. We also hear that he was one of Mandela's young men — Umkhonto we Sizwe — the ones who set fire to the white man's beard.'

The Master of Ceremonies, Asquith Thula Goba, found me carrying a pot of African beer to a group of visitors outside and he indicated he wanted a word with me. I placed the pot in front of my visitors, took a sip, and joined him. He said I was wanted in the tent to speak to the people about my travels and experiences.

'I must warn you, though, Thula, that there are ANC as well as IFP people here. I don't know what you intend to tell them, but keep that in mind.'

The buzz of conversation subsided as I entered the tent. About 150 pairs of eyes were staring at me. A guy I had gone to primary school with, Erwin Nkabinde, shouted out.

'Yes, it's him, that's Thula. He hasn't changed much. Hi, Thula. Do you still remember me?'

'Yes, of course I do, Erwin. How could I forget you when we had so many fist fights as boys?'

He laughed with joy and the people buzzed with excitement.

'*Sanibonani maQadi*', I said, greeting them by the traditional name of the people who live in that area.

'*Sawubona*' (hello), came the reply.

Someone remarked that I could still speak Zulu well despite my long absence.

I nodded and said I would address them in that language. I had decided to tell them a political story, but one they wouldn't immediately identify as such. And its meaning wouldn't be partisan to one organisation or the other.

'During my primary school days the teachers used parables, short stories and fairy tales to teach us some of the more important lessons in life', I started. 'I have something important to tell you, so I'll also use a parable. It contains a moral lesson which you can work out for yourselves.

'A long time ago dogs went and told their masters, the human beings, that they no longer wanted to be referred to as dogs. They said it was derogatory and insulting. They also said they no longer wanted to be referred to by the names given to them by their masters — names like Spotty, Bingo, Fido and whatever. They pointed out that they had names in their own language which they called each other by.

"The next problem is that when we try to enter your houses you drive us outside, saying that's where dogs should be", the spokesman for the dogs continued. "Yet, while you're sleeping or away at work we guard your homes and make sure that burglars don't break in. You take us hunting and we spend the whole day chasing buck and rabbits for you. We bring you what we catch and you gorge it along with your friends and families. When you have finished eating you throw the cleaned bones to us. Only the bones are good enough for us. This exploitation must stop!"

'The spokesdog closed his speech on an ominous note:

"If this doesn't stop immediately there'll be war between us."

'The other dogs were shouting political slogans.

"We want freedom! We want equality! Down with human tyranny!"

'The masters didn't even bother to hold a meeting to consider their response. They gave the dogs short shrift. As far as they were concerned a dog was a dog and its master could call it by whatever name he liked. And they were still barred from entering their masters' houses. They chased the dogs away, kicking them and yelling "*voetsek*!"

'Then war broke out. The dogs waited until the men had gone to work, then they attacked the women and children. The attacks were vicious and many humans were bitten to death. When the masters returned home the dogs attacked them as they got out of their cars. Some dogs were shot and killed and others were wounded. The war raged for many days. When the masters left their homes to go to work, the dogs stood aside and allowed burglars to break in and steal property. The burglars had heard the dogs were on strike and they pillaged with impunity. The situation deteriorated every day and there was fear in the masters' households.

'After weeks of chaos the masters called a truce and asked the dogs to send a delegation to discuss terms. The dogs came, small ones and big ones and bitches too, because while the fighting was going on the bitches had begun to press for female rights. The spokesperson for the masters said:

"We have lived in harmony for many centuries and we can return to that peaceful way of life if we use our heads and not our emotions. A conference room is being made ready for our delegations to settle our problems. You have not eaten for several days while the fighting has been going on and we know that hungry creatures are angry creatures. We'll bring you meat that will quiet your hunger pains. Will that satisfy you?"

"Okay, but no bones. We'll only accept meat", the dogs barked back.

'The masters' spokesman returned to his group. "Our plan is working", he said. "We'll demonstrate that whatever they might think, they are they are still dogs. Let's take meat to them."

'Huge dishes of meat were placed before the dogs. The dogs had never seen such large quantities of meat. The masters went into the conference hall and looked out through the windows. The dogs began feasting, but it wasn't long before trouble started. The big dogs grabbed a greater share than the smaller ones and when they complained they were bitten. Then the bigger dogs began fighting each other to get the largest portions. Soon, it was a free-for-all.

'The masters rubbed their hands with glee.

"Look at them. Didn't we tell them they are dogs and dogs will be dogs until they die? They want equality with us, but they can't even share a plate of meat without fighting over it. They had us cornered and we were about to accept their terms. But after tossing plenty of meat at them they have forgotten what they fought us for in the first place. That's dogs for you!"

'Many dogs were dead and others had fled, bleeding profusely. Many were still fighting and the meat lay there forgotten. The masters left the conference room with sticks and sjamboks and beat the dogs mercilessly, causing them to scatter in all directions. Many returned to their masters and begged forgiveness. They were accepted back on condition that they forgot their nonsense of demanding equality with humans. They quickly agreed to the terms — which explains why dogs are still the servants of human beings to this day.

'Their mistake was that they forgot what they had set out to fight for in the first place — which was dignity, fair treatment and equal rights. When they saw the meat their unity vanished and they became deadly enemies, killing each other for their share. And these were not just common dogs, but leadership dogs elected to represent the others. When the ordinary dogs heard that their leaders had not even sat down with their masters around the conference table, they also started fighting among themselves.'

I ended my story and asked them to reflect on the moral. There was absolute silence and I walked out. Asquith Goba gave me feedback afterwards.

'*Udlale ngathi lomfana kaBopela*" (Bopela's son is playing games with us), some said. 'We thought he was going to tell us about his training in Russia and how he had fought the white Rhodesians. Instead, he tells us a fairy story about dogs wanting to be treated like humans.'

'You missed the whole point, Mr Mkhize', someone remarked. 'That boy is far more mature than any of us. The dogs he spoke about are the African leaders who mobilised us to fight and free ourselves from white oppression. Now, just as we have won our freedom, they have started fighting again. This time it's over power. The dogs fought over meat and African leaders fight over power. The whites have promised to hand over their power to the black leaders and now they're fighting over it. Why do you think UDF and IFP are fighting? And look who is dying. Is it the white people? No, it's us, the blacks.'

The feast went on until early evening. When people started to leave they were still talking at the tops of their voices and arguing about what I had told them. It was wonderful to be in the New South Africa, but it was shameful that many of the old problems were still with us.

That night I heard the sounds of guns firing in the distance. The black-on-black violence was continuing. People were dying, but what for?

Shortly afterwards I left my brother's home and went to live in Umlazi with my cousin, Nonkosi Queen Mfeka. Her father was my uncle — my mother's brother — and we had been close friends since childhood. Each morning she left for the school where she taught and I went to town job hunting. This continued for several months, but I couldn't find work. Some employers said I was far too qualified for their vacancies, while others complained about my lack of employment history. I still hadn't pinned down a job when Cherry and the children returned from Holland and joined me. They also moved in with cousin Nonkosi and the children attended school at Bhekithemba Primary.

Violence continued unabated at Malukazi and Folweni which were close to where we were living. When gunfire crackled at night the children used to cry with fright, rush from their bedrooms and climb into our bed. Sometimes it sounded as if the gunshots were coming from the yard outside. To reassure the children and demonstrate that it was safe, I would walk into the yard and back. But I was more than a little worried about the situation myself.

In September 1992 I received a call from Eskom, the electricity utility, asking me to come for an interview. Don Mkhwanazi, an old friend, had sent my CV to many companies. Don lived in Westville and at the time was the ANC's economic advisor and a highly paid consultant. I had no intention of approaching the ANC for help and decided I would take my chances in the private sector using the qualifications I possessed.

Eskom's offices were on the 8th and 9th floors of the BP Centre in West Street, Durban. I was interviewed by Hugh McGibbon — a Scotsman and my future boss — and by Brian Anderson from Eskom's Human Resources Department. I had never been interviewed for a job before, so I didn't know how to prepare myself. Furthermore, I knew nothing about the company and even less about electrification. I cannot remember their questions, let alone my answers but and it all seems irrelevant now. The two men assumed on the spot that I was the person they wanted. They introduced me to Doug Dewey whose shoes I would be filling. He was emigrating to Australia and I sometimes wonder what happened to him. I was appointed Electrification Manager, Coastal. I began to read everything relating to electrification.

A few days later Hugh gave me a job contract and asked me to sign it. At the bottom it read: 'If I am provoked by a conservative white South African, I will curb my natural aggression and not resort to violence.' I refused to sign.

'What do you mean by a white, conservative South African, Hugh?' I asked, confronting him in his office. 'Do you mean a white racist? What do you mean by me curbing my natural aggression? Who said I'm naturally aggressive? You don't know me. I'm not signing that contract unless that clause is removed.'

It was removed and I signed.

Hugh knew there were plenty of white racists in Eskom and he was conditioning me to react tamely so his white friends wouldn't have their noses put out of joint. He thought that because I needed a job I would be prepared to put up with racism — something I had spent 27 years resisting. Well, I told myself, he has another think coming. Indeed it didn't take me long to discover that many whites employed by Eskom were not ready for my kind of person and they didn't quite know how to handle me. But it was they who would have to change their attitudes, not me.

'I have been told that you were a terrorist, Mr Bopela, and that you're now a senior man at Eskom. Is that true?' a lady phoning from Eskom in Newcastle asked.

'Yes, Ma'am', I replied.

There was a choking sound on the other end of the line and the phone was put down abruptly. I smiled to myself and continued with my work. I have never been a terrorist and I believe that word has no real meaning. It's used by right-wing governments in the West when they refer to freedom fighters who oppose governments they support. When the same Western governments train and equip people to topple governments they disapprove of, they call such people rebels or guerrillas.

Jonas Savimbi and his men were always rebels and never terrorists. RENAMO who sought to destabilise the Mozambican government were also rebels. The Contras who fought against the Nicaraguan government of Daniel Ortega were trained and equipped by the Americans so how could they be terrorists? Even Osama bin Laden — in his earlier days when he fought the Red Army in Afghanistan — was never a terrorist. He only became one when he began to target the Americans and the West. At one stage Nelson Mandela was definitely a terrorist and the ANC was a terrorist organisation in the eyes of white right-wing governments. Now those same administrations have diplomatic relations with the ANC government.

In 1993 I moved my family to Pinetown, a lovely, quiet town about 20 kilometres from Durban. We put the children in school at Pinetown Primary where a first-rate white lady, whose name I have forgotten, was principal. Cherry found a teaching post at Bongo Higher Primary. We bought a house at Caversham Glen. In the same year I bought my first car, a Ford Sapphire, and we began to live like normal people. Cherry told me that although she'd had serious doubts about the correctness of my decision to leave Holland, she was now sure I was right. It was very gratifying.

I decided one day I'd read enough about electrification and needed to go out in the field to see how it was done in practice. I phoned Blackie Swart at Pinetown and asked him to take me to where connections were being made. He collected me the next morning and we headed for the Cato Ridge depot. I told Blackie not to tell anyone that I was a manager.

'Just give my name and say I've just joined Eskom.'

'But, sir, if they don't know your position they won't behave correctly towards you', Blackie objected.

'Just tell them my name, Blackie, and leave it at that.'

We walked into the Cato Ridge Depot and there was a chorus of greetings for Blackie. Some of his friends jokingly said 'Blackie, *jou gat jong*' (your arse man). It was all good fun although Blackie frantically tried to signal that such language was inappropriate, but they ignored him. After all, he was white and the black guy with him was presumably one of his workers. It never ceases to amuse me how South Africans automatically assume that when a black and a white are working together, the latter is the senior. Everybody in the office was white except for the cleaners and those who served tea. Blacks worked in the field.

I needed to fetch something from the van and while I was out Blackie apparently enlightened everyone about who I was. Within minutes the supervisor of the depot came through and invited me in for tea. I politely declined but he was quite insistent .I had to be blunt which probably offended him. I got hold of Blackie and we left.

We drove to Hammarsdale where we found several huge Eskom trucks complete with steel ladders and crews. Blackie explained that they were engaged in connecting customers to our grid. There were three or four white senior distribution officers (SDOs) dressed in khaki and wearing boots. Blackie tried to introduce me, but they showed absolutely no interest. They were obviously wondering why Blackie was paying so much attention to a black guy. We walked into a small spaza shop where a connection was being made.

There were two black technicians working there. I saw one hurriedly conceal something behind a big deepfreeze. Blackie introduced me and told them I had recently joined Eskom and was keen to see how power lines were connected. They nodded politely and continued with their work, explaining what they were doing. A white SDO shouted for Blackie and he went outside.

As he left the room the black technician reached behind the freezer and brought out a quart of Black Label beer. He took a long swig and handed it to his mate who did likewise. He asked if I felt like a drink and I said I didn't.

'Okay, then', he went on, 'can you stand by the door and warn us when Blackie comes back?'

I agreed and took up station by the door. They finished the bottle, discarded the empty and retrieved a second one. While they were busy with it I warned them that Blackie was returning. The bottle was quickly concealed and work continued. Fifteen minutes later they had completed the installation. They switched on the lights and the freezer throbbed with power. We applauded and left.

While driving back to town I described to Blackie what had happened. He laughed so much he almost lost control of the vehicle. I told him that on his next visit he should identify my position to the black technicians. I got the chance to meet the two fellows again. They were penitent and wringing their hands with embarrassment.

'We had no idea who you were, Mr Bopela', Mhlongo said. 'We thought you were one of Blackie's workers. We know you can fire us, Mr Bopela, because we did a wrong thing. But please think of the children who will suffer if we lose our jobs. Please forgive us.'

It was pathetic listening to the two guys pleading for their jobs.

'It's true you two could be fired, but I want you to listen carefully. If you drink while working with electricity you can cause a fatal accident, killing either yourself or someone else. And if you die like that the autopsy will show you were drunk which means your children won't get compensation. On the other hand, if you cause the death of someone else, it will result in Eskom having to pay out a fortune in claims. Do you understand? I won't have you fired but I will submit a report. If you are caught drinking during working hours again, you will mostly certainly be fired.'

The men had worked for Eskom doing hard manual labour for many years. I had just joined and hadn't yet made a significant contribution to the company, so I left the matter at that.

I worked for Eskom for ten years and learned a lot about the way financial and human resources are managed. Eskom is a microcosm of South African society, so the positive and negative things that happen there also occur in the wider society. Many white Eskomites still refuse to reconcile with their black fellow workers and continue with their racial prejudices, but this also happens in the country at large.

'Thula, when will *your* [meaning black] government rid South Africa of crime?' a white colleague asked.

'When *my* government, as you call it, has expanded the economy to a point where there is employment for almost everyone', I responded.

'But when will that be? Your government must reinstate the death penalty and hang the criminals.'

'You must be patient, my friend. The present levels of crime are the result of the systematic dispossession and exploitation of Africans by *your* successive white governments. *My* government, as you choose to call it, believes that the remedy lies in empowering blacks economically and enabling them to earn a decent living without resorting to crime.'

'You cannot blame whites for everything, Thula. It's time that blacks take responsibility for failing to run the country properly.'

'We can blame the whites for taking our land and cattle away from us. We weren't a nation of criminals and beggars before the whites arrived. That's why there were no policemen and prisons then. The whites plundered and impoverished us and we became criminals and prostitutes as a result. So you can blame the rising crime on the whites because they caused it. How can you blame the ANC government for failing to eradicate crime in such a short space of time when it took centuries of white oppression and discrimination to cause it?'

It would be wrong to suggest that all the whites at Eskom thought like this, because they didn't. By the same token, it would be inaccurate to describe all whites in South Africa as racist.

35

Let's stop the killing

With the return of the Caprivians from training, the IFP gained the capacity to strike back with great violence against the UDF. Historians will argue about who struck the first blow — the UDF or the IFP. The answer will solve nothing. What can be said with certainty is that the two organisations set out to settle their differences with violence. The world looked on as black people who had been oppressed for centuries attacked each other. However, instead of their long-term Afrikaner oppressors just looking on impassively as the violence escalated around the country, they set out to fuel it.

The violence didn't happen in KwaZulu alone — it was countrywide. Since 1948 the National Party's legislation had been designed to oppress the black people. They introduced laws and carried out acts that disadvantaged the blacks at every turn. They created an education system — Bantu Education — deliberately planned to give blacks an inferior education. They promulgated laws that excluded blacks from all but the lowest categories of jobs and prevented competition with whites in the workplace. They excluded blacks from voting and allowed them to become lawyers serving other blacks, but barred them from becoming magistrates or judges. Blacks were not allowed to own property or do business in urban areas. The list of restrictions was endless.

Yet when the National Party government enacted the Territorial Authorities Act, traditional leaders fell over themselves to support it, arguing like their white masters that it would empower black people. The traditional leaders who opposed it were deposed from their positions. The most significant example was the removal of Chief Albert Luthuli from chieftainship of the Amakholwa (Christian) people of Groutville. He was by then president of the ANC and opposed to legislation that clearly disadvantaged his people. The apartheid government might have thought he would rot and be forgotten in the political wilderness, but internationally the view was otherwise. He was awarded the Nobel Peace Prize — but the government refused him permission to personally collect it.

In KwaZulu-Natal Chief Mangosotho Buthelezi (he preferred Mangosotho to Gatsha by then) accepted — whilst protesting loudly that he didn't — something close to a Bantustan arrangement. In the Transkei, Chief Kaizer Matanzima agreed to the Bantustan system on behalf of the Xhosa people, and Lennox Sebe did the same in the Ciskei. Chief Mphephu roped his people into the Venda 'homeland'. Chief Lucas Mangope accepted on behalf of the Batswana what he called the 'Independent State of Bophuthatswana'. Its little enclaves of territory were spread all over the countryside.

Hardly any of the so-called 'homelands' had the infrastructure or economic base to support their populations. When the people rose in protest against the Bantustan system, the chiefs and their sycophants chose to support the apartheid enemy. So in their hour of need, the black people found themselves trapped in an unworkable system by people who were only after political advantage and personal wealth.

The chiefs and later the urban councillors were seen by the people as stooges, traitors. When black people in all the provinces rebelled under the leadership of the UDF to make South Africa ungovernable, they found themselves opposed by the army, police and vigilantes who owed loyalty to chiefs and councillors.

The worst thing about Bantustans was that they were ethnically-based, while organisations like the ANC, PAC and the South African Congress of Trade Unions (SACTU) had worked for unity among the black people for decades regardless of tribal affiliations. The government had always feared the power of black nationalist movements. To combat them they sought to promote ethnic divisions by playing off one traditional ruler against another; the idea was to cause friction between them and the democratic movements. The ANC created a House of Chiefs as part of their political structure and all chiefs were made honorary vice-presidents of the ANC. The aim was to take the chiefs along the path of the national struggle for freedom.

The Bantustans were purposefully created to strike at the heart of black national unity. The National Party government had to wean the chiefs away from involvement with organisations like the ANC. They succeeded beyond their wildest dreams because many chiefs saw the Bantustans rightly as the route to personal power and much wealth. In another move, urban councillors were appointed mayors of townships and by this route also became wealthy — something most could not have achieved without the support of the national government.

It became clear that there was widespread opposition by urban blacks to the idea of community councillors. Vigilante death squads began to appear in the townships. When the local authority structures broke down, the state used its security and administrative organs to clamp down on the disruptive elements and restore order.

Who were the vigilantes and why did they fight and kill to uphold National Party policies? They were mostly so-called migrant workers who lived in township hostels with their roots firmly in the tribal areas. Chiefs, under the traditional ruler system, have the right to call on people from their areas of tribal jurisdiction to support causes or political parties they themselves espouse. Even where a man lives in an urban area but has rural roots — perhaps a house, a wife, children and livestock — the power of the chief still reaches out to him. The IFP is an ethnic-based organisation and in the culture of the Zulus, the chief is the recognised leader. Thus it was normal for a chief who supported the IFP to compel his people to join that party. Punishments, even expulsion from the chief's area of jurisdiction, can be imposed on those who refuse to obey orders. So it follows that when one has control over a chief by whatever means — financial or otherwise — then one has control over the people under him. This is the lock that holds rural people in the traditional system. No wonder the National Party government was in favour of retaining traditional leaders!

Hostel dwellers by and large are illiterate and unskilled because of their rural origins. They perform manual low-paid jobs and are frequently looked down on by educated and skilled urban blacks. They never feel welcome or at home amongst city dwellers, especially with the youths who never seem to lose an opportunity to make these deprived people feel inferior and stupid. This creates a resentment between the two groups and conflict is never more than a breath away.

The rural people are still mostly culture-bound and conservative. The young people respect and obey their elders and look to them for guidance. Political leadership among blacks in the countryside can only come from the elders — never the youth.

The UDF, on the other hand, was mostly led by young upwardly mobile urban blacks. The hostel dwellers looked sideways at them and muttered angrily: '*Sideleliswa ngabantwana bethu*' (the UDF teaches our children to disrespect us). Indeed, some of the young UDF lions had no understanding whatsoever of the cultural ways and mannerisms that the hostel dwellers cherished. The hostel dwellers for their part, wondered how the UDF could be a worthwhile organisation when it was led by children.

'What do children know?' the exasperated elderly people asked.

There were many instances where UDF youths publicly paraded older people naked in township streets and whipped and humiliated them. This added to the impotent fury felt by older people. The youthful comrades regarded the IFP as a traitor organisation. They declared that its members were sell-outs and attacked them. The most diabolical form was necklacing — placing a petrol-filled car tyre around their necks, setting it alight and burning them to death. The youth chanted and danced around the victims as they screamed in their death agonies. The elders people shook their heads and shivered with disgust and fear at such an atrocious fate.

In 1984 the ANC instructed its supporters to make the country ungovernable. Community councils were brought to a standstill and popularly nominated people's committees replaced them. The government responded by declaring a state of emergency and sent the SADF and the police into the townships to quell the unrest. The state of emergency gave the police sweeping powers to arrest and detain people indefinitely. People identified as leaders or even supporters of the revolt were arrested, sometimes murdered.

The vigilantes were unleashed on the youth to make it appear the fighting was amongst the blacks and the police were purely there to keep the peace. Yet when vigilantes launched attacks against the UDF, the police — sometimes wearing uniform and sometimes not — fought on their side.

It's interesting to analyse the motives that drove the participants in the conflict. The government had the imperative to crush the liberation movement, both internally and externally. The breakdown of the community councils in the townships was regarded by the government as part of the 'Total Onslaught'. The Bantustan leaders sought to defend their power and crush opposition to their claims that they were the legitimate leaders of the African people. The hostel dwellers saw it as an opportunity to vent their pent up fury and resentment against 'these insolent young upstarts'. The government used them to crush the revolt against white power.

The South African and international media saw it as 'black-on-black violence' — which is what the apartheid government's propaganda machine put out. The hidden hand of the State behind the melee remained concealed. The government didn't want the uprising to be seen as a revolt by black people against an oppressive state. They used the fighting as conclusive evidence to prove what they had been saying all along — that blacks are incapable of governing themselves and need the whites to get them to toe the line.

Daluxolo described in his testimony to the Truth and Reconciliation Commission the special assistance and support the IFP death squads got from the state. The police raided settlements and townships where UDF supporters were believed to be paramount, confiscated their weapons and arrested their leaders. The police then left the targeted area and gave pinpoint intelligence to IFP vigilantes which allowed them to launch attacks against the unarmed comrades. Afterwards members of Military Intelligence who worked closely with the IFP together with the Security Police, moved in and erased any evidence that might incriminate the IFP. Only then would the regular police, hardly any of whom showed much enthusiasm, be allowed into the area to investigate the murders.

Vigilantes wore red or white cloths wound around their heads so that they could identify each other in the heat of battle. They became known as *rooidoekies* or *witdoekies* (red or white bandanas). Another more sinister but practical reason was that it allowed the police to identify friend from foe — it indicated who they should shoot and who they shouldn't. In the vocabulary of the white policemen, the *rooidoekies* or *witdoekies* became 'our blacks' and care was taken not to arrest or injure them. This left them free to march, chant and attack the UDF with impunity.

The return of the 200 men from Caprivi marked the start of an escalation in bloodletting to a level never before reached in KwaZulu. They were highly trained fighters under the orders of a seasoned and battle hardened commander, Daluxolo. He had trained in the USSR, had seen action in Wankie and was recognised as one of the best shots in the country. The UDF, to our knowledge, didn't have fighters of this calibre in its ranks and at best they used inexperienced internally trained fighters. The UDF also didn't have the police on its side, which meant that their firepower was generally inferior.

To suppress the revolt the state ignored its own laws, murdering, maiming and massacring its citizens. What kind of state is it that releases criminals from its prisons and arms them against citizens who are demanding legitimate human rights . . . where the police are no longer law enforcement agents and keepers of the peace . . . where even the courts are vicariously criminalized by enforcing unjust laws? It becomes a pariah state. It was to this kind of state that the Bantustan leaders aligned themselves and by association became criminalized themselves.

We are not going to relate particular incidents that happened during this terrible time. They were just too many to detail: the killings at the Crossroads squatter camp in the Cape, Mpumalanga in KwaZulu, Katlehong, Sebokeng and Tembisa in Gauteng, reveal how widespread the conflict became.

One day Daluxolo was commanding his IFP forces who had been fighting a pitched battle against the UDF in Mpumalanga for three days. The ferocity of the fighting drove him to conclude that it couldn't last much longer. Nevertheless neither his forces nor the UDF's appeared to be gaining the upper hand and he wondered why.

While the fighting was raging, Daluxolo told a Major Pollberry (Paul Berry?) of Military Intelligence — attached to his forces for liaison purposes — that he was planning to attack a squatter settlement known as '25 Rand'. It got its name from the people who had bought their residential stands there for R25. The major's job was to ensure that the IFP got every assistance in their quest to crush the UDF. When he heard about Daluxolo's plans he asked for a postponement of the attack.

'Why?' Daluxolo asked.

'I will first have to withdraw my men. I don't want them killed.'

'Major', Daluxolo asked incredulously, 'you have men at 25 Rand?'

'Yes, I have, Commander Luthuli', the major responded.

'What are they doing there, Major? The people who have mounted attack after attack against Mlaba's house live there. What's the role of your men?'

Mlaba was the IFP chairman in Mpumalanga.

'Military Intelligence's role is to keep balance and ensure that neither side wipes out the other. If that happens the fighting will stop. In a nutshell, if the IFP gains the upper hand our men intervene on the side of the UDF and vice versa.'

Daluxolo stood there flabbergasted and speechless.

'You seem surprised Commander Luthuli. I felt sure you knew this.'

'So the people at 25 Rand who've been attacking and killing our supporters could be your men?'

'It's possible', the Major responded diffidently.

Daluxolo kept quiet for a very long time, digesting what he had just heard. He found it difficult to control his temper. He had suspected for a long time that his white Military Intelligence colleagues had been double dealing. Now, it was out in the open. To these whites the IFP and the UDF supporters were the same — just natives fighting among themselves. Who killed who didn't really matter.

He wondered whether his leaders at Ulundi knew or suspected this, or like him did they believe the SADF was their ally in the fight against the UDF? It seemed to him that the hypocrisy and duplicity of those whites knew no bounds. And what about the naivete of the IFP leadership? Hadn't they learned after all the centuries of conflict that the whites would never support a black leader unless it suited their self interest?

That evening at a meeting at Mr Mlaba's house, Daluxolo explained what had happened and why he had called off the attack on 25 Rand.

'The time has come, Ximba (clan name of the Mlabas) for us to question the relationship between ourselves, the government and the UDF,' Daluxolo said.

'From what you have told me, Daluxolo, we are being used as pawns in a game the whites have successfully played from the day they first set foot on this continent. They concentrate on the political differences between blacks to weaken both parties', Mlaba remarked, shaking his head.

'Should we go to Ulundi and tell our leaders what Pollberry told me?' Daluxolo asked. 'The question is, will they believe me? And if they do, will they be prepared to disengage from the clutches of the apartheid government? Or will they decide to sacrifice both of us and continue their relationship with the Boers?'

Mlaba rooted out a bottle of Limosin Brandy and two glasses and passed them to Daluxolo. He poured two generous tots and they drank thoughtfully. They were not the first Africans to find themselves in such a predicament. When one has committed oneself to the cause of a black leader that involves fighting one's own people, it's extremely painful to discover that the leadership got it entirely wrong in the first place. How then does one rectify such a primary error? Many people had died already and one couldn't just call their relatives, apologise and say it was all a dreadful mistake.

The two men sat talking into the early hours of the morning, planning what to do. They decided to call off all anti-UDF operations immediately. Contact would be opened between them and the UDF with a view to ending hostilities. They would tell the UDF's leadership in Mpumalanga what Daluxolo had learned and propose an immediate cease-fire. Both sides were tired of war and somebody had to make the first move to stop the fighting.

The meeting was arranged and the opposing sides met. At first the UDF's youthful leaders displayed distrust and scepticism, but after long discussions the older and wiser men realised it was an unexpected opportunity to bring peace to Mpumalanga. They embraced the IFP position and agreed to end hostilities. Leaders from both sides would call rallies and address their supporters about the peace plan. This would be followed by joint rallies where leaders from both groups addressed the people alongside their erstwhile enemies. From the same platform they would mutually declare that the war between them was over.

Everyone knew it would be touch and go. All that was needed to rekindle the blaze was a single shot by a rogue individual. Fortunately, though, things stayed calm and the agreement held. The guns fell silent and areas that had been no-go for one faction or the other could be visited by anyone without taking their lives in their hands.

Several months passed and still the peace remained in place. The people of Mpumalanga have never forgotten the Christmas of that year. It was their most peaceful for many years. Former enemies invited each other to parties where they drank and danced the night away. Lovers strolled the streets without the fear of being attacked by unidentified gunmen. Life gradually started to return to normal.

When the IFP wanted to hold a rally, they informed their UDF counterparts who organised their own marshals to guard against miscreants who might want to destroy the peace. UDF rallies got the same protection from the IFP.

New slogans appeared on each side's placards: 'It's your right to be IFP and my right to be UDF'; 'Leaders unite us — don't divide us'; 'The enemy is in Pretoria, not Mpumalanga'.

Mpumalanga was healed and funerals of murdered victims became rare. But it was too good to last, at least for Daluxolo. Word soon reached Ulundi that he was no longer a hit squad leader, but the peacemaker. The IFP's leadership was alarmed. How dare he make peace with the UDF without permission. He was recalled to Ulundi and put behind a desk. Fighting between the IFP and UDF was ongoing in other areas, notably Pietermaritzburg, the South Coast, Esikhawini in Durban and in Katlehong, Tembisa and Sebokeng on the East Rand.

Meanwhile, the IFP entered into a pact with white right-wingers. They would jointly start a civil war during the democratic election — which was still a year away — to stop the ANC from gaining power. Truckloads of weapons were moved from Pretoria to IFP training camps. Widespread weapons training courses were being conducted by right wingers, Military Intelligence operatives and according to Peter Stiff in his *Warfare by Other Means*, even by Rob Brown, the founder of Veterans for Victory — an SADF front organisation put in place to stymie the End Conscription Campaign.

The plan called for the IFP to trigger the civil war and the South African news media would tell the world that the Zulus were fighting the ANC because the latter were communists. Meanwhile, backing the IFP would be crack units of the SADF, the Afrikaner Weerstandsbeweging (AWB) and the Afrikaner Volksfront. The key element was the participation of the Zulus, for without them the whole plot would be exposed for what it really was — a white counter-revolution to restore apartheid.

Daluxolo stood on the sidelines and watched helplessly as the weapons came in and preparations were made for war. The Caprivians would be in the thick of the fighting and he knew he would have to lead them in the coming conflict. He didn't know how, but he intended to try and stop the bloodshed. He was still directing hit squad activities in areas where war between the IFP and the UDF/ANC alliance raged on. He was hungry for peace, but had no option but to continue making war on his own people. He also knew that he was being watched like a hawk by Military Intelligence. He spent sleepless nights tossing and turning in his bed next to his wife, wondering what to do.

Eventually, he decided to pay a covert visit to the ANC offices in Durban in the hope of meeting some of his former comrades so he could put the matter before them. He went alone, unarmed and unprotected. But his former comrades recognised him as a deadly enemy and avoided him, fearing an IFP attack. This almost caused his demise because the Security Police kept the ANC offices under constant surveillance and he was spotted entering and leaving.

Word was immediately passed on to the IFP that Daluxolo had defected back to the ANC. A decision was made to assassinate him. His membership of the IFP's Central Committee was withdrawn and he was placed under surveillance. Fortunately he had friends in Military Intelligence and they warned him of the danger he was facing. He clearly had to make a move and quickly.

An Eskom employee, Ndelu, who belonged to the IFP, happened to mention to him that there was a manager at Eskom by the name of Thula Bopela. Ndelu said he was well liked by the black staff because he stood up to the whites and didn't take any nonsense from them like the other black managers did. Daluxolo could scarcely credit that it was *his* Thula — whom he had last seen fighting with two Rhodesian policemen back in 1967. Maybe, just maybe, if it was his old comrade he might help him out of his deadly predicament. He would try to locate him on the morrow. That night Daluxolo slept peacefully.

It was a Thursday morning when the phone in my office rang. I picked it up.

'Eskom, can I help you?'

The person on the end of the line started laughing. I was not only puzzled but irritated.

'Can I help you?' I repeated, but the caller was still laughing.

'Who the hell are you and what do you want?' I asked getting really cross.

'It's Daluxolo. How the hell are you? I thought you would recognise my voice.'

'26 years is a long time', I replied. 'Where are you calling from?'

'I'm at Ulundi and I need to talk to you urgently. When could we meet?'

'I hope you're not suggesting I come to Ulundi! When will you be in Durban?'

'How about Tuesday next week? Can we meet at the Royal Hotel in Smith Street at 13:00?'

'That shouldn't be a problem. I heard you've become a big Inkatha politician. What happened?'

'It's a long story. I'll tell you about it when we meet on Tuesday.'

Daluxolo was not at Ulundi but in Durban when he made the call. He had fled there because of the dangers he was facing. Lying about his immediate whereabouts had become second nature. He also needed the interim period before our meeting to conduct his own observations on me before we met face-to-face. He wanted to be sure that I had really returned to civilian life and was no longer an MK cadre. He briefed three of his trusted Caprivians, gave them my description and told them where I worked.

'Follow him when he goes to lunch and find out who he talks to. If he goes to a restaurant, get a table nearby. See who is with him and try to pick up the conversation. Follow him wherever he goes and make notes on who he meets. Follow him home from work and find out his address. Try to confirm that he really is an electrification manager at Eskom.'

The Caprivians did their job and reported accordingly. But when they followed me after work they lost my car in the heavy Durban traffic. By Tuesday they still had not discovered where I lived. They took up stations and observed me as I stood reading a newspaper and waiting for Daluxolo in front of the Royal Hotel. They phoned him and reported what I was doing. Everything seemed okay but Daluxolo decided not to keep the appointment, fearing an ambush.

'Why are checking on this guy, commander?' one of his Caprivians asked. 'He looks a fairly harmless sort of chap to me.'

'That's why I'm checking. He looks too damned harmless for my liking', Daluxolo replied. 'He's one of the few men in MK who could kill me if he was given such a mission. I know him too well to underestimate him. If MK has told him to execute me he will do it in style.'

'Are you afraid of him? I have never known you to be afraid of anyone', the Caprivian said in astonishment.

'I fear nobody, Sosha, but if he is MK and I make one mistake, I won't get the chance to make another. We were very close in the old days and MK knows it. If they have chosen somebody to assassinate me, he is likely to be the one because they know I would be at ease with him. The people you trust always pose the greatest danger to you. Remember that Sosha.'

Daluxolo phoned me the following morning and apologised for not keeping the appointment. I accepted his apology and we agreed to meet on Friday the same week. Once more he didn't turn up. He knew my temper and that I had a short fuse. He judged correctly that making and breaking appointments would annoy me. He reasoned that if I lost my temper and refused to meet him, he would know he was not a target. If I was patient and conciliatory he would have good reason to suspect I had been tasked to assassinate him. He phoned me the following Monday, and I growled like an angry bear.

'Listen Daluxolo', I began, 'maybe you are the biggest warlord in South Africa but you're not going to have me hanging around the front of a hotel like a lemon for nothing. I'm older than you and I take great exception to being sent on wild goose chases. I don't like being messed around. Do you understand?'

'I'm so sorry, my brother, please listen. I had to rush my son to hospital only 15 minutes before I was due to meet you. Can we meet tomorrow? I promise I'll be there. Please, Thula.'

'Where? Same place same time?' I asked sullenly but softening.

'Same place, same time', Daluxolo said, winking at one of his Caprivians.

'Now I'm sure he's not after me', Daluxolo said to nobody in particular.

At exactly 13:00 the next day a white Kombi drew up in front of the Royal Hotel and Daluxolo stepped out grinning broadly. We stood looking at each other for some seconds and then spontaneously put our arms around each other. Me — hugging a man who was arguably one of the most dangerous men in South Africa at the time! When I suggested we lunch at the hotel he said he had made other arrangements and I should get in the Kombi.

There were three other men in the vehicle. They were Caprivians but I didn't know that then. I didn't see any guns, but they must have been armed. I greeted them and sat next to Daluxolo. I had not seen him for 26 years but he still looked pretty much the same, just a bit older. The driver swung out of the parking place and sped down Smith Street.

Daluxolo told me how he had been captured, taken to South Africa, tried and sentenced to ten years on Robben Island. He explained how and why he changed sides and became a member of the Inkatha Freedom Party.

'I couldn't understand and I still don't, Thula, why attacks against the homeland leaders occur only in KwaZulu. Chief Buthelezi is one of many homeland leaders but the rest have never been attacked. I asked myself — is the ANC intent on targeting Zulus? After all, Chief Kaiser Matanzima of Transkei was the first to accept homeland rule. Why wasn't he or Lucas Mangope of Bophuthatswana targeted?' Why only Buthelezi?

We didn't know it then but the State Security Council of the apartheid government had approved a plan called *Project Katzen* to assassinate President Lennox Sebe using ex-Rhodesian mercenaries based in neighbouring Transkei. The idea was to amalgamate Ciskei with Transkei and place both territories under the control of the hopelessly corrupt Kaizer Matanzima. The attack turned out to be an abysmal failure and resulted in a military clique led by Major-General Holomisa mounting a coup and taking control of Transkei.

'Perhaps', I suggested, 'it's because Buthelezi was the most confrontational. Why did the police suddenly allow the IFP to carry traditional weapons while marching and demonstrating in the cities when this had always been illegal? If other organisations dare to do the same they are promptly arrested. Surely heavily armed IFP men can hardly claim they're in danger from students and run-of-the-mill township dwellers?'

'We'll never know for sure who struck the first blow, but we in the IFP believe that it started when our members were attacked by people calling us sell-outs. Sell-outs to what? All I knew was that Zulus were being attacked and as a Zulu I felt it was my duty to defend ourselves', Daluxolo said.

'What about the people in the UDF and ANC?' I asked. 'Weren't a lot of them also Zulus? It doesn't make much sense for Zulu to attack Zulu.'

'The people instructing them to target the IFP were not Zulus. You'll remember in MK how Zulus were marginalised even at camp commander level, with appointments being made on a tribal basis.'

'Well, as you said Daluxolo, we'll never know who struck the first blow. But I cannot accept all this killing and bloodshed with blacks fighting blacks. The whites who have oppressed us for centuries are being left untouched by the violence. Why are blacks finding it so easy to shed each other's blood?'

'It's because the instigators directing this so-called black-on-black violence are whites. I'm fully aware of that now. That's what I'm here to discuss. The killing must stop.'

'I thought you said it's the UDF and ANC people who are attacking you. Where do the whites come in? And if you think the whites are directing it, what's the point of telling someone like me?'

'The apartheid state has helped homeland leaders like Buthelezi to acquire a military capability so that they can be used as surrogate forces to fight the liberation movement. I've discovered that right-wing whites are getting ready to fight to prevent the ANC from assuming power. But they want the Zulus to start the war, then the whites will do the rest. The world will be told that the Zulus are rejecting ANC rule because it's communist.'

'Come on, Daluxolo, if you think this, why are you still fighting for the IFP against the UDF/ANC alliance? You have me totally confused!'

'I found out not long ago that Military Intelligence is supporting both the IFP and the UDF to keep the fighting on the boil. In Mpumalanga I initiated peace moves and the fighting stopped. Now I've been told that Military Intelligence is gunning for me because I was seen going into the ANC offices. I wanted to persuade them to get the UDF/ANC alliance people to suspend all anti-IFP operations. If they agreed, I would have guaranteed the immediate halt of all IFP operations against them. But they wouldn't even talk to me because they know me as an IFP warlord.'

I sensed his inner turmoil. He was no longer smiling but had the face of a man who had resigned himself to die. I had seen the same look on the faces of men in Death Row. I began to understand his problem. He was IFP, but the IFP was with the Boers who were using Zulus to stem the liberation movement's revolution. Now he wanted to change sides and throw in his lot with the UDF/ANC, but understandably they wanted nothing to do with him.

'You say you can guarantee the immediate cessation of all anti-UDF/ANC operations. How can one man achieve such a major task?' I asked.

'Because I'm the commander-in-chief of all IFP hit squads', he answered quietly. 'If I tell my men to stop fighting the UDF, they'll obey me.'

'Okay, but who'll guarantee the cessation of the alliance's anti-IFP operations?' I asked, more to myself than him. I thought for a few moments. 'Maybe you should talk to Joe Modise.'

'I'm talking to you.'

'That's not much use. I left MK a long time ago.'

'Look, Military Intelligence is planning to assassinate me and the ANC will have nothing to do with me. The Boers are delivering large quantities of weapons to the IFP. When the civil war starts, as it most surely will, our people, the Zulus, will die like flies. If you can't see your way clear to helping me stop this bloodshed, I'll have no option but to return to the IFP and fight to the finish. At least I'll have a clean conscience because I will have done my best to save innocent lives. You'll be all right. You'll be able to sit in your posh office, drive your new blue Ford Sapphire and live peacefully in Pinetown with your wife and children. You'll be well away from the trouble.'

'What the hell do you expect of me?' I demanded in exasperation. 'I told you I'm no longer MK or an ANC office bearer, so I don't know how I can help — even if I wanted to.'

'I want you to say to yourself quite honestly that there is absolutely nothing you can do to stop the planned carnage against our people. If you can say that, I'll leave you alone. You'll wonder later, of course, after rivers of blood start to flow, if you could have done more. But that will be on your conscience.'

I lit a cigarette and smoked for a long while. I lit another and finished it without saying a word. In truth I didn't know what to do or say. The problem was so great that I was certain I was not the right person to deal with it. I had to speak to somebody high up in MK, but who? I thought of Baleka Mbete, but I didn't even know if she had returned to the country. Where was our old Wankie commander, Mjojo Mxwaku or Zola Bona alias Zola Skweyiya? My problem was that I was out of touch and didn't even know who was around. I thought of Ronnie Kasrils but he was a wanted man and in hiding. Suddenly it occurred to me. I would speak to Jacob Zuma.

The Kombi had been driven aimlessly around for two hours. We finally stopped close to the beach at La Mercy. We got out and looked at the sea. The waves were rising and the crests were a milky white. A strong wind was blowing and the seagulls screamed, seemingly aware that we were facing critical decisions.

'I accept that I have betrayed the ANC, Thula', said Daluxolo, ' but that's history. We should now focus on the future and decide what to do to frustrate the strategies of the apartheid government. We cannot allow them to roll back the liberation struggle. I'll leave it in your hands. See Zuma and explain things. Let him decide what should be done.'

We shook hands and the years seemed to disappear. It was as if we were back in Wankie in 1967. We had lacked the advantage of numbers then and were no better off now. But despite that, I felt confident that the two of us were still capable of cocking a snook at the Boers.

As an afterthought I asked him how he knew where my office was, that I drove a new blue Sapphire and that I lived in Pinetown.

'I didn't keep those earlier appointments because I was checking on you. I couldn't meet you until my men were sure of you', he told me.

'Oh, so you have been spying on me, you bastard. Was that necessary?'

'I also have a wife and children now, Thula. I have travelled a long and hard road and it's my ambition to be alive when Freedom Day comes.'

'How can you be sure I won't kill you for betraying the cause?'

'I know you well enough. If given the choice of killing me or stopping a counter-revolution, I think that both you and Jacob Zuma will opt for the latter. I could be wrong, of course.'

'Yes, you just might', I laughed.

We got back in the Kombi and I was driven to my office in West Street. I had been away for several hours and if my manager, Hugh McGibbon, had found out what I had been up to, there would surely have been trouble.

36

War clouds gather

It's no exaggeration to say that between 1992 and 1994 South Africa teetered on the brink of full-out civil war. A low intensity war had already begun with the apartheid state and the surrogate armies of the homeland territories on the one side, and the liberation forces on the other. The release from prison of Nelson Mandela and the unbanning of the liberation organisations were viewed differently by different sections of the South African population. Some groups were jubilant and others dismayed, depending on their expectations.

The blacks supporting the ANC/UDF/COSATU alliance were triumphant because they could sense that victory was in sight. They knew that the De Klerk government had not released their leader out of compassion, but because it saw this action as a major step on the road to conciliation. The alliance supporters knew it signalled that the ANC would form the next government and realised that the years of bitter struggle had not been in vain.

The National Party government had painted itself into a corner. PW Botha had started negotiations with the ANC externally and with Nelson Mandela in prison. Having been forced to withdraw from Angola and Namibia, its politicians finally realised that it would be impossible for South Africa to survive as a white state on a black continent. After the collapse of the Soviet Bloc, South Africa lost its importance to its allies in the West as guardian of the Cape sea route and supplier of strategic materials. The West believed that if change didn't come peacefully, it would inevitably mean that a black army comprising Angolans, Namibians, Mozambicans and probably Zimbabweans — with the support of the Cubans — would march south to free their black brothers from apartheid. Of course, the whites would put up a grim fight and the country, along with its surrounding territories, would be left a blackened smoking ruin. Western countries owned much of South Africa's economy and they certainly wouldn't want to see a war like that. So De Klerk was nudged towards the negotiating table and Nelson Mandela needed to be sitting there with him.

The homeland leaders, with the exception of Major-General Bantu Holomisa in Transkei, were dismayed. How could the government assure them at one moment that it would crush the liberation movement and the next moment release their jailed leadership?

The homeland leaders had not even been informed, let alone consulted about what was happening. They felt that the government was betraying them to the communists. There had long been rumours in Bisho, Ulundi and Mmabatho that the government had been secretly meeting and having discussions with the ANC. They began to feel like a wife who discovers that her husband is having an affair with a woman far younger and prettier than herself — a feeling of desperation and deep disillusionment.

The white right-wingers were also alarmed. The *Volk* was about to be betrayed by the politicians who were making a deal with the communists. They had to do something because they couldn't just sit around and wait for their Afrikaner heritage to be traded for a red flag. They had to mobilise, but who was there to take the lead? It couldn't be their former National Party leaders because those were the people selling them out.

The white right-wingers found themselves in the same position as their forebears at the beginning of the 20th century. They had fought the Anglo-Boer War to defend their freedom and independence, only to finish up being ruled by the foe. They were not of a mind to let that happen again and if it took another war, so be it.

Politicians are devious characters. They urge their people to rally around and fight for a cause, only to backtrack later and try to persuade the same people that it's the wrong cause to fight for. Afrikaner right-wingers had been raised to believe in the superiority of the white race and the inferiority of the black one. Their Dutch Reformed Church had even given apartheid divine sanction. So they had gone and fought the 'kaffirs' in Angola, Namibia and Rhodesia — and now they were about to be ruled by Nelson Mandela. What had their sons fought and died for?

Most Afrikaners had been raised to hate the ANC from childhood. They were told it was anti-Christ and communist — the two greatest sins on earth. If it took power it would abolish all social, economic, cultural and political values held dear by them. It would ban their language and religious worship and nationalise their farms. It would encourage marriage between the races and within two or three generations the whites would disappear. The ANC meant the end of life as they knew it.

Their eyes turned towards one man, General Constand Viljoen — a well-salted battle veteran and a former Chief of the SADF. He had fought to defend the *Volk* and they were confident he wouldn't turn his back on them in their hour of need. If they couldn't have the whole country, what they wanted was a *volkstaat* (a people's state) where Afrikaners could live, govern themselves and protect their culture and language. General Viljoen fully embraced the idea of a *volkstaat*. He was also confident that if there was a need to fight, he could draw 50 000 men to his banner.

Then there was Dr Ferdi Hartzenberg, the dour Conservative Party leader who was totally against black rule. There was Eugene TerreBlanche, fiery and charismatic leader of the fascist AWB. History has proven him to be a loud-mouth and a coward, but at that time his compelling oratory drew a small but committed and highly vocal support group. He has since been declared a *verraaier* (traitor) by the very people he used to enthral with his fiery rhetoric. Prison has taken its toll on both him and his ideology and he now claims to be a changed man. He has never explained publicly what he changed from and what to.

The *volkstaat* idea had never been well-reasoned and objectively developed. It was the product of the Afrikaner's fear and distrust of a future black government. If they had formed a sort of independent homeland, say in the Western Transvaal as was suggested, they would have been hemmed in with Botswana to their north, Namibia to their west and a black South Africa on the other sides. Survival would depend on trading and dealing with their black neighbours. But what if their neighbours ignored them? They wouldn't have lasted long. This was amply demonstrated during the days of consumer boycotts when white businesses went bankrupt because blacks stopped buying.

The ideology of apartheid conferred a privileged status on whites and they benefited hugely from it. They had the advantages of job reservation, superior subsidised education, access to capital, access to land , freedom of movement, and the rest of it. Change threatened this privileged way of life. That's why many whites are opposed to the ANC government to this day and refuse to live in an atmosphere of equality with other races.

During 1993 some retired SADF generals formed the Afrikaner Volksfront (AVF) in an attempt to bring together right-wing Afrikaners and build a significant power bloc. Prominent among them were Generals Constand Viljoen and Tienie Groenewald. It was a movement of Afrikaners unhappy with the National Party's handling of the political situation. They believed the only solution was the formation of an Afrikaner homeland autonomous from the South African State.

The emotions of many Afrikaners were so aroused by the possibility of coming under ANC rule that they were ready to fight and die for this hopeless cause. In August 1993 General Groenewald said South Africa had never been closer to a civil war. A surprising claim emerged when he said: 'The AVF was involved in intensive bilateral talks and the ANC and the government realised that Afrikaners and the Zulus wouldn't permit a communist government to take power'.

How could the Zulus, who had fought and died at the Battle of Blood River to defend their land from Afrikaner colonisation, make common purpose with a racist Afrikaner organisation like the AVF? In any case, why would Zulus want to oppose communism? The Zulus of the 1990s were factory, farm and domestic workers — not the tillers of land and livestock owners they once were. That economic status was lost when those very Afrikaners had stolen their land and livestock from them. It was not Zulus who were opposed to the ANC and communism, but wealthy Afrikaner landowners who hired them to work on their farms at miserable wages and in atrocious conditions. Some Zulu leaders who had decided to make common cause with these racists, wanted to promote their own private interests by involving Zulus in a war that had nothing to do with them. They were good enough to fight the ANC, but would be relegated to votelessness after the ANC had been defeated.

When De Klerk's National Party government passed the Transitional Executive Council Bill in September 1993, General Groenewald declared its adoption would be considered a declaration of war. The Conservative Party and the IFP also opposed the bill, declaring it to be a 'constitutional revolution that will transfer power to the ANC/SACP alliance.' It would apply to South Africa and all homeland states and its purpose would be to ease the transition from National Party rule to democracy after the elections.

From this moment the AVF and the AWB began to prepare for war.

General Viljoen said he would be prepared to fight if he was convinced that no alternative existed. Having known war personally he was less hotheaded about starting it than the AWB and the CP. They seemed to relish the prospect of starting another Anglo-Boer War. It seems remarkable that they got their inspiration from a war that had ended in their defeat.

General Viljoen, in our view, posed the most serious threat if he decided to go to war. If his claim to have the backing of 50 000 men could be believed, then nobody could doubt that he needed to be treated with great circumspection. He was a combat general and when it came to directing a war, he would undoubtedly have proved formidable. When asked whether the SADF would have moved against him he was explicit: 'My personal feeling was that loyalty to me still existed in the SADF'. I believe it was an honest answer.

His strategy would have been different from the AWB's. He would probably have opted to mass his men and occupy a specific area, then declare it a *volkstaat* and demand recognition. The AWB was different — they saw the coming conflict as one where they could go out and kill as many black people as they wished with no thought of the consequences.

Peter Stiff explains how AWB Chief Commandant Phil Kloppers of Randfontein told his men that orders had come from Eugene Terre'Blanche that the AWB should prepare for war.

> I received an order that the revolution will start that night [12 December 1993]. Our duty was to sow chaos in the urban areas. All the men understood what I meant by 'the real McCoy' because General Oelofse wanted to see corpses. Our target group was the ANC/SACP alliance. The revolution was scheduled to commence countrywide that night.

A roadblock was set up at Ridora Crossing and three black students travelling from Mafikeng to Springs were stopped. They were punched, kicked, beaten with rifle butts and robbed. A second vehicle, a Cressida with more blacks aboard, was also stopped. The occupants were dragged from the vehicle, asked why they supported the ANC, and assaulted. In the end the occupants of both cars were shot. Not all of them died at the scene. Some with serious wounds were taken to hospital where they died from loss of blood.

One vehicle was ablaze either because its fuel tank had been shot up or because it had been deliberately set alight. A victims' ear was cut off and taken as a trophy by the attackers because their commander had demanded to see one.

The Ridora Crossing massacre was hailed by the AWB as a great victory where 'communists' had been killed. Their leader, Terre'Blanche, inspected a guard of honour formed by the butchers of Ridora Crossing and he congratulated the commander, General Oelofse. Within 20 days most had been arrested and charged with murder.

That's how the AWB fought — by hatching murderous madcap schemes to protect their narrow extremist interests. They considered unarmed and innocent people fair targets as long as they were black. In their view every black person was a supporter of the ANC and thus a communist.

Of course, not all Afrikaners were like that. National Party politicians like President De Klerk, Roelf Meyer, Pik Botha and others were at that very time negotiating a constitution with the ANC that would secure the safety and rights of all whites in a South Africa under ANC rule.

Peter Stiff in his *Warfare by Other Means*, explains how General Georg Meiring, the newly appointed Chief of the SADF, was visited by an AVF deputation in January 1994. Their aim was to discover where his sympathies and intentions lay with regard to the right wing. CP leader Dr Ferdi Hartzenberg, his deputy Dr Willie Snyman, Agricultural Union leader Dries Bruwer, the general secretary of the AVF Joseph Chiole and Colonel Piet Uys assembled at the SADF's Intelligence College. Terre'Blanche had not been invited, which tells us the AVF's opinion of the AWB.

They asked General Meiring whether he was prepared to serve under an ANC President like Nelson Mandela who was a communist. The general was incensed and told the questioner that he took orders from the president of the day. When asked what he would do if the AVF embarked on an armed struggle against the political process, his answer was abruptly simple.

'I will shoot you!'

Someone demanded to know which soldiers he would use since Afrikaners would not kill their fellow Afrikaners.

'I will use my English [Citizen Force] regiments.'

'And then?'

'I will use my black soldiers.'

Meiring had also on another occasion cautioned General Viljoen, making it plain to him that 'If you are really going to do what you say you are going to do, we'll have to stop you'.

Before the elections he had warned everybody who wanted to derail the electoral process to be careful. '*As julle 'n ding gaan doen gaan ons julle opvok. Julle moet pasop*' (If you are going to do something, we'll fuck you up. You'd better watch out).

He had other discussions with General Viljoen where things were thrashed out between them. Viljoen went away from these meetings knowing that he stood no chance of getting his *volkstaat* by force. Even his 50 000 men with their rifles and machine guns would have been no match against a disciplined army backed by tanks and heavy artillery. He understood that he had been checkmated. Good generals can see an inevitable outcome before a shot has been fired.

Later, when Viljoen went to try and rescue President Lucas Mangope of Bophuthatswana from the political ruins of his collapsing government, he kept his head. The deaths that occurred during that doomed undertaking were the direct result of the reckless activities of the AWB.

We mention General Georg Meiring because at thr time he was the most powerful man in the land. He stood at the head of an army whose military power was unsurpassed in Africa. Although he was an Afrikaner general, he resisted the call of his people to use the force at his disposal to derail a legitimate political process. Above all, he was a professional soldier who chose to abide by the oath of allegiance he had taken. There has been speculation as to how General Viljoen would have acted had he been in Meiring's shoes. Suffice it to say that at the time Meiring saw things more clearly and realistically than Viljoen.

37

Rocky road to peace

Why didn't civil war erupt in South Africa prior to or after the 1994 election? There are those who attribute the prevalence of peace in South Africa to the spirit and wisdom of former President Nelson Mandela. His contribution to tranquillity in the country is indeed unsurpassed and this was recognised internationally by him being awarded a Nobel Prize for Peace.

Former President FW De Klerk was honoured in the same way. Zealots like us who would have preferred only one messiah — Nelson Rolihlahla Mandela — were disappointed by the accolade given to De Klerk. How could Mandela share a pedestal with one who had waged war against the liberation struggle? When Mandela invited De Klerk to participate in a government of national unity, we were outraged.

Our vote in the democratic elections of 1994 gave Mandela a clear majority and a mandate to rule alone. 'There he goes', we said, 'inviting the enemies of the black people to take part in a government of national unity. What is the matter with the man?', we asked.

Our exasperation with the ANC leadership was caused by our inability to see the bigger picture. Mandela well knew the role that De Klerk had played in paving the road to peace. His decision to release Mandela from prison had scandalised most Afrikaners. The two leaders went through tough negotiations together at Kempton Park at what became known as Codesa. Despite disruptions like the AWB crashing an armoured vehicle into the conference centre, the process went forward.

The South African Police and the Defence Force remained loyal to the political process, thanks to the influence of President De Klerk. He had also retired certain SADF generals who were known to have strong right wing sympathies. And what about the Afrikaners who refused to answer the AVF's and AWB's call to arms? Did they contribute to peace simply by not flocking to the standards of men determined to set the country aflame in a racial war? In my view they did and they deserve the credit for it.

Jan Smuts Airport (now Johannesburg International) was rocked by AWB-rigged explosions. They hoped that this kind of visible action would bring the entire Afrikaner nation to the AWB flag. It didn't. Then came the assassination by members of the CP of the darling of the revolution, Chris Hani. They expected this to trigger black rage followed by indiscriminate retaliation against whites that would start a racial free-for-all. It didn't happen, largely due to Nelson Mandela's conciliatory hand. The ANC leaders kept a tight leash on their furious cadres and averted disaster.

Who else contributed to a transition from violent confrontation to peaceful resolution and democratic elections in 1994? Well, Daluxolo alias Daluxolo Wordsworth Luthuli did.

After our meeting I went home and thought about what I should do. I had to try and find Jacob Zuma and talk to him. Days passed and I still had not located him. No one was willing to volunteer information on his whereabouts. Times were dangerous and such information was never divulged unless one knew the questioner well and trusted him implicitly. It took a week before I got wind of where he was going to be the following day and I managed to arrange a meeting. I got right down to business and explained who I was. He listened carefully, particularly when I mentioned that I had fought in the Wankie Campaign of 1967. Whatever suspicions he might have harboured about me vanished immediately.

'So, you were with Comrade Chris in Wankie?' Jacob asked.

'Yes, Msholozi', I replied, using his clan name. 'But that's not what I have come to talk about. There is a more urgent and important matter.'

'It must be urgent if it's being brought by one of our tried and tested cadres. I'm listening, Comrade Thula.'

'A guy who was with me at Wankie and who was detained with you on Robben Island has told me that the IFP, AWB and AVF are preparing to launch a civil war to disrupt the elections. Their plans are well advanced and huge quantities of weapons have already been stockpiled in KwaZulu. He wants to stop the war. I think you should have a word with him, comrade.'

'We know those groups are planning to start a civil war, Comrade Thula, but we lack detail. Who is this man who thinks he can put a stop to it?'

'He's Daluxolo Luthuli, Msholozi, the commander of all IFP hit-squads. He says he has convinced his men that they should pull out of the IFP and expose hit squad activity to the newspapers and the TEC [Transitional Executive Council]. He is willing to do this on condition that all ANC military activities against the IFP are also stopped. I couldn't give him guarantees on that, which is why I brought the matter to you.'

Jacob Zuma was silent for a moment, looking over my head at nothing in particular. I wished at the time that I had been an artist so I could have captured the faraway look on his face which gave no clue to what was going on in his mind.

'Have you mentioned this to anybody else, Comrade Thula?'

'I have not, Msholozi.'

'Good, let's keep it that way, *zikhali zamaNtungwa lezi* [an expression used by Zulus to indicate that something is of extreme importance). I think I should meet this Daluxolo and find out more. Can you arrange a meeting?'

'I will do so, Msholozi.'

'Thank you. Phone me at this number when you are ready.'

He wrote a number on a piece of paper and told me to memorise it. He then took it back and destroyed it. I took my leave, the meeting having lasted exactly five minutes.

I contacted Daluxolo immediately and venue, date and time were agreed on. The meeting took place at the Albany Hotel in Smith Street, Durban. Zuma was accompanied by Eric 'Khehla' Mtshali who I think was in charge of intelligence in KwaZulu-Natal. I had last seen him in Zambia in 1966.

'The IFP has sufficient capacity to cause widespread chaos, Msholozi', Daluxolo explained. 'Its hit squads are a vital part of the operation because the plan is to project the fighting so that it appears to be between the ANC and the Zulus and not the Boers. I'm in command of the hit squads and I can bring them over to the ANC. That will mean the Boers will have to find their own Zulus to do the dirty work for them.'

There was an in-depth discussion for over an hour. I didn't say anything because I had no contribution to make. After the meeting Daluxolo drove off in his car, Zuma left with Eric and I went home to Pinetown. Several days passed without any contact, but before the week was over, Zuma phoned.

'President Mandela will be coming to Durban within the next fortnight. This will give Daluxolo an opportunity to personally place the matter before him. The president has agreed to meet him. Let's see what comes of it.'

'That's good, Msholozi. Shall I tell Daluxolo now or later?'

'I don't have a problem if you tell him now, but ask him to confirm that he will attend. Tell him to use the phone number I gave you.'

'I'll do that, Msholozi. I don't believe I'll be of any use to you after this, so may I be excused from the meeting between the president and Daluxolo?'

'That's fine, Comrade Thula, and thank you for your intervention'.

Daluxolo phoned Jacob Zuma and confirmed that he was prepared to meet Mandela. I almost forgot about the whole thing and got on with my work at Eskom. A week passed and I heard nothing. Just before the end of the second week Zuma called.

'There's a problem', he said.

'Daluxolo has said he wants to pull out of the meeting which is scheduled for tomorrow. What do we do, Comrade Thula?'

'Why is he pulling out? Only a week ago he agreed to meet the president. What's happened to make him change his mind?'

He believes he'll be assassinated by ANC security if he goes.'

'Is he going to be killed, Msholozi? You should know. How can I persuade him that it won't happen?'

'I can assure you, Comrade Thula that as much as our men would love to take him out, it won't happen as long as he agrees to meet the old man.'

'So how do I convince him, Msholozi?'

'He says he will go on one condition.'

'What's that?' I asked, sensing trouble.

'He wants you to accompany him because he doesn't think the ANC will hit him if you're there. It's up to you, but I cannot compel you, Comrade Thula. But I think you know how important this meeting will be.'

Damn Daluxolo, I thought. What gives him the right to involve me in his affairs any time he chooses? I didn't tell him to join the IFP and become a death squad commander. How does he know they won't kill him if he's with me, anyway? They could hit us both. Damn him again!

'So what do you think, Comrade Thula?'

'I don't like the way he's using me. How can he use me as his shield just because I was stupid enough to get involved?'

'I understand how you feel, but what can I say to the old man? Shall I say that his veteran MK soldiers no longer wish to meet their supreme commander? How can I do that?'

'Well, I'll come, but I don't like it. Damn that man! Tell him I'll be there.'

Zuma made a brief phone call. I thought I heard suppressed laughter at the other end but I couldn't be sure.

'Thank you, Comrade Thula. The meeting will be at the Royal Hotel tomorrow at noon. We'll be expecting the two of you. Please phone me before you arrive. I'll come out and meet you personally to allay any fears you might still have.'

I phoned Daluxolo and demanded an explanation for his latest ploy.

'*Uyadelela wena mfana, ucabanga ukuthi ngiyinto yakho yokudlala*' (you're a very insolent young man, Daluxolo, treating me like your toy).

'Thula, it's not like that. I was given information that some chaps in Zuma's outfit were discussing the question of shooting me if I went to meet the president. I want to meet the old man, but I don't want to run into trouble.'

'So you decide to enlist me as your bodyguard. Damn you, Daluxolo, saving your hide isn't my life's work. It was your decision to join the IFP and go toe-to-toe with MK. It was nothing to do with me. Now when they might want to get you, you crawl under me and hide. I saved you from arrest in Rhodesia and you abandoned me that time. Are you planning to do the same again? Well my friend, you won't get me to play Jesus Christ and die for your sins this time. What makes you think that Zuma's guys won't shoot you even if I'm with you?'

'Zuma has a great deal of respect for you. He told me so. I'm certain he won't let anything happen to me if you're there.'

'*Ag* man, I feel like throwing up', I told him. 'I'm going to do it, but I'm not doing it for you. I'm doing it for the president and for peace.'

That night I had a nightmare. I dreamt we were at the meeting and that Daluxolo murdered Mandela. I jumped out of bed, switched on the bedside lamp and stood there trembling. I could hardly believe it had only been a bad dream. Cherry stirred and opened her eyes.

'Is there anything wrong?' she asked.

'Just a bad dream, my dear. Go back to sleep.'

I walked to the lounge and lit a cigarette. What was the meaning of the dream? Was it a warning? Did Daluxolo harbour sinister thoughts about Madiba? How could I really know? If he harmed the old man how could I explain why I had brought him into contact with Zuma? In such an atmosphere no one would believe a word I said. I decided to phone Zuma, but I couldn't raise him. I tried again in the morning and got him.

'Tell me Msholozi, how well do you know Daluxolo?'

'Not much. Why do you ask?'

'I have been out of contact with him for almost 26 years. He has fought against the ANC and killed many of our comrades. Can we be sure of his state of mind? What if has been given the mission to kill Mandela? We are putting them together tomorrow. If such a terrible thing happened, how could we ever explain it to the ANC or live with ourselves?'

'Do you suspect he might attempt such a thing, Comrade Thula?'

I didn't want to tell Zuma about my dream. Soldiers work with facts and information, not dreams.

'It's just a concern, Msholozi. I have no evidence to suggest it's likely.'

'You have caught me off guard, Comrade Thula. I don't know what to say, but I agree a possibility always exists. What do you suggest?'

'Conceal a .38 Special in the toilet of the President's hotel room and I'll get it as soon as we enter the room. I'll watch Daluxolo's every movement. If he tries anything, it will be the last thing he ever does', I growled.

'But what if *you* use the gun to shoot the President, Comrade Thula? How will I explain that?'

We both started laughing. We were being ridiculous. The three of us had come a long way in this peace process and we were still asking questions about each other.

Zuma controlled his bout of laughter first.

'Now what will you do if *I* shoot the President!' Zuma asked.

We embarked on another bout of almost hysterical laughter.

The meeting took place in Madiba's suite and, of course, there were no incidents. The President was gracious, embarrassing Zuma and myself by the sheer trust and confidence he displayed towards Daluxolo. For his part, Duluxolo was overcome with emotion and wept openly. It was an amazing moment. There was this great man, tall and upright, accepting the apologies of a man who had once been his soldier — but who had defected to the enemy. Now he had returned to the ANC fold. All was forgiven, but there were others out there who would neither forgive nor forget.

'I must warn you, Comrade Daluxolo', Madiba said. 'You'll antagonise many people and they'll want to kill you for what you have done. Many will be very powerful and the ANC will be unable to protect you because it is not yet the government. I will arrange for you to enter the witness protection programme and leave the country until the ANC is in a position to shield you. I wish to thank you on behalf of the people of South Africa. *Amandla*!'

Daluxolo entered the witness protection programme and was sent to Denmark. He was later granted amnesty by the Truth and Reconciliation Commission for his actions while commander-in-chief of the Caprivi hit squads.

The IFP agreed, at the very last moment, to enter the negotiations and participate in the election. In his *Warfare by Other Means*, Peter Stiff attributes this to the amendment made to the new constitution that would recognise the institution of the Zulu monarchy, its role, authority and status. Or perhaps it was a face saver for the IFP when they realised that with Daluxolo's defection and the exposure of IFP hit squad activity, it would no longer be possible to project a civil conflict as a Zulu uprising against the ANC? However, on 28 March 1994 there was another attempt to stir IFP enmity against the ANC. Thousands of Zulus, mostly armed with traditional weapons but many with automatic rifles, launched an attack on the ANC's headquarters at Shell House in Johannesburg. In the exchanges of fire that followed 11 Zulus were killed and 276 wounded. Nobody quite knew where to lay the blame, but maybe it was the last concerted effort of white right-wingers to camouflage their operations with the cloak of Zulu warriors.

Whichever way, the power of the white right had finally been broken, allowing the country to move from near anarchy to the democratic rule we see today.

Afterword

On 5 November 1995, more than 10 years after it had happened, 20 people appeared in the Durban Supreme Court for remand on charges relating to the murder of 13 people during the KwaMakutha massacre. They were:

Accused 1   Major Louis Botha, formerly head of the Security Police in Durban and liaison officer for *Operation Marion*.
Accused 2   Brigadier John Reeves More, formerly a colonel in the Chief of Staff Intelligence's Directorate of Special Tasks.
Accused 3   Zakhele 'MZ' Khumalo, former personal assistant to Chief Buthelezi who was in charge of the Caprivi trainees.
Accused 4   Peter Msane, Caprivi graduate and alleged hit squad member.
Accused 5   Celukwanda Ndhlovu, Caprivi graduate and alleged hit squad member.
Accused 6   Martin Thulani Khanyile, Caprivi graduate and alleged hit squad member.
Accused 7   Prince Phezukwendoda Mkhize, Caprivi graduate and alleged hit squad member.
Accused 8   General Magnus Malan, former Minister of Defence.
Accused 9   General Kat Liebenberg, former Chief of the Army.
Accused 10 General Jannie Geldenhuys, former Chief of the SADF.
Accused 11 General Tienie Groenewald, former Director of Military Intelligence.
Accused 12 General Neels van Tonder, former Director of Intelligence Operations.
Accused 13 Vice Admiral Dries Putter, former Chief of Staff Intelligence.
Accused 14 Brigadier Cor van Niekerk, former Director of Special Tasks – Unit 2 – in the office of the Chief of Staff Intelligence.
Accused 15 Colonel Johannes Victor, former senior Military Intelligence Chief of Natal Command.
Accused 16 Colonel Jake Jacobs, chief instructor of the Caprivi trainees when still a major.
Accused 17 Colonel Jan van der Merwe, a Military Intelligence operative as a commandant.

Accused 18 Colonel Dan Griesel, former commander of the secret Ferntree military base.
Accused 19 Hloni Andreas Mbuyazi, Caprivi graduate and alleged hit squad member.
Accused 20 Alex Vulindiela Biyela, Caprivi graduate and alleged hit squad member.

They were all acquitted after a lengthy trial.

INDEX

25 Rand squatter settlement, 24
5-Brigade, atrocities, 215-217

African Democratic Movement, 180
Afrikaner Volksfront, 249, 257-262
Afrikaner Weerstandsbeweging, (AWB), 249, 256, 258-261
Ama-Afrika, SADF front, 180
ANC's House of Chiefs, 244
ANC/ZAPU alliance, 53
ANC's Working Committee (WC) of the NEC, 174
Angola, 45, 91, 173-175, 177, 180, 189, 203, 219, 220, 222, 255, 256
ANC's HQ Shell House, attack, 266
Aucamp, Col, SA Correctional Services, 152, 154
AVF (See Afrikaner Volksfront)

Baloyi, Robert, MK KIA, 60, 68
Bam, Enock and Bongie, 226-229
Banana, Rev Canaan, Zimbabwe President, 183
Banda, Dr Hastings Kamuzu of Malawi, 49, 52
Barayl, Elijah, COSATU president, 197, 198
Barker, Supt Salisbury Maximum Security Prison, 113
Batoka Gorge, Zambezi River, 61
Bhengu, Sbu, Inkatha Youth Brigade, 210
Bhengu, Siegfried, MK and IFP, 201
Biyela, Alex Vulindiela, Caprivi graduate, 268
Biyela, Philimon 'Pangaman, MK, 46
Bona, Zola Bona (Zola Skweyiya), ANC, 46, 233, 253
Bopela, Blanjan Mhlathini, 17, 19-21, 147
Bopela, Mrs Cherry Duduzile Khoza, 223-234, 239, 240, 264
Bopela, Mduduzi, 236
Bopela, Nandi, 231
Bopela, Nombali, 231
Bopela, Simo Pascoe, 17-20, 23, 28
Bopela, Tshitshi, 224, 225, 227, 231
Bopela, Vusumuzi, 20, 81, 86-88, 219
Bophuthatswana, 195, 210, 243, 244, 252, 259
Bosman, Theron, Rhodesian Attorney General, 113
Boston, MK guerrilla, 61
Botha, Major Louis, Security Police Durban, 206, 210, 211, 267
Botha, President PW, 192, 255
Botha, Pik, SA Foreign Minister, 259
Botswana, 28, 29, 33, 49, 75, 86, 89, 93, 122, 123, 162, 189, 220, 223, 257
Breytenbach, Colonel Jan 'Mehlwensimbi', 202, 205
British South Africa Police (BSAP), Rhodesia, 95-97, 105, 114, 125, 190
Bruwer, Dries, General Secretary AVF, 259
Buchner, General, KwaZulu Police Commissioner, 211
Buciko, Boysie, MK, 47
Bulawayo, 23, 74, 81, 83-87, 93, 103, 105, 113, 122, 123, 164, 183, 184, 214-216, 219-22
Buthelezi, Chief Mangosuthu Gatshe, 188, 191-193, 196-201, 205-207, 209, 219-222, 226, 243, 251, 252, 267

Caculama, Angola, MK military training camp, 173, 174, 177
Caprivi, 205, 209, 246, 267
Caprivians, IFP hit squad trainees, 243, 249-251
Castro, President Fidel, Cuba, 32, 49, 50, 55, 60, 147
Caxito, Angola, 174
Central Intelligence Organisation, Rhodesia (CIO), 53, 213
Chibuwe, BSAP Stn, 97, 105, 121
Chifombo, ZANLA Base, Mozambique, 178
Chikadaya, Lovemore, ZANLA commander, 178
Chikerema, James, ZAPU, 52, 53, 181
Chikore Mission, Rhodesia, 88, 122
Chimsoro, Chirisa, ZAPU, Death Row prisoner, 147-150
Chiole, Joseph, General Secretary AVF, 259
Chipinga (now Chipinge), 94, 99, 102, 106, 160
Chisumbanje, Rhodesia, 88, 90, 93, 94, 102, 121, 183
Chitepo, Adv Herbert, ZANU's director of operations in Zambia, 52, 53, 178
Cienfuegos, Camillo, Cuban revolutionary commander, 49
CIO (See Central Intelligence Organisation)
Clarke, Rev, prison chaplain, Salisbury Maximum Security Prison, 113, 149, 157
Cloete, Sgt, Military Intelligence, 202, 204, 208
Congress of South African Students (COSAS), 192
Conservative Party, 258
Contra-Mobilisation group of the Caprivians, 203-205, 207
COSATU (Congress of SA Trade Unions), 194, 197, 198, 201
Crater, prison officer, 165-167
Cuba, 32, 41, 50, 226

Dabengwa, Dumiso 'Black Russian', ZIPRA, 216
Dancer, Detective Inspector, BSAP, 99-102, 105, 106, 112, 122
Dar-es-Salaam, Tanzania, 28, 35, 40, 45, 49, 51, 146
De Arriaga, General Kaulza, Portuguese general, 51
De Klerk, President FW, 236, 255, 257, 259, 261
Death Row, 117, 120, 145, 146, 183
Defensive Group, Caprivians, 204
Derek, Chief of staff of Luthuli Detachment, traitor, 75-77, 79-81, 83, 84, 88, 91, 93-95, 108, 121, 123, 128
Dett (now Dete), 63
Dhlomo, Oscar, Sec-Gen of IFP, 192
Dingane ka Senzangakhona, Zulu King, 17, 19, 20, 61, 162, 235
Dlamini, Linus Themba, ANC prisoner, 151, 156
Dlamini, Victor, MK, 50
Donda, Nicholas, MK, KIA, 73, 74
Driver, George, MK, 73, 74
Du Plooy, Rhodesian prison officer, 166, 167
Dube, Dr John Langalibalele, 13, 17, 22, 43
Dube, John, ZIPRA commander, 64, 66, 72, 75
Dube, Kayeni, ZIPRA prisoner, 60, 112, 161
Duma, Edgar 'Problem', MK, 48
Dunge, Capt KwaZulu Police, 205

Entumbane, fighting between ZIPRA and ZANLA, 222
Eric 'Khehla', ANC Intelligence, 263

Ferreira, Lt, SAP Security Branch, 125-127
Forster, Marshall, MK prisoner, 168, 181
FRELIMO, (Front Lib Mozambique), 45, 51, 114, 180, 203
FROLIZI (Front for the Liberation of Zimbabwe), 180
Front for the Liberation of Mozambique (see FRELIMO)

Geldenhuys, General Jannie, SADF Chief, 200, 210, 267
Georgedale, 14, 26, 186-188, 190
Goba, Asquith Goba, 23, 236, 238
Gomomo, John, COSATU, 198
Goniwe, Jacques, MK, 49, 63
Gqabi, Joe, ANC and MK rep in Zimbabwe, 190

269

Gqozo, Brigadier Oupa, Ciskei, 204
Grey Street Prison, Byo, 183, 220
Griesel, Col Dan, commander of Ferntree military base, 208, 268
Groenewald, General Tienie, Director of Military Intelligence, 199, 200, 205, 257 267
Guevara, Che, Cuban revolutionary, 32, 49, 55
Gulalikabili Village, Rhodesia, 78, 81, 83, 84, 86, 94
Guluva, MK guerrilla, 61
Gumede, MK guerrilla, 49
Gwala, Harry, ANC, 154

Hadebe, Harry, ZIPRA fighter, captured, 112
Hadebe, Moffat, ZIPRA fighter, captured, 182
Hambanathi Township, 196
Hani, Chris, 54, 55, 59-61, 63-66, 69, 70, 73, 75, 156, 188-194, 261
Hartzenberg, Dr Ferdi, Conservative Party leader, 256, 259
Hippo Base, Caprivi, 202
Hlatshwayo, Petrus, MK died in prison, 168
Hlekani, Gandhi, MK (nom de guerre Marcus Chilemba), 41, 63, 64
Hlengwa, Capt, KwaZulu Police, 205
Hofman, Rev Auke, Chaplain at ISS, 231, 234
Holomisa, Major-General Bantu, 252, 256

Inkatha Freedom Party (IFP), 156, 180, 187, 191, 193, 194, 196, 199-204, 207, 211, 236, 239, 243-247, 252, 253, 258, 264
Ilanga Lase Natal (The Natal Sun newspaper), 18
Iliso Lomzi, SADF front, 180
Inanda Mission, 17, 22-24
Inkatha Youth Brigade, 192, 198

Jackie Selebi, SAPS Commissioner, 126
Jacobs, Col Jake, chief instructor Caprivi trainees, 202, 203, 267
Jeqe, MK base commander Kaluwa, Zambia, 57, 58
Jonathan, Chief Leabua, Lesotho, cooperation with ANC, 189
Joyi, Thwalimfene, MK prisoner, 151
Jwili, Mtu, member of ANC's Stuart Commission, 174

Kaluwa Base, Zambia, MK, 56
Kasrils, Ronnie, ANC, 254
Katenga, Novo, Angola, MK camp attacked by SAAF, 173
Kathrada, Ahmed, ANC, 27, 114, 155
Katlehong, 247, 249
Kaunda, Dr Kenneth, Zambian president, 52, 179
Kgositsile, Baleka (Baleka Mbete, later Speaker of Parliament), 233
Khami Maximum Security Prison, 111, 112, 164, 183
Khanyile, Martin Thulani, IFP, Caprivi graduate, 267
Khombisa, Alfred, MK, 40
Khoza, Duncan 'Sigh No More', MK, 46, 48, 55
Khoza, Ntshingwayo ka Mahole ka, Zulu general, 147
Khoza, Vincent, MK, 40
Khumalo, Bhekisisa Alex, Caprivians' Defensive Group, 207, 208
Khumalo, Melchizedeck Zakhele 'MZ', IFP, 188, 201, 203, 205-209, 211, 267
Khumalo, Tennis Nkonkoni, ZIPRA fighter, 112, 119
Kloppers, Phil, AWB Chief Commandant, 258
Kongwa Camp, Tanzania, 40, 41, 48, 49, 51, 53, 210, 233
Kwamakuta Massacre, 207, 209
KwaMashu Township, 191-192

Lancaster House negotiations, Rhodesian settlement, 180, 181
Lengisi, Amos, MK prisoner, 151
Lesotho, 91, 156, 189
Lewis, Mr Justice, Rhodesian judge, 114, 115
Liebenberg, General Kat, Chief of the Army, 267
Lobengula, Ndebele king, 61, 82, 119
Louis Botha Airport (now Durban International), 201
Lupane MK group, 63, 64
Lusaka, 28, 29, 89, 124, 178, 180, 183, 220, 233
Luthuli Camp, Tanzania, 26, 27
Luthuli Detachment, 59, 68, 220, 230
Luthuli, Chief Albert, 43, 57, 243
Luthuli, Col, KwaZulu Police, 206
Luthuli, Japhta Skhumbuzo, 13-16, 25, 26, 187
Luthuli, Jimson, 14
Luthuli, John, 14
Luthuli, Zebulon, 14

Mabhida, Moses, MK's Chief political commissar, 40, 190
Machel, Samora, guerrilla and Pres Mozambique, 51, 60, 114
Madziba, David, ZAPU, 161
Mafole, Ntwe, Publicity secretary IFP Youth Brigade, 201
Mafukuzela, Dr John, 17, 18
Majola, Nomthandazo, Daluxolo's mother, 13, 16, 25
Makhasi, Shuda, MK, 73
Makhoba, Wana, MK, 32
Makiwane, Ambrose, MK comp commander at Kongwa, 41, 45, 47
Makumbe, Sgt BSAP, 97, 99-103
Makwetu, Clarence, PAC leader, 155
Malan, Dr Daniel, 22
Malan, General Magnus, SA Minister of Defence, 200, 210, 267,
Malinga, Kenneth, MK, 46, 48
Mambazo (true name Patrick Mathanjana) MK, captured, 64
Mampuru, Chris, MK, KIA, 65
Mandela, Nelson, 26-32, 34, 43, 55, 114, 146, 152, 155, 171, 235, 236, 240, 255, 256, 259, 261, 262, 265
Mandela Camp, Tanzania, 26
Mangope, Lucas, Pres Bophuthatswana, 210, 244, 259
Mantashe, Gwede, COSATU, 198
Manzonzo, ZIPRA prisoner, 167
Mapoto, Isaac, MK prisoner, 168
Mapoto, MK fighter, 184
Mariri, Happy, MK prisoner, 169, 183
Marks, JB, communist, 35-37, 48
Martinenko, Lt Col Yuri, Red Army, 43
Masango, TEBA agent, 91
Mashengele, Oscar 'Mash', 88-90, 93, 95, 99, 101, 102, 121, 122, 183
Mashigo, Comrade, MK regional commander, Angola, 177
Masimini, James, MK, died covering retreat of his comrades, 63, 64
Masipa, Barry, MK, KIA, 65
Massangena, Mozambique, 90-92
Masuku, Lieutenant-General Lookout, ZIPRA commdr, 216
Matanzima, President Kaiser, Transkei, 195, 210, 244, 252
Mathanjana, Patrick, MK, 151
Mathe, General Sipho, KwaZulu Police Commissioner, 202, 204-206
Mathengele, Donald, MK, 151
Maycock, Patrol Officer, BSAP, 85, 198
Mbeki, Govan, ANC leader, 27, 114, 155
Mbeki, Thabo, ANC leader, 199
Mbijana, MK fighter, 75
Mbokodo, ANC's Security Dept, 173, 174, 176, 177
Mbongwa, Masiphula, ANC, 232, 233

Mbuya Nehanda (Shona spirit medium hanged in Salisbury Prison), 61, 19, 117, 118
Mbuyazi, Hloni Andreas, Caprivi graduate, 268
McGuinness, Mac, Chief Superintendent, BSAP, 111
Mdletshe, Aubrey, MK cadre, 168, 184, 219
Mdletshe, Gideon, MK and IFP, 188
Mdletshe, ZIPRA prisoner, 181
Meiring, General Georg, SADF commander, 259-260
Melane, MK, KIA, 63
Metal and Allied Workers Union (MAWU), 195, 198
Mfeka, Grace, 17
Mfeka, Nonkosi Queen, 239
Mfusi, Maud, MK, (nom de guerre Maud Manyoni), 30, 33
Mhlauli, Goodman, MK (nom de guerre Rashidi), 30, 41
Mhlongo, Peter, MK died of wounds, 68, 71, 74
MK cadres, murdered by ANC, 222
Mkhaba, Zinakile, MK, executed by apartheid regime, 41
Mkhizi, Goina Brian, IFP, Caprivian, 211
Mkhizi, Prince Phezukwendoda, IFP Caprivi graduate, 267
Mkhulisi, Leslie, Caprivian, Offensive Group, 204
Mkhwanazi, Sitwell, IFP, Caprivian, Defensive Group, 204
Mlaba, IFP chairman Mpumalanga, 247, 248
Mncwango, Mangaga, executive committee member IFP Youth Bd and Central Committee, 201
Mnikathi, Filomena, murdered by IFP, 198
Mninzi, Freddy, MK prisoner, 63, 168
Mnyandu, Victor, ANC, 28
Modise, Joe, MK Commander-in-Chief, 26, 39, 40, 47-49, 55-57, 59, 60, 68, 71, 210, 219, 220, 222, 224, 236, 253
Modulo, Ernest, MK, KIA, 65
Moema, MK, (real name Ramano, later SA's army chief), 47
Mogotsi, Silas, ANC, 151
Molefe, Blackie, MK prisoner, 168
Moloi, Lambert, MK, (later Lt Gen SANDF), 47
Moloi, Sparks, MK, 68, 71
Mongalo, Antony, ANC, 174
Mopedi, Jimmy, MK, 50
More, Col John, Military Intelligence, 206-208
Morogoro Camp, Tanzania, 53, 56
Mosedi, Patrick, 40

Motau, William, MK, prisoner, 112, 118, 168, 184
Mothopeng, Zeph, PAC official, 155
Mothusi, George, MK, captured, 63
Motsepe, Godfrey, ANC rep Benelux countries, 232, 233
Motsoaledi, Elias, ANC official, 155
Moyo, Abel, ZIPRA prisoner, 112
Moyo, George, ZIPRA, 167, 168
Moyo, Jason 'JZ', ZAPU, 178, 181
Moyo, Jonathan, MK, captured, 63
Mozambique, 51, 60, 89, 91, 190, 203
MPLA (See Popular Movement for the Liberation of Angola)
Mpofu, Robert, ZAPU, 212, 213
Mpopoma BSAP Station, 111, 112
Mpumalanga, KwaZulu, 247-249
Msane, Peter, IFP Caprivi graduate, 204, 267
Mshengu, Phumalani Xolani, IFP Caprivi graduate, 204, 209
Msimang, Mendi, ANC rep in London (later ANC Treasurer-General), 27, 34, 233
Msimang, Walter, MK, 227, 233
Mthembu, Sipho, MK, 48
Mthcthwa, Joyful, IFP comm Contra-Mobilisation Group, IFP, 203
Mtoni, Tanzania, 26, 28, 30, 34
Mugabe, Robert, President of Zimbabwe, 52, 158, 163, 180-183, 212, 214, 215, 218, 230
Muzorewa, Bishop, 163, 181, 212
Mxwaku, Mjojo (later Major-General Lennox Tjali SANDF), 54, 59, 60, 71, 73-75, 253
Mzamo, Ralph, MK prisoner, 168, 169
Mzilikazi, Ndebele king, 61, 162
Mzondeni, Templeton, MK, (nom de guerre Alfred Sharp), 41-43, 63
Mzondiwa, Boniface, prisoner in Khami, 166, 167

National Executive Committee (NEC), ANC, 26, 40, 47, 48, 50, 55, 127, 174, 176
National Party, 28, 36, 54, 210, 243-245
Ncube, Morris, ZIPRA prisoner, 112
Ndhlovu, Celukwanda, IFP Caprivi graduate, 267
Ndlovu, Akim, ZIPRA commander-in-chief, 60
Ndlovu, Curnick, ANC, 156
NEC (see National Executive Committee)
Ngcakani, Zola, MK, later Inspector General of Intelligence, 227, 233
Ngcobo, Matthews, ANC, 151
Ngcobo, Nomsa, 184
Ngcobo, Pamela, 86

Ngcobo, Prof Selby, 86
Ngendane, Selby, PAC official, 155
Ngubane, Simon, murdered by IFP, 198
Ngwenya, Peter, ZANLA commander, 178
Nhari, Thomas, ZANLA commander, 178
Nhlabathi, Reuben 'Kulak', MK, 48, 66, 73
Nhlanhla, Joe, ANC, 31
Nhlungwane IFP Camp near Ulundi, 201
Nkala, Enos, ZANU-PF's Min of Fin, Zimbabwe, 154, 158, 214
Nkomo, Joshua, ZAPU leader, 52, 54, 84, 91, 113, 160, 169, 170, 182, 212, 214, 215, 218
Nkonkoni, ZIPRA guerrilla, 112
Nkosi, Leonard Mandla, (real name Derek), 151
Nokwe, Advocate Duma, ANC Sec General, 27
Nomthandazo, Daluxolo's mother, 186
Novo Katenga Camp, Angola, MK, 175
Nsele, Henry, MK, died in RSA, 168
Ntshangase, John Bhekuyise, NUM official murdered by UWUSA, 198
Ntuli, Rev Willie, 208
Ntuli, Victor, 207, 208
Ntumbane Township, Bulawayo, 214, 215
Nyamandhlovu, Rhodesia, 79, 81, 84, 85, 108

OAU (Organisation of African Unity), 36, 53, 113, 127
Odessa Military Academy, Ukraine, 38, 43
Ohlange Institute, Inanda, 13, 17, 18, 22
Operation Lebanta, SADF raid on Maseru, 190
Operation Marion, SADF assistance to IFP, 200, 202, 205, 267
Opperman, Captain, Military Intelligence, 204, 206, 207, 211
Organisation of African Unity (OAU)

PAC (See Pan Africanist Congress)
Pahad, Aziz, ANC, 174
Pan Africanist Congress (PAC), 25, 27, 45, 53, 54, 108, 180, 213, 244
Pango Quibaxe MK Camp, Angola, 173, 174
Pasques, Dr L, 204
Peters, Detective Inspector Ronald Stanley, BSAP, 74, 105, 107-111, 113, 114, 116
Phokanoka, Lawrence, ANC, 151
Pollberry, Major, (Paul Berry?),

Military Intelligence, 247, 248
Popular Movement for the Liberation of Angola (MPLA), 45, 51, 202, 203
Project Katzen, SADF plan to murder Lennox Sebe, 252
Putter, Vice-Admiral Dries, SADF's Chief of Staff Intelligence, 200
Putterill, General Sam, Rhodesian Army Commander, 55

Quatro MK Camp, Angola, 173
Quibaxe, MK Camp, Angola, 174

Radebe, James, ANC, 27, 34
Ramaphosa, Cyril, ANC. 198
RAR (Rhodesian African Rifles), 66, 68, 70, 72, 114
Rashidi (Goodman Mhlauli), 64
RENAMO, (Mozambique National Resistance Movement), 176, 180, 201-203, 240
Report of ANC Commission, 176
Revolutionary Committee of the ANC, 220
Rhodesian African Rifles (see RAR)
Rhodesian Light Infantry, 72
Ridora Crossing, AWB murders at, 258
Robben Island, 27, 32, 65, 151, 152, 154-156, 171, 178, 186-188, 251

SAAF (South African Air Force), 173, 201
SACP (South African Communist Party), 189, 258
SACTU (South African Congress of Trade Unions), 189, 244
SADF (South African Def Force), 30, 36, 48, 180, 201, 203, 206, 218, 245, 247, 249, 257-259, 261
Salisbury Maximum Security Prison, 113, 119
San Michelle guerrilla training base, Caprivi, 202
SAP (See South African Police)
Savimbi, Jonas, UNITA, 45, 240
Sebe, President Lennox of Ciskei, 244, 252
Security Branch, 25, 109, 124, 127, 186, 190, 192, 208, 211, 246, 249
Sello, Mogalake, ANC, 188
Shiri, Col Perence, Butcher of Bhalagwe, 217
Sibanyoni, Delmas, MK, KIA, 63, 64
Sibeko, Archie, (nom de guerre Zola Zembe) commander MK's Kongwa Camp, 45, 46
Sibiya, Phineas, murdered by IFP, 198
Sigwela, Ezra, Robben Island prisoner, 151, 188
Sigxashe, Sizakele, ANC, 174

Simelane, Jack, MK, 73, 74
Sishuba, MK, KIA, 68
Sisulu, Walter, ANC, 27, 114, 155
Sithole, Joe, MK prisoner, 168
Sithole, Rev Ndabaningi, ZANU, 52, 113,158-161, 163, 182, 213
Skhosana, ZAPU, 118
Smith, Ian Douglas, Prime Minister, 33, 52, 53, 84,115, 122, 182
Smith, Lt John, RAR, KIA, 66-71
Soames, Lord, British governor in Rhodesia, 181, 182
Sobukwe, Robert, PAC leader, 155
South African Air Force (See SAAF)
South African Defence Force (See SADF)
South African Police (SAP), 95, 107, 261, 245
South African Special Forces, 190
Soweto Students' Uprising, 54, 173
Special Branch, Rhodesian, 158, 213
Stuart Commission, 41, 174, 176
Swanepoel, Major 'Rooi Rus' (Red Russian), 125-127, 152, 246
SWAPO (SWA People's Organisation), 28, 45, 51, 202
Swart, Col, 203-205
Swaziland, 33, 189, 190, 194, 195

Tamana, Bothwell, MK prisoner, 63, 119
Tambo, Oliver, ANC President, 27, 33, 34, 48-50, 55, 58-62, 111, 127, 223, 229
Tau, George, MK captured, 63, 168
Tekere, Edgar, ZANU PF, 158
TerreBlanche, Eugene, AWB leader, 256, 258, 259
Thomas, Patrol Officer BSAP, KIA, 74
Thomson, Cyril, hangman, 150
Timitiya, Sergeant Major, RAR, KIA, 66, 69, 71, 166
Tladi, Peter, MK captured, 64
Tongogara, Josiah, ZANLA commander-in-chief, 178
Transitional Executive Council, 257
Transkei, 195, 252, 256
Treacy, BJ, Director of Prosecutions, Rhodesia, 159
Truth and Reconciliation Com, RSA, 199, 209, 246, 265
Tjolotjo (Now Tsholotsho), 63, 78, 79, 88, 92, 107, 117
Tshwete, Steve, ANC, 154

UDF (United Dem Front, 191, 193, 197, 199, 200, 204, 209, 210, 236, 239, 243, 245, 247-253
UDI (Unilateral Dec Independence), Rhodesia, 52, 179
Ulundi, 192, 206, 247, 249, 250

Umlazi township, Natal, 191, 239
Umtali (now Mutare), Rhodesia, 86, 88, 93, 94, 105, 122
Underground High Command in South Africa, ANC, 50
United Nations High Commission for Refugees (UNHCR), 108
UWUSA (See United Worker's Union of South Africa)
Uys, Col Piet, AVF, 259

Van der Merwe, Col Jan, Military Intelligence, 267
Van der Merwe, General Johan, Commissioner SAP, 210
Van Niekerk, Brig Cor, Dir Special Tasks, 202, 203, 205, 206, 267
Van Rensburg, Capt, SAP Security Branch, 125
Van Tonder Gen Neels, Director of Intelligence, 202, 267
Viana Transit Camp, MK, 173, 174
Victor, Col Johannes, Military Intelligence, 267
Victoria Falls, 29, 60, 179
Viljoen, Gen Constand, 256-260
Volkstaat, 256-258
Vorster, BJ, Prime Minister, 59, 179

Wankie (now Hwange), 63, 64, 79, 80, 87, 102, 116, 160, 188, 230, 246, 254, 262
Willar, Major, 67
Witdoekies, 180, 246

Xesibe, Thompson, IFP commander, 202

Zambezi River, 59-61, 162
Zambia, 28, 29, 53, 60, 103, 189,
ZANLA (Zimbabwe African National Liberation Army), 52, 53, 179, 180, 215, 222
ZANU (Zimbabwe African National Union), 45, 52, 54, 91, 92, 110, 169, 180, 219
Zimbabwe African People's Union (ZAPU), 45, 52-54, 79, 108, 110, 169, 180, 215
ZIPA (Zimbabwe People's Army), 178
ZIPRA (Zimbabwe People's Revolutionary Army), 51-55, 60, 63, 64, 179, 180, 214-216, 222
Zondi, Musi, National Chairman IFP Youth Brigade, 201
Zuma, Jacob, ANC, 254, 262-265